Ludics

"*Ludics: Play as Humanistic Inquiry* is a valuable resource, re-centering play as essential to the humanities. Working through a bracingly diverse set of examples, the contributors put flesh on co-editor Eric Gordon's concept of *meaningful inefficiencies*—the ways in which understanding, inspiration and learning all arise through the messy process of play. Where play and work are often portrayed as being in opposition, this volume illustrates how meaning is often made through playfulness in the work of scholars, philosophers, and artists. In recent decades, corporatist models of productivity in the academy have too often lead to a diminished role for humanistic study. This book is a cogent argument for humanities reinvigorated through a return to their playful roots. At a time when all institutions of learning are undergoing dramatic transformation, this volume is a vital tool for those of us trying to imagine a better future."

—Scot Osterweil, *Game Designer, Research Scientist, MIT, USA*

"This passionate volume invites us to see play at the center of the humanities. We can find it in the connections we make between ideas and with each other, both within and across disciplines. And we find it here on full display: leading scholars from an impressive cross-section of disciplines from Classics to Computer Game Research, Architecture to Archaeology, Religious Studies, Comparative Literature, Philosophy, and many more—as well as practicing poets, performers, and artists—all exploring ludic topics from the angle of their own scholarly interests. What emerges from the individual essays and the many connections between them is not only a rich source of scholarship about play, but a vision of play at the creative heart of scholarly endeavor."

—Stephen E. Kidd, *Associate Professor of Classics, Brown University, USA*

Vassiliki Rapti · Eric Gordon
Editors

Ludics

Play as Humanistic Inquiry

palgrave
macmillan

Editors
Vassiliki Rapti
Classical Studies
Boston University
Boston, MA, USA

Eric Gordon
Visual and Media Arts
Emerson College
Boston, MA, USA

ISBN 978-981-15-7434-4 ISBN 978-981-15-7435-1 (eBook)
https://doi.org/10.1007/978-981-15-7435-1

Cover image: courtesy of Gentleman's Game and Octavia Art Gallery

This Palgrave Macmillan imprint is published by the registered company Springer Nature Singapore Pte Ltd.
The registered company address is: 152 Beach Road, #21-01/04 Gateway East, Singapore 189721, Singapore

Acknowledgments

We would like to express our profound gratitude to the Mahindra Humanities Center, Harvard University, its past and current directors, Homi K. Bhabha and Sunil Amrith, respectively, its executive director Steven Biel, and all its staff members, especially, Neal Adolph Akatsuka and Laura Sargent, for providing an intellectual space to the Ludics Seminar since its inception in 2013, in order to explore the concept of play across disciplines, out of which this edited volume was born. A great deal of debt goes to Professor Kathleen M. Coleman, co-founder and co-chair of the Ludics Seminar during its first two years, for her generosity, encouragement and hard work to identify and invite guest speakers inspired by the ludic drive in their research. To all Ludics guest speakers and its diverse audiences, along with its graduate coordinators for the last seven years, Ilana Freedman, Effie Gonis, and Bella Bennett, we extend our warmest thanks, in particular, to the contributors to this volume in alphabetical order: Yiorgos Anagnostou, Danuta Fjellestad, Catalina Florina Florescu, Leslie Frost, Sarah Green, Stephen Kidd, Peter Levine, Timothy Moore, Gabriel Mugar, Nicole Nolette, Brigitte Pitarakis, Diana Ramírez-Jasso, Johnathon Robinson-Appels,

Arthur Louis Ruprecht Jr., Miguel Sicart, Doris Sommer, Chrysostomos A. Stamoulis, Pierre Taminiaux, Zenovia Toloudi, and Mary J. Yossi. We would like to also acknowledge the many blind reviewers whose feedback and constructive criticism was of paramount importance in the process of collecting and finalizing the papers included in this volume.

We are grateful to Gentleman's Game, a partnership of artists Brandon Friend and Jason Douglas Griffin, for granting us permission to use their work "The Child, 2015," represented by Octavia Gallery and its owner Pamela Bryan and its director Emily Siekkinen, who made every effort to smooth the process of copyright clearance.

Our thanks also go to our student assistant Kara Jackson, for assisting us in stylistic matters. And of course, boundless gratitude to Palgrave-MacMillan commission editor Joshua Pitt, for his trust, patience and understanding. Many special thanks go to all our friends who helped us in various ways throughout this project; in particular, to Peter Bottéas, Carmen-Francesca Banciu, Julia Dubnoff, Meral Ekincioglu, Susan Husserl-Kapit, Maria Kakavas, Maria Koundoura, Elena Mancini, Ivaana Muse, Maklena Nika, Stella Tiratsuyan, Hannah Trivilino and Vinia Tsopelas, for their constant support and for being inexhaustible sources of wisdom and encouragement.

We are thankful to the institutions and collectives with which we are affiliated, Emerson College with its Engagement Lab and *Citizen* TALES Commons, Harvard University and Boston University for providing us with a most playful intellectual environment to work in.

Last but not least, we are grateful to our families for their patience and steady support during the various stages devoted to the completion of this project.

It has been an extremely rewarding ludic journey for both of us that we will always cherish and which helped us to gain insights in our future research and joint endeavors.

Boston, USA
May 2020

Vassiliki Rapti
Eric Gordon

Contents

INTRODUCTION: Ludics—Play as Humanistic Inquiry 1
Vassiliki Rapti and Eric Gordon

Playspace, Ethics & Engagement

Toward an Ethics of *Homo Ludens* 21
Miguel Sicart

SPORT MATTERS: On Art, Social Artifice, and the Rules of the Game, or, the Politics of Sport 47
Louis A. Ruprecht

Pre-Texts: Press Play to Teach Anything 73
Doris Sommer

Work, Play, and Civic Engagement 85
Peter Levine

Technoecologies: The Interplay of Space and Its Perception 95
Zenovia Toloudi

Meaningful Inefficiencies: Incorporating Play into Civic Design 125
Eric Gordon and Gabriel Mugar

Playthings, Comedy & Laughter

"Let Us Laugh and Play": Laughter in Greek Lyric Poetry 155
Mary J. Yossi

Ludic Music in Ancient Greek and Roman Theater 181
Timothy J. Moore

Did Christ Laugh? Umberto Eco's Question and Saint John Chrysostom's Response 213
Chrysostomos A. Stamoulis

Comedy, Physicality, and Ludic Dance Gestures: The Comic in Ballet and Tai Chi? 227
Jonathon Robinson-Appels

Toys, Childhood, and Material Culture in Byzantium 243
Brigitte Pitarakis

Language & Poetics of Play

"How to Catch a Falling Knife:" Poetic Play as the Practice of Negative Capability 277
Sarah Green

The Ludic Impulse in Post-Postmodern Fiction 293
Danuta Fjellestad

Games Translators Play in French-Canadian Theatre 317
Nicole Nolette

Immigraνt Poetics: Play as Performativity of the Liminal Self 339
Yiorgos Anagnostou

Play(Modes) & Performance as Transgression

Ludics as Transgression: From Surrealism to the Absurd to Pataphysics 361
Pierre Taminiaux

2 Sisters, 2 Stories: Breast Cancer, Femininity, and Body Ownership 377
Catalina Florina Florescu

"Don't Be Mean" and Other Lessons from Children's Plays of the Federal Theatre Project 403
Leslie Frost

The Republic of Childhood: Friedrich Froebel's Kindergarten and *Naturphilosophie* 427
Diana Ramírez-Jasso

Oscillating Between Tag and Hopscotch: Theo Angelopoulos' Playful Aesthetics 447
Vassiliki Rapti

Author Index 463

Subject Index 467

Notes on Contributors

Yiorgos Anagnostou is Professor of transnational and diaspora modern Greek studies at Ohio State University. His work is interdisciplinary and has been published in a wide range of scholarly journals (see, http://www.mgsa.org/faculty/anagnost.html). He is the author of *Contours of White Ethnicity: Popular Ethnography and the Making of Usable Pasts in Greek America* (Ohio University Press, 2009), now under translation into Greek (εκδόσεις Νήσος, 2017). He has also published two poetry collections, "Διασπορικές Διαδρομές" (Απόπειρα 2012, http://apopeirates.blogspot.com/2012/04/blog-post_20.html), and «rλωσσες X Επαφης, Επιστολšς εξ Αμερικης» (Ενδυμιων 2016, http://endymionpublic.blogspot.com/). He is the co-editor of the upcoming online *Ergon: Greek/American Arts and Letters* (Autumn 2017). He writes for Greek and Greek American media, and occasionally blogs on Greek America (http://immigrations-ethnicities-racial.blogspot.com/), and diaspora poetry (http://diasporic-skopia.blogspot.com/). His poetry in English has been published in *Transnational Literature and Voices of Hellenism.*

Danuta Fjellestad is Chair and Professor of American Literature and Culture, Uppsala University. Professor Fjellestad's main research interests are twentieth- and twenty-first-century American fiction, in particular postmodern and post-postmodern texts; visual culture; literary theory; intellectual auto/biography; ethnic studies; new media; electronic literature. She is also keenly interested in pedagogy and organization of higher education. Her present book-length study, *The Pictorial Turn in Literature: Reading Fiction Today*, focuses on word–image interactions in contemporary American literature. Professor Fjellestad is the recipient of several grants and scholarships, among others from the Bank of Sweden Tercentenary Foundation (RJ) and the Swedish Agency for Innovation Systems (2004), Fulbright (2000–2001), the Swedish Research Council (1995–1997), ACLS (1989), and Vilas (1986). Since 2010 Fjellestad has been a member of the Board of the Swedish Research Council (VR).

Catalina Florina Florescu holds a Ph.D. in Comparative Literature (Medical Humanities and Comparative Theater). She teaches at Pace University in Downtown Manhattan. She is the curator for the New Plays Festival at Jersey City Theater Center whose second edition is titled "Return to Love." She is working on several projects, one of which is under contract with Routledge, *Female Playwrights Intersectionality in Contemporary Romanian Theater*. More here: http://www.catalinaflorescu.com/.

Leslie Frost is a Teaching Associate Professor at the University of North Carolina at Chapel Hill. In *Dreaming America: Popular Front Ideals an Aesthetics in Children's Plays of the Federal Theatre Project* (2013) Frost traces the how the tumultuous politics of the late 1930s shaped the stories and staging of Federal Theater Project (1935–1939) children's plays. In 2016, Frost adapted and produced the Federal Theater Project's *It Can't Happen Here* for an anniversary staged reading at Historic Playmakers Theater at UNC-Chapel Hill. She is currently working on a project centered on New Deal U.S. Post Office murals.

Eric Gordon is a professor and Founding Director of the Engagement Lab at Emerson. In 2020–21, he is a visiting professor in the Department of Comparative Media Studies / Writing at the Massachusetts Institute of Technology. Eric studies civic media and public engagement within the United States and around the world. He is specifically interested in the application of games and play in these contexts. In addition to being a researcher, he is also the designer of award-winning "engagement games," which are games that facilitate civic participation. He has served as an expert advisor for the UN Development Program, the International Red Cross/Red Crescent, the World Bank, as well as municipal governments throughout the United States. In addition to articles and chapters on games, digital media, urbanism and civic engagement, he is the author of three books: *Meaningful Inefficiencies: Civic Design in an Age of Digital Expediency* (Oxford University Press 2020, with Gabriel Mugar), *Net Locality: Why Location Matters in a Networked World* (Blackwell 2011, with Adriana de Souza e Silva) and *The Urban Spectator: American Concept Cities From Kodak to Google* (Dartmouth 2010). His edited volume (with Paul Mihailidis) entitled *Civic Media: Technology, Design, Practice* was published by MIT Press in 2016.

Sarah Green is the Author of *Earth Science* (421 Atlanta, 2016). Her previous chapbook, *Skeleton Evenings*(Finishing Line Press, 2015) won the 2014 New Women's Voices prize. Poems of hers have appeared in *Best New Poets 2012, the Incredible Sestina Anthology, Pleiades, FIELD, Passages North, Mid-American Review, Gettysburg Review, Redivider, Ruminate,* and elsewhere. A Pushcart Prize winner, she holds both an MFA and Ph.D. in Poetry. Sarah has 14 years of creative writing teaching experience, in settings ranging from higher ed (Oberlin College, Emerson College) to nonprofits (Grub Street, The Loft Literary Center) to artists' retreats in France and Italy. Enthusiastic about engaging with students at all experience levels and coming from all styles, as an instructor she emphasizes play, intuition, precision, and musicality. She is currently compiling a multi-genre anthology called *Welcome To The Neighborhood.*

Peter Levine is the Academic Dean and Lincoln Filene Professor of Citizenship & Public Affairs in Tufts University's Jonathan Tisch College of Civic Life. He has tenure in Tufts' Political Science Department, and he also has secondary appointments in the Tufts Philosophy Department and the Tufts Clinical and Translational Sciences Institute. He directs the Civic Studies Major at Tufts.

Levine graduated from Yale in 1989 with a degree in philosophy. He studied philosophy at Oxford on a Rhodes Scholarship, receiving his doctorate in 1992. From 1991 until 1993, he was a research associate at Common Cause. From 1993 to 2008, he was a member of the Institute for Philosophy & Public Policy in the University of Maryland's School of Public Policy. During the late 1990s, he was also Deputy Director of the National Commission on Civic Renewal. Levine was the founding deputy director (2001–2006) and then the second director (2006–2015) of Tisch College's CIRCLE, The Center for Information and Research on Civic Learning and Engagement.

Levine is the author of *We Are the Ones We Have Been Waiting For: The Promise of Civic Renewal in America* (Oxford University Press, 2013), five other scholarly books on philosophy and politics, and a novel. He has served on the boards or steering committees of AmericaSpeaks, Street Law Inc., the Newspaper Association of America Foundation, the Campaign for the Civic Mission of Schools, Discovering Justice, the Kettering Foundation, the American Bar Association's Committee for Public Education, the Paul J. Aicher Foundation, and the Deliberative Democracy Consortium.

Timothy J. Moore is John and Penelope Biggs Distinguished Professor of Classics at Washington University in St. Louis. His publications include *Artistry and Ideology: Livy's Vocabulary of Virtue, The Theater of Plautus, Music in Roman Comedy, Roman Theatre*, a translation of Terence's *Phormio*, and articles on Latin literature, the teaching of Greek and Latin, ancient music, American Musical Theater, and Japanese comedy.

Gabriel Mugar is a Senior Design Researcher at IDEO Cambridge, where he works with communities and organizations to design opportunities for learning, collaboration, and storytelling. He received his Ph.D. from the Syracuse University School of Information Studies.

Nicole Nolette is a Postdoctoral Fellow (SSHRC 2014–2016) associated with Harvard University. She has a Ph.D. in French language and literature from McGill University (Montreal). Her dissertation focuses on the games of translation and the issues at stake with translation in multilingual plays from Canada's Francophone minorities. She is interested in ludics, multilingual theater, Translation Studies, Performance

Studies, and Canadian Francophone Literature. She has published articles in *Inquire: Journal of Comparative Literature, Jeu: revue de théâtre,* and *Theatre Research in Canada*, as well as book chapters in *La Traduction dans les cultures plurilingues, Staging and Performing Translation: Text and Theatre Practice,* and *Translation and the Reconfiguration of Power.*

Brigitte Pitarakis is a Byzantine Art Researcher at the CNRS in Paris, France, with numerous contributions to the field.

Diana Ramírez-Jasso is Dean of the School of Architecture, Art, and Design in the Southern Region of the Tecnológico de Monterrey. Her research interests span the history and theory of interiors, buildings, gardens, and landscapes, particularly as they intersect with discourses stemming from literature, philosophy, pedagogy, and art. She received the Doctor of Philosophy degree in the History and Theory of Architecture from Harvard University in 2012. She also holds a Master of Arts in Architecture from Harvard University and a Master of Science in the History, Theory, and Criticism of Architecture from the Massachusetts Institute of Technology. Her recent work has focused on the perceived contributions of designed spaces to the shaping of modern subjectivity, a topic that she has explored by interrogating historical intersections between architecture, gardens, education, and the history of childhood.

Vassiliki Rapti is a Professor of comparative literature, curator, editor and translator and currently is a Visiting Lecturer in Modern Greek Studies at Boston University. She holds a Ph.D. in Comparative Literature with an Emphasis in Drama and an M.A. in Civic Media: Art and Practice from Emerson College, U.S.A, where she has taught courses on global literature, especially women's writing and literary theory, and theories of new media. During the years 2008–2016 she has served as Preceptor in Modern Greek at Harvard University, where in 2013 she co-founded and co-chaired the Ludics Seminar at the Mahindra Humanities Center and the Advanced Training in Greek Poetry Translation and Performance Workshop, which she has been running since then along with Citizen *TALES* Commons, an open platform and collective of independent scholars and artists, based in Cambridge, MA.

Her publications and research interests center around ludic theory, avant-garde theater and performance with an emphasis on Surrealism, literary theory and gender studies. She is the author of *Ludics in Surrealist Theatre and Beyond* (Ashgate, 2013) and of several edited books and translation volumes including *Nanos Valaoritis's "Nightfall Hotel": A Surrealist Romeo and Juliet* (Somerset Hall Press, 2017) and of several poetry collections including *Transitorium* (Somerset Hall Press, 2015). She co-founded and co-edited the journal *Theatron* during the years 2002–2004 and she is currently the editor of *The Journal of Civic Media* at Emerson College.

Jonathon Robinson-Appels is the Artistic Director and Choreographer of Company Appels, a modern ballet company founded in 1979. The Company has toured seventeen countries on three continents. He has received the William Como Award for Choreography, and has received an award from The Foundation for Contemporary Performance Arts. He teaches at Columbia University in the departments of English and Comparative Literature, French and Romance Philology, and Anthropology.

Louis A. Ruprecht Jr. is the inaugural holder of the William M. Suttles Chair in Religious Studies as well as Director of the Center for Hellenic Studies. His doctoral concentration was in the area of philosophical and religious ethics, with special emphasis on classical literature and philosophy. His work covers a wide range of topics but may best be characterized as a historical study of the appropriation of Greek themes in a number of subsequent historical periods, especially the Early Modern period. He interrogates this classical legacy in areas ranging from ethics and politics, to psychology and sexuality, to drama and film. For the past ten years he has been a Research Fellow at the Vatican Library and the Vatican Secret Archives, where he has extended these research interests to the emergence of the Early Modern conception of Art, and the privileging of classical art as embodied in that preeminent institution, the Vatican Museums. His recent books include: *Winckelmann and the Vatican's First Profane Museum* (Palgrave Macmillan, 2011), *Policing the State: Democratic Reflections on Police Power Gone Awry, in Memory of Kathryn Johnston* (Wipf and Stock, 2013) and *Classics at the Dawn of the*

Museum Era: The Life and Times of Antoine Chrysostome Quatremere de Quincy (Palgrave Macmillan, 2014).

Miguel Sicart is an Associate Professor at the Center for Computer Games, IT University of Copenhagen. His research has focused on the ethics of digital games and game design. His more recent work explores the nature of play, with a particular interest in the ludic aspects of computational technologies. He is the author of *The Ethics of Computer Games*, *Beyond Choices: The Design of Ethical Gameplay*, and *Play Matters* (The MIT Press, 2009, 2013, 2014).

Doris Sommer, Director of the Cultural Agents Initiative at Harvard University, is Ira and Jewell Williams Professor of Romance Languages and Literatures and of African and African American Studies. Her academic and outreach work promotes development through arts and humanities, specifically through "Pre-Texts" in Boston Public Schools, throughout Latin America and beyond. Pre-Texts is an arts-based training program for teachers of literacy, critical thinking, and citizenship. Among her books are *Foundational Fictions: The National Romances of Latin America* (1991) about novels that helped to consolidate new republics; *Proceed with Caution when Engaged by Minority Literature* (1999) on a rhetoric of particularism; *Bilingual Aesthetics: A New Sentimental Education* (2004); and *The Work of Art in the World: Civic Agency and Public Humanities* (2014). Sommer has enjoyed and is dedicated to developing good public school education. She has a B.A. from New Jersey's Douglass College for Women, and Ph.D. from Rutgers University.

Chrysostomos A. Stamoulis is Professor of Dogmatic and Symbolic Theology at the Department of Theology of the Aristotle University of Thessaloniki. He studied Theology at the Universities of Thessaloniki (Greece), Belgrade (Serbia) and Durham (UK) and teaches the core module of Dogmatic and Symbolic Theology. His major works include: *Theotokos and Orthodox Dogma. A Study in the Theology of St. Cyril of Alexandria*, Palimpseston Publications, Thessaloniki 2003 (1996). *On Light. Personal or Natural Energies? A Contribution to the Contemporary*

Debate on the Holy Trinity in the Orthodox world, Palimpseston Publications, Thessaloniki 2007 (1999). *Sacred Beauty. An Introduction to the Philocalic Aesthetics of Orthodoxy*, Akritas Publications 2010 (2004, 2005, 2008). *Lot's Wife and Contemporary Theology*, Indictos Publications, Athens 2008. *Eros and Thanatos. Essay for a Culture of Incarnation*, Akritas Publications, Athens 2009. *As if I were a Stranger and a Wanderer, Or, Incarnation: The migration of Love*, Akritas Publications, Athens 2011. Further papers and essays have been published in English, French, Italian, German, Serbian, Romanian, and Russian. In 2011–2013 he served his first term in office as Head of the Department of Theology and was reelected for a further term (2013–2015). He undertook musical studies at the Macedonian and State Conservatories in Thessaloniki. He is principally engaged in choral music and composition and has made 5 CDs.

Pierre Taminiaux is actively involved in university teaching, research, and service at Georgetown since the fall of 1991. In addition, he pursues a wide range of creative activities, both in literature and the visual arts. In this regard, he has recently given several poetry readings of his own work, in particular a series of four readings at the Alliance Française of Washington, DC, between 2008 and 2014, and has also exhibited some 100 artworks (paintings, drawings and photographs) both in his native Belgium and in the United States. Moreover, he has presented a series of 12 art projects in the field of conceptual photography in various graduate seminars and international conferences both on the East Coast of the United States and in Europe. The wide range of his academic interests is also reflected in his teaching. Professor Taminiaux concentrates particularly in his advanced courses on the relationship between twentieth century French literature and the visual arts, with a specific emphasis on poetry and photography. At the same time, Professor Taminiaux serves as a student advisor and on various committees in both the French Department and at the University level.

Zenovia Toloudi is an Architect, Artist, and Associate Professor at Studio Art, Dartmouth College. Her work critiques the contemporary alienation of humans from nature and sociability in architecture and public space, and investigates spatial typologies to reestablish cohabitation, inclusion, and participation through digital, physical, and organic media. The founder of Studio Z, a creative research practice on art, architecture, and urbanism, Zenovia has exhibited internationally, including at the Biennale in Venice, the Center for Architecture, the Athens Byzantine Museum, the Thessaloniki Biennale of Contemporary Art and the Onassis Cultural Center. She has won commissions from Illuminus Boston, The Lab at Harvard, and the Leslie Center for Humanities at Dartmouth. Zenovia's work belongs to permanent collections at Aristotle University (AUTh) and the Thracian Pinacotheca. Her essays have been published in Routledge, Technoetic Arts, and MAS Context. Zenovia is the recipient of The Class of 1962 Fellowship. She was a Public Voices Fellow; a Research Fellow at Art, Culture, and Technology Program at MIT; and a Fulbright Fellow. Zenovia received her Doctor of Design degree from Harvard's GSD (2011), a Master of Architecture degree as a Fulbright Fellow at the Illinois Institute of Technology (2006), and in 2003, she graduated from the AUTh in Architectural Engineering. Website: http://zenovia.net/.

Mary J. Yossi is Professor of the Classics at the National and Kapodistrian University of Athens, Greece. She has written extensively on Greek tragedy and human rights and besides her scholarship she is also a poet. Among her poetry collections are *Sunken Sky*, *Special Itinerary* and *Wedding*.

List of Figures

Technoecologies: The Interplay of Space and Its Perception

Fig. 1 Zenovia Toloudi, Maria Stefanidis, 10 models/visions (view of one model) as part of *Amour-Amour, Exhibition of Architectural translations of "Oktana" by the poet Andreas Empeirikos* 99

Fig. 2 Zenovia Toloudi / Studio Z, 4 models/visions for Aegean Metapolis (view of one model) as part of *The Dispersed Urbanity of the Aegean Archipelago*: 10th International Exhibition of Architecture Venice Biennale: Greek Participation 100

Fig. 3 **a**,**b** Zenovia Toloudi, Maria Stefanidis, Chrysa Lekka, *The Cage*. Thessaloniki, Greece, 2001. In collaboration with George Toloudis and Costas Varotsos 101

Fig. 4 Welding shop in Alexandroupolis, Evros, Greece, 1999/2000 103

Fig. 5 *Invisible Cities* project as part of Introduction to Architecture course by Zenovia Toloudi, Dartmouth College. Project by student Sam Gochman 104

Fig. 6 *A Temporary Museum of Ideas in the Making* exhibition curated by Zenovia Toloudi and Gerald A. Auten, Strauss Gallery, Dartmouth College, 2018 (*Source* © Photograph by Gerald D. Auten) 105
Fig. 7 Zenovia Toloudi / Studio Z, *Technoecologies* solo exhibition (initial sketch layout), Storrs Gallery, UNC-Charlotte, NC, 2018 107
Fig. 8 **a,b** Zenovia Toloudi / Studio Z, *Technoecologies* solo exhibition (exhibition overview), Storrs Gallery, UNC-Charlotte, NC, 2018 108
Fig. 9 Zenovia Toloudi / Studio Z, *Micro-Ceasefire Under Shadow V* 108
Fig. 10 Zenovia Toloudi / Studio Z, *Photodotes I.* Boston, MA, 2012. Installation was first part of Garden Lab exhibition (2012), Brant Gallery, Massachusetts College of Art and Design (*Source* © Photograph by Dominic Tschoepe) 111
Fig. 11 **a,b** Zenovia Toloudi / Studio Z, *Photodotes II: Light Garden.* Boston, MA, 2012. Installation was part of Garden Lab exhibition (2012), Brant Gallery, Massachusetts College of Art and Design (*Source* © Photograph by Dominic Tschoepe) 112
Fig. 12 Zenovia Toloudi / Studio Z, *Photodotes III: Plug-n-Plant.* Cambridge, MA, 2013. Installation was first part of solo exhibition at Industry Lab 114
Fig. 13 An example of *Photodotes* installation transforming into a structural wall of a building (*Source* © Zenovia Toloudi / Studio Z) 115
Fig. 14 Zenovia Toloudi / Studio Z, *Photodotes V: Cyborg Garden.* Boston, MA, 2012. Interaction Design: Spyridon Ampanavos. Installation as part of Illuminus Boston event at Fenway (*Source* © Photograph by Dimitris Papanikolaou) 117
Fig. 15 **a,b** Zenovia Toloudi / Studio Z, *Silo(e)scapes* (interior view) Athens, Greece, 2017. Installation as part of Tomorrows: Urban Fictions for Possible Futures exhibition 119
Fig. 16 Zenovia Toloudi / Studio Z, *Silo(e)scapes* (exterior view) Athens, Greece, 2017. Installation as part of Tomorrows: Urban Fictions for Possible Futures exhibition 120

Meaningful Inefficiencies: Incorporating Play into Civic Design

Fig. 1 Screenshot of faces of Dudley mural Pokéstop before and after the workshop 147

Comedy, Physicality, and Ludic Dance Gestures: The Comic in Ballet and Tai Chi?

Fig. 1 Elinor Hitt moving from the tragic, and toward the ludic gesture, personal archive 233
Fig. 2 Adison Martin contemplating the inner smile, personal archive 235
Fig. 3 The spring, cushion, and buoyancy: Company Appels, Princeton University, April 23, 2007, personal archive, Photo Credit: Gene Schiavone 239

Toys, Childhood, and Material Culture in Byzantium

Fig. 1 *Toy in the Shape of a Rider and Two Horses on Wheels*, fourth century AD, Wood 14.2 cm (5 9/16 in.), The J. Paul Getty Museum, Getty Villa, Pacific Palisades, CA, inv, 82.AI.76.22 (Digital image courtesy of the Getty's Open Content Program) 244
Fig. 2 Bone doll with a body made of rags, eighth or ninth century AD, Egypt. H. 11 cm; W. 8 cm. Benaki Museum, Athens, inv. 10390 (*Source* © Benaki Museum) 245
Fig. 3 Bone doll Fatimid period (909–1171), Egypt. Benaki Museum, Athens, inv. 10737. **a.** Naked bone figurine, front and back views. H. 13.5 cm; W. 3 cm. **b.** Bone doll dressed in fourteen layers of tunics (*Source* © Benaki Museum) 246
Fig. 4 Miniature wooden boat found during the excavations of the Theodosian harbor (Theodosios I, r. 379–395) of Yenikapı, Marmaray Excavations, Istanbul, 2008. Late fifth or sixth century AD (?). Length 17.2 cm; Width 7.1 cm. Istanbul Archaeological Museum, inv. MRY'08-9060. **a.** side view **b.** view from above (*Source* © Istanbul Archaeological Museums) 247

2 Sisters, 2 Stories: Breast Cancer, Femininity, and Body Ownership

Fig. 1 Thedra Cullar-Ledford, *Bedroom Gaberdine* (2016) 388
Fig. 2 Humument 1, personal archive 396
Fig. 3 Humument 2, personal archive 397
Fig. 4 Scrabble Cancer Project, personal archive 399

The Republic of Childhood: Friedrich Froebel's Kindergarten and *Naturphilosophie*

Fig. 1 Friedrich Froebel, "Übungsplatz für kleine Kinder zu Blankenburg" (ca. 1839) 436

List of Tables

Ludic Music in Ancient Greek and Roman Theater

Table 1 Musical patterns in Plautus' *Mostellaria* 196
Table 2 Plautus, *Mostellaria*: metrical structure 198

INTRODUCTION: Ludics—Play as Humanistic Inquiry

Vassiliki Rapti and Eric Gordon

"Play taunts us with its inaccessibility. We feel that something is behind it all, but we do not know, or have forgotten how to see it," Robert Fagan claims.[1] Play is an integral part of being human. It is how we learn, explore, how we imagine, and experience joy. But then we grow up. And the mystery of play ceases to matter. In most cultures, excluding competitive sports and gambling, play is largely detached from the "serious" matters of adulthood. It is an escape hatch, a safety valve, a mere retreat from the official structures of modern adult life. "All serious activities," writes Hannah Arendt in *The Human Condition*, "irrespective

[1]Quoted in Sutton-Smith, Brian, *The Ambiguity of Play* (Harvard University Press, May 15, 2001), 2. https://www.hup.harvard.edu/catalog.php?isbn=9780674005815.

V. Rapti (✉)
Classical Studies, Boston University, Boston, MA, USA

E. Gordon
Visual and Media Arts, Emerson College, Boston, MA, USA
e-mail: eric_gordon@emerson.edu

V. Rapti and E. Gordon (eds.), *Ludics*,
https://doi.org/10.1007/978-981-15-7435-1_1

of their fruits, are called labor, and every activity which is not necessary either for the life of the individual or the life process of society is subsumed under playfulness."[2] So there is labor—that which is directly applicable to personal or social goals, and everything else is play, which is marginalized and frivolous. In an extended footnote, Arendt equates this to another binary between necessity and freedom, wherein everything becomes either an activity to meet one's needs (i.e., we work in order to be able to live) or to be free from that necessity. Not even the "work" of the artist is left, she says: "It is dissolved into play and has lost its worldly meaning."[3]

By maligning play, confining it into the "non-serious" and the frivolous, society continues down its violent path of rationalization. The space of childhood discovery, the foundation of learning, becomes meaningless. The arts are further marginalized as neatly distinct from productive labor, and child's play is quickly forgotten as a fleeting stage of human development. Play is the label society puts on the frivolous, and as such Arendt is not interested in salvaging it. Instead she turns to the concept of action. She argues that the human condition, or the *vita activa*, consists of three parts: labor, work, and action. Labor is life itself, it is the physical effort involved in getting things done. Work "provides an 'artificial' world of things."[4] It is the product of human labor. Action is the perpetual process of creation, of invention, of putting new things into motion. It "corresponds to the human condition of plurality," which, she argues, "is the condition of human action, because we are all the same, that is, human, in such a way that nobody is ever the same as anyone else who ever lived, lives or will live."[5] Action is social. It is worldly. It describes the connections between individuals that are created through expression, experimentation, exploration, and play. But, she laments, it is also at risk. It is being squeezed out of a rational, laboring society,

[2]Arendt, Hannah, *The Human Condition*, 2nd Edition (8601300156224) (Chicago, IL: University of Chicago Press, 1998), 127. https://www.amazon.com/Human-Condition-2nd-Hannah-Arendt/dp/0226025985. Accessed 29 May 2020.

[3]Ibid., 128.

[4]Ibid., 7.

[5]Ibid., 7–8.

and relegated to the irrelevant. So while she never makes the connection between action and play, we embrace Arendt's idea of action as a powerful form of play.

We have called this book *Ludics* because of its expansive meaning. Ludics derives from the Latin *ludus* (plural *ludi*), a direct derivative of the verb *ludere*, meaning "to play," on which the Dutch anthropologist Johan Huizinga comments as follows:

> In remarkable contrast to Greek with its changing and heterogeneous terms for the play-function, Latin has really only one word to cover the whole field of play*: ludus*, from *ludere*, of which *ludus* is a direct derivative. We should observe that *jocus, jocari* in the special sense of joking and jesting does not mean play proper in classical Latin. Though *ludere* may be used for the leaping of fishes, the fluttering of birds and the splashing of water, its etymology does not appear to lie in the sphere of rapid movement, flashing, etc., but in that of non-seriousness, and particularly of "semblance" or "deception." *Ludus* covers children's games, recreation, contests, liturgical and theatrical representations, and games of chance. In the expression *lares ludentes* it means "dancing."[6]

The slippage of meaning in the word *ludus* corresponds perfectly not only to the interdisciplinary character of this edited volume but also to our take on play as a *sine qua non* of humanistic inquiry. Play's association with "deception," and "semblance," pointed out by Huizinga further implies "mischievousness," "bringing to light," or "leisure," as opposed to seriousness, and alludes to its potential for new beginnings, setting into motion new realities, new inquiries, and new discoveries. Hence *ludus* shares the root of the word *leid*, which means to "let go frequently," which is common in many other languages, including the Latvian *laist*, which means "to let, publish," or "set in motion." The concept of ludics much like Arendt's action, suggests opportunity for new beginnings, for the unleashing of meaning into the world of discourse. Understood as poetics of play, ludics has deep connections to learning,

[6]Huizinga, Johan, *Homo Ludens: A Study of the Play-Element in Culture* (Boston, MA: Beacon Press, 1955), 35. Amazon.com. https://www.amazon.com/Homo-Ludens-Study-Play-Element-Culture/dp/1621389995. Accessed 28 May 2020.

knowledge creation and its dissemination. In fact, we argue that the ludic drive, or the desire to play, is an essential part of humanistic inquiry and in this respect we align with Huizinga who claimed that culture arises in and as play. Also, in his definition of the humanities, Geofrey Galt Harpham argues that the "scholarly study of documents and artifacts produced by human beings in the past enables us to see the world from different points of view so that we may better understand ourselves."[7] Unlike the sciences that generate understanding through narrowing and refining, the humanities is the art of sensemaking, of interpretation, of generating discourse. But many disciplines representing the humanities have become so thoroughly disciplined in the modern university that they have little room to acknowledge their common connection to *ludere*. The humanities has trended toward putting objects on *dis*play—to immobilize, to capture meaning in time and space. Where play invites new beginnings, display invites reflection. Where play means activity and engagement, display calls for inactivity and speculation.

Through discipline and professionalization, the humanities risks losing sight of its simple goal of "understanding ourselves in the world." Arendt defines the world as all the ways in which people interact with each other and produce meaning through action. What she famously labeled "dark times" is a state in which people are increasingly alienated from the world, or the structures that comprise the space in between individuals. We are now living in dark times. As we write this introduction, the world is in the midst of the Covid-19 pandemic, wherein space between individuals is mandated as a public health requirement. We are literally distanced from one another as a means of keeping each other safe. But when Arendt speaks of the world as the space between individuals, she is not referring to physical space, she is referring to discourse, the generative play of meaning that happens through art, culture, conversation, love, and shared experience. Even when we are physically close, we can be void of connections. When the world is filled with misinformation, mistrust, and missed opportunities, then we are distanced. When public sector institutions fail to represent the public, when art speaks only for

[7]Harpham, Geoffrey Galt, *The Humanities and the Dream of America* (Chicago, IL: University of Chicago Press, 2011), 23. https://press.uchicago.edu/ucp/books/book/chicago/H/bo10774861.html.

the artist, when weaponized Tweets are mistaken for dialogue, and when the pursuit of truth is just another lie, then the social distance grows. Dark times prevail.

This book takes the bold position that *play is an antidote to dark times*. Rather than an escape hatch, it provides opportunity for discovery, connection, joy, care, and relational aesthetics—conditions that are central to worldliness, not extraneous to it. Even though play is often characterized as distinct from "everyday life," such as Huizinga's concept of the *magic circle*, it should be seen as a persistent fluctuation as opposed to a constant state.[8] Huizinga defines play as "a free activity standing quite consciously outside 'ordinary' life as being 'not serious' but at the same time absorbing the player intensely and utterly."[9] Stepping into the magic circle does not need to be premeditated. Play can happen within a well-organized game, or it can happen spontaneously in a moment and just as quickly subside. It can take recognizable form (games, sport, imaginative exploration), or it can look like something else entirely (deliberation, interpretation, discovery, flirting). Brian Sutton-Smith argues that play is not one thing or another, it is a set of competing rhetorics, most commonly split between the "rhetoric of progress" (play teaches and builds life skills), and the "rhetoric of fate," (play is the "illusion of mastery over life's circumstances").[10] These rhetorics are the ways academics, educators, policymakers, speak about the affordances or dangers of play. They are descriptive of the position of the player, as well as those looking at play from the outside. But Sutton-Smith also introduces the rhetoric of resistance, which represents how players make sense of the power dynamics in a playspace and how play is used as an oppositional strategy to fixed structures. Miguel Sicart characterizes this kind of resistance as playfulness. "To be playful is to appropriate a context that is not created or intended for play. Playfulness is the play-like appropriation of what should not be play."[11] From a unique flourish in a dance, to uneven rhymes in poetry, to a bold interpretation of a

---

[8]Huizinga, Johan, *Homo Ludens: A Study of the Play-Element in Culture*.

[9]Ibid., 13.

[10]Sutton-Smith, Brian, *The Ambiguity of Play*. Accessed 28 May 2020.

[11]Sicart, Miguel, *Play Matters* (Cambridge: MIT Press, 2014), 27. https://mitpress.mit.edu/books/play-matters.

biblical text, to a surprise kiss between new lovers, playfulness defines a whole slate of actions that are outside of what typically gets labeled as labor or serious work. Play is where and when we learn. According to Douglas Thomas and John Seely Brown, "All systems of play are, at base, learning systems. They are ways of engaging in complicated negotiations of meaning, interaction and competition, not only for entertainment, but also for creating meaning. Most critically, play reveals a structure of learning that is radically different from the one most schools or other formal learning environments provide, and which is well suited to the notions of a world in constant flux."[12]

David Staley, in his book *Alternative Universities,* develops this idea further. He proposes a model of a university he calls "the Institute for Advanced Play," where play is acknowledged as the "highest form of learning, placed well above the acquisition and production of knowledge."[13] This institute is designed as a playground and encourages imaginative exploration. There is no specific goal for the acquisition of knowledge. It is for its own sake. Play always exists within structure. Staley's Institute is an imaginative articulation of that. Whether it's the structure of a board game, a playing field, a poem, the shared imagination of a group of children at a playground, within a dance, a conversation, flirtation, or even the laboratory, play is never completely free. Either the players themselves or the architects of the playspace create a space for play to happen. This can be entirely within the imagination of one person, or in a codified rule book. The Institute accommodates all forms. As play is enveloped by its own facilitating structure, it can be mobile—following players around from school to home, from peace to war. Staley continues in his explanation: the Institute is a "space for unlearning and failure. Unlearning implies the opposite of a specialist, who is someone with deep knowledge…Failure is a natural outcome of pure play. Freed from any pressure to perform or produce, [participants] explore and

[12]Thomas and Brown, *A New Culture of Learning: Cultivating the Imagination for a World of Constant Change*, 97. https://www.amazon.com/New-Culture-Learning-Cultivating-Imagination/dp/1456458884.

[13]*Alternative Universities: Speculative Design for Innovation in Higher Education* (Johns Hopkins University Press, 2019), 161. https://www.amazon.com/Alternative-Universities-Speculative-Innovation-Education/dp/1421427419. Accessed 29 May 2020.

appropriate and fail."[14] This space of play, removed from the pressures of industrial productivity, activates players toward discovering worldly meaning, without mind to specific outcomes. Play, when structured appropriately, provides a safe space to fail.[15] While Staley's speculative designs are fictional, untethered by the practicalities of tuition, grant funding, and the needs of benefactors, it provides a useful object from which to imagine other futures where ludics is aligned with humanistic inquiry.

This book is not a critique of the humanities, but rather a celebration of the play drive, "the core of humanity," in Friedrich Schiller's words, which binds humanistic inquiry together. Take notice of Schiller's famous quote, for instance: "Man plays only when he is in the full sense of the word man, and he is only wholly Man when he is playing" (qtd. in Frissen, Valerie, Jos De Mul, and Joost Raessens, 76). Since Schiller an entire tradition in favor of play has been established in the humanities, from the rise of modernity to today's ludic century,[16] which is well summarized by Valerie Frissen, Jos De Mul, and Joost Raessens as the ludic turn:

> Alongside reasoning (Homo sapiens) and making (Homo faber), playing (Homo ludens) now advanced to the centre of attention. Philosophers such as Nietzsche, Wittgenstein, Heidegger, Gadamer, Marcuse, Deleuze and Derrida (most of them considered as forerunners or representatives of postmodern culture) followed the ludological footprints of Heraclitus and Schiller in their attempts to transform modern, predominantly rationalistic and utilitarian ontology and anthropology. But in the natural sciences, social sciences and humanities, a strong interest in play – and the related phenomenon game – grew as well. One can think, for example, of the implementation of game theory in biology, economics and cultural anthropology. In addition to the interest in the phenomena of play and

---

[14]Ibid., 163.

[15]Juul, Jesper, *The Art of Failure* (Cambridge: MIT Press, 2013). https://mitpress.mit.edu/books/art-failure. Accessed 29 May 2020.

[16]Zimmerman, Eric, "Position Statement: Manifesto for a Ludic Century," In *The Gameful World: Approaches, Issues, Applications,* edited by Steffen P. Walz and Deterding Sebastian (Cambridge, MA and London, UK: MIT Press, 2014), 19–22. https://doi.org/10.2307/j.ctt1287hcd.5. Accessed 30 May 2020.

> games in these already existing disciplines, in the last decades – motivated by the substantial growth of leisure time and the growth of ludo-industry and ludo-capitalism – several new disciplines entirely devoted to the study of play and (computer) games have emerged.[17]

Sensing the resurgence of the ludic turn then, the editors of this volume in 2013 established a forum that would focus primarily on play and the cross-pollination it could potentially engender in the current humanities. They sought a kind of language very close to Mary Flanagan's ludic language that draws on Nicolas Bourriaud's cited relational aesthetics: "In this, the people involved in relational works together craft a dynamic disruption of the mundane and reconnect with humanness. In a sense, relational works are in direct opposition to abstractions and disembodied experience" (Flanagan 261).[18] Such disruption of the mundane could potentially disrupt the status quo of the traditionally understood humanities that this edited volume aspires to offer, by making room for embodied experiences of play as humanistic inquiry that encompasses poetry, performance, philosophy, and other disciplines. The essays collected in this volume were all presented at the *Ludics* seminar as part of the Harvard Mahindra Humanities Center,[19] which is co-chaired by the editors of this book. Each of the contributors was invited to present new work that examined the role of play in humanistic inquiry—from disciplines well beyond those typically associated with the humanities.

[17]See p. 76. in Frissen, Valerie, Jos De Mul, and Joost Raessens, "Homo Ludens 2.0: Play, Media and Identity," In *Contemporary Culture: New Directions in Art and Humanities Research*, edited by Thissen Judith, Zwijnenberg Robert, and Zijlmans Kitty (Amsterdam University Press, 2013), 75–92. https://doi.org/10.2307/j.ctt6wp6n0.8. Accessed 30 May 2020.

[18]Flanagan, Mary, "Playful Aesthetics: Toward a Ludic Language," In *The Gameful World: Approaches, Issues, Applications*, edited by Steffen P. Walz and Deterding Sebastian (Cambridge, MA and London, UK: MIT Press, 2014), 249–272. https://doi.org/10.2307/j.ctt1287hcd.19. Accessed 30 May 2020.

Mary Flanagan delivered the talk "Purposeful Gaming" in a joint presentation with Constance Rinaldo at the Ludics Seminar on September 14, 2015. Their talk focused on the Biodiversity Heritage Library (BHL), an international consortium of the world's leading natural history libraries that has the goal of improving research methodology by collaboratively making biodiversity literature openly available to the world as part of a global biodiversity community.

[19]"Ludics—Mahindra Humanities Center—Harvard University." http://mahindrahumanities.fas.harvard.edu/content/ludics. Accessed 27 May 2020.

Over the years, the seminar has welcomed historians, literary critics, theologians, classicists, dancers, visual artists, philosophers, educators, entrepreneurs, translators, activists, and physicists. Each participant was asked to reflect on the role of play in their object of study, or in their process of inquiry and each one came up with their own ludic language, and in many cases, with their own *sui generis* embodied experiences as it is exemplified in the sections of poetics and performance of this book. The result is a playbook of distinct ludic narratives that together constitute aspects of ludic language situated in an eternal present and that oscillates between what Roger Callois calls free play (*paidia*) and constrained play (*ludus*),[20] between one discipline and another, in the hope to further advance a dialogue that will lead to a cross-pollination of thought. Together, the essays collected here represent a range of perspectives and approaches to humanistic inquiry where *ludics* is a common thread expressed in a ludic language.

The opening section of the book is called the "Playspace, Ethics and Engagement." Here the authors ask questions such as: Who benefits from play? Can play transform the structures of institutions? Who gets to be a player? And who makes those decisions? Miguel Sicart's essay, "Toward an Ethics of *Homo Ludens*," reflects on what happens when computers become the players and create worlds. More specifically, Sicart claims that, as we live in a historical moment defined by the ubiquitous presence of computers—playful machines that shape our experience of computers from video games and gamification to other forms of leisure, play has a fundamental role in shaping the cultures of the information age and therefore it has profound social, cultural, and ethical implications. Such an example is offered from another era by Arthur Louis Ruprecht, Jr., in his essay "SPORT MATTERS: On Art, Social Artifice and the Rules of the Game, or, the Politics of Sport." Ruprecht's essay showcases how C. L. R. James's *Beyond a Boundary* connects race, class, nation, and sport and emphasizes the moral and political meaning of organized sport.

Doris Sommer's "PreText: Press Play to Teach Anything," is a descriptive analysis of her play-based curriculum that uses playful humanistic

---

[20]Caillois, *Roger, Man, Play and Games* (Chicago, IL: University of Illinois Press, 1961). https://www.amazon.com/Man-Play-Games-Roger-Caillois/dp/025207033X. Accessed 28 May 2020.

inquiry to generate discourse. The curriculum invites participants to design activities, to create interpretations, and then pause to reflect. Speculations, readings that converge or diverge, and admiration for different points of view all come from the players in *eureka* moments that glow with pleasure. They add up to an aesthetic education in deep reading and in broad civility that can revive the school of Athens and Schiller's Enlightenment. Next is an article by political philosopher and civic engagement scholar, Peter Levine. "Work, Play and Civic Engagement" juxtaposes *homo ludens* with *homo faber*, contrasting the player with the public worker and artisan in the world. Being critical of civic engagement designed to be more play-like or game-like, Levine dismantles the relationship between work and play in the civic domain and discusses what may happen to that relationship if work disappears for many human beings while opportunities for play expand. The following essay is by scholar-architect Zenovia Toloudi. Her essay "Technoecologies: The Interplay of Space and its Perception" examines how play is used as a tactic in architecture and urban design. Here the author, through an examination of her own architectural work, reimagines a playful symbiosis that begins with language, between people and the environment. By working through tangible media (models and installations) with a grounded vision and through concepts/modes such, experiment and experience, metabolic aesthetics, ordinary and illusionary, empathy and vulnerability, public participation and user engagement, the living can be imagined as possible, positive, and even playful. Play with language is crucial for Toloudi's work and opens up possibilities for the perception of space. The section concludes with Eric Gordon and Gabriel Mugar's essay "Meaningful Inefficiencies: Incorporating Play into Civic Design" that examines play as a logic of civic design. Through play, they argue, it is possible to create spaces for trust between institutions and constituents. Based on research with civic organizations ranging from public newsrooms to municipal governments, they identify how practitioners are using play to scaffold community interactions. The essay concludes with a brief case study of a project called *Participatory Pokémon Go*, where play was used as a backdrop to engage youth in repairing data inequities in Boston.

The second section, "Playthings, Comedy and Laughter," comprises five essays that span three millennia from various disciplines, including theology, philosophy, classics, archaeology, music, theater, and dance, with a particular emphasis on laughter as a manifestation of play. Within this frame, Mary J. Yossi's "'Let Us Laugh and Play': Laughter in Greek Lyric Poetry" shows how laughter connects with play. Through a short selection of fragments of Archilochus, Theognis, Semonides, Sappho, and Pindar, with reference to genre and occasion, modes of behavior, and systems of value that the vocabulary of laughter reveals, Yossi shows that, apart from its principal function as a weapon for derision or blame (*psogos*), laughter in Ancient Greek Lyric Poetry can assume various meanings depending on the context (sympotic, erotic, ritual, etc.) within which the term (*gelōs*) is used.

Similarly, in his essay "Ludic Music in Ancient Greek and Roman Theater," Timothy Moore argues that that ancient theater's music was not just for fun but its ludic element is undeniable in any play we consider. In some, like *Mostellaria*, music carried audiences into a realm of playfulness that would be impossible in drama that was merely spoken.

The inherent connection between the ludic and comedy is also extended to our modern era. In his essay, "Comedy, Physicality, and Ludic Dance Gestures: The Comic in Ballet and Tai Chi?," John Robinson-Appels juxtaposes the training and performing traditions of ballet and Tai Chi only to see that the smile, as is true with the Mona Lisa's smile, is an enigmatic gesture in which both the tragic and the comic are interpreted. The physical action of producing a smile is a ludic operation filled with both hope and trepidation, and is deployed upon the domains of the tragic and the comic. The comic, Robinson-Appels argues, is a byproduct of the ludic gesture, the result of a ludic action, the aftereffect, the afterglow, of a committed physical gesture which has been enacted.

Laughter is also discussed in a theological context. In his essay, "Did Jesus Christ Laugh? Umberto Eco's Question and Saint John Chrysostom's Response," Chrysonstomos A. Stamoulis delves deep into John Chrysostom's views on laughter and argues that what bothered the Father of the Church is the inopportune and measureless laughter that distances man from Godly mourning, not laughter itself. On the contrary, laughter when manifested at the appropriate moment is what allows the flourishing of the mystery of friendship and community essential for the resurrection of the human soul. This reality presents joy, mixed with sorrow and pain which moves beyond theories of purity and fleshless idolatry of "types and forms." Interestingly, a reality that presents joy and laughter in the lives of children who are instructed to seek the divine is also reflected in the material culture of children's toys during the Byzantine era. In her essay, "Toys, Childhood and Material Culture in Byzantium," Brigitte Pitarakis argues that the universe of children's play offers a valuable tool for a new reading of Byzantine artistic production, as abstraction and phantasm, the two central elements in children's play, regulate exchanges between the sensible and the intelligible in all aspects of secular and religious life in Byzantium. Her examination of how toys mediated children's interactions with nature and animals, as well as their social interactions with children and adults, show how they were used as vehicles in the quest of divine knowledge.

The third section is called "Language and Poetics of Play." It delves into the playful and ironic intricacies of language, identity, and poetic art as defined by perception of space and the slippage of language. Starting with a reference to Johan Huizinga's *Homo Ludens* and diving into a detailed comparative poetry analysis, Sarah Green's essay "How to Catch a Falling Knife: Poetic Play as the Practice of Negative Capability," demonstrates how play activates poetic imagination and discloses *ars poetica* as negative capability. The endless capability to activate creative imagination is also demonstrated by Danuta Fjellestad in her essay "The Ludic Impulse in Postmodern Fiction," which is informed by Zimmerman's *Ludic Manifesto* and (re)claims a place for post-postmodern fiction in the so-called ludic turn. Focusing on the *Gameful World* collection, Fjellestad proposes that while postmodern fiction is high on cognitive ludicity, post-postmodernism is high on ergodic ludicity. It shows that the ludic impulse in post-postmodern fiction reconceptualizes the format of the codex: the gaming elements are recast from the diegetic level, the level of the story, onto the material machine or platform for telling stories, the book.

Yorgos Anagnostou in his *sui generis* autobiographical account "Immigraνт Poetics: Play as Performativity of the Liminal Self" reveals from within how *ars poetica* is instinctively unleashed through play and how this process automatically creates the immigrant's oscillating self in an effort to constantly negotiate a sense of belonging and non-belonging, a sense of constant wrestling with language(s) and a sense of endless possibilities due to the constant slippage of meaning, where freeplay is seen as disruption of presence, an interplay between absence and presence.

In her essay, "Games Translators Play in Bilingual French-Canadian Theater," Nicole Nolette discloses how playful language in translation helps us understand how target-oriented practices can resemble a bow and arrow, and how translation can be a pointed trajectory toward purposeful exclusion. Such a conception of translation reminds us that translation doesn't have to occur between two languages and cultures, that it can even play across the two to consolidate a single community. Through playful translation, bilingualism and translation intersect, creating different versions of bilingual performances that cater to specific audiences in a gesture of resistance while accommodating unilingual spectators whose presence is considered to be necessary to become legitimate. Thus, the partial translation process points to its own bias, its own partiality and fondness for a particular ideal spectator, its own intended circulation from the margins. It is a jolting reminder that terms need not be deemed untranslatable, but that translation itself can engage with their resistance to substitution. In other words, it calls on us to take up what Apter refers to as "a linguistic form of creative failure with homeopathic uses" within the context of translation rather than without it.

The last section of this book is called "Play (Modes) & Performance as Transgression." It opens with Pierre Taminiaux's essay, "Ludics as Transgression: From Surrealism to the Absurd to Pataphysics," which analyzes the critical power of ludics in six of his plays, influenced by surrealism, the theater of the absurd and pataphysics, published in the last decade. These works constitute a metaphorical representation of twenty-first century French culture and of some of the main issues that characterize it, from random violence to the overall decline of the French social contract. Ludics is conceived here as an important tool for the expression of a social and political discourse that is rooted in the community. Ludics is introduced to question ways of thinking that are based on purely objective and rational language.

In her turn, Catalina Florina Florescu's autobiographical play "2 Sisters, 2 Stories: Breast Cancer, Femininity, and Body Ownership" which is a tribute to her mother, a victim of breast cancer, uses the fluidity of ludics in order to talk freely and raise awareness about women's ill bodies. Inscribed in a feminist discourse informed by the transformational power of games in performance, Florescu created the game "Scrabble-Cancer Project" that encapsulates the playful dimension of people's lives and exposes and challenges the linguistic impact of the illness. This adapted scrabble game conceives of bodies and words as open, associative structures that connect through people's bodies via sensations and experiences in an infinity of connective tissues. For Florescu, games and exercises have the capacity to ease the embarrassment and pain of difficult conversations.

The next piece is called "'Don't Be Mean' and Other Lessons from Children's Play of the Federal Theater Project." Leslie Frost takes us back to children's theater in the 1930s, which seldom engaged with the most controversial political issues of its time, such as labor justice, anti-racism, and anti-fascism. Yet she discovered three children's plays of the Federal Theater Project (1935–1939) that explore how children's play and childhood imagination vanquish forces of violence, oppression, and inequality. The cultivation of civic virtue in early childhood education is the focus of the next chapter coming from the field of early childhood education and landscape architecture. Historian of architecture Diana Ramírez-Jasso in her article, "The Republic of Childhood: Friedrich Froebel's Kindergarten and *Naturphilosophie*" walks us through Friedrich Froebel's Kindergarten model, established during the Enlightenment. According to that model the garden functioned as a miniature state for children, since they were engaged in gardening practices that allowed for an engagement with objects, people, and nature that emerged out of the child's own desire. Such a recognition of the benefits of harnessing the child's natural curiosity and discoverability as a conduit for genuine artistic expression is undertaken in the final chapter of this edited volume. Vassiliki Rapti's essay, "Oscillating Between Tag and Hopscotch:

Theo Angelopoulos' Playful Aesthetics," examines how the Greek auteur-cineaste uses the children's games, specifically tag and hopscotch, as cinematic tropes for autobiographical reflection and reflection upon Greece's bleak history across his films.

The essays collected in this volume began as presentations at the *Ludics* Seminar. Each is engaged in the project of centering play in humanistic inquiry. Most of the essays are not traditional in format or subject. They span the range of the humanities disciplines, but they share the play drive,[21] the motivation for understanding the human condition that is more concerned with the connectivity of discourse than the capture of knowledge. In this spirit, we also introduce the artwork on the cover of the book. The piece is called *Gentleman's Game* and it is a collaboration between two artists, Brandon Friend and Jason Douglas Griffin. According to Pamela Bryan, the owner of the Octavia gallery, "In their signature technique, Friend and Griffin collaborate and create works by combining mixed-media that is unlike any other. *Gentleman's Game* has a unique process of turn-based mark making that results in arresting pieces rich with depth and texture. This process employs various methodologies rooted in painting, printmaking, collage, drawing and image transfer. Each mark on the canvas, whether unintentional or deliberate, forces the painting into a new context that is non-linear and shifting. The emergence of recognizable images or gestures is intended to provoke a sense of familiarity that echoes throughout the works. *Gentleman's Game* provides an aesthetic that explores themes in pop culture and mythology, which seamlessly fuses together a partnership built on individual approach, mutual respect, trust, and fair play."[22] The piece represents a give and take between two artists, a playful array of references, that seems not to lead any place in particular, but invites the viewer into the playspace to explore.

---

[21]This is inspired by philosopher Bernard Suits' notion of the "ludic attitude." He explains how players need to approach games with a desire to play the game. He declares that all games are voluntary. Indeed, we assert that must be voluntary as well, otherwise it drifts into the realm of labor. See Suits, Bernard, *The Grasshopper* (New York: Broadview Press, 2005). https://www.amazon.com/Grasshopper-Games-Life-Utopia/dp/155111772X.

[22]https://medium.com/@__Portia/gentlemans-game-4b9b87adf694. Accessed 29 May 2020.

As you, dear reader, explore this book, we hope that you approach it playfully. Don't look for specific outcomes; don't merely skim for a reference in the paper you're writing. Instead, look for connections between essays, imagine implicit connotations, find allusions to long-forgotten ideas of yours that have been gathering dust in your memory. We are living in dark times. Humanistic inquiry, guided by *ludere*, is more important now than ever before. Play invites new beginnings. We hope that you welcome them.

References

Arendt, Hannah. 1998. *The Human Condition.* Chicago, IL: University of Chicago Press. https://www.amazon.com/Human-Condition-2nd-Hannah-Arendt/dp/0226025985. Accessed 29 May 2020.

Brown, John Seely and Thomas, Douglas. 2011. *A New Culture of Learning: Cultivating the Imagination for a World of Constant Change.* https://www.amazon.com/New-Culture-Learning-Cultivating-Imagination/dp/1456458884.

Callois, Roger. 1961. *Man, Play and Games.* Chicago, IL: University of Illinois Press. https://www.amazon.com/Man-Play-Games-Roger-Caillois/dp/025207033X. Accessed 28 May 2020.

Flanagan, Mary. 2014. "Playful Aesthetics: Toward a Ludic Language." In *The Gameful World: Approaches, Issues, Applications*, edited by Steffen P. Walz and Deterding Sebastian, 249–272. Cambridge, MA and London, UK: MIT Press. https://doi.org/10.2307/j.ctt1287hcd.19. Accessed 30 May 2020.

Frissen, Valerie, Jos De Mul, and Joost Raessens. 2013. "Homo Ludens 2.0: Play, Media and Identity." In *Contemporary Culture: New Directions in Art and Humanities Research*, edited by Thissen Judith, Zwijnenberg Robert, and Zijlmans Kitty, 75–92. Amsterdam University Press. https://doi.org/10.2307/j.ctt6wp6n0.8. Accessed 30 May 2020.

Harpham, Geoffrey Galt. 2011. *The Humanities and the Dream of America.* Chicago, IL: University of Chicago Press. https://press.uchicago.edu/ucp/books/book/chicago/H/bo10774861.html.

Huizinga, Johan. 1955. *Homo Ludens: A Study of the Play-Element in Culture.* Boston, MA: Beacon Press. Amazon.com. https://www.amazon.com/Homo-Ludens-Study-Play-Element-Culture/dp/1621389995. Accessed 28 May 2020.

Juul, Jesper. 2013. *The Art of Failure*. Cambridge: MIT Press. https://mitpress.mit.edu/books/art-failure. Accessed 29 May 2020.

Sicart, Miguel. 2014. *Play Matters*. Cambridge: MIT Press. https://mitpress.mit.edu/books/play-matters.

Staley, David J. 2019. *Alternative Universities: Speculative Design for Innovation in Higher Education*. Baltimore: Johns Hopkins University Press. https://www.amazon.com/Alternative-Universities-Speculative-Innovation-Education/dp/1421427419. Accessed 29 May 2020.

Suits, Bernard. 2005. *The Grasshopper: Games, Life, and Utopia*. New York: Broadview Press.

Sutton-Smith, Brian. 2001. *The Ambiguity of Play*. Cambridge: Harvard University Press. https://www.hup.harvard.edu/catalog.php?isbn=9780674005815.

Zimmerman, Eric. 2014. "Position Statement: Manifesto for a Ludic Century." In *The Gameful World: Approaches, Issues, Applications*, edited by Steffen P. Walz and Deterding Sebastian. Cambridge, MA and London, UK: MIT Press. https://doi.org/10.2307/j.ctt1287hcd.5. Accessed 30 May 2020.

Playspace, Ethics & Engagement

Toward an Ethics of *Homo Ludens*

Miguel Sicart

Introduction

There is a long history of accusing videogames of societal ills. From violence to addiction, videogames have been in the crosshairs of legislators, psychologists, and moralists of all kinds. Often, there is no proof of the evil deeds of games, and probably these moral panics are fueled more by a contempt about the idea of play as escapism, than triggered by evidence of social decay caused by games.

However, these moral panics have had a large effect in the way we study games and ethics. It seems that the very idea of questioning the ethics of games needs to revolve around how the content of games, or the activity of playing games, affect our capacity as players to distinguish between the real and the virtual. This single-minded, simplistic approach

M. Sicart (✉)
University of Copenhagen, Copenhagen, Denmark
e-mail: miguel@itu.dk

V. Rapti and E. Gordon (eds.), *Ludics*,
https://doi.org/10.1007/978-981-15-7435-1_2

has left many questions and many approaches to the ethics of games underdeveloped.

In this chapter, I will present a theoretical argument to overcome the limitations of those "sensationalist" approaches to game ethics, and will use it to illustrate what new ethical issues may arise if we transcend the theoretical and cultural parameters in which we have situated play, games, and all ludic forms, when it comes to their morality.

My theoretical argument is simple: I propose that Huizinga's *homo ludens* is an instantiation of a broader conceptual category of ethical agency proposed by Floridi[1]: the *homo poieticus*. The *homo poieticus*[2] is a creative, moral agent who inhabits the infosphere, an environment "constituted by the totality of information entities, including all agents – processes, their properties and mutual relations."[3]

If we consider the *homo ludens* as a category or variation of *homo poieticus*, we can then pose new questions and analyze new ethical challenges from a perspective that is both based on solid philosophy, and on classic play theory. This chapter applies a constructivist ethics approach to look for trouble, to seek those ethical challenges that might define a generation of players and several generations of game designs, but that so far has been camouflaged under old concerns about the morality of play.

The structure of the chapter is as follows: I will start with a brief presentation of the concept of *homo ludens* as *homo poeiticus*, introducing both classic play theory, Philosophy of Information, and how these two perspectives can be combined in an original perspective on play. After that, in the second part of the chapter, I will present two different ethical questions that this perspective allows us to identify, and to propose answers to. This chapter outlines a research program on the ethics of computer games that calls for an extension of the breadth and depth of our ethical analysis of games and playable media, so we can better understand their role in culture and society.

---

[1] Floridi, *The ethics of information* (Oxford University Press, 2013).

[2] Ibid., 161–179.

[3] Floridi, Information ethics: On the philosophical foundation of computer ethics, *Ethics and Information Technology* (1999), 1(1), 37–56.

From *Homo Ludens* to *Homo Poieticus*

Tinkering with one of the key concepts in play theory is always a risky maneuver. If it doesn't work, the proposed ideas will not catch on, and the research program will fail. If it works, and a valid alternative is adopted by different communities, there will still be years of formal debates around the validity of the new terminology. It is not my intention to perform such exhaustive and exhausting work. Therefore, I do not want to argue that we should start using *homo poieticus* instead of *homo ludens*. The goal is simpler: to argue that *homo ludens* is a type of *homo poeiticus*, a subclass of a more general category or concept of human that is not defined by playing, but that uses playing to express, to construct their own relations to others and the world. Let's start, then, with the classic concept from play theory.

Understanding *Homo Ludens*

To make things easy, let's start with the concept of play. Since play is inherently ambiguous and resists definitions,[4] I will limit myself to providing an instrumental definition of play that allows me to engage with the ethics of *homo ludens*. This instrumental definition is phenomenological in nature, as I am mostly interested in *homo ludens* as a mode of explaining how humans interact and relate with the world.

Play is a way of organizing our experience of the world: "Summing up the formal characteristics of play we might call it a free activity standing quite consciously outside 'ordinary' life as being 'not serious,' but at the same time absorbing the player intensely and utterly. It is an activity connected with no material interest, and no profit can be gained by it. It proceeds within its own proper boundaries of time and space according to fixed rules and in an orderly manner. It promotes the formation of social groupings which tend to surround themselves with secrecy and to stress their difference from the common world by disguise or other

[4] Sutton-Smith, *The ambiguity of play* (Cambridge: Cambridge University Press, 1997).

means."[5] In my own[6] theory of play, I propose that that play is a mode of being in the world that structures both reality and agency: "To play is to be in the world. Playing is a form of understanding what surrounds us and who we are, and a way of engaging with others. Play is a mode of being human."[7] Play's structuring of reality and agency creates worlds that have their own purpose and seriousness.[8] These are the encapsulated worlds of dollhouses and *The Sims*, of the beauty of a ball bouncing off a wall, of the pleasure of skateboarding downhill, of making Amazon's voice controller Artificial Intelligence (AI henceforth) assistant Alexa tell a joke. The worlds created by play are not worlds of productivity, defined by their end goals and results. The worlds of play have meaning on and of their own. Play is ultimately a free activity we voluntarily engage with,[9] an activity that is separate from the world, but that is also deeply engaged with creating a world, a possible network of connections and relations based on the imposition of order through rules, the creation of behaviors through mechanics, and pleasure as a driving principle for action.

In Philosophy of Information terms, this concept of play as world-building and establishing new relations between agents can be described as re-ontologization. To play is to re-ontologize the world so we can give it a different meaning than the conventional one. This new world is open for expression, pleasure, and interrogation: "(…) play is a rebellion against the forms and forces of the world. Players confront and challenge 'claims' coming from their own bodies, the environment, the social world, and culture. In those confrontations, they try to manage behavior their way."[10] Playing is re-ontologizing the world with the purpose of appropriating it for expressive, personal reasons.

---

[5]Huizinga, *Homo ludens: A study of the play-element in culture* (Boston: Beacon Press, 1992[1938]), 13.

[6]Sicart, Playing the good life: Gamification and ethics, in *The gameful world: Approaches, issues, applications* (2014a), 225–244.

[7]Ibid., 1.

[8]Henricks, *Play and the human condition* (University of Illinois Press, 2016).

[9]Caillois, *Man, play and games* (Urbana and Chicago: University of Illinois Press, 2001[1958]); Bogost, *Play anything: The pleasure of limits, the uses of boredom, and the secret of games* (New York: Basic Books, 2016).

[10]Henricks, *Play and the human condition*, 1451–1453.

Play and the Ethics of Information

Let's look at this process of world creation from the perspective of Information Ethics and the Philosophy of Information. More specifically, let's lay the groundwork for understanding how the concept of re-ontologization can be used for the ethical inquiry on games and play. Floridi argues that one of the unique capabilities of information technologies is their capacity to re-ontologize: "re-ontologizing [...] refer[s] to a very radical form of re-engineering, one that not only designs, constructs, or structures a system (...) anew, but one that also fundamentally transforms its intrinsic nature, that is, its ontology or essence."[11] That process of representation[12] is similar to a process of creating a world: "computational model-building proceeds through the application of a repertoire of schemata, each of which joins a metaphor to a bit of mathematics that can be realized on a computer."[13]

Since the world created by this process of re-ontologization is inhabited by agents, both human and nonhuman, that relate and interact with each other,[14] any ethical approach requires to consider what happens when a world is re-ontologized. Most of the work in Philosophy of Information refers specifically to those instances in which a computer is creating a re-ontologized environment (a world). This chapter focuses mostly on the ethics of videogames, so that should not be problematic, though I admit that the applicability of these ideas to board games and other forms of non-digital play might be more complicated to argue for.

In any case, since play consists of a process of creation, of re-ontologization, it is fitting to take a constructivist approach to the

---

[11]Floridi, *The ethics of Information,* 6.

[12]Cantwell Smith, *On the origin of objects* (Cambridge, MA: MIT Press, 1996).

[13]Agre, *Computation and human experience* (Cambridge: Cambridge University Press, 1997), 38.

[14]Bynum, Flourishing ethics, *Ethics and Information Technology* (2006), *8*(4), 157–173. https://doi.org/10.1007/s10676-006-9107-1; Volkman, Why information ethics must begin with virtue ethics. *Metaphilosophy* (2010), *41*(3), 380-401; Volkman, Being a good computer professional: The advantages of virtue ethics in computing, *Professionalism in the Information and Communication Technology Industry* (2013), *3*, 109.

ethics of play. Information Ethics (IE henceforth) provides a method[15] to address some complexities of ethical constructives. Even though it implies an inflation of terminology, Information Ethics allows us to deploy a very specific framework to explain what happens when re-ontologization takes command: agents in the infosphere, be those human or artificial, like the non-playing-characters in videogames, should proactively contribute to maintaining the balance of the infosphere: "By placing value in the infosphere and in the informational nature of entities, regarded ontologically as the primary, fundamental, and constituent element of our new element and its artificial agents, it is possible to elaborate a constructionist strategy that supports an ecopoietic approach."[16] The infosphere requires constructivist ethics because it needs to be developed by all the informational agents that inhabit it: "[…] IE is an ethics addressed not just to 'users' of the world, but also to producers or demiurges, who are 'divinely' responsible for its creation and well-being."[17]

According to Floridi, humans in the infosphere should be considered *homo poieticus*, stewards of an environment in which they should act so they can thrive: "*Homo poieticus* concentrates not merely on the final result, but on the dynamic, on-going process through which the result is achieved. *Homo poieticus* is a demiurge, who takes care of reality, today conceptualized as the infosphere, to protect it and make it flourish."[18]

What do we have so far? Play is a form of creating worlds so we can establish new relations and appropriate existing world structures. This process can be defined as re-ontologization, leading us to the possibility of using Philosophy of Information to analyze what happens during these processes of re-ontologization. *Homo poieticus*, therefore, becomes a model to understand the creative stewardship of humans in these environments, be those infospheres, or game worlds. It is time to look at the ethics of *homo ludens*, so we can draw the comparison between *homo poieticus* and *homo ludens*.

---

[15]Floridi, The method of levels of abstraction, *Minds and Machines* (2008), *18*(3), 303–329. https://doi.org/10.1007/s11023-008-9113-7.

[16]Floridi, *The ethics of information*, 178–179.

[17]Ibid., 168.

[18]Ibid., 175.

Homo Ludens as Ethical Agent

The analysis of the ethics of *homo ludens* has been largely influenced by Huizinga's insistence on situating play outside the domain of morality: "Play lies outside the antithesis of wisdom and folly, and equally outside those of truth and falsehood, good and evil."[19] For Huizinga, it is important to keep the integrity of the experience of play as a separated activity, even if that means creating an uneasy contradiction with the broader argument that play creates culture.

If play is outside morality, is *homo ludens* (the player) a moral agent? And if play is outside ethics, what is the moral value and status of the culture it produces? Huizinga created these problems by insisting that play is a disinterested activity, that play produces nothing quantifiable, and that play is separate from real life. The core of the problem, then, is the issue of the *separateness* of play. And therefore, we must try to overcome this limitation by thinking within the framework proposed by Huizinga, but also in a different way. We need to redefine the separateness of play not as a formal property of play, but as the description of a process. Let's start by reassessing the very concept of play as separate from other activities.

Huizinga was adamant in his considering of play to be ontologically separated from real life due to his reading of Schiller's interpretation of Kant. In Schiller's *On the Aesthetic Education of Man*,[20] he writes: "(…) in every condition of humanity it is precisely play, and play alone, that makes man complete."[21] Schiller's argument is a reading of Kantian aesthetics.[22] This Kantian "play" is a detached activity outside of the domain of productivity.

[19]Huizinga, *Homo ludens: A study of the play-element in culture*, 6.

[20]Schiller, *Dover Books on Western Philosophy: On the aesthetic education of man* (Mineola, New York: Dover Publications, 1794 [2012]).

[21]Ibid., 79.

[22]Kant, *The Cambridge edition of the works of Immanuel Kant: Critique of judgement* (Cambridge: Cambridge University Press, 1790 [2001]); see also Laxton, From judgement to process: The modern ludic field, in D. J. Getsy (Ed.), *Refiguring modernism: From diversion to subversion, games, play, and twentieth-century art* (Pennsylvania: Pennsylvania State University Press, 2011), 3–24.

For Huizinga, play creates culture as a function of its disinterestedness, as a result of its (Kantian) aesthetic engagement with the world. This argument complicates the moral position of the concept of *homo ludens*, since any attempt to do so would break the disinterested, separate, aesthetic engagement with the world that constitutes the very essence of play. Play is paradoxical, but it should not be to the extent that we cannot think about its role in shaping the ethical behavior of those who play, or the moral impact of their actions. If we accept play's separateness as an unnegotiable ontological quality, then we are accepting a paradoxical position: play creates culture, but if we accept that play is outside morality, then the culture it creates is also outside the scope of moral scrutiny.

Creating an order in the world by applying a play lens to it is what makes *homo ludens* a creator of culture. Play can create worlds, and these worlds reflect the values of *homo ludens*. That is why we need to inquire on the moral foundation of *homo ludens*: to understand the ethical challenges of a playful computational culture, and the ways in which we can intervene to analyze problems and effect change.

Play is a moral action because it re-ontologizes the world for the purpose of playing. Play creates encapsulated worlds through the use of rules, social norms, and mutually agreed goals, in order to achieve a (shared) pleasurable experience.[23] This process of appropriation is not morally neutral: games and other play technologies have embedded values[24] that affect the way the world is re-ontologized. At the same time, players have values they bring to the activity of play.[25] The worlds created at play are assemblages[26] of technologies and agencies, human and artificial.

Any ethical discourse about *homo ludens* needs to reflect both the informational nature of being, the infosphere as the space in which informational agents live and thrive, and the creative, appropriative capacities

---

[23] Goffman, *Encounters, two studies in the sociology of interaction* (Indianapolis: Bobbs-Merrill, 1961); Henricks, *Play and the human condition.*

[24] Sicart, *The ethics of computer games.*

[25] Ibid.

[26] De Landa, *A new philosophy of society: Assemblage theory and social complexity* (Bloomsbury Publishing, 2006); Taylor, The assemblage of play, *Games and Culture* (2009), *4*(4), 331–339.

of *homo ludens*. An ethical understanding of *homo ludens* needs to be flexible enough to allow for understanding how play is both separate from the conventional structuring of reality and reflecting the social structures in which it takes place.

Homo Ludens as *Homo Poeiticus*

To play is to create worlds. *Homo ludens* is a creator of worlds in which rules and actions are giving purposes and consistency to the very existence of that world. To play by the rules, and to change those rules so all players are welcome and they can enjoy the pleasures of play, is to act *poietically* in the world of play. Playing is *poiesis*: the creation of infospheres to inhabit, within this world, for ourselves and others to enjoy. Playing is a carefully balanced activity that proposes a world, gives it a consistency through rules and props, and gives agents the responsibility of keeping that world alive.

Both *homo poieticus* and *homo ludens* are concepts that describe agency in the infosphere. They are both models of constructivist beings, creators, and preservers of worlds. Because of their central role in creating and preserving these worlds, both *homo ludens* and *homo poieticus* as agents who should have moral responsibility toward the world they inhabit and the agents they interact with. *Homo poieticus* is a steward of the values and informational integrity of the environment in which they inhabit. Similarly, *homo ludens* is responsible for the values that define the encapsulated infosphere created when playing. As Goffman observed, many of the activities that we engage with when we play have to do with collectively negotiating the purpose of our actions while maintaining the integrity of the separated world in which we play: "Speaking more strictly, we can think of inhibitory rules that tell participants what they must not attend to and of facilitating rules that tell them what they may recognize."[27] To play is to create and sustain an encapsulated infosphere. *Homo ludens* has creative stewardship in the infospheres of play.

---

[27]Goffman, *Encounters, two studies in the sociology of interaction* (Indianapolis: Bobbs-Merrill, 1961), 31.

Playing is a way of manifesting the ethical nature of *homo poieticus*. This encapsulated play infosphere is separate but not unrelated to the world. Playing is constructing worlds. Most research on the ethics of games has focused on the gameworld as a finished manifestation. In this chapter I encourage a shift of perspective toward the analysis of the processes that lead to the creation of gameworlds, from rules and social norms to the broader ecologies of media and culture in which games can be found. Games are encapsulated infospheres, and we should analyze the relations between the encapsulated gameworld, and the world at large.

An ethical *homo ludens* is in creative charge of the values that structure the re-ontologization process that creates the encapsulated infosphere. *Homo ludens* is also in charge of upholding those values and contributing to the experience of the ludic in a creative way. If we are to understand how *homo ludens* can act ethically in the Information Age, we need to address its *poietic* actions, and develop the kind of constructivist ethics that will allow us to better engage with these play worlds and the ways they have an effect in computational culture.

I propose then that the ethical analysis of *homo ludens* focuses on how to create worlds through play by specifying the values of those worlds, the values of the actions that can take place in that world, and how they relate to the infosphere. It is the moral duty of *homo ludens* to make these values public, to share them, to reflect upon them, and to ensure that they contribute to the well-being of every agent in the playworld. By public here I refer to a double position: public within the gameworld, so communities of play can be created around those values; and public from the gameworld toward the world outside of the game, so it is possible to understand, analyze, and critique the values of the game within the broader cultural discourses in which they are situated.

To play is to create worlds within this world, creating culture and human forms of expression. In our era of ubiquitous computer machines, questioning the ethics of *homo ludens* is fundamental to understand some of the ethical challenges posed by videogames. But most interestingly, which new ethical challenges does this perspective, of *homo ludens* as *homo poieticus*, allow us to analyze?

Changing Topics: New Horizons for Ethical Inquiries in Videogames

The purpose of this chapter is to move on from the classic, tried and tired topics that have dominated the discourse on the philosophy and ethics of games.[28] Considering that the ethical responsibility of *homo ludens* is to practice creative stewardship of the playworld that is created when playing, I propose to look at two different new ethical challenges that, if we focused exclusively on analyzing the game as object, and not the capacity of players to act and enact values, would be invisible for ethical analysis.

Videogames Are Culture

To put this approach to the ethics of videogames to test, let me return to the question of violent videogames, and let's explore them as ethical challenges. First of all, it is imperative to start by acknowledging that violent videogames are extraordinarily popular, both in terms of their commercial impact and of their cultural relevance. Even in the age of the independent videogames as a form of exploration of a medium, the popular discourse around videogames often pays extraordinary attention to games in which violence is a key element of gameplay.

One way of explaining the popularity of these games could be through the application of Huizinga's ideas, who argued that play was a formal structuring of conflict within accepted boundaries and separate from the real world. But that does not answer the actual ethical question these violent games raise: why does Western culture embrace violent and militaristic metaphors as the dominant rhetoric to embody the artificial conflict of play?

[28] McCormick, Is it wrong to play violent video games? *Ethics and Information Technology* (2001), *3*, 277–287; Coeckelbergh, Violent computer games, empathy, and cosmopolitanism, *Ethics and Information Technology* (2007), *9*, 219–231; Waddington, Locating the wrongness in ultra-violent video games, *Ethics and Information Technology* (2007), *9*, 121–128; Wonderly, A Humean approach to assessing the moral significance of ultra-violent video games, *Ethics and Information Technology* (2008), *10*, 1–10.

Videogames cannot be isolated from the culture that creates them, and trying to answer this ethical issue by looking exclusively at what the player does in one of these games will only give us a partial, limited, narrow-scoped answer. So let me try to approach this question from a different angle: the problem of violent videogames is not the problem of violent videogames. Violent videogames are a symptom of a culture obsessed with violence. And their negative effects are not so much training players to kill, which they don't, but forcing the creative stewardship of homo ludens to the limited spectrum of relating to others through the metaphors of dominance, violence, death, and conquer. Violent videogames are an act of violence on our ethical standing as moral *homo ludens*.

The argument that we, understood as the wealthy west, live in a culture of violence should surprise nobody. From *Game of Thrones* to *Westworld*, violence dominates the discourse in fiction. And, of course, in real life, where conflicts are escalated, where the news is a parade of threats, where the violence we inflict on those in the margins is ever-present, without remorse. This ambient violence, this permanent thrill and allure of blood and the dead, they are the cornerstone of cultural expression in our days.

Violence in videogames is problematic, yes. But not because of what it makes us do—or not just because of that, but because it reflects and contributes to broader cultural conversations, using the power of play and the rhetorics of technological prowess to promote, like propaganda, a glorification of violence as the only mode of engaging with conflict, and resolving it. The actual ethical question should not be what do violent videogames do to us, but what do violent videogames say about us, as individuals and as culture.

From the perspective of *homo ludens* as *homo poeiticus*, we can phrase this dilemma as follows: the worlds created by play are reflections of the world outside of them. The act of creating these worlds, of maintaining them by playing, of giving them meaning, is an act of reproducing the violent actions and harming inequalities of the world. Violent videogames exploit the stewardship of *homo ludens* to colonize games as a form of expression with a rhetoric of violence.

I am aware that violence has always been connected to videogames, and that there are of course arguments that consider violence to be just a metaphor for conflict. I believe this argument does not break my premises: videogames have always used violence because they partially reflect the culture of violence from which they come from. The worlds we are stewards of when playing are worlds of violence, and that is the ethical issue that needs addressing.

What are the alternatives, then? Are all games, or all mainstream games, violent or reflecting this culture of violence? Fortunately, we have historical examples of mainstream games that are more popular than their violent counterparts, and that do not make us stewards of a world of conflict. From *The Sims* to the *Animal Crossing* series, or *Stardew Valley*, there is a large number of examples of games that use other metaphors to provide players with challenges that are pleasurable, and with worlds that, while they still reflect capitalist and wealth-extractive ideologies that are questionable, are not founded on discourses of conquer and domination. Other worlds are possible in games, other worlds should be given to us in games, so the act of playing as stewardship is not the act of taking care of a cult-of-death-like aesthetic, but a practice of virtues and an opening for the imagination of social, political, and human alternatives.

Videogames in the Digital Stream

I want to extend this review of the ethical challenges of videogames from the perspective of culture to highlight other ethical issues that are not central to game studies at the moment, but that is relevant when trying to make sense of the ethics of computer games. For example, we should start questioning the position and role of videogames in the digital stream, that is, in the multimedia environment of images and services that are now shaping the specific culture of videogames, from *Twitch* to *YouTube*.

Let me start with a popular example from the game *Red Dead Redemption 2*, an open-world Western that allows players to explore the myth of the Far West and to interact with a richly crafted cast of non-player characters that create a multitude of stories in that virtual world. The player and the story she triggers in the game is the common element in the simulated lives of all these non-player characters. *Red Dead Redemption 2* has been designed to have fairly coherent AI-controlled characters, that not only react to players' actions, but also keep a schedule outside of the players' influence. For example, the farmer will spend most of the virtual day farming, and the village drunk will be drunk or waiting eagerly for the saloon to open. These complex systems create a coherent sense of place, that help players engage with the world beyond the narrative lines they have to perform. These are cues that encourage exploration, and in that exploration, I find my example.

In order to give coherence to this virtual world, the developers decided to include the character of a suffragette. This character is interactive. It has lines of dialogue that explain the critical role of these women in extending the right to vote to women in the United States. This suffragette is also the main character in a series of *YouTube* videos in which players try out different cruel ways of killing this suffragette. The videos are horrible, and the comments tend to reveal the worst of human nature.

This example shows the complexity of analyzing the ethics of a computer game, if we insist on looking exclusively at their content, or even at what an abstract, ideal player could do. We could argue that the mere presence of this possibility in the game is ethically questionable and should be prevented. After all, in *Red Dead Redemption 2* there are characters who are children, and it is impossible, by design, to kill them. Rockstar, the developers of the game, could have done the same with a character that should have been obvious was going to be targeted by the sad, angry mobs of *GamerGate* and similar misogynistic communities gathered in and around games. On the other hand, one could also argue that what Rockstar gives is a possibility for players to *not* do those horrible actions. It's a cynical argument, but a possible one: nobody is forcing players to do any act of violence with that character, and the game cannot be responsible for those whose morals are not developed enough.

This argument displaces responsibility from the game to the player. Players are then responsible for creating the discourses around the game, they are the creative stewards of the world they have been given, and they should act ethically. This is the key argument in a creative stewardship understanding of games.

And yet, there is also something about the value of games as places in which we can freely explore consequences and choices, in which we can safely fantasize about *what if*. There is a pleasure in these explorations of imagination, and while they may be questionable, they are also a part of practicing the stewardship of the world we are given. However, these explorations need limits: they cannot harm others, and they shouldn't promote or contribute to discourses of hate. The tension here is between the act of playing unethical actions *privately* and the act of doing so *publicly*. A lot of "immoral" play happens in private. Why is then something like the suffragette death videos in *Red Dead Redemption* ethically questionable?

The answer is cultural. Videogames are not individual, isolated consumer products. They are cultural objects that are played and enjoyed in public, that are an integral part of the ecosystem of discourses in the digital stream. Videogames shape and are shaped by *YouTube*, *Twitch*, *reddit*. Publishing these videos in these digital streams means having an effect in the culture of games, and in the cultural role given to games.

The ethical dilemma here is not so much whether we should or not act unethically in a game, but how will that action become a part of a digital stream that creates cultural interpretations and understandings of games. We need to study not what the game allows us to do, but when are we doing what the game allow us to do, and for whom are we doing it. If the action is private, the conversation is different. The act of playing these games in isolation, or as a practice of few individuals bound together by friendship or other strong social bonds, might call for a different perspective on the ethics of games. But few games are played in private. Videogames are a public performance of play in the digital stream. Our stewardship does not end in the game—it extends toward this stream; it considers the whole set of discourses around play and games. By playing, we are becoming stewards of a world presented to us but interconnected and related to all the other players and their worlds out there, a part of the global discourse around games, a part of the global culture of games.

Videogames and Data Transactions

Understanding *homo ludens* as *homo poieticus* is a productive perspective shift if we want to look at games within a broader ecology of media and entertainment. Some of the dilemmas about the content of videogames, about the actions they represent, and they force players to make, are part of an ecosystem of digital communication and data transactions that need to be taken into account when analyzing the ethics of videogames. When videogames become a part of the attention economy of *YouTube*, when the actions taken by players are rewarded by comments, likes, and also by economic rewards to that attention; when videogames become funded by the data markets that fuel the attention economy, the question of the ethics of content and the ethics of game design needs to be extended beyond what *a* player does, but how a player is given agency and stewardship over a game, and in exchange of what data that stewardship is assigned.

Videogames are part of what Srnicek[29] described as platform capitalism: the economic context in which technological platforms, from Apple to Amazon and Google, use their system to extract data from users, so it can be sold to advertisers who in turn try to get the attention of users to sell them products, from port-a-potties to presidents. The complexity of platform capitalism is too great to be addressed in this chapter, but I still want to mention it as one of the areas in which ethical inquiry on *homo ludens* as *homo poieticus* needs to be carried out.

For example, what are the ethics of the economic model of *free to play*, in which players are given free access to a game, while offering them the possibility of purchasing small game elements to improve gameplay, or the aesthetics of the game. *Free to play* is an economic model that, in the context of the current economics of capitalism, is encouraged to create engaging experiences that are abruptly cut so that players spend some money so they can keep on playing. *Free to play* commodifies the act of play. From this perspective, it might be the case that this economic model monetizes stewardship itself, breaking the possibility of creating a

---

[29] Srincek, *Platform capitalism* (London: Wiley, 2016).

healthy and constructive relation with and through the activity of play, since it will be interrupted by economic requirements.

And there's another element to the *free to play* economy. As the saying goes, if you don't have to pay for it, you are the product. So these games are also often used to syphon user data and sell it to data brokers. In fact, these games have the ability to capture data of extreme value: attention span, interest in certain topics, willingness to spend money, the time dedicated to play, ... Videogames are used in platform capitalism as pleasurable instruments that break privacy through play so data can become a part of an economic transaction. And we accept it, as players, because we like free things, but also because we are hesitant to look at videogames from the same perspective, we apply to question Facebook and other algorithmic machines of data extraction. Understanding the ethics of videogames is also understanding videogames as a platform in the economy of data extraction. This requires extending our perspective, looking at videogames as data systems that monitor users and try to extract data for selling it. The challenge is preserving the positive elements of creative play, of the creative stewardship of virtual worlds, while managing to protect the privacy and autonomy of players. Only when both are met, can we truly speak about ethical approaches to videogame playing and design.

(Temporary) Conclusions

I started this chapter by challenging our understanding of the ethical nature of *homo ludens*. By adopting a philosophy of information perspective on the activity of playing games, and specifically of playing videogames, I wanted to change the focus of the ethical inquiries on players. This chapter proposes a perspective that allows us to move beyond the analysis of the actions of players in gameworlds. The focus of ethical inquiry is not what players do according to the rules of the game in these gameworlds, but more their role as being critically engaged with the very act of creating meaning and enacting values in those games. Players do not perform actions: they are the stewards of gameworlds that require their effort to exist, and that should be open to the values that emerge from the creative appropriation of that world.

I followed this move from locating the ethics of players in actions to locating them in their relations to gamewolds to a similar change of perspective with regards to games and their position in culture. *Homo ludens* was described by Huizinga as a creator of culture, and therefore games were also origins of culture. However, games were also considered to be separate from the world, as if they were reflections of a world from which they were isolated. My move from the separateness of *homo ludens* to the relationality of *homo poieticus* should be followed by a relational approach to games as culture. The stewardship implied in the playing of games requires us to see them in the larger contexts of culture in which they are inserted, understanding how games are connected and related to the world outside them, how they have an effect in larger forms of culture. This article proposed two different domains in which an approach to the ethics of games from a perspective of informational stewardship allows us to formulate novel questions and see new moral dilemmas: videogames as part of a broader digital ecology in which broadcasting play in platforms of surveillance capitalism is affected by the logics of attention-seeking algorithms; and videogames as part of an economy of data extraction in which players' privacy becomes commercial interest, in a free-to-play market.

The perspective on *homo ludens* I have sketched in this chapter requires us to apply ethical thinking about videogames in the context of the societies, economics, and cultures in which these games are developed and consumed. The ethics of games cannot be reduced to the ethics of their content, isolated in individual moments of play. All play is public, all play is social, all play is part of a culture and an economy. The true challenges of the ethics of play are not the analysis of what happens on one screen at a time. For us to truly engage with the ethical challenges of games, we need to see them not as worlds separate from this one, but as cultural forces that are inserted in the same ebbs and flows of data, money, and attention than other digital media. Let's keep Huizinga's intuition that play is at the heart of culture, that *homo ludens* creates culture; but let's question the ethics of this player as a *homo poieticus*, a creator of worlds in the crossroads of many worlds.

References

Aarseth, E. (2001). Computer game studies, year one. *Game Studies, 1*(1). Retrieved from http://www.gamestudies.org/0101/editorial.html.

Adorno, T., & Horkheimer, M. (2010). *The dialectic of enlightenment*. London and New York: Verso (Original work published 1944).

Albrechtslund, A., & Dubbeld, L. (2006). The plays and arts of surveillance: Studying surveillance as entertainment. *Surveillance and Society, 3*(2–3), 216–221.

Agre, P. (1997). *Computation and human experience*. Cambridge: Cambridge University Press.

Arafat, O., & Riehle, D. (2009). *The commenting practice of open source* (pp. 857–864). Presented at the Proceedings of the 24th ACM SIGPLAN Conference Companion on Object Oriented Programming Systems Languages and Applications, New York, NY, USA: ACM. http://doi.org/10.1145/1639950.1640047.

Arnoldi, J. (2016). Computer algorithms, market manipulation and the institutionalization of high frequency trading. *Theory, Culture & Society, 33*(1), 29–52. http://doi.org/10.1177/0263276414566642.

Avedon, E. M. (1971). *The structural elements of games*. New York: Wiley.

Bakhtin, M. M. (1984). *Rabelais and his world*. Bloomington: Indiana University Press.

Bardzell, J., & Bardzell, S. (2011). *Pleasure is your birthright: Digitally enabled designer sex toys as a case of third-wave HCI*. In Proceedings of the SIGCHI Conference on Human Factors in Computing Systems (pp. 257–266). Retrieved from Google Scholar.

Bateson, G. (2000). *Steps to an ecology of mind: Collected essays in anthropology, psychiatry, evolution, and epistemology*. Chicago: University of Chicago Press.

Berkowitz, D., & Schwartz, D. A. (2016). Miley, CNN and the onion. *Journalism Practice, 10*(1), 1–17.

Bishop, R., Gansing, K., Parikka, J., & Wilk, E. (Eds.). (2017). *Across and beyond: Post-digital practices, concepts, and institutions*. Berlin: Sternberg Press.

Bogost, I. A. (2014). Why gamification is bullshit. In S. Deterding & S. Walz (Eds.), *The gameful world approaches, issues, applications* (pp. 65–80). Cambridge, MA: MIT Press.

Bogost, I. A. (2016). *Play anything: The pleasure of limits, the uses of boredom, and the secret of games.* New York: Basic Books.

Bynum, T. W. (2006). Flourishing ethics. *Ethics and Information Technology, 8*(4), 157–173. https://doi.org/10.1007/s10676-006-9107-1.

Caillois, R. (2001). *Man, play and games.* Urbana and Chicago: University of Illinois Press (Original work published 1958).

Cantwell Smith, B. (1996). *On the origin of objects.* Cambridge, MA: MIT Press.

Chess, S., & Shaw, A. (2015). A conspiracy of fishes, or, how we learned to stop worrying about #gamergate and embrace hegemonic masculinity. *Journal of Broadcasting & Electronic Media, 59*(1), 208–220. https://doi.org/10.1080/08838151.2014.999917.

Coeckelbergh, M. (2007). Violent computer games, empathy, and cosmopolitanism. *Ethics and Information Technology, 9*, 219–231.

Consalvo, M. (2007). *Cheating: Gaining advantage in videogames.* Cambridge, MA: MIT Press.

Consalvo, M. (2009). There is no magic circle. *Games and Culture, 4*(4), 408–417.

Corneliussen, H. G., & Rettberg, J. W. (2008). *Digital culture, play, and identity: A world of Warcraft® reader*. Cambridge: MIT Press.

D'Angour, A. (2013). Plato and play: Taking education seriously in ancient Greece. *American Journal of Play, 5*(3), 1–15.

Deci, E. L., & Ryan, R. M. (2008). Hedonia, eudaimonia, and well-being: An introduction. *Journal of Happiness Studies, 9*(1), 1–11. https://doi.org/10.1007/s10902-006-9018-1.

DeLanda, M. (2006). *A new philosophy of society: Assemblage theory and social complexity.* London: Bloomsbury Publishing.

Demir, H. (2010). The fourth revolution: Philosophical foundations and technological implications. *Knowledge, Technology & Policy, 23*(1–2), 1–6. https://doi.org/10.1007/s12130-010-9095-7.

Deterding, S., & Walz, S. P. (Eds.). (2015). The gameful world. Cambridge, MA: MIT Press.

Deterding, S., Sicart, M., Nacke, L., O'Hara, K., & Dixon, D. (2011). *Gamification: Using game-design elements in non-gaming contexts.* In *PART 2*—Proceedings of the 2011 Annual Conference Extended Abstracts on Human Factors in Computing Systems (pp. 2425–2428).

Dodig-Crnkovic, G., & Larsson, T. (2005). Game ethics-homo ludens as a computer game designer and consumer. *International Review of Information Ethics*, *4*(12), 19–23.

Farwell, J. P., & Rohozinski, R. (2011). Stuxnet and the future of cyber war. *Survival*, *53*(1), 23–40. http://doi.org/10.1080/00396338.2011.555586.

Feezell, R. (2006). *Sport, play, and ethical reflection*. Chicago: University of Illinois Press.

Ferrara, J. (2012). *Playful design*. New York: Rosenfeld Media.

Floridi, L. (1999). Information ethics: On the philosophical foundation of computer ethics. *Ethics and Information Technology*, *1*(1), 37–56.

Floridi, L. (2002). On the intrinsic value of information objects and the infosphere. *Ethics and Information Technology*, *4*(4), 287–304.

Floridi, L. (2008). The method of levels of abstraction. *Minds and Machines*, *18*(3), 303–329. https://doi.org/10.1007/s11023-008-9113-7.

Floridi, L. (2013). *The ethics of information*. Oxford: Oxford University Press.

Floridi, L. (2014). *The 4th revolution : How the infosphere is reshaping human reality*. Oxford: Oxford University Press (Kindle edition).

Floridi, L., & Sanders, J. W. (2005). Internet ethics: The constructionist values of homo poieticus. In R. J. Cavalier (Ed.), *The impact of the internet on our moral lives* (pp. 195–213). Albany: SUNY.

Frissen, V., Lammes, S., de Lange, M., de Mul, J., & Raessens, J. (2015). *Playful identities: The ludification of digital media cultures*. Amsterdam: Amsterdam University Press.

Galloway, A. R. (2006). *Gaming: Essays on algorithmic culture* (Vol. 18). Minneapolis: University of Minnesota Press.

Galloway, A. R. (2012). *The interface effect*. New York: Polity.

Gaver, W. (2009). Designing for homo ludens, still. In T. Binder, J. Löwgren, & L. Malmborg (Eds.), *(Re)searching the digital Bauhaus* (pp. 163–178). London: Springer. Retrieved from http://www.gold.ac.uk/media/46gaver-ludens-still.pdf.

Geertz, C. (1972). Deep play: Notes on the Balinese cockfight. Indianapolis: Bobbs-Merrill.

Getsy, D. (2011). *From diversion to subversion. Games, play, and twentieth-century art*. Pennsylvania: Penn State University Press.

Giddings, S. (2007). A 'pataphysics engine: Technology, play, and realities. *Games and Culture*, *2*(4), 392–404. https://doi.org/10.1177/1555412007309534.

Goffman, E. (1961). *Encounters. Two studies in the sociology of interaction*. Indianapolis: Bobbs-Merrill.

Golumbia, D. (2009). Games without play. *New Literary History, 40*(1), 179–204.
Henricks, T. (2008). The nature of play: An overview. *American Journal of Play, 1*(2), 157–180.
Henricks, T. S. (2009). Orderly and disorderly play: A comparison. *American Journal of Play, 2*, 12–40.
Henricks, T. S. (2016). *Play and the human condition.* Chicago: University of Illinois Press.
Huizinga, J. (1992). *Homo ludens: A study of the play-element in culture.* Boston: Beacon Press (Original work published 1938).
Johnson, S. (2016). *Wonderland: How play made the modern world.* New York: Riverhead Books.
Juul, J. (2005). *Half-real: Videogames between real rules and fictional worlds.* Cambridge, MA: MIT Press.
Kant, I. (2001). *The Cambridge edition of the works of Immanuel Kant: Critique of judgement.* Cambridge: Cambridge University Press (Original work published 1790).
Khaldarova, I., & Pantti, M. (2016). Fake news. *Journalism Practice, 10*(7), 891–901. https://doi.org/10.1080/17512786.2016.1163237.
Knight, T., & Vardouli, T. (2015). Computational making. *Design Studies, 41*, 1–7. https://doi.org/10.1016/j.destud.2015.09.003.
Laxton, S. (2011). From judgement to process: The modern ludic field. In D. J. Getsy (Ed.), *Refiguring Modernism: From diversion to subversion: Games, play, and twentieth-century art* (pp. 3–24). Pennsylvania: Pennsylvania State University Press.
Lehdonvirta, V., & Castronova, E. (2014). *Virtual economies: Design and analysis.* Cambridge, Massachusetts: MIT Press. 0262027259.
Lieberoth, A. (2014). Shallow gamification: Testing psychological effects of framing an activity as a game. *Games and Culture.* https://doi.org/10.1177/1555412014559978.
Mallaband, P. (2002). Understanding Kant's distinction between free and dependent beauty. *The Philosophical Quarterly, 52*(206), 66–81. Retrieved from Google Scholar.
Marenko, B., & van Allen, P. (2016). Animistic design: How to reimagine digital interaction between the human and the nonhuman. *Digital Creativity, 27*(1), 52–70. http://doi.org/10.1080/14626268.2016.1145127.
Massanari, A. (2015). #Gamergate and the fappening: How reddit's algorithm, governance, and culture support toxic technocultures. *New Media & Society.* https://doi.org/10.1177/1461444815608807.

May, H. (2010). *Continuum series in ancient philosophy: Aristotle's ethics: Moral development and human nature.* New York: Continuum.

McCormick, M. (2001). Is it wrong to play violent video games? *Ethics and Information Technology, 3*, 277–287.

McNamee, M. (2007). Sport, ethics and philosophy; Context, history, prospects. *Sport, Ethics and Philosophy*, *1*(1), 1–6. https://doi.org/10.1080/17511320601173329.

Montola, M., Stenros, J., & Waern, A. (2009). *Pervasive games: Theory and design.* London: Morgan Kaufmann Publishers.

Nijholt, A. (2016). *Playable cities.* London: Springer.

Norman, D. A. (2004). *Emotional design: Why we love (or hate) everyday things* (Vol. 2004, pp. 1–1). New York, NY: Basic Books. http://doi.org/10.1145/966012.966013.

Phillips, W., & Milner, R.N. (2017). *The ambivalent internet: Mischief, oddity, and antagonism online*. New York: Polity.

Phillips, W. (2015). *This is why we can't have nice things: Mapping the relationship between online trolling and mainstream culture.* Cambridge, MA: MIT Press.

Piaget, J. (1997). *The moral judgement of the child.* New York: Simon & Schuster.

Postman, N. (2005). *Amusing ourselves to death: Public discourse in the age of show business* (20th ed.). London: Penguin Books.

Ratto, M. (2011). Critical making: Conceptual and material studies in technology and social life. *The Information Society, 27*(4), 252–260. http://doi.org/10.1080/01972243.2011.583819.

Raessens, J. (2006). Playful identities, or the ludification of culture. *Games and Culture, 1*(1), 52. https://doi.org/10.1177/1555412005281779.

Rodriguez, H. (2006). The playful and the serious: An approximation to Huizinga's homo ludens. *Game Studies, 6*(1), 1604.

Schechner, R. (1988). Playing. *Play & Culture, 1*, 3–19.

Schiller, F. (2012). *Dover books on western philosophy: On the aesthetic education of man.* Mineola, New York: Dover Publications (Original work published 1794).

Seo, Y., & Jung, S.-U. (2014). Beyond solitary play in computer games: The social practices of eSports. *Journal of Consumer Culture, 16*(3), 635–655. http://doi.org/10.1177/1469540514553711.

Seward, G. (1944). Play as art. *The Journal of Philosophy, 41*(7), 178. https://doi.org/10.2307/2020303.

Sherrick, B., & Hoewe, J. (2017). The effect of explicit online comment moderation on three spiral of silence outcomes. *New Media & Society*, *25*(1), 146144481666247. http://doi.org/10.1177/1461444816662477.
Shields, R. (2015). Ludic ontology: Play's relationship to language, cultural forms, and transformative politics. *American Journal of Play*, *7*(3), 298–321.
Sicart, M. (2009). *The ethics of computer games*. Cambridge, MA: MIT Press.
Sicart, M. (2014a). Playing the good life: Gamification and ethics. In *The gameful world: Approaches, issues, applications* (pp. 225–244).
Sicart, M. (2014b). *Playful thinking: Play matters*. Cambridge, MA: MIT Press.
Srincek, N. (2016). *Platform capitalism*. London: Wiley.
Suits. (2005). *The grasshopper: Games, life and Utopia*. Peterborough, ON: Broadview Press.
Sutton-Smith, B. (1997). *The ambiguity of play*. Cambridge: Cambridge University Press.
Taylor, T. L. (2006). *Play between worlds: Exploring online game culture*. Cambridge, MA: MIT Press.
Taylor, T. L. (2009). The assemblage of play. *Games and Culture*, *4*(4), 331–339.
Taylor, T. L. (2012). *Raising the stakes: E-Sports and the professionalization of computer gaming*. Cambridge, MA: MIT Press.
Vallor, S. (2016). *Technology and the virtues: A philosophical guide to a future worth wanting*. Oxford: Oxford University Press.
Verbeek, P. P (2006). *What things do: Philosophical reflections on technology, agency, and design*. Pennsylvania: Pennsylvania State University Press.
Volkman, R. (2010). Why information ethics must begin with virtue ethics. *Metaphilosophy*, *41*(3), 380–401.
Volkman, R. (2013). 7. Being a good computer professional: The advantages of virtue ethics in computing. *Professionalism in the Information and Communication Technology Industry*, *3*, 109.
Waddington, D. I. (2007). Locating the wrongness in ultra-violent video games. *Ethics and Information Technology*, *9*, 121–128.
Walz, S. P., & Deterding, S. (2014). *The gameful world : Approaches, issues, applications*. Cambridge, MA: MIT Press.
Whitson, J. (2014). Foucault's fitbit: Governance and gamification. In S. Deterding & S. Walz (Eds.), *The gameful world approaches, issues, applications* (pp 339–359). Cambridge, MA: MIT Press.
Wonderly, M. A. (2008). Humean approach to assessing the moral significance of ultra-violent video games. *Ethics and Information Technology*, *10*, 1–10.

Zimmerman, E. (2013). Manifesto for a ludic century. In S. Deterding & S. Walz (Eds.), *The gameful world approaches, issues, applications* (pp 19–23). Cambridge, MA: MIT Press.

SPORT MATTERS: On Art, Social Artifice, and the Rules of the Game, or, the Politics of Sport

Louis A. Ruprecht

I have made great claims for cricket. As firmly as I am able and is here possible, I have integrated it in the historical movement of the times. The question remains: What is it? Is it mere entertainment or is it an art?… The aestheticians have scorned to take notice of popular sports and games--to their own detriment. The aridity and confusion of which they so mournfully complain will continue until they include organized games *and the people who watch them* as an integral part of their data.… [C]ricket is an art, not a bastard or a poor relation, but a full member of the community.

The approach must be direct. Too long has it been impressionistic or apologetic, timid or defiant, always ready to take refuge in the mysticism

This essay is dedicated to the memory of Mr. Edward Scott (1931–2018).

L. A. Ruprecht (✉)
Georgia State University, Atlanta, GA, USA
e-mail: lruprecht@gsu.edu

V. Rapti and E. Gordon (eds.), *Ludics*,
https://doi.org/10.1007/978-981-15-7435-1_3

of metaphor. It is a game and we have to compare it with other games. It is an art and we have to compare it with other arts.

C. L. R. James, *Beyond a Boundary*, 195–196

* * *

Sport as Social Artifice

There is an artifice, an arbitrary artifice, about sport. This is a central aspect of its social, cultural, and especially its moral, value. The man or woman who crossed the tape first at the one-hundred-meter mark might have placed third if the course were one hundred-and-ten-meters long, instead. The victory has an essential arbitrariness about it, one determined by the conventional placement of a line on a field of play. From an anthropological or ethnographic perspective, if alien visitors were to observe our species for any length of time, two features would presumably stand out immediately to them: first, how much time we appear to spend engaged in talk, simply talk; and second, how many complicated bounded spaces we create in which to engage in some highly complex social rituals. (There is a lot of talk that takes place inside these bounded spaces as well, some of it quite animated, hence the elective affinity many observe between baseball and democracy.) A tennis or basketball court, like a football field (of both the American and European kinds), and also like a baseball diamond, is, strictly speaking, illegible to the anthropological outsider. The more you know about the boundaries, the better an observer of the game you will be. The better you are at finessing those boundaries, the better an athletic participant you will be.[1] There is a great deal to ponder in that only apparently simple observation. And that is

[1]Pierre de Coubertin, to whose Olympic Revival I will turn in the second part of this essay, knew this well:

> What is a sporting result? It is a figure or a fact. You have a maximum height above which you cannot jump, a minimum time below which you cannot sprint a hundred meters. The weight which you lift and the rope which you climb also express in kilos or in metres the value of your effort.... On all sides you encounter restrictions of a more or less mathematical severity. But you could not see them when you began. Nobody knows his exact limitation in advance. Only one road leads there--training and hard work....

where I would like to begin my reflections on sporting matters, and why they matter in the ways they do.

The religious ethicist, Jeffrey Stout, *emeritus* professor of religion at Princeton University, has utilized this observation to mount a post-Kantian critique of traditional Social Contract theory. The crude version of that theory, as well as its more creative iterations by more recent political philosophers like John Rawls,[2] presupposes individual rational agents who come together to establish the rules by which they will play the game of politics. A constitution, like a contract, is a rule-book of sorts; a complex, socially differentiated modern society is a carefully choreographed and tightly bounded field of democratic play. It was Hegel's great step forward, first enunciated in his 1807 *Phenomenology of Spirit*,[3] to note that human beings are fundamentally social and historical creatures, such that no such primordially individual rational agents of the sort imagined by Social Contract theories really exist. Where, Hegel wonders, do such individuals come from? In short, they emerge from a social and historical matrix, something he somewhat mystically referred to as "Spirit" (*Geist*). "It takes a village," and it takes Spirit. Art, Religion, and Philosophy were, for Hegel (and significant other Romantic philosophers, like Schelling[4]), the primary works of Spirit. We might well add sport to that august list.

There, incidentally--if you will allow me this parenthesis--is the whole secret of sporting education.

Pierre de Coubertin, *What We Can Now Ask of Sport* [1918], in *The Olympic Idea: Discourses and Essays* (Stuttgart: Carl Diem Institute, 1964), 47–48.

[2]John Rawls, *A Theory of Justice* (Cambridge: Harvard University Press, 1979), 11–22.

[3]G. W. F. Hegel, *Phänomenologie des Geistes* [1807], Volume 3 of the 20-volume *Werke* (Frankfurt am Main: Surhkamp Verlag, 1970). Three important English versions are: *The Phenomenology of Mind*, J. B. Baillie, trans. (London: Humanities Press, 1910); *The Phenomenology of Spirit*, A. V. Miller, trans. (Oxford: Oxford University Press, 1977); and a more recent (2010, 2013) translation by Terry Pinkard, *The Phenomenology of Spirit*, available online at https://www.marxists.org/reference/archive/hegel/works/ph/pinkard-translation-of-phenomenology.pdf.

[4]A superb retrieval of Schelling's importance as a thinker of profound contemporary relevance is offered by Jason M. Wirth in *The Conspiracy of Life: Meditations on Schelling and His Time* (Albany, NY: State University of New York Press, 2003); *Schelling's Practice of the Wild: Time, Art, Imagination* (Albany, NY: State University of New York Press, 2015). Wirth's edited volume, *Schelling Now: Contemporary Readings* (Indianapolis, IN: Indiana University Press, 2005) is also excellent and insightful.

Inspired largely by his reading of Hegel, Stout utilizes the example of soccer to illustrate the value of Hegel's intervention.[5] On the Social Contract model, we are invited to imagine a group of playful folk who set down the rules of the game, and sketched out the boundaries of the field of play, after which they began playing soccer together. Historically speaking, that is not how soccer (or any other sport of any real complexity) emerged. Rather, people already committed to playing a game together learned through long experience what sorts of things were acceptable, what problematic, and what dangerous or disruptive to the game. Their purpose was to enhance the quality, complexity, and competitiveness of the game.

Some of the rules have an obviousness about them; others are meaningful only within the confines of play. It became clear early on that a player who is tripped (or "hacked") while running at full speed could be seriously injured. There are elaborate rules to deal with that infraction: yellow and red cards, penalty kicks, and the like. It presumably became clear more slowly what the ideal size of a goal should be: too large, and it is too easy to score; too small, and most games will end in a zero-zero tie (this would be simply uninteresting, ethically equatable to Tic-Tac-Toe, rather than Chess or the Game of Go). Rules regulating the treatment of opponents, mostly designed to avoid injury and to promote a level of courtesy within the competition, are meaningful outside the field of play; other rules have meaning strictly within the field of play. Sorting out the relationship between inside and outside will be the stuff of most philosophical and ethical reflection about sport. From the standpoint of political theory, then, "the rules [like the constitutions] come later,"[6] after long social and historical experience of playing a game together. And, like the US Constitution, such rules are never set in stone; they are amenable to amendment.

---

[5] I am here rehearsing the argument laid out in Jeffrey Stout, *Democracy and Tradition* (Princeton, NJ: Princeton University Press, 2004), 272–274.

[6] I develop this idea at greater length in the context of Stout's analysis of democratic grassroots organizing: Jeffrey Stout, *Blessed Are the Organized* (Princeton, NJ: Princeton University Press, 2010) in "The Rules Come Later: The Priority of Practices in a Grass Roots Democracy, Soundings" 95.1, 2012, 98–129.

Arbitrary limits—boundaries, again—also set the conditions in which athletic excellence may be most artfully displayed. A sonnet is difficult to produce, and especially pleasing when done well, precisely because of the existence of an arbitrary set of rules. A tennis player who is especially good at "hugging the line" does not just increase his or her chance of winning a match; he or she creates a game that is pleasing, and even moving, to watch. These boundaries are partially constitutive of the beauty we associate with sport. In short, these are all arbitrary limits placed upon the athlete by the game. *The experience of limit* is one essential point of the game. There is a unique grace in the finessing of a boundary. Echoing the Romantics, we might use the spiritual language of "transcendence" here: we must have a boundary in order to have something to transcend. Another common language used for the especially gifted player who demonstrates such finesse is "fluidity." There is a logic to this Romantic trope as well.

Consider the metaphor of water.[7] What is most striking about water is that it possesses a form, and hence visibility, in its solid and gaseous states. The jagged edge of a glacier has a sublime and ominous power. Finding the shapes in clouds is a form of child's play that requires no field other than the boundless youthful imagination. But water in its liquid form takes the shape of whatever contains it. The *boundary* is what gives it shape and form. That is water's unique quality and signature. As Grant Farred's work on what he considers to be the rarified athletic "event" which organized sport makes possible,[8] the athletic body—especially to the degree that it is also a racialized body—is housed in an implicit container defined by written rules of the game and unwritten codes of ethno-racial conduct that make the athlete legible, rendering him or her

---

[7]Here I am summarizing an argument made at greater length in Louis A. Ruprecht Jr., *An Elemental Life* (Collegeville, MN: Liturgical Press, 2018).

[8]Grant Farred, *In Motion, At Rest: The Event of the Athletic Body* (Minneapolis, MN: University of Minnesota Press, 2014). To rehearse his striking examples in playful brief: first, X lies motionless on a scorer's table, then rebounds into the stands to kick the crap out of some boozy fans; next, Y confronts a fan who is doing little more than playing his part in the scripted drama of opposition that is modern fandom, pitting one city against another, and drops him like a stone; and finally, Z head butts an opponent in the World Cup Final, receives a red card, and is ceremoniously ejected in the final game of his storied career.

visible. That is to say, the rules and norms construct the container that gives the athlete shape, and form, and canons of excellence.

When the athlete escapes the confines of the container, then we are confronted with something more than transgression; the athletic body has suddenly become evanescent. It has liquified, and in the context of such a strange metamorphosis, it has slipped the bonds of the reigning regimes. It has, to use a phrase from the classic study of sport by C. L. R. James to which I will turn later in this essay (and which Farred has recapitulated with great subtlety) moved "beyond a boundary."[9] Quite suddenly—in the instant that is the athletic "event"— we do not know what we are looking at, and failing that, we will have great difficulty in finding the right things to say about it, in knowing what to call it. As the fluid athlete escapes the regulatory regime, finessing the boundary in some striking and original manner (like the first basketball player to "dunk," or the first person to run a mile in under four minutes), he or she becomes harder to comprehend or appreciate. Such an athlete has been rendered questionable [*fragwurdig*].[10] Grant Farred's work highlights the unwritten racial norms that inform such athletic experience on the contemporary scene; I will return to the complex relation between racialized scripts, racism and modern sports when I turn to the work of C. L. R. James. But first, I wish to make a detour of sorts, to discuss the moral meaning of the modern Olympic movement. As Edward Albee cautions, "sometimes a person has to go a very long distance out of his way to come back a short distance correctly."[11]

[9]C. L. R. James, *Beyond a Boundary* (Durham, NC: Duke University Press, 1963, 1993). Farred offers a fascinating reading of James's luminous account of cricket, colonialism, and moral formation, one which underlines some critical, if implicit, class concerns, in "Maple Man: How Cricket Made a Postcolonial Intellectua", in Grant Farred, ed., *Rethinking C. L. R. James* (Cambridge, MA: Blackwell Publishers, 1996), 165–186.

[10]Farred gets at much the same problem of a liquid (and racialized) being escaping its containment in his meditation on *Martin Heidegger Saved My Life* (Minneapolis, MN: University of Minnesota Press, 2015). Only in this instance, *he* is the figure—not quite an athlete, but a professor in the curious role of a day laborer—one whose ethno-racial identification enables (or forces?) him to slip from one social-professional container to another, and back again.

[11]Edward Albee, *The Zoo Story* (1959). The idea is used to great effect by Jeffrey Stout in *Democracy and Tradition* (Princeton: Princeton UP in association with Hebrew Union College Press, 2004), 226.

Modern Olympism as Neohellenic Revival

How to revive a dormant tradition? How to bring the past, not just to light, but to life? The first task, bringing to light, is largely an archaeological matter; the second task, bringing to life, requires more artful forms of cultural engagement. As the man largely credited with the revival of the Modern Olympics,[12] Pierre de Coubertin (1863–1937), put the matter in the early years of the Modern Olympic revival, "Germany had brought to light what remained of Olympia; why should not France succeed in rebuilding its splendours?"[13] He was referring to the extensive German excavation at ancient Olympia which began in the 1870s,[14] and intended his revival of the Olympic "Games"[15] as a religious supplement to that largely scientific endeavor, what he would later call the *religio athletae*. And therein lies a tale.

Consider the following historical facts. According to the Greeks' own reckoning—that is, the story they told themselves about themselves—the ancient Olympic Games were held in honor of Zeus for the first time in 776 BCE.[16] They eventually emerged as the preeminent panhellenic ritual contests (*agônes*) and were held quadrennially, without significant

[12]There has been some quarrel about that attestation, mostly from the perspective of Modern Greek Studies, but I think the quarrel is largely unfounded. A good introduction to the criticism is David C. Young, "How the Amateurs Won the Olympics", in Wendy Raschke, ed., *The Archaeology of the Olympics: The Olympics and Other Festivals in Antiquity* (Madison, WI: University of Wisconsin Press, 1988), 55–75, esp. 65–69.

The essential starting point for appreciating Coubertin and his Olympic achievement is John J. MacAloon, *This Great Symbol: Pierre de Coubertin and the Origins of the Modern Olympic Games* (Chicago, IL: University of Chicago Press, 1981, 1984). His more recently edited volume, *Bearing Light: Flame Relays and the Struggle for the Olympic Movement* (New York, NY: Routledge, 2013), is also germane to this discussion.

[13]Pierre de Coubertin, *What Germany Had Brought to Light* (1908), in *The Olympic Idea: Discourses and Essays* (Köln: Carl-Diem Institut, 1967), 1.

[14]Tellingly, the first brief archaeological work at the Temple of Zeus was undertaken in 1829 by French troops which had come to Greece in support of the War of Independence against the Ottomans.

[15]To call these ancient Greek (or modern) *agônes* "games" is a translational misnomer which tends to trivialize what is in play here. The German *Spiele* and French *jeux*—that is to say, "play"—comes closer to the ritual, theatrical and socially performative dimension of both the ancient and modern "games." That some play can be deeply serious is a central assumption of the most scholarly studies of sport: *homo ludens*.

[16]For the history of this claim, see Hugh M. Lee, "The 'First' Olympic Games of 776 B.C.", in Raschke, ed., *The Archaeology of the Olympics*, 110–118.

interruption, until the Roman emperor Theodosius formally closed all "pagan" sanctuaries in the Roman Empire in 393 CE.[17] The Olympics were thus to lie dormant for more than fifteen hundred years, prior to the Modern Olympic Revival, in Athens, in 1896. This enormous historical lacuna raises the central Neohellenic question: how do you revive something after so long a rupture? What evidence do we have for what happened in such an ancient past and, still more, how may we account for how the Olympics changed over their more-than-eleven-hundred-year ancient career? One answer to these questions we have already confronted. The *archaeological record* at Olympia (as well as at Delphi, Isthmia, and Nemea) offers a great deal of evidence about what took place at the site of ancient Olympia. So too does the *written record*: especially Pindar's epinikian "victory songs"[18] from the fifth century BCE, and Pausanias's extensive description of the sanctuary[19] in the second century CE. We also possess an extensive *visual record* in the material culture of Greek antiquity: vase paintings, sculptures, friezes, statue bases, sarcophagi, and the like. All that said, the overall evidence for ancient athletics is pretty sketchy and rather thin. It was Coubertin's genius (or hubris, for those who do not like him) to see that the ancient record

---

[17]The Theodosian edicts may be found in Clyde Pharr, ed., *The Theodosian Code and Novels and the Sirnondian Constitutions* (Princeton, NJ: Princeton University Press, 1952), 440–476, and in Michael Maas, ed., *Readings in Late Antiquity: A Sourcebook* (New York, NY: Routledge, 2000), 166–191.

[18]See Frank Nisetich, trans., *Pindar's Victory Songs* (Baltimore, MD: Johns Hopkins Press, 1971), especially the Olympian poems, 81–150.

For the Greek version, I am using William H. Race, trans. of *Pindar* (Cambridge, MA: Loeb Classical Library of Harvard University Press, 1997), 2 volumes.

[19]See Peter Levi, trans., *Pausanias: Guide to Greece* (New York: Penguin Books, 1971), 2 volumes, especially Books 5–6 on Elis, Volume 2, 195–368.

It is instructive that the description of Olympia takes up 20% of Pausanias's entire text since, in his words, while "there are many wonders to see and hear about in Greece, there is more divine care taken for the *drômenois* at Eleusis and the *agôni* at Olympia than for anything else in the world" (*Description of Greece* V.10.1).

For the Greek version, I am using W. H. S. Jones trans., *Pausanias: Description of Greece* (Cambridge, MA: Loeb Classical Library of Harvard University Press, 1992), 5 volumes.

For more on Pausanias at Olympia and elsewhere, see Louis A. Ruprecht Jr., *Was Greek Thought Religious? On the Use and Abuse of Hellenism, for Rome to Romanticism* (New York, NY: Palgrave Macmillan, 2002), 39–58.

needed a supplement; as a figure of the late nineteenth century, *Romanticism* provided the primary imaginative lens through which Coubertin viewed the task of his revival.[20]

Before we condemn this unapologetic insertion of the Romantic imagination into the work of Neohellenic revival, we should take note of something that Coubertin saw, and said, with great clarity. The ancient Olympics were established for *religious* reasons: as a ritual and pilgrimage event arranged in honor of Zeus. The ancient Olympics were shut down for religious reasons: as an enduring (and therefore dangerously tempting) example of the wrong kind of religion, from the imperial Christian standpoint. The Olympic Revival, for Coubertin, needed to take religion into account; it was indeed a "revival" in the nineteenth-century sense of the term. Coubertin's Modern Olympics was designed to do precisely that, staging a stunningly original and self-conscious intervention in the nineteenth-century religious culture of northern Europe. European Christians–Protestant and Catholic alike, in his view[21]—had been trained to be virtually embarrassed about natural forms of human competitiveness, and virtually scandalized by the fact of their embodiment. Central to the Modern Olympic Revival, then, lay a theory of embodiment and an embrace of a certain kind of ritualized competition. The ancient Greeks, Coubertin observed, knew well that if agonism were not socially and culturally inscribed, then a community would suffer antagonism (literally, "instead of agonism") instead. The ancient Greeks were also almost astonishingly casual and accepting of their embodiment: athletics, erotics, and all. These were the religious supplements needed to revive a dying Christian culture in Europe, Coubertin believed.

In short, the pagans and the Christians need not be at war. In perhaps his most striking and original presentation of this idea, Coubertin observed the following, risking what he understood might be seen by some as "blasphemy":

[20]For further explanation of that claim see Ruprecht, *Was Greek Thought Religious?* 156–161.

[21]Coubertin was and remained French Catholic, but was deeply informed by various Anglican cultural forms, most notably Thomas Arnold's athletic reforms at the Rugby School. See MacAloon, *This Great Symbol*, 50–55, 60–70.

> Our over-simple habit of cataloguing things leads us to call paganism the worship of idols; as though every religion, even the most materialist, did not have its spiritual followers, and as though every religion, even the most mystical, did not have its idolators, if only of the golden calf which today is more powerful and more incense-wreathed than ever. *But there is a paganism--the true form--which humanity will never shake off*, and from which--*I will risk this seeming blasphemy*--it would not be well for it to free itself completely: *and that is the cult of the human being*, of the human body, mind and flesh, feeling and will, instinct and conscience. Sometimes flesh, feeling and instinct have the upper hand, and sometimes mind, will and conscience, for these are the two despots who strive for primacy within us, and whose conflict often rends us cruelly. We have to attain a balance. We reach it, but we cannot hold it....
>
> It was the immortal glory of Hellenism to imagine the codification of the pursuit of balance and to make it into a prescription for social greatness. Here--at Olympia--we are on the ruins of the first capital of eurhythmy, for eurhythmy does not belong to the art-world alone; *there is also a eurhythmy of life*.
>
> Let us therefore meditate among the ruins of Olympia, ruins which are still alive, as is indicated by the [Opening] ceremony which I recalled just now. And from there we perceive the *alternations between paganism and asceticism* which form the warp and woof in history, a warp and woof neglected by historians because in order to see it one must look beneath the events which cover it, *and proceed more in the manner of an archaeologist than a historian.*[22]

Paganism and asceticism: the "warp and woof" of religious history. If Greek religion could seem quite alien to the competitive and bodily sensibilities of modern Christians, Coubertin realized, then one thing these religious cultures clearly shared was a taste for ritual (and, at least in the Catholic case, a taste for anthropomorphic religious imagery).

Consider the following paradox. What is the most expensive ticket at the Modern Olympics, and the most difficult to obtain? That for the Opening Ceremonies... where, precisely, nothing athletic happens at all. Without a ritual-religious frame, Coubertin observed, the Modern

[22]Coubertin, "Olympia" (1929), in *The Olympic Idea*, 106–119, quote at 110.

Olympics would simply become another version of World Championships, and the world already had enough of those. The Olympics were designed to be something different, and the ritual framing was designed to set the terms of that religious difference. As John J. MacAloon has observed through careful ethnographic study, the ritual framing of the Opening Ceremonies and the Medal Award Ceremonies choreograph soaring flights of ecstatic emotion for which most modern athletes can only turn to the language of spirituality and sublimity.

A final issue deeply implicated in Coubertin's Olympic revival concerns the troubled modern concept of "identity." Here too Coubertin was both provocative and prescient. The ancient Olympics were open to any Greek participant from anywhere in the larger colonized Greek Mediterranean, a world running from Sicily and southern Italy to Asia Minor and the Black Sea coast. But what constituted Greekness, and how was participation in the Olympics regulated? We do not know precisely, but an obvious answer likely involved two features: the Olympic athlete must have spoken some form of Greek, and must have accepted the central ritual features of the Olympic religion, whatever that entailed (in practice, or belief). In other words, the crucial ancient identity categories were language and religion.

Coubertin developed that insight in a fascinating political direction. If the Olympic sanctuary and its rituals were indeed organized in the eighth century BCE, then this corresponded with the early emergence of the Greek *polis* as the dominant form of political organization around the Mediterranean basin. The Greeks, Coubertin observed, recognized that the natural competition between rival Greek *poleis* needed some ritual and religious outlet if war were not to be the only means of resolving inter-*polis* disputes. Olympia and Delphi were to emerge as the two premier inter-*polis*, that is, "panhellenic," sanctuaries in the ancient world.

In the nineteenth century, Coubertin analogized, the nation-state was rapidly emerging as the dominant form of political organization, worldwide. There was thus an analogous need for certain vibrant international institutions to serve a role similar to that served by Olympia in antiquity. This is precisely what the Modern Olympics were designed to be[23]: intentionally international, open to any citizen of any nation, and emphatically "ambulatory,"[24] that is, designed to move to a new city every four years, belonging to no one nation (not even Greece). In this, Coubertin staged what was arguably his most creative adaptation of an ancient Greek form, suiting it to modern needs and modern political realities.

The issues at stake were three-fold. First, nationalism had emerged in the early nineteenth century, especially after the political fallout from the Napoleonic Wars, as the dominant revolutionary, anti-imperial ideology in Europe and its global colonial holdings. Nationalism would fuel postcolonial revolutions throughout the later nineteenth and early twentieth centuries. And yet, at the same time, a form of nationalism quite different from the one Coubertin had in view was emerging: a nationalism grounded in a conception of national identity, which identity was founded on notions of "blood and soil," not language or religion, nor anti-imperial demands for the increased liberty and autonomy of all citizens. This more recent iteration of nationalism—let's call it fascism, for now—was ironically to develop in precisely the same period, and in parallel to, the Modern Olympic Revival. The other dominant revolutionary ideology that emerged in this same period, one that understood itself in direct opposition to these new nationalisms, was communism. These two ideologies were to set the terms of political debate for the interwar years in Europe, and it is more than historically ironic that the last Olympics Coubertin lived to see (though he

[23]And he would later brag that his version of a modern international institution had proven far more effective than its alternative, the League of Nations:

> The members of the I.O.C. are in no way delegates to this Committee. They are even forbidden to accept from their fellow-citizens any imperative mandate likely to fetter their liberty. They must consider themselves as ambassadors of the Olympic idea within their respective countries... Being subsidised by no one, their independence is absolute... A short time ago a certain high personage regretted at Geneva that the League of Nations could not have been organised in a similar way.

Coubertin, "Olympia" (1929), in *The Olympic Idea*, 117.

[24]Coubertin, "Letter to the Honourable Members of the International Olympic Committee" (1919), in *The Olympic Idea*, 67–72.

was too ill to travel to them) were the 1936 Berlin Games.[25] After the chaos unleashed by the fascist irruption in Europe, and the dissolution of the European gunpowder empires that ensued, nationalism was to re-emerge—especially in European colonies in India, Sub-Saharan Africa, and the Caribbean—as the anti-imperial ideological foundation for freedom movements that bore a striking resemblance to earlier nineteenth-century versions inspired by the French Revolution and its "Declaration of the Rights of Man and Citizen" in 1789.

I have now traveled a long distance out of my way. And so the stage is set for me to turn to what is arguably the finest book on sport and its relation to political and moral formation ever written: C. L. R. James's classic study of cricket in *Beyond a Boundary*. This remarkable text, technically but not exclusively devoted to the close study of cricket, actually expresses the authorial ambition to do a great deal more; its ultimate aim is to liken a sport unto the world. The whole world, we should add: playing on Rudyard Kipling's famous 1891 poetic paean to the English flag, borne around the world by a far-flung naval empire ("Of what should they know of England who only England know?"), James challenges his reader to consider a question in parallel, one that Kipling would not have comprehended as implicated in his own: "*What do they know of cricket who only cricket know?*"[26] In James's wisened authorial hands, that question proves to seep into virtually everything of moral importance. He or she who knows only cricket—the callow cast of sports fandom—will never come to see how modern team sports is indelibly bound up in such politically momentous matters as race, class, nation, empire, and the lifelong quest of ethical formation. To explain how and

---

[25]There is further irony in the fact that the most trenchant symbol of the Opening Ceremonies, the Olympic Flame, was invented by the German Olympic Committee for the 1936 Games, an invention which provides the beginning for Leni Riefenstahl's remarkable 1938 film, "Olympia."

For more on these ironies, see MacAloon, ed., *Bearing Light*, 1–20.

[26]C. L. R. James, *Beyond a Boundary*, Preface; the line is italicized in the original.

The complex intertextual play between James's query and Kipling's rather fluid English nationalism are nicely laid out by Michael Brearley in "Socrates and C. L. R. James," where he notes that James toyed with this line as a title for the book, and essentially wrote the book as if this were its subtitle; see David Featherstone, Christopher Gair, Christian Høgsbjerg, and Andrew Sith, eds., *Marxism, Colonialism and Cricket: CLR James Beyond a Boundary* (Durham, NC: Duke University Press, 2018), 223–239.

why this is so required James to devote an entire book, and an entire lifetime, to the task. "To answer involves ideas as well as facts."[27]

Sport and Postcolonial Identity in the Work of C. L. R. James

James's literary and political identity is difficult to nail down, in part because he was subject to several self-conscious shifts in his commitments. As we will see, his passionate commitment to cricket was decisive to several of these shifts. James is also utterly singular as a stylist in the English language. For my purposes in this essay, I wish to consider James as a virtue ethicist who gradually became committed to the cause of Trinidadian national independence for reasons that had everything to do with his passion for cricket and his understanding of the ethical relevance of obedience to the rules of the game, any game. These views were also filtered through his profound understanding of the seismic political permutations in the first half of the twentieth century which I mentioned above and, in particular, the role of modern racism[28] in the unfolding political changes accompanying those shifts.

James launched his literary career with an important study of the slave revolt led by Toussaint L'Ouverture (1743–1803), which resulted in the formation of an independent Haitian state in 1804.[29] James brilliantly captures the paradoxes of the French Revolution and its Napoleonic aftermath: the French Assembly originally recognized that the abolition of human enslavement was a natural extension of its "Declaration of the Rights of Man," but later rescinded this liberty upon recognizing that it

---

[27]C. L. R. James, *Beyond a Boundary*, Preface.

[28]An excellent summary of what this political color-consciousness entails is Cornel West's, "A Genealogy of Modern Racism", in *Prophesy Deliverance! An Afro-American Revolutionary Christianity* (Louisville, KY: Westminster John Knox Press, 2002), Edition 2, 47–65.

[29]C. L. R. James, *The Black Jacobins: Toussaint L'Ouverture and the San Domingo Revolution,* [1938] (New York, NY: Random House, Inc., 1963, 1989), Edition 2.

could not afford to lose the enormous income from its Caribbean plantation colonies.[30] Toussaint L'Ouverture emerges as the tragic figure[31] at the heart of this vast political paradox: understanding himself to be a free French citizen, as well as a passionate believer in the ideals of the French Revolution, he was shocked to discover the French Republic unwilling to play by the rules of the very political game it had set in motion. He refused to believe that the French government would not recognize its unsportsmanlike inconsistency and redress the matter; he witnessed the arrival of a French fleet sent to squash the rebellion with heartsickness as well as dread. Agreeing to a negotiation under the conditions of truce, he was kidnaped, imprisoned, and died in jail, writing plaintive epistles to Napoleon to the end, attempting to make the Emperor see the error of his vicious (that is, virtueless) rendering of the principles of the Revolution. But the diasporic African freedom movement Toussaint helped set in motion would eventually prevail.

The lines of political, philosophical, and moral commitment that connect this early work to James's remarkable book nominally dedicated to sport and published[32] more than twenty years later, are relatively clear,

[30]For more on the paradoxes lying at the heart of the 1789 Declaration and its immediate interpretations (i.e., should these rights be extended to executioners, actors, slaves, women, or the poor?), see Lynn Hunt, ed., *The French Revolution and Human Rights: A Brief Documentary History* (Boston, MA: St. Martin's, 1996), Edition 2.

[31]James had already written a play to highlight the tragic dimension of his career: *Toussaint L'Ouverture: The Story of the Only Successful Slave Revolt in History; A Play in Three Acts* (1934) (Durham, NC: Duke University Press, 2013). Also germane here is James's classic study, *A History of Negro Revolt* (Chicago, IL: Frontline Books, 2004), Edition 5.

[32]The complicated publication history of this important text is nicely laid out with the aid of archival evidence from James's own correspondence by Roy McCree in "The Boundaries of Publication: The Making of Beyond a Boundary", in David Featherstone, Christopher Gair, Christian Høgsbjerg, and Andrew Sith, eds., *Marxism, Colonialism and Cricket: CLR James Beyond a Boundary* (Durham, NC: Duke University Press, 2018), 72–87.

James struggled for several years to find a publisher willing to take a risk on such a hybrid manuscript—one part a study of cricket as sport and art-form, and one part ethical and social commentary. James's friend, George Lamming, was responsible for connecting him to the London publisher (Hutchinson) that eventually agreed to publish the book, but with a new title. James had submitted the manuscript with the title *Who Only Cricket Know* (a phrase which echoes Rudyard Kipling's famously unimperial question, "What should they know of England who only England know?"), and he later suggested *WG, A West Indian Grace* and *West Indian Progeny of WG* and *The Cricket Crusaders*, but the publisher balked at these as well. It was Lamming who suggested *Beyond the Boundary*, which the editors altered to *Beyond a Boundary*; James was delighted with the new title.

but they are developed here in large part through the lens of personal autobiography.[33]

James was interested in the history of emancipatory political transformations, and he became more finely aware of the role racism played in the hindrance of such transformations—not only in Haiti, but also in Trinidad, in England, and far more dramatically for him personally, in the United States. Clearly, attitudes as well as political institutions required moral transformation. His emerging view was that there is a close connection between those two practical forms of transformation, such that James's formation in the game of cricket was at least as determinative as his formation by school, and by later readings of Marx in London, had been. Put more pointedly, the cricket pitch *was itself* home to a form of schooling. As he confesses early in the book, James thought very little of cheating at school, but such a thing was unthinkable when he was playing cricket.[34] That paradox is the essential mystery which *Beyond a Boundary* is designed to describe, if not resolve. The book was published in 1963, just one year after Trinidad had won its independence; given James's long involvement in the movement for West Indian independence, the book is thus also intended as a cautionary tale of sorts. Without the requisite virtues, James believed, no revolution could succeed for long—as in France, as in the United States, so in Trinidad.

The personal story told in *Beyond a Boundary* is the story of an ambitious and highly talented young man, a colonial subject who thought of himself, and who aspired to be, British; we are meant to see the parallels to Toussaint L'Ouverture's complex revolutionary and postcolonial identity here. In James's case, they were two eminently British, and eminently imperial, institutions that would eventually radicalize him: Victorian novels, a taste he took from his mother; and the game of cricket, which

[33]Of course, it is autobiographical in a highly selective manner, one supplemented with sporting biographies (five chapters dedicated to William Grace alone), literary criticism (claiming Thackeray as more important to the book than Marx) and social–political commentary designed to illustrate his own slowly emerging class-and-color consciousness. James famously summarizes his entire five-year sojourn in London (1933–1938), where he became a Marxist and lived for some time with Learie Constantine, in a single paragraph (CLR James, *Beyond a Boundary*, 151).

[34]C. L. R. James, *Beyond a Boundary*, 24–25.

passion was all his own.[35] James was positively addicted to the game, and since a cricket match can last for days, it takes real commitment to play or to spectate. James did both. He graduated in 1918, played for a league team from 1919 to 1932,[36] then reported on the game in London from 1933 to 1938. He appreciated the subtle artistry of cricket, the "Homeric" choreography which pitted a bowler against a batsman, as well as the ways in which personality and character were intimately connected to sporting success and failure.

When the West Indian team was scheduled to play a match in England in 1957, James and others were mystified to discover that the captain of the West Indian team had been selected and that the team's most gifted black batsman had been passed over for a less talented white player. "I

[35]C. L. R. James, *Beyond a Boundary*, 18, 21. There is also the matter of his mother's Puritanism in play, as well as his father's long family involvement with cricket, but in any case James's combination of these traditions was *sui generis*.

[36]While this issue lies outside my present purposes, Grant Farred has brilliantly shown how unconscious class interests were the subtle drivers behind James's nominally color-conscious decision to play for the team he eventually chose. As a man of color, he had three choices: Maple, a team of the bourgeoisie, composed of teachers and journalists mainly, and primarily composed of light-skinned players; Shannon, composed of working class and lower middle class players who were largely dark-skinned; and Stingo, composed of laborers and oil field workers largely without social status. James, a talented player with significant social status, could have chosen either Maple or Shannon, despite being dark-skinned. To his later shame, he chose Maple—for what Farred outlines as unconsciously class-based reasons. Shannon was the better team, so James had unconsciously made something else (namely, class) more important than the virtues of the game; this is the moral lesson that would drive the later composition of *Beyond a Boundary*. Shannon was the team with Trinidad's greatest cricketers: the bowler Learie Constantine, and the batter Wilton St. Clair. James would devote an entire chapter of *Beyond a Boundary* to each man. In a sense, then, every Shannon victory over Maple was a victory in a class war, and a rough personal reminder. But James did not see the symbolic importance of such games at the time. He saw it later, when he came to see color more clearly, and its relation to the (post)colonial mentality. James's trajectory to radical independence movements began then. His later readings of Marx in London, and long discussion with Learie Constantine there (he was ghost-writing Constantine's memoir, *Cricket and I*) would bring those unconscious class forces to the surface, a consciousness-raising that contributed to his political radicalization.

See Farred's *Maple Man*, 185–186, which concludes with a fascinating historical juxtaposition: the Trinidadian team attracts hundreds of thousands of spectators in Melbourne, Australia, in 1961; Trinidad achieves its independence in 1962; and *Beyond a Boundary* is published in 1963.

For more on James's understanding of the philosophy of Shannonism, and his attempts to atone for sins against cricket and Constantine, see Clem Seecharan, "Shannonism: Learie Constantine and the Origins of C. L. R. James's Worrell Captaincy Campaign of 1959–1960: A Preliminary Assessment", in David Featherstone, Christopher Gair, Christian Høgsbjerg, and Andrew Sith, eds., *Marxism, Colonialism and Cricket*, 153–169.

adhere stubbornly to my juvenile ethics," James tells us, "that the captain should not be [a black or white] man but the best man."[37] The stakes of such international games are high, of course: to beat the empire at its own game is a vastly symbolic colonial victory. But the West Indian team seemed to care more about looking like the imperial center than the colonial periphery… and thus James's identity-cum-moral crisis was born.

In short, the attentive practices of close reading—of cricket and Victorian prose—radicalized C. L. R. James. He took the rules of the game seriously, off the pitch and on it. To fail to live up to the code of honor of the game had always been virtually unthinkable to him. The British empire failed this test, but so too would some of James's fellow revolutionaries.

James's radicalization through cricket first drew him to be a Marxist critic of economic injustice, and later to be a postcolonial critic of imperialism. While the experience of the West Indian cricket team had made him aware of race, and of his own blackness, it was a fifteen-year sojourn in the United States, between 1938 and 1953, that made him aware of a still more virulent, and explicitly violent, form of segregated color consciousness. He puts his expatriate conundrum in poignantly personal terms: "[I] stayed there for fifteen years and I never saw a cricket match."[38]

His long sojourn in the United States bore other lessons for James as well. He quickly came to see that he was far more similar to his British than to his American friends. Americans raged at the umpires of sporting events, especially in baseball of all things (the closest North American equivalent to cricket), something he had vowed never to do (as we will recall, James admitted that he had cheated wildly in school as a child, but on the field of play, never). His American friends also raged at racism, but in unproductive and vicious ways. Most pointedly, James felt that the Americans he met had no sense of loyalty to a team, or a school, or much of anything. Two experiences made the issue clear: a pervasive cheating scandal which was uncovered in college basketball; and James's six-month

[37]C. L. R. James, *Beyond a Boundary*, 135.

[38]C. L. R. James, *Beyond a Boundary*, 19.

internment at Ellis Island while his communist credentials were examined by the Departments of Justice and Immigration. *No respect for the rules.* At this point, James broke with the whole show, and promptly returned to Trinidad... where he began working on West Indian independence, a book on Hermann Melville,[39] and another on the game of cricket. We might consider these the moral triptych that defined both his life and his career.[40]

Other changes were in the offing in this same period, most of them inspired by this same schooling on the cricket pitch. James broke with Soviet-style Marxism in 1940 when Stalin made his pact with Hitler: utilitarian politics of convenience were as venal and as vicious as anything he had seen in the United States. He would become a staunch critic even of the Trotskyite position for this same reason.

James left the United States in 1953, just one year before the landmark *Brown v Board of Education* ruling by the US Supreme Court. More significant than Supreme Court decisions, to James, was the moral formation provided by his beloved game. Virtues enacted on the field of play were enacted in the realm of politics too, or at least they were supposed to be. James was to break with many of his independence-minded colleagues over questions of tactics and the vicious compromises they deemed necessary, justified in terms similar to the ones the Trotskyites had made in Russia. For James, a revolution without virtue was no revolution, just a moral perpetuation, more of the same. The Caribbean test-case had ever been his primary education. In the end, however, success was achieved in terms he could accept: "'The Case for West

[39]C. L. R. James, *Mariners, Renegades & Castaways: The Story of Hermann Melville and the World We Live in* (Hanover, NH: Dartmouth College Press, 1953, 1978). The book brilliantly summarizes lectures on Melville which he had given throughout the United States during his fifteen-year sojourn. *Moby Dick's* main theme, James argued, was "how the society of free individualism would give birth to totalitarianism and be unable to defend itself against it" (54). That thesis is filtered through James's experience of imprisonment on Ellis Island, which he chronicles in the last chapter of the book (125–167).

An important collection of James's occasional writings, especially those relating to racism and the question of political liberty, is Anna Grimshaw, ed., *The C. L. R. James Reader* (Oxford: Blackwell, 1992).

[40]C. L. R. James, *Beyond a Boundary*, 19.

Indian Self-Government' and 'It isn't cricket' had come together at last and together had won a signal victory."[41]

The whole enterprise hinges on a simple idea, but like most simple things, the moral reach of a simple idea can be long. The rules matter. They matter whether you are oppressed or not; they matter whether you win or lose. They matter whether the umpires and courts are ones you like or not. To violate the rules in order to win would be to strip the victory of its value. That is as true for a committed revolutionary as it is for a passionate cricketer. To cheat is quite literally to fail to understand the nature of the game and its values. "Cricket had plunged me into politics long before I was aware of it,"[42] James concludes in retrospect.

Apart from semi-autobiography, *Beyond a Boundary* offers up a spirited catalogue of the greatest players James ever saw or studied: the great bowler, George John; the great batsman, George Headley; and Learie Constantine, who excelled at both. Fully one-quarter of the book is an encomium to one man, W. G. Grace (1848–1915). "Grasp the fact that a whole nation had prepared the way for [W.G. Grace]," James observes, "and you begin to see his stature as a national embodiment."[43] And once again, in terms echoing Coubertin's great intervention in sporting philosophy: "Cricket was a religion and W.G. stood next to the Deity."[44]

James's reasons for writing in this mingled biographical/autobiographical manner are complex.[45] On the one hand, he was clearly participating in the Renaissance and Humanist essayist's tradition

---

[41] C. L. R. James, *Beyond a Boundary*, 241.

[42] C. L. R. James, *Beyond a Boundary*, 65.

[43] C. L. R. James, *Beyond a Boundary*, 170.

[44] C. L. R. James, *Beyond a Boundary*, 165.

[45] And in particular his encomium of W. G. Grace has received criticism for various reasons: that it relied on uncritical acceptance of newspaper reporting, since James never saw Grace play; that it failed to see how Grace's apotheosis in 1895 was designed to defend and promote a form of masculinity in opposition to Oscar Wilde's at the height of the Wilde scandal; and that it engaged in suspect Hegelian lionization of world-historical persons without the proper dialectical Marxist attention to society and political context.

See Neil Washburne, "C. L. R. James, W. G. Grace and the Representative Claim", and Claire Westall, "C. L. R. James and the Arts of Beyond a Boundary: Literary Lessons, Cricketing Aesthetics, and World Historical Heroes", in David Featherstone, Christopher Gair, Christian Høgsbjerg, and Andrew Sith, eds., *Marxism, Colonialism and Cricket*, 137–152, 173–190.

of teaching through exemplary persons.[46] A virtue exists, if and only as it is displayed in action. James was also attempting to explain the unique thrill and moral passion that sports can inspire. He wishes, then, for us to understand how a game can produce forms of excellence (the Greek word, *aretê*, possesses an overlapping sense of both virtue and excellence).

James, who admired the ancient Olympics much as he admired cricket, was shocked to note that so few intellectuals took such play seriously; this is a fact of academic and scholarly culture well worth considering in greater depth.

> All art, science, philosophy, are modes of apprehending the world, history and society. As one of these, cricket in the West Indies at least could hold its own. A professor of political science publicly bewailed that a man of my known political interests should believe that cricket had ethical and social values. I had no wish to answer. I was just sorry for the guy.[47]

Sport—as I noted at the outset, and as James knew very well—is organized, ritualized, and subtly choreographed social activity. It is very much like religion, in that way. James also recognized that the Olympic religious festivals in ancient Greece were a magnet for much else that we admire and hold dear: the philosophy, the politics, even the art. As a product of British schooling, as well as of the Empire's novels and games, James was deeply informed by the character of Greek athletics. The first two Trinidadian character sketches he offers make this plain: first we meet Matthew Bondman, a marvelous batsman whose natural talent was nonetheless squandered by vicious character flaws[48]; and Arthur Jones, whom James deems a "Phidias in form."[49] As the Greeks knew well, exemplary characters offer negative as well as positive object lessons.

---

[46]This is an insight I owe to Jeffrey Stout. I had the privilege of attending three of his latter seminars at Princeton University, in which readings of Montaigne, Machiavelli, Milton, and Emerson drove this point home.

[47]C. L. R. James, *Beyond a Boundary*, 249–250.

I have for many years offered an upper-level seminar on the ancient and modern Olympics for this very reason, one which concludes with a close reading of James's text. I take the work of Harvard University's Ludics seminar to be dedicated to very similar work.

[48]C. L. R. James, *Beyond a Boundary*, 3–5.

[49]C. L. R. James, *Beyond a Boundary*, 5–7.

In two luminous passages, one early and one late,[50] James tries to make sense of his rebelliousness at school in contrast to his virtually Puritan obedience on the cricket pitch. "The first task was to get Greece clear," he observes.[51] What James inherited from his schooling was not philological skill in ancient languages so much as an *internalization* of the Greek model of areteic education, one in which *poetry and games* were essential, and essentially linked. Greek athletics, James concludes, were "co-birthed" in Athens, together with democracy, tragedy, and philosophy. Ancient sport thus had a great deal to do with teaching us about poetry in motion, tragedy in experience, and wisdom in practical life.[52] "The end of democracy is a more complete existence,"[53] James will conclude. Like Coubertin, James recognized that contests in poetry were joined to athletic contests at Olympia and Delphi, both. Like Coubertin, James understood the role of "eurhythmy" in sport, as in life. His was a moral philosophy that aimed to link art, to philosophy, to religion, much as the Romantic philosophers had done in Hegel's day, after the French Revolution. Developing this essentially moral connection, James notes that what the Olympics had been to ancient Greece, cricket was to the British empire in the nineteenth century (and, as I have tried to suggest, what modern Olympism was to become in the twentieth). Athletes and umpires all swear a sacred oath; cheating is quite literally the blasphemy that would undo the game.

For many young men and women around the world, sport is as crucial a source of moral formation as it is physically liberating. James would have understood Coubertin, who insisted repeatedly that his Olympic Revival had simply been one piece of a lifelong project in educational

[50]C. L. R. James, *Beyond a Boundary*, 32–34, 154–158.

[51]C. L. R. James, *Beyond a Boundary*, 154.

[52]This idea was developed with great insight in the work of Cornelius Castoriadis. See, for instance, "The Greek Polis and the Creation of Democracy", in David Ames Curtis, ed. and trans., *Philosophy, Politics, Autonomy* (New York, NY: Oxford University Press, 1991), 81–123, and discussion from David Ames Curtis, ed. and trans., *World in Fragments: Writings on Politics, Society, Psychoanalysis and the Imagination* (Stanford, CA: Stanford University Press, 1997), 74, and *The Greek and the Modern Political Imaginary*, 84–107.

[53]C. L. R. James, *Beyond a Boundary*, 210.

reform.[54] Athletes learn discipline, learn how to appreciate excellence—that is, the excellence of any performance, not just their own. Perhaps most significantly of all, athletes learn how to lose charitably, as well as how to win. Thus athletes are schooled to see that winning is not valuable at all costs. Athletes learn how to recognize when a game, or a career, is over. These are deeply significant lessons to learn.

And that is why sport matters. In the hands of a batter like William Grace (cricket's Babe Ruth) or George Headley,[55] or a bowler like Wilton St. Hill (Trinidad's Sandy Koufax),[56] or an all-around virtuoso like Learie Constantine (Trinidad's Willie Mays),[57] or even a coach with rarified gifts of moral and personal discernment,[58] sport is not just an arena for transcendent performance and the thrill of spectacle; it is quite literally a school of virtue. Here is how James ultimately came to understand cricket's place in his own formation:

> The aesthetics of cricket demand first that you master the game, and, preferably, have played it, if not well, at least in good company. And that is not the easy acquisition outsiders think it to be.[59]

In C. L. R. James, then, we are learning far more than how to master a game. James was one of the most remarkable moral teachers this, or any, game has produced. And he produced it, always, by recognizing and promoting good company.

Conclusion

I suggested at the outset that James might best be considered "a virtue ethicist who gradually became committed to the cause of Trinidadian

[54]See MacAloon, *This Great Symbol*, 83–112.

[55]C. L. R. James, *Beyond a Boundary*, 171–185 and 139–148, respectively.

[56]C. L. R. James, *Beyond a Boundary*, 82–97.

[57]C. L. R. James, *Beyond a Boundary*, 101–135.

[58]See Michael Lewis's encomium to his baseball Coach Fitz, *Coach: Lessons on the Game of Life* (New York, NY: W. W. Norton & Company, Inc., 2005).

[59]C. L. R. James, *Beyond a Boundary*, 207n1.

national independence for reasons that had everything to do with his passion for cricket and his understanding of the ethical relevance of obedience to the rules of the game." I would like to concretize that claim by looking briefly at the retrieval of "the tradition of the virtues" enunciated by Alasdair MacIntyre in his now-classic study, *After Virtue*. While there have been many iterations of the virtue tradition, and many incompatible lists of requisite virtues, MacIntyre suggests, there is nonetheless a family resemblance among these various traditions, one which hinges on several interlocking ideas. The first of these is what he refers to as a notion of "internal goods"[60]—goods, that is, that are internal to certain elaborated social practices, like sports.

To illustrate the point, MacIntyre offers the analogy of teaching a young child to play chess. In the beginning, the child must be bribed to play the game, with the promise of candy to be rewarded at the end of the game. However, after long experience of playing the game, and recognizing the expansive opportunities for increasing his or her excellence in playing it, the child will eventually come to see goods that are only recognizable, and understandable, in the context of playing the game (here once again, presumably in good company). At some point the child no longer needs the promise of candy, a good entirely external to the game of chess. He or she has come to recognize, and to appreciate, goods and excellences created by the elaborate and rather arbitrary rules that constitute the game, its field of play, and its unique satisfactions. The analogy to what James experienced here is clear, I hope. The player who plays a game strictly for money, or fame, or victory, will be blinded to the

[60]Alasdair MacIntyre, *After Virtue* (South Bend, IN: University of Notre Dame Press, 1984), 187–188, Edition 2. The other two features MacIntyre identifies are the narrative conception of the unity of a human life, and the concept of participating in an historical tradition. These issues have more to do with his larger critique of an allegedly fragmented modern society and modern life, views I do not endorse.

For criticism of that broader anti-modern project, see Louis A. Ruprecht Jr., *Afterwords: Hellenism, Modernism and the Myth of Decadence* (Albany, NY: State University of New York Press, 1996), 91–123; Jeffrey Stout, *Democracy and Tradition*, 118–139.

Earlier interventions by Stout include: "Virtue Among the Ruins", in *Ethics After Babel: The Languages of Morals and Their Discontents* (Boston, NY: Beacon Press, 1988), 333–358; "Homeward Bound: MacIntyre on Liberal Society and the History of Ethics," *Journal of Religion* 69, 1989, 220–232; and "Commitments and Traditions in the Study of Religious Ethics," *Journal of Religious Ethics* 25.3, 1998, 23–56.

virtues of the game by the distraction of these external goods. Such an athlete will also have very little incentive not to cheat if victory or fortune can be achieved in this way (hence James's dismay with North American sports). In this sense, *Beyond a Boundary* attempts to describe the goods internal to the game of cricket, and how the gradual habituation into the game's singular virtues can play an essential role in the moral formation of a young adult. James became who he was to become largely through indoctrination into the rules and roles of the game, the virtues attendant upon playing it well, and the goods internal to the practice. What he learned within the cricket boundary was to have great moral consequence for him outside of that boundary, later in his life.

The book concludes with a chapter fittingly entitled "Epilogue and Apotheosis." It describes the last, and perhaps the most salient, exemplar James will present to us: Frank Worrell, whom he deems a Pindaric apotheosis of the virtues of cricket, and of life. Worrell was a black Trinidadian who captained the team that toured Australia in 1961. James had lobbied on Worrell's behalf ever since returning to Trinidad in 1958, in the pages of the *Nation* (the literary organ of the People's National Movement) which he had been invited to serve as editor. Worrell's captaincy was a symbolic social event in many ways—racially (post)colonially, dramatically. And it began quite badly. Yet Worrell, captain and coach in one,[61] did not panic. "If something was wrong I told them what was right and left it to them," he observed almost casually.[62] But in fact Frank Worrell did far more, James tells us; he led

[61]I had the great personal gift of being trained by such a coach during my formative high school years running for my school's track team. He was Mr. Edward Scott of Elizabeth, New Jersey (1931–2018); this essay is dedicated to his memory.

[62]C. L. R. James, *Beyond a Boundary*, 258. James continues:

> Those words will always ring in my ears. They are something new, not only in West Indies cricket but in West Indies life. West Indians can often tell you what is wrong and some even what will make it right, but they can't leave it to you. Worrell did. It is the ultimate expression of a most finished personality, who knows his business, theory and practice, and knows modern men.

by example, playing the game to perfection. And all the world saw it. Trinidadian independence was achieved the next year.[63]

There are certainly meaner legacies, and meaner forms of art, to which to commit oneself. It was the moral pedagogy of cricket that helped James to see this so.

[63]As I noted earlier (Note #36) Grant Farred notes this same connection, making it central to his understanding of James and his maturing political views.

Pre-Texts: Press Play to Teach Anything

Doris Sommer

I extend a perhaps paradoxical invitation to educators who face new challenges of migration, technological advances, and a general erosion of sociability, because what I offer is hardly new. Instead, it is a methodology that gathers useful lessons and distills them into a single prompt that works like pedagogical acupuncture. "Use this text to make art" is an invitation that fires up cognitive, creative, emotional, and communicative systems. We need this simplicity now that teachers face overwhelming flows of new knowledge and disorienting flows of unfamiliar people. The methodology is called *Pre-Texts* because texts become excuses for making something else. And the work of creative, often irreverent, translation of text into something else is both intellectually challenging and emotionally empowering. Artists own their raw material, even if it seems difficult or boring. Pre-Texts is a handy and portable approach to teach practically any curriculum in almost any environment. The

D. Sommer (✉)
Harvard University, Cambridge, MA, USA
e-mail: dsommer@fas.harvard.edu

V. Rapti and E. Gordon (eds.), *Ludics*,
https://doi.org/10.1007/978-981-15-7435-1_4

acupuncture lights up three general lessons for Pre-Texts: (1) Integrate skill sets; (2) Play; (3) Customize activities.

Rather than clear the decks of past experiments that didn't make migration and technology central concerns, Pre-Texts extracted advice from past masters. The most distinguished among them is Paulo Freire, not only because *Pedagogy of the Oppressed* teaches how to reduce the distance between the poor and the powerful—between migrants and the native born—but also because education in general depends on non-hierarchical interactions. John Dewey called this dynamic "transactional."[1]

Freire's fan and follower, theater director Augusto Boal, grounded his friend's philosophical principles into a simple arts-based activity. Boal produced political education in *Theater of the Oppressed* with a step by step approach that almost anyone can follow: (1) Ask people to identify a collective problem; (2) support them to script the problem into a staged tragedy; (3) invite to play-act adjustments on stage that may derail the tragedy. The sequence requires little cultural competence on the part of facilitators. Instead, it counts on their humility and curiosity. Facilitators ask and listen; they don't presume to know. Knowing about different groups of people is, in any case, practically impossible given our heterogeneous and changing environments. And in some cases the presumption promotes a kind of unfounded confidence that can confirm existing hierarchies.

Boal's improvised plays are a prompt to create the protocol for Pre-Texts to teach, starting with language arts. Today, literacy is a foundation for all human development (cognitive, political, economic, social, emotional, health). Reimagining migration and democracy should, necessarily, target learning at least a *lingua franca* in the multilingual environments of our schools and refugee camps. If people don't share a language, how can educators support learning or promote other human rights? Pre-Texts responds to the challenge with neutral Boal-inspired steps to teach anything, anywhere: (1) Take a required text, say something imposed by authorities, (2) invite students and teachers to propose

---

[1] John Dewey and Arthur Fisher Bentley, *Knowing and the Known* (Boston, Beacon Press, 1949), vi.

interpretive activities, (3) Then pause for all to reflect on "What did we do?" The series ignites collaborations among autonomous agents who learn deeply and enjoy one another.

When local authorities choose the reading material, curricular requirements are satisfied. This gives teachers a margin of liberty to decide how to present the material. In this margin, teachers and students have opportunities to play. Cultural differences in the classroom then become resources for multiplying creative practices that can fuel fun. And the fun generates a taste for difference along with admiration for classmates. If one session turns the required text into an American football game, another may use the material to create Arabic style calligraphy, or Kathak inspired choreography. Difficult or boring texts become artistic challenges, raw material for play, through rap, dance, music, murals, fashion, sport, theater, etc. Participants enjoy manipulating the text on their own terms, even taking revenge on it. Text, after all, means a weave (textile) whose threads can loosen and tie up in various ways. During the process, students read closely, practice critical distance, and make personal connections to possibly foreign texts and to each other.

Lessons Learned

Integrate

Learning a language through art-making engages all the learner's faculties and skill sets; it is not merely technical work. Along with the mechanics of language, students learn communication skills which are the core of socio-emotional development. They also learn to innovate, because language is an art form that recombines available elements into new sentences and new thoughts. Close-reading assumes a multiplicity of viewpoints and depends on creative interpretation. With literacy and innovation, citizenship thrives because speakers come to anticipate the creativity of others and to admire their differences.

Literacy, Innovation, and Citizenship describe the gears of a holistic education which is both simple and profound (see www.pre-texts.org).

Pre-Texts develops these three goals as interlocking areas of human development—cognitive, creative, and socio-emotional—through student-centered activities. They resemble solutions reached by some seasoned educators to the challenges of overwork, large classes, and student indifference. But effective practices sometimes develop late in professional life, and then the teachers retire. Pre-Texts makes good on the accumulated wisdom to invite all teachers to "work less and achieve more."

The recent and still current emphasis on socio-emotional learning (SEL) is an understandable corrective to education by numbers, a trend that proposed to improve outcomes in literacy and numeracy by vigilant measurement of advances. But the therapy for having ignored students' psychological wellbeing in favor of academic performance can be as dangerous as the now disqualified use of metrics. One approach and the other targets a particular set of human faculties and brackets many more, even though the human condition is a dynamic combination of cognitive, emotional, creative, and social capacities. Wisely, Carola Suárez-Orozco collects all these dimensions in her essay on the "Ecologies of care: addressing the needs of immigrant origin children and youth."[2] To single out one focus runs the risk of crippling the complex interactions. There is hardly a teacher—or parent—who hasn't experienced the joy that a child feels when he or she learns a new word, or puts a puzzle together, or discovers the mechanism of a machine. Is this emotion different from feeling self-efficacy or personal worth? Our challenge should not be to distinguish one dimension of education from others, but to develop opportunities for students to flourish as integral human beings. Play provides endless opportunities for this.

A corollary concern to SEL is the often unexamined value of empathy. The well-intentioned objective to promote empathy among students and teachers assumes, ideally, that one human being can and should feel the feelings of another. Whether or not this is feasible, or ethical, is a question I raise here and revisit on considering how to customize education as we reimagine migration. Is it possible that wanting to cancel distances of feelings among people is—in fact—to wish their differences away?

---

[2]Carola Suárez-Orozco, Ecologies of Care: Addressing the Needs of Immigrant Origin Children and Youth (*Journal of Global Ethics*, Published online: 22 August 2018), 47–53 at https://doi.org/10.1080/17449626.2018.1496348.

Can the words compassion or love (to revive Freire's advice) lead to more ethical and nuanced relationships that appreciate difference rather than overcome it?

Play

People learn through play, after all; it frees the faculties to engage in the safe space of fiction. Play creates room for multiple perspectives that bypass the mono-vision of base sensuality or of heartless reason. The opposite of play is not work or seriousness, Gregory Bateson explained; it's not even depression. For Bateson, the opposite is mental constriction. Play interrupts the one-dimensionality or literal-mindedness that leads a species to extinction.[3] One virtue of play is that it explores possible relationships among people and animals; it stages virtual engagements instead of producing the real thing that can cause damage. Donald Winnicott based his entire project of psychotherapy for children on play. At the thrilling border between subjective fantasy and objective reality, play is the fundamental activity of human development and of sustained psychic health. Real therapists get down on the floor with children and take turns leading a game or a fantasy.

Winnicott drew a connection between play and art-making, which he called "symbolic violence," thereby recovering an Enlightenment legacy of education. I refer to Friedrich Schiller's *Letters on the Aesthetic Education of Man* (1793), written during the terror of the French revolution. In that daring book, Schiller admitted that aesthetics probably seemed "unseasonable" during the reign of terror. But thinking about and making art was urgent, he insisted, because only art can de-escalate violence. Art deflects compromised emotions and it recombines familiar materials to create surprising new forms that stop opponents in their tracks, make them reflect on meaning and maybe even talk to one another. Who are the artists capable of this maneuver? All human beings are artists for Schiller. Our complex condition includes the conflicting

[3]Gregory Bateson, *Steps to an Ecology of Mind* (Chicago, University of Chicago Press, 1972), 180.

instincts of reason and passion. But it also includes the "Playdrive" (*Speil-trieb*) to invent new forms in response to conflict. Schiller wrote "man is truly human when he plays, and he plays when he is truly human," (letter 15) as if conjuring Winnicott's future work.

"There is no anger in the destruction of the object to which I (Winnicott) am referring, though there could be said to be a joy at the object's survival."[4] Healthy, symbolic destruction opens routes to integrate the subject with the objective environment and with emotional maturity, while pathological and truly destructive acting-out keeps the immature subject split off from the world. Much of Winnicott's work describes a structural link between healthy living and art-making: "Through artistic expression we can hope to keep in touch with our primitive selves whence the most intense feelings and even fearfully acute sensations derive, and we are poor indeed if we are only sane."[5] "Psychotherapy has to do with two people playing together."[6] This means free and non-purposive communication, which the analyst must not force into reasonable sequences.

If curiosity and potentially explosive emotions can ignite play, it is pleasure that keeps it going.[7] Winnicott's clinical advice is to promote non-purposive pleasure through play, and thereby to foster healthy integration of students to their surroundings. Otherwise we block learning and development in general. Pleasure is a condition [and also an effect] of real learning, as neuroscience has confirmed.[8] So, when good intentions become too purposive, too earnest to instigate fun, we run the risk of

---

[4]D. W. Winnicott, The Use of an Object (*International Journal of Psycho-Analysis*, 1969), 50: 711–716.

[5]D. W. Winnicott, Lesley Caldwell, and Robert Adès, *The Collected Works of D.W. Winnicott* (Oxford University Press, 2016), 368.

[6]D. W. Winnicott, *Playing and Reality* (London, Tavistock, 1971), 38–52. The therapist included his own practice among the playful and creative (that is, human) activities he studied: "Psychotherapy takes place in the overlap of two areas of playing, that of the patient and that of the therapist."

[7]D. W. Winnicott, *Playing: Its Theoretical Status in the Clinical Situation* (*International Journal of Psycho- Analysts*, 1968), 48, 49.

[8]Kent A. Berridge and Morten Kringelbach, Affective Neuroscience of Pleasure: Reward in Humans and Animals (*Psychopharmacology*, August 2008), Volume 199, Issue 3, 457–480. https://www.ncbi.nlm.nih.gov/pmc/articles/PMC3004012/ "A particularly important topic for affective neuroscience is to understand how brains generate pleasure and other psychological components of reward because reward is important in daily life. Pleasure is essential to a normal

derailing socio-emotional development. Unhappy emotions of displaced and perhaps traumatized children, angry or depressive responses to the exclusion they often experience before and after they arrive, can set off dangerously destructive and self-destructive dynamics if anger and anxiety don't find outlets through "symbolic destruction" as play and art. The practically joyless and earnest effort that seems to drive SEL, should raise a worry as it works to prepare children for global citizenship by soberly teaching them empathy and ethics. There is hardly any fun here, either for teachers or for students. Better citizenship would follow from an indirect approach, Schiller explained, because appeals to reason and to obligation can be met with resentment and maybe even resistance. But the pleasure of making new creations promotes connections with the world and with fellow artists who admire one another precisely for their differences. Difference in art-making classrooms becomes delightful rather than burdensome.

I am saying that SEL implies, perhaps counterproductively, an obligation to feel good toward other people instead of just feeling good. "**Social** and **emotional learning** (SEL) is the process through which children and adults acquire and effectively apply the knowledge, attitudes, and skills necessary to understand and manage **emotions**, set and achieve positive goals, feel and show empathy for others, establish and maintain positive relationships, and make responsible decisions."[9] Neither joy nor admiration appears among the sober competencies set forth in programs for hire in professional development. By definition, research in SEL recognizes its object as an established practice and often shares the providers' almost Victorian tone of moral improvement. See for example, "Risks and Benefits to Teaching Children about Intergroup Biases."[10]

---

sense of well-being. Pathological losses of pleasure may be a devastating part of many affective disorders ranging from depression to schizophrenia and addiction."

Piotr Wozniak, "Pleasure of learning" https://supermemo.guru/wiki/Pleasure_of_learning. "Language and reward: Study examines the pleasure of learning new words" (University of Barcelona, *PsyPost*, October 26, 2014). https://www.psypost.org/2014/10/study-e-28987.

[9]https://casel.org/what-is-sel/.

[10]Rebecca S. Bigler and Yamanda F. Wright, Reading, Writing, Arithmetic, and Racism? Risks and Benefits to Teaching Children About Intergroup Biases (*Child Development Perspectives*, March 2014), Volume 8, Issue 1, 18–23. https://onlinelibrary.wiley.com/doi/abs/10.1111/cdep.12057.

Why not instead invite children to play with one another and then to reflect on experience, including possible bias? Prepare fun activities that honor differences as well as commonalities, and then measure the degree of bias, before and after.

The circularity of existing research about established questions confirms a particular line of enquiry, rather than raise alternative questions, so that conclusions seem self-evident: Schools *should* build SEL into classrooms and safeguard developments by appointing experts with an institutional mandate. (See the Rennie Center for Research's *Policy Brief* for the State of Massachusetts.) The policy recommendations claim support from neuroscience which "demonstrates that emotion and cognition are inextricably linked; (note #5) in fact, emotions are critical for all people to understand, organize, and make connections between even 'pure' academic concepts (note #6)." But *pleasure*—the very emotion that neuroscience has long associated with learning—is glaringly absent from this *Brief* and from SEL in general.[11] Is there perhaps a stigma against pleasure in our sincere mission to educate? Does the stigma participate in a general drive to develop and to modernize society at the expense of human feelings? (See Max Weber's *The Protestant Ethic and the Spirit of Capitalism*, 1905). Of course SEL rejects that human cost, to its credit. But it may have inherited a rationalizing rigor that isolates one human faculty from another to favor emotions over cognition, this time. Either choice is crippling for the complex human condition; and downplaying the pleasure of learning, when it should be the driving emotion at school, aggravates unintended damages.

School means leisure, and the activities that leisure permits. This is a strictly etymological reference to the ancient Greek foundation (σχολή) for our contemporary classrooms. *Skholḗ* was where the privileged youth of Athens gathered to develop games and conversation, to stroll, meditate, debate, and reflect. Hanna Arendt hoped to revive that charmed tradition of speaking freely and listening carefully. It's worth

[11] http://www.ascd.org/ASCD/pdf/siteASCD/policy/SEL_PolicyBrief_Final_11-16-15.pdf. https://www.google.com/search?q=social+emotional+education&rlz=1C1G GRV_enUS751US759&oq=socio-emotional+edu&aqs=chrome.1.69i57j0.7095j1j7&sourceid =chrome&ie =UTF-8.

another try. The term she recovers to name political life is "vita activa."[12] It was a response to the trial of Socrates and to the general conflict between philosophy and the polis. An active life, like that of Socrates, is devoted to public-political matters. And to the degree that it chooses freedom (unavailable to slaves, craftsmen, merchants, women, anyone bound to prescribed activities), it has three options: physical, political, and contemplative. What the three have in common is a dedication to "beauty" which by definition is neither necessary nor useful. It is precisely the undetermined and useless quality of beauty that safeguards freedom. Medieval interpretations of "vita activa" would add praxis to political life, but not in antiquity when philosophy defended purposeless freedom.[13]

The Greek word *skholḗ* has hardly changed phonetically. It sounds as familiar in Romance languages as it does in English, though lamentably—its original use is now almost unrecognizable, except for experimental recoveries by Maria Montessori, John Dewey, Rudolf Steiner, and Reggio Emilia, all of which have congealed into boutique options. More promisingly, the entire country of Finland demonstrates that play pays off in education. But the promise is blunted elsewhere when decision makers miss the magic of leisure's activities, and attribute Finland's educational advances primarily to pay raises for teachers.

As we reimagine migrations to consider refugees and host communities, we will face children and their families in camps such as Cox's Bazaar in Bangladesh, where more than a million Rohingya crowd a liminal space of permanent statelessness, if the authorities stay their course. One immediate danger is violence in the camp. The hopeless conditions fueled by frustrated resistance sow suspicion and hostility among the Rohingya themselves. Is this explosive context an appropriate setting for SEL that would encourage children and their families to care for one another as a moral imperative? Or is the indirect arts-based approach to diffusing tensions more practical? Does normative ethical behavior follow from reasoning about rights and responsibilities, or does civility develop in response to enjoying oneself in the company of playmates? Absurdly,

---

[12] Hannah Arendt, *The Human Condition*, with an introduction by Margaret Canovan (Chicago, University of Chicago Press, 1998, orig, 1958), 12.

[13] Arendt, *The Human Condition*, 13.

and tragically, Rohingya children and adults live the kind of "purposeless" life that an elite vita activa had represented. Since the Middle Ages we know that active life has pursued productive employment and purposive social movements. Today, productivity survives as a personal goal even as sociability wanes, along with predictable jobs for the future.

Maybe now, facing the crisis of shrinking labor markets worldwide that historian Yuval Harari says will raise the few survivors to god-like status and leave the rest of us to obey or to grovel, maybe now that jobs and goals evaporate among the masses, and—without wishing the losses on anyone—there may be an opportunity and even a mandate to establish the new *skholḗ*.[14] Will refugee camps be a vanguard for the future post-work economy, literally a utopia or "no place" for self-fashioning when other jobs vanish? This perverse utopia would occupy the empty space between endless human creativity and depleted opportunities for productive work. A renewed non-productive schooling may lead the way, as we wonder what to do with more and more leisure time that advancing technology will impose on us, or gift to us. If we cannot learn to play again, to enjoy doubt and differences among fellow artists, Gregory Bateson warned, we'll face extermination as a species.

Customize

Let me assume, optimistically, that you acknowledge my line of thinking so far as we reimagine migration: The line connects dots between high order literacy and socio-emotional development to foster the pleasure of learning, good feelings that undergird civility among migrants and nationals. Education is a complex improvisation of cognitive, emotional, and creative faculties that together generate a virtuous cycle of learning as play. But how does one promote pleasurable activity among students whose cultures may differ significantly? Fun is culturally constructed, after all. One response has been to encourage teachers to achieve "cultural competence," as if that were possible in multi-cultural settings. How competent can anyone become about even one more culture beside one's

[14] Yuval Harari, *Homo Deus: A Brief History of Tomorrow* (London, Vintage, 2017).

own? It is time to question whether the goal itself is desirable, because—without wanting to—the effort to close the culture gap confirms a teacher's authority over students since teachers will continue to know best.

Massive and dynamic migrations today overwhelm our capacity to be competent, so that pursuing proficiency can amount to underestimating the challenge and over-estimating our aptitude.

Sometimes the gap is decried as a lack of empathy to be filled in. Here too, the laudable objective to overcome indifference raises ethical dilemmas and professional burdens that may backfire. Love was what Freire called the care that teachers feel for students, not empathy. And Boal explicitly rejected the word, preferring sympathy or compassion, because empathy in theater is designed to reduce spectators to clones for heroes who speak for us all. Rowan Williams, Archbishop of Canterbury from 2002–2012 considered "The Paradoxes of Empathy" in his 2014 Tanner Lectures, to urge caution about closing in on others' feelings.[15] "An ethical discourse which gives central place to empathy as emotional identification draws our attention away from questions of culture and power." Referring to Jewish born Edith Stein (1891–1942; canonized by the Catholic Church as Saint Theresa Benedicta of the Cross), Williams argued that true empathy honors the unbridgeable distance between one consciousness and another. Stein wrote, "The empathic position is one in which we know that we *are not* the other." And her disciple "cautioned against a colonizing mindset that too readily collapses the distance between one's self and another." Williams concludes that "The ethically significant expression of this sort of empathy would be in saying not, 'I know how you feel, but, 'I have no idea how you feel.'"

Given the risks of pursuing competence and empathy in unexamined ways, we might prefer to stay close to Freire and simply to love our students. Along with him, we can become facilitators for learning. This is a democratic option for education, and one that is professionally more modest and more manageable. Instead of trying to master how students will learn best, rather than struggle under the burden of

---

[15]Harvard Magazine, *I Have No Idea How You Feel.* April 15, 2014. https://harvardmagazine.com/2014/04/paradoxes-of-empathy.

choosing the right activity, a teacher can just ask students how they want to tackle a text. We can become "ignorant schoolmasters." I owe the charming oxymoron to Jacques Rancière's biography of a French philosophy teacher who urgently needed to leave France after the Revolution.[16] Jean Joseph Jacotot accepted a friend's invitation to teach in Belgium, though he knew no Dutch. The desperate man preferred to risk incompetence over risking his life. Luckily for him, a bilingual edition of a popular novel came out that year; and to his delight, Jacotot found that his students could teach themselves French by pouring over that book. Students teach themselves when they have the tools and when you have high expectations.

Pre-Texts takes these lessons to heart by inviting participants to design activities, to create interpretations, and then pause to reflect. Speculations, readings that converge or diverge, and admiration for different points of view all come from the players in eureka moments that glow with pleasure. They add up to an aesthetic education in deep reading and in broad civility that can revive the school of Athens and Schiller's Enlightenment.

[16]Jacques Rancière, *The Ignorant Schoolmaster: Five Lessons in Intellectual Emancipation*, trans. with an introduction by Kristin Ross (Stanford, CA: Stanford University Press, [1987]1991).

Work, Play, and Civic Engagement

Peter Levine

It has long been standard practice to distinguish politics or civic life from both work and play.[1]

Aristotle provides an early example of the distinction between work and politics. He begins with the premise that "the citizen's function" is "deliberating and judging (whether on all issues or only a few)."[2] In other words, to act as a citizen means to talk, to listen, and to vote. Citizenship is discursive and cognitive. Citizens, understood as deliberators and judges, must be free from doing the necessary tasks of life, which are done by slaves (who work for individuals) and by mechanics and laborers (who work for the community). Aristotle advises: "The best form of

[1]The words "politics" and "civic" have overlapping meanings, coming respectively from Greek and Latin, and I'll use them interchangeably here.

[2]Aristotle, *Politics*, Book III (1275b), author's translation.

P. Levine (✉)
Tisch College, Tufts University, Medford, MA, USA
e-mail: peter.levine@tufts.edu

V. Rapti and E. Gordon (eds.), *Ludics*,
https://doi.org/10.1007/978-981-15-7435-1_5

city will not make the mechanic a citizen."[3] Note that the mechanic or laborer is not defined by poverty, for some are very rich, but by participation in the marketplace. Working distorts people's values and goals and makes them bad at deliberation about the public good, perhaps because they focus on their economic interests. Governance is best reserved for a class that has enough wealth *not* to work.

I cannot think of anyone today who would openly disenfranchise workers for the reasons that Aristotle cites. However, the same distinction between work and politics is evident in several political traditions that make the opposite value-judgment from Aristotle's. Like him, they presume that politics is about talking, listening, and deciding, and it's done outside of work. But unlike Aristotle, they think that *only* those who work are worthy of politics, because they alone have the appropriate values or because their productive labor gives them the *right* to rule.

One version holds that people of industry and thrift are worthy of governing a republic. This idea is familiar from the English Revolution, the Dutch Republic, and Colonial New England. It associates the bourgeois work ethic with republican virtues.

A different version is agrarian populism, which sees the stalwart farmer as the most legitimate citizen. Like Cincinnatus, a republican farmer puts down his plow to govern and fight, but he hastens back to his fields when his civic duty is done. Jeffersonian American populism and Russian *Narodnism* are examples.

A third version is Marxist. The workers form a class, distinguished from the bourgeoisie, who merely claim a "work ethic" while they exploit the actual laborers. The working class should rule. Marx offers the resonant ideal of *unifying* work with Aristotelian politics, removing the alienation between ruling and making. But my impression is that Marxist reforms—from mild democratic socialism all the way to Maoism—have hardly ever realized that ideal. Instead, they have tended to distinguish—just as Aristotle did—between work and governance, but they make the workers into the governors. You work in the factory by day, and after the whistle blows, you attend a workers' council meeting to make decisions.

[3]Aristotle, *Politics*, Book III (1278a).

In fact, the problem with socialism, according to Oscar Wilde, is that it occupies too many evenings.

Two additional strands of reform have developed since the Industrial Revolution. I endorse both, but they are not my main subject here. One aims to democratize the workplace by creating coops and other alternative enterprises that are governed on the basis of one-worker, one-vote. The other puts democratic pressure on the workforce by forming an independent association of workers than can negotiate and strike—a union. Both reforms narrow the gap between work and politics, but not in the way that I will describe.

Harry Boyte advocates a different ideal, which he calls Public Work. He has uncovered many precedents for it from around the world.[4] Public Work begins with a conceptual shift. We should no longer distinguish deliberating and judging from designing and making. They are all aspects of building our public world, our *res publica* or commonwealth.

For example, the democracy of ancient Athens was not just a discussion among gentlemen; it was also a set of physical spaces—like the Pnyx, where the discussions occurred—that people had built with their hands. The workers and the deliberators were jointly responsible, and their tasks were not sharply distinguishable. Talking in a forum is one kind of work; building the forum requires deliberation and judgment as well as skill and sweat.

Closer to our time and place: Harvard Square is the joint creation of the Cambridge City Council (which deliberates and judges about things like zoning rules), many firms and corporations (including the Harvard Corporation), workers who do everything from drawing blueprints to pouring cement, and the people who put their bodies onto the streets for a wide variety of reasons, including the homeless who sleep there. All of them create common space.

Public Work disputes the standard definition of "civic engagement" as activities that people undertake voluntarily without being paid, such as voting, protest, or discussing issues. That definition trivializes civic life by reducing it to after-work voluntarism and marginalizes the many ways

[4]Harry Chatten Boyte and Nancy N. Kari, *Building America: The Democratic Promise of Public Work* (Temple University Press, 1996); Harry C. Boyte, "Constructive Politics as Public Work: Organizing the Literature," *Political Theory* 39, no. 5 (October 2011).

that people contribute to public spaces and institutions. Public Work also disputes the distinctions among public, private, and nonprofit sectors. A private enterprise might turn out to contribute more and better to a public good than a government does.

We do need a definition of the word "public" in "Public Work," or else the phrase threatens to encompass all work and ceases to guide judgments and reforms. Perhaps to be public, work must involve intentional efforts to create public goods (at least as byproducts) and must be responsive to other citizens. If you run a bank in Harvard Square, you strive to make a profit; but if you also ensure that the facade of your building is attractive and harmonious with the other structures in the Square and you take advice and feedback from other people, including the homeless who sleep on your doorsteps, you have made your work more *public*. If everyone behaves like that, we have a democratic commonwealth.

This ideal suggests a whole range of reforms, from regulations that compel consultation to changes in the training and education of professionals. We might also reconceive some policy proposals, such as the Green New Deal, as opportunities for many people in many sectors to do Public Work. Reducing greenhouse emissions and mitigating the damage of climate change are public goods. People can contribute to these goods by paying taxes, supporting regulations, participating in local planning processes, volunteering after work, reorienting their businesses, conducting research, refraining from certain purchases, and educating their own children. All of this—together—can be seen as Public Work and promoted (but not fully realized) by federal policy.

So far, I have discussed work and tried to soften the distinction between work and politics or civic engagement. But we are not only workers and artisans; we also like to play. We are *homo ludens* as well as *homo faber*.

In *Making Democracy Fun*, Josh Lerner argues that civic and political leaders should learn from people who know how to make good games. For instance, in an enjoyable game, you glean the information you need as you go along. You needn't study for months before you can begin to play. But we tend to assume that you can't be a good voter until you have already studied many details about government and policy. Couldn't we integrate learning into political participation?[5]

Likewise, fun games give most of the players something satisfying to do all the way through. If only a few get to play, or if the game continues long after the result is obvious, people drop off. Couldn't we redesign civic processes so that everyone has interesting roles all the way through?

Eric Gordon has contributed excellent examples of such redesigns and important theoretical insights, such as his idea of "meaningful inefficiencies":

> Well designed human systems are indeed comprised of efficient transactions, but they should also include encounter, wonder, relation and caring, experiences largely absent from the smart city paradigm. Borrowing from game design, where players are provided with goals, and confronted with unnecessary obstacles that make their striving for that goal meaningful, I suggest that these *meaningful inefficiencies* are necessary for making a city smart. When there is room for play in the systems with which we interact, there is opportunity for people to form relationships, build trust, care for one another, and make shared meaning — all of which comprise the foundation for resilient communities.[6]

To summarize the argument so far: Most people reflexively distinguish citizenship and politics from work *and* from play. When you're on the job or having fun, you are not involved in politics or civic engagement. If you get paid for public service, that is work; but if you help others for free, that is volunteering, which is an example of civic engagement. If your after-work activity is a game, it is not service. The standard view is a three-way distinction: work, play, politics.

Harry Boyte and others reject one of these distinctions, the one between work and politics. For Boyte, politics is Public Work. In passing, he sometimes complains that we have reduced it to mere play. "It is as if

---

[5]Josh Lerner, *Making Democracy Fun: How Game Design Can Empower Citizens and Transform Politics* (Cambridge: MIT Press, 2014), p. 61.

[6]Eric Gordon, *Meaningful Inefficiencies: Caring for Civics in an Age of Smart Cities* (Synopsis). http://mahindrahumanities.fas.harvard.edu/content/meaningful-inefficiencies-caring-civics-age-smart-cities.

citizens have been consigned to the playground of civil society after they have been chased off everywhere else."[7]

Josh Lerner, Eric Gordon, and others reject the other distinction: between play and politics. In passing, Lerner suggests that we have made politics too much like work (in a bad sense). He cites Erik Erikson for the idea that play involves self-imposed rules. So does democratic politics, because the people are supposed to make the rules that govern them. In contrast, work is defined by externally imposed rules.[8]

Must these two critical positions conflict? It may depend on how we define play or games and work. These particular definitions are notoriously difficult. In the great text of his late phase, *The Philosophical Investigations*, Wittgenstein uses "game" as his primary example of a word that functions very well for communication even though it cannot be defined with necessary and sufficient conditions. We can learn what the word "game" means. We can use it correctly or incorrectly. Mistakes in our use of the word can be demonstrated. Yet the dictionary's definition will not teach us how to use it, basically because it is a family-resemblance term. It encompasses many types of behavior that cluster together without having one common denominator.

The same is likely true of the word "work." In fact, Wittgenstein gives examples of games that *are* work. Already on the first page of the main text of the *Investigations*, he asks us to imagine,

> [A] language that is meant to serve for communication between a builder A and an assistant B. A is building with building stones: there are blocks, pillars, slabs and beams. B has to pass the stones, and that in the order in which A needs them. For this purpose they use a language consisting of the words "block", "pillar", "slab", "beam". A calls them out;—B brings the stone which he has learnt to bring at such-and-such a call.——Conceive this as a complete primitive language.[9]

---

[7]Harry C. Boyte, *Off the Playground of Civil Society: Freeing Democracy's Powers for the 21st Century* (Civic Engagement, Paper 20, 1998), http://digitalcommons.unomaha.edu/slcecivic eng/20.

[8]Josh Lerner, *Making Democracy Fun: How Game Design Can Empower Citizens and Transform Politics* (Cambridge: MIT Press, 2014), p. 61.

[9]Ludwig Wittgenstein, "*Philosophical Investigations* 2:1," translated by G.E.M. Anscombe (London: Blackwell, 1986).

This example is also a game, and it is also work. Wittgenstein presents the example as he begins to analogize all language to games, and all purposive human behavior to language.

To explore the similarities further: Both work and game-play usually involve interactions among multiple parties, although at the limit, one can work alone or play solitaire. Both require planning and execution. Both can result in success or failure. Both can either satisfy or bore and alienate. (Similar design features may increase the odds of satisfaction.) Both imply agency: purposive action within a larger structure. Both depend on rules, but the rules must permit innovation and judgment. Both usually develop as traditional structures that newcomers can learn, but we can invent new forms of work and new games. We can find what Mihály Csíkszentmihályi and colleagues call "flow" in either work or play.[10]

The overlap is large and important, but I would like to conclude with a difference that inclines me to favor Public Work.

Characteristically, work produces things of market value (even if the producer does not choose to sell or trade them). This is not characteristic of play. Borderline forms of play, such as professional athletics, hunting, and such hobbies as knitting may produce tradable goods, but in each case, we wonder whether "play" is really the right word.

Producing things with market value generates political power or leverage over systems. Once producers organize themselves, they can refuse to provide goods or deploy their revenue to influence politics. By these means, workers have been able to win a share of political power. They haven't been *granted* power because they deserve it as a matter of fairness; they have demanded and seized it.

The classic case is an organized strike, but workers have many other ways to influence states. I believe that democracy arose basically because elites in certain countries (beginning with Holland and England) offered segments of their productive classes political voice in return for a willingness to pay taxes, purchase government bonds, and enlist in the military. These countries then decisively defeated monarchies because they could

---

[10]Jeanne Nakamura and Mihaly Csikszentmihalyi, *Flow and the Foundations of Positive Psychology* (Springer, Dordrecht, 2014), pp. 239–263.

field much larger and better armies and navies. The nascent democracies had a Darwinian advantage over monarchies; they spread because their workers and elites cooperated.

This means that work tends to promote democracy. I don't see the same pattern for play. Josh Lerner offers excellent advice to benign political leaders (including the organizers of insurgent social movements) whose goal is to engage the people. Such leaders should learn from game design and create opportunities for play. But I don't see an equally viable strategy for using play to combat obstinate power, whether in the state or in popular movements (which tend to turn into oligarchies).

It is worth thinking about some interesting cases in which play does seem to confer power. Lerner[11] cites the *Theater of the Oppressed* of Augusto Boal: poor people improvise public theatrical performances. Their activities can be classified as "play," and they contribute to radical social reforms. But I suspect that they only succeed when poor people *also* use their work for leverage.

Another interesting example is Participatory Budgeting, which invites the public to develop and choose proposals that get public funding. It is somewhat game-like and it turns out better to the extent that it uses good practices of game design. It originated with an elite: the leaders of the newly elected Workers party in Porto Alegre, Brazil. But it proved so popular that succeeding governments retained it. That suggests that the popularity of play generated some power.

On the other hand, Participatory Budgeting can be interpreted as Public Work.[12] The play aspect makes PB enjoyable, but the work aspect makes it powerful.

I mention all of this because automation and artificial intelligence may worsen the scarcity of work, yet human needs may continue to be met by an increasingly productive economy, giving more people more time for play. If play conferred power and tended to strengthen democracy, this would be good news. But if democracy depends on work—on

[11]Josh Lerner, *Making Democracy Fun: How Game Design Can Empower Citizens and Transform Politics* (Cambridge: MIT Press, 2014), pp. 43–44.

[12]Peter Levine, "Social Accountability as Public Work," in Sina Odugbemi and Taeku Lee, eds., *Accountability Through Public Opinion: From Inertia to Public Action* (Washington, DC: The World Bank, 2011), pp. 291–306.

elites needing the support of workers—then the news is bad. We may be heading for authoritarian oligarchies that rely on machines and very high-skilled labor to generate wealth and that offer play to keep most people compliant. To respond to that threat, we probably ought to save work rather than expand play.

Technoecologies: The Interplay of Space and Its Perception

Zenovia Toloudi

Introduction

The dystopia of our emergent ecological catastrophe has excluded the right to imagine and envision a future playful symbiosis between humankind and the environment. Within this context, many visual artists have delegated themselves to make work that brings awareness about this catastrophic landscape, relying on seductive sci-fi art (Liam Young) shifting the attention from thinking solutions and working synthetically, to mostly narrate visually the situation. My work, poised at the intersection of art and architecture, participates in this discourse: On one hand it critiques the alienation of humans from nature and each other (therefore bringing awareness); and on the other hand it strives to restore broken relationships (therefore also proposing ideas for the present and future). In doing so it investigates playful spatial typologies to reestablish cohabitation, inclusion, and participation through

Z. Toloudi (✉)
Department of Studio Art, Dartmouth College, Hanover, NH, USA

V. Rapti and E. Gordon (eds.), *Ludics*,
https://doi.org/10.1007/978-981-15-7435-1_6

digital, physical, and organic media. As many other creators who are also academics, I follow a triple process to develop my work: materializing the ideas (through my creative practice), writing about the ideas (through essays and talks), and cultivating these ideas (through teaching). I rely on a constellation of concepts, at the intersection of art, architecture, and humanities, that guide me to work and think synthetically, toward reshaping the present and future. These concepts/modes of working range from working with models and installations (what I call *metamaquettes*), to having a *techno-utopian* vision, to shifting between *experiment and experience*, to working through *metabolic aesthetics*, which cultivate *empathy and vulnerability*, to thinking binary through the *ordinary and illusionary*, and to ensuring *public participation* and *user engagement*. In this chapter I will present the general context of my work through my overall methodology (*metamaquettes*) and vision (*techno-utopia*), and how within this context I materialize my ideas in response to the environmental matters (*technoecologies*).

Why Metamaquettes?

The last decades, the genre of Installation Art has become a shared domain for creators coming not only from visual arts and sculpture, but also from architecture and computation. This interest in installations by architects and technologists can be explained due to the rapidly evolving field of digital fabrication, but it also relates to a recent trend within architecture to be more involved with research and academia, working with grants and funds, and therefore developing another type of practice, independent from clients and the model architecture as service. But one can track the origin of installations, in both art and architecture worlds. In the art world, the beginning of installation is considered either as an expansion of the painting (El Lissitzky's Proun Room) or as the merge of art studio and artwork (Melzbau's art studio). Claire Bishop positions the spectator in installations as an integral part of the work.[1] Without the spectator, the work does not exist. In the architecture world, the history

[1] Bishop, C., *Installation Art: A Critical History* (London: Tate Publishing, 2014).

of "installations" relates to the big mock-ups and prototypes by architects to test particular structures (Antoni Gaudi), as well as lifestyles (Le Corbusier). But the case of Diller and Scofidio is an interesting one for the genre, as it signified a period of 70s crisis, an alternative approach of making architecture—opposite to "paper architecture" aligning with happenings, events, and real experiences.[2] Within this discourse, I have developed the concept of *metamaquette.*[3]

Metamaquettes (or metamodels) are installations, models, and mock-ups which explore subjective perceptions of space and user engagement.[4] *Metamaquettes* question their own nature yet create playful spaces in which to explore cognition/perception, scale, light, and (im)materiality. *Metamaquettes* invite us to investigate subjectivity, neglected notions about sensory experiences, communal habits, and the ordinary and vernacular elements of culture. Being a composite word that derives from the Greek μετά/meta, and the French maquette, *Metamaquette* literally translates as after/post/among/beyond models. By positioning installations as meta-spaces that depart from the service model of architecture practice, *Metamaquettes* lend a fresh perspective on the influence of installations in contemporary architecture. This discourse of installations expands beyond the artists, architects, and makers, to all creators and thinkers invested in exploring the crisis of our time through spatial practices.

Techno-Utopia

If *metamaquette* represents my method and process, *techno-utopia* stands for the vision I hope to create for (near) future architecture. I am interested how, in an era of societal and ecological crises, architecture

---

[2]The interview can be found at: Incerti, G., Ricchi, D., and Simpson, D., "*Diller + Scofidio (+ Renfro): The Ciliary Function; Works and Projects 1979–2007*" (Milan: Skira, 2007).

[3]Toloudi, Z., "*Metamaquette* exhibition" (Strauss Gallery, Dartmouth College, 2015). https://studioart.dartmouth.edu/news/2014/09/zenovia-toloudi-metamaquette. Accessed March 6, 2019.

[4]Toloudi, Z., "*Metamaquettes: Between the Lab and the Site* exhibition" (2019). https://the-bac.edu/experience-the-bac/news-and-events/events/metamaquettes-exhibition. Accessed March 6, 2019.

thoughtfully blended with our environment offers us the chance to rediscover, nurture, and activate our (lost) public selves. I am invested in architecture's ability to animate the social imaginary and reinforce the civic self. To establish this new civic vocabulary and fresh chances to establish rituals building courage, empathy, and connection, I ground my approach to the etymology of the word technology, which in Greek, *Technae* translates to Τέχνη, meaning art, and therefore linking to making and craft. In addition I draw inspiration from the Japanese Metabolists' grounded approach to future as something tangible[5]; and my own training as an architect in Thessaloniki, Greece. This context brought opportunities to participate in architectural exhibitions, with emphasis in visualizing surrealistic poetry and literature such as the case of *Amour-Amour, Exhibition of Architectural translations of "Oktana" by the poet Andreas Empeirikos*. and *The Dispersed Urbanity of the Aegean Archipelago*: 10th International Exhibition of Architecture Venice Biennale: Greek Participation (Figs. 1 and 2).

In parallel, professors and artists such as Costas Varotsos and Yorgos Lazongas, have inspired me, respectively, to think of real scale and building the ideas, even in a guerilla-manner, and to relate to the real, socio-political events around, while making art.[6] Architecture in a way had offered fiction, and architecture the reality (Fig. 3).

However what is crucial here, is not which world represents what, but mostly being able to move between the two.

I make my work in both North America and Northern Greece by collaborating with craftspeople in each region who focus on particular materials and techniques. Finding these individuals for the work that I do is essential. Making, constructing, and producing are important aspects of creativity, and learning our existence and our identity. It is an act of resistance against the virtual era we experience, as well an act of resistance

[5]Bijutsukan, M., "*Metabolism, the City of the Future: Dreams and Visions of Reconstruction in Postwar and Present-day Japan*" (Tokyo: Mori Art Museum, 2011).

[6]By guerilla-manner, I mean how the project transforms from temporary to almost permanent: we had suggested the project to stay there for one month and it stayed for more than fifteen years (with the exception of moving to another location due to underground work for metro public transportation).

Fig. 1 Zenovia Toloudi, Maria Stefanidis, 10 models/visions (view of one model) as part of *Amour-Amour, Exhibition of Architectural translations of "Oktana" by the poet Andreas Empeirikos*

to times of a crisis where workshops and individual makers disappear (in Greece), or becomes a luxurious activity (in USA) (Fig. 4).

In my pedagogy, I follow the same emphasis in this dipole of making and imagining, craft and fantasy, or techno-utopia. One example is the *Invisible Cities* project where I ask my students to draw, and make models, analyze the writing, and create new cities, based on needs and desires often neglected by architects and planners (Fig. 5).

Then they return and write their own text for what they design. We work with models, physical models which we often exhibit in order to

Fig. 2 Zenovia Toloudi / Studio Z, 4 models/visions for Aegean Metapolis (view of one model) as part of *The Dispersed Urbanity of the Aegean Archipelago*: 10th International Exhibition of Architecture Venice Biennale: Greek Participation

communicate the ideas behind. These models are small worlds, they are seductive. They are both fantasy and reality[7] (Fig. 6).

Exhibitions have been used in architecture throughout its history as a general rule to present unbuilt projects, competitions, retrospectives of architects, and particular histories and future visions. At the same time, in periods of bad economies and crises, exhibitions have served as alternative practices. Even if they have typically focused on the final outcome, well-crafted representations of architecture through pristine models and drawings, in many occasions, exhibitions have been more experimental. Herzog and De Meuron have used exhibition as an opportunity to test an idea (for future projects), or to promote an approach to architecture

[7] *A Temporary Museum of Ideas in the Making* exhibition, hosted by Strauss Gallery at Dartmouth College in 2018, presented this manifesto. Visit the link: https://studioart.dartmouth.edu/news/2018/01/temporary-museum-ideas-making.

a

Fig. 3 **a,b** Zenovia Toloudi, Maria Stefanidis, Chrysa Lekka, *The Cage*. Thessaloniki, Greece, 2001. In collaboration with George Toloudis and Costas Varotsos

b

Fig. 3 (continued)

in certain audiences.[8] Such exhibitions, being simultaneously final and in process, are a tautology.[9]

Technoecologies body of works is an example of a *technoutopian* vision realized through a series of *metamaquettes*, and having been presented to the public through the mode of exhibition.[10]

---

[8]To learn more about the experimental aspect in the exhibitions of Herzog and de Meuron, find the book of Ursprung, P., *Herzog & De Meuron: Natural History* (Montréal: Canadian Centre for Architecture, 2002).

[9]Metamaquette exhibition, hosted by Strauss Gallery at Dartmouth College in 2015, showcased this tautology.

[10](UNCC, UMass).

Fig. 4 Welding shop in Alexandroupolis, Evros, Greece, 1999/2000

Technoecologies Exhibition Manifesto[11]

Technoecologies reconceives the relationship between humans and their environment in architecture through prototypes and models that explore emerging forms of bioarchitecture, living systems, and evolving environments. The exhibition critiques the performance-driven corporate architecture of "sealed" envelopes and controlled environments, which disconnect users from natural air, light, and exposure to public activity while contributing to spatial homogeneity and dullness, possibly triggering psychobiological disorders.

By contrast, *Technoecologies* proposes a metabolic architecture as a provocative alternative approach, being manifested in speculative yet

[11]The first version of *Technoecologies* was hosted in Storrs Gallery of University of North Carolina at Charlotte, during 2018. Visit the website: https://inside.uncc.edu/news-features/2018-01-23/storrs-gallery-exhibit-%E2%80%98technoecologies%E2%80%99.

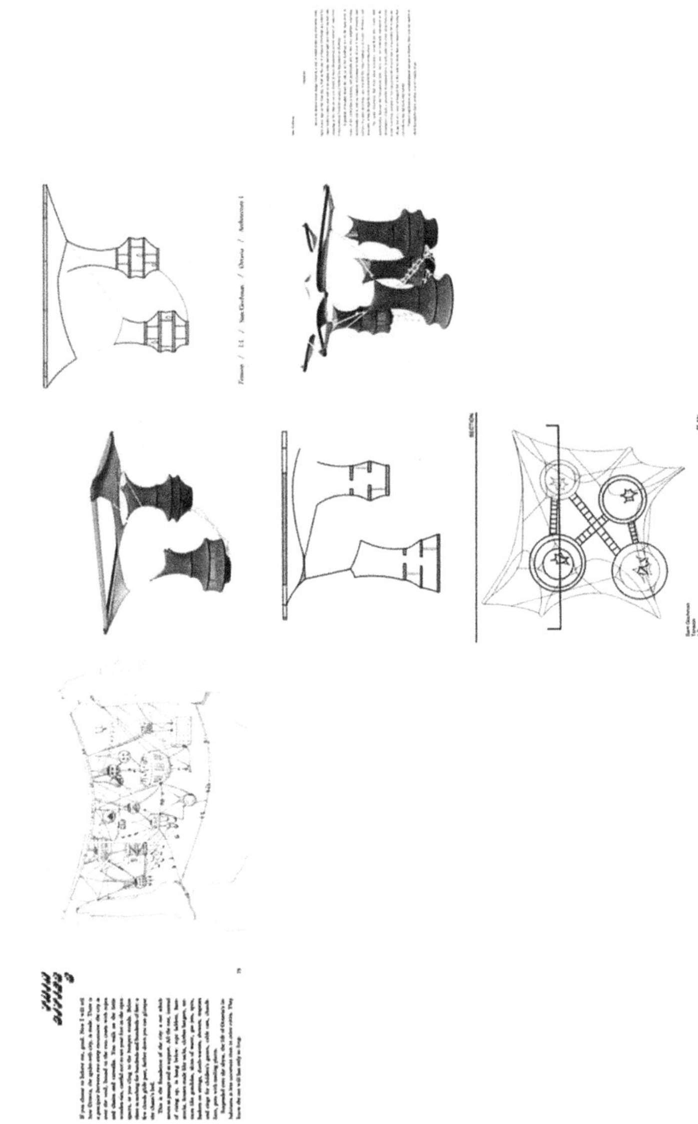

Fig. 5 *Invisible Cities* project as part of Introduction to Architecture course by Zenovia Toloudi, Dartmouth College. Project by student Sam Gochman

Fig. 6 *A Temporary Museum of Ideas in the Making* exhibition curated by Zenovia Toloudi and Gerald A. Auten, Strauss Gallery, Dartmouth College, 2018 (*Source* © Photograph by Gerald D. Auten)

tangible ways. In architecture, metabolism is connected to the neoavant-garde design strategies of the Asian postwar movement of the 1960's known as Japanese Metabolism, a movement grounded in the idea that, rather than being fixed machines, buildings and cities should be organic and constantly grow, change, and renew. *Technoecologies* shares that vision and aligns, too, with that of architect and artist Gordon Matta-Clark, who also deployed the concept of metabolism in his work, using the medium of the art installation as a means of tangible experimentation and real-time intervention in existing buildings.

Metabolic architecture is contemplated here both literally and metaphorically. Literally, it deals with material transformations caused by either the growth or decay of organic matter. Metaphorically, it relates to immaterial transformations of light or sound caused by environmental or artificial stimuli. Through these processes, metabolism within architecture becomes an apparatus that produces constant changes in form, space, and user perception. *Technoecologies* bridges the gap between technophilia and technophobia. While acknowledging the rapid technological changes of the present and future, *Technoecologies* also projects roots into tradition and society to reinterpret in contemporary terms past history, culture, and traditional habits. With examples ranging from artificial sonic gardens and living wall prototypes to interactive models of seed banks, the projects in *Technoecologies* examine processes of material transformation, eventually generating a series of themes for architecture to consider, such as laboratory experimentation, objectification of nature, temporality and theatricality, the vernacular and cultural, modular and infrastructural elements, vulnerability and voyeurism, autonomy and complexity, and user participation. This exploration forms both a theory and a design approach, which subsequently advocate how art, technology, and architecture might progressively transform the environment, society, and culture (Figs. 7 and 8).

Between Experiment and Experience

How can we rethink nature within the context of the Chicago metropolis? Is there an alternative to the green roofs and green facades movement when surfaces to be greened are not available? One of the first projects of *Technoecologies* responds to this question, by investigating the objectification of nature. By looking into examples such as the Dan Kiley's South Garden in The Art Institute, *Micro-Ceasefire Under Shadow* (MCUS) series explores how citizens can rethink issues of sound, ecology, technology, and the metropolis. This series of micro-sonic installations imagines a new typology for streetscapes that is a hybrid between an artificial garden or tree and an urban canopy. The busy and noisy daily life in a metropolis calls for a spot where the urban dweller can stop for a second, feel the city, the ever-changing weather, and take a break. Inspired by the naive and picturesque happy moment of a man enjoying life under a shade tree, "MCUS" is a small city garden growing next to the streets. "MCUS" evokes qualities that trees provide, such as rich shade and sound absorption/noise reflection, and uses rustle and warble

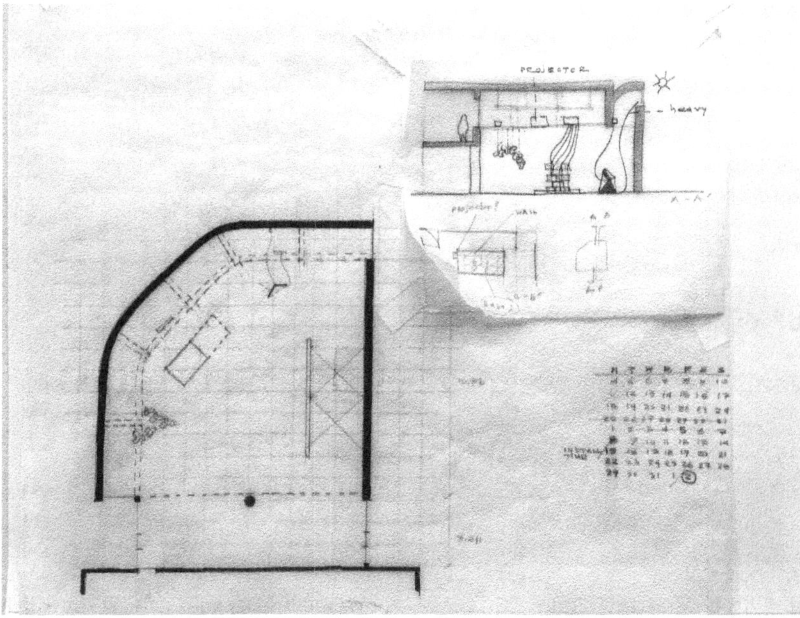

Fig. 7 Zenovia Toloudi / Studio Z, *Technoecologies* solo exhibition (initial sketch layout), Storrs Gallery, UNC-Charlotte, NC, 2018

sounds to attract the ear. Variations of this installation include mechanisms for water evaporation, sound transmitters, lights, and electronics to engage people interactively, as well as solar panels for energy harvesting. "MCUS" is a breath within the megalopolis where people can escape from the hostile urban environment to eat a snack, chat, meet, talk on the phone, or simply loaf (Fig. 9).

The project is presented through the medium of art installation. Its sounds can be activated once each spectator approaches the work. Curator Hans Ulrich Obrist presents art installations, and experimental exhibitions (such as installations as network, exhibition as laboratory, live exhibition, exhibition within exhibition, self-organized exhibition, display which grow in time, etc.) as the media to expand beyond the object and objecthood to interactions, relationships, events, intensities,

a
b

Fig. 8 a,b Zenovia Toloudi / Studio Z, *Technoecologies* solo exhibition (exhibition overview), Storrs Gallery, UNC-Charlotte, NC, 2018

Fig. 9 Zenovia Toloudi / Studio Z, *Micro-Ceasefire Under Shadow V*

and processes.[12] *Micro-Ceasefire Under Shadow* is an experiment set up in the public exhibition to be experienced by the city inhabitants. This idea of experiment and experience is present in Bruno Latour's *World Wide Lab*.[13] According to this, the old divisions between, (a) wild and domesticated, (b) private and public, and (c) technical and organic no longer exist. Due to science experimentation, which has now moved outside the laboratory, to the world wide lab, we all engage in a series of experiments. There is no dichotomy between inside and outside. We all collectively attempt to survive within the atmospheres. Laboratories are atmospheres, and experiments become spatial. In these we collectively participate to test an idea. Peter Slotredijk also considers art installations as between observation and participation. They "force the observer to take a far less dominating role and compels them to enter the work."[14] Similar merging between the object and the experience have occurred through the visual environments of the 60s, in which artists had been inviting spectators to touch and transform the art through objects (Lygia Clark) or to transform the spaces through environments and happenings (Davide Boriani, Allan Kaprow).[15]

Metabolic Aesthetics

A major part of *Technoecologies* unfolds around art installations and speculative projects that embody processes of material transformation.[16] These projects are named as *Photodotes*, meaning Light Donors. The idea of metabolic architecture is analogous to life itself in its unfolding

---

[12]Obrist, H., Installations Are the Answer, What Is the Question? (*Oxford Art Journal*, 2001), *24(*2), 95–101.

[13]The concept of Bruno Latour, "*World Wide Lab*": https://www.wired.com/2003/06/research-spc/.

[14]See Sloterdijk, P., Atmospheric Politics, ed. B. Latour and P. Weibel, *Making Things Public. Atmospheres of Democracy* (Cambridge, MA, The MIT Press, 2005), 944–951.

[15]See the book by Popper F., *Art—Action and Participation* (New York, New York University Press, 1975).

[16]The language of metabolic aesthetics is presented thoroughly in the chapter: Toloudi, Z., *Architecture and Living Matter(s): From Art/Architectural Installations to Metabolic Aesthetics*, The Routledge Companion to Biology in Art and Architecture, ed. Charissa Terranova and Meredith Tromble (New York: Routledge Press), 197–217.

according to four fundamental states of development: birth and growth; digestion and nutrition; motion and action; and finally, decay and recycling. The context for this body of works is the Northern America sealed buildings, such as glass towers for offices and apartments.

The disconnection from the living element has given birth to the idea of rethinking spatial light within given problematic spaces. Certain observations, such as disconnection between daytime light experience, and nighttime experience (such as the example of the Aghia Sophia); the different explorations between architectural light (through sophisticated windows) and artistic light (expressive forms of light to be experienced in black box); as well the extremes of either pollution or lack of light, along with a series of 56 playful light experiments, have resulted in the design of Photodotes I (Fig. 10).

Photodotes I: Light Donors is a mixed media installation that critiques the disconnection from natural light in windowless workplaces, resulting in phenomena such as disrupted circadian rhythms and depression, by channeling light into dark places remotely, both from natural and artificial sources. Through the process of collecting, transferring, and diffusing light in space, *Photodotes* augments the individual and collective perceptual mechanism, to emphasize how light's relation to energy and the survival leads to well-being of people. Capturing kinesis as a form of metabolism is present in Otto Piene's Lightballet (subtle movements of light in space, as a reaction to the cacophony of the war), Hans Haacke's systems of the 1960, as well Olafur Eliasson's recent projects (such as the documentation of the spectrum of light variations occurring within a day in the landscape). To capture these light variations I have connected the cable to the sky.[17] When the light and the change is subtle, it requires investigation to unpack the aesthetics, to find the essential infrastructure needed to create the phenomena, and to experience all other immaterial properties. Testing this process in real space, such as the building of Mass Art in Boston, and realizing that the little amount of natural light,

[17]The analysis of the first experiments as part of the Garden Lab exhibition at Mass Art can be found: Toloudi, Z., Natural and Artificial Light as Energy: Experiments in Space, in *Proceedings of ACSA 101: New Constellations, New Ecologies* (Washington, DC: ASCA Press, 2013), 219–225.

Fig. 10 Zenovia Toloudi / Studio Z, *Photodotes I*. Boston, MA, 2012. Installation was first part of Garden Lab exhibition (2012), Brant Gallery, Massachusetts College of Art and Design (*Source* © Photograph by Dominic Tschoepe)

as well as its small changes over time, made it difficult to be perceived by the visitors.

This led to the idea of integrating plants into the *Photodotes*' structures to show the effect of light into plants' life (Fig. 11).

The idea here has been to incorporate the plants from the beginning, not as an aftermath addition. Also, emphasis has been given to edible matter, to think of plants as a source of energy and food for survival.

a

Fig. 11 **a,b** Zenovia Toloudi / Studio Z, *Photodotes II: Light Garden*. Boston, MA, 2012. Installation was part of Garden Lab exhibition (2012), Brant Gallery, Massachusetts College of Art and Design (*Source* © Photograph by Dominic Tschoepe)

b

Fig. 11 (continued)

The use of capsule(s) relates both to the vernacular, as a portable and build-able module that you can stack, but also to the petri-dish, where nature becomes objectified.

I created the *Photodotes III: Plug-n-Plant* and experimented its evolution over time in the co-working Industry Lab for three months (Fig. 12).

Photodotes Plug-n-Plant is a modular structural system whose blocks are hybrids of water, light, and potential food volumes. The whole system acts both as a spatial element that brings natural light in dark spaces, and also as a living or edible structure. *Plug-n-Plant* seeks to redefine

Fig. 12 Zenovia Toloudi / Studio Z, *Photodotes III: Plug-n-Plant*. Cambridge, MA, 2013. Installation was first part of solo exhibition at Industry Lab

the nature—tectonic relationship where one does not erase the other but they simply coexist and coevolve.

Each exhibition becomes an opportunity to grow it in size or test different formations, or plants such as the case of *Photodotes IV: Living Wall* in Storrs Gallery at University of North Carolina in Charlotte which proposes new typologies of living modular walls that combine hydroponics and fiberoptic cables to bring natural light in dark spaces, while illustrating how light accelerates growth of living organisms such as edible plants. The ultimate goal has been to move from the "table experimentation" to the actual world and integrate this wall into an existing or new building (Fig. 13).

One component that becomes evident in this work is the decay and decomposition of matter. The vulnerability of plants due to contamination from air and their nutrition has questioned the autonomy of such a symbiosis. Even if there is always a request to find more self-sufficient

Fig. 13 An example of *Photodotes* installation transforming into a structural wall of a building (*Source* © Zenovia Toloudi / Studio Z)

plants (e.g., bamboos as autotrophs), at the end, this project is about interdependence between plants and people.

Ordinary and Illusionary

In Japanese streets and architecture, the vernacular appears through informal small gardens. In those, the random has eventual surgical precision and becomes theatrical in the eyes of the citizen. The role of small and repetition emphasizes the social and the presence of users within this architecture.[18] The dipole of ordinary/illusionary is explored in the *Photodotes V: Cyborg Garden* project in which the plants become species of extinction, museum display, and their survival depends on users' movements (Fig. 14).

Photodotes V: Cyborg Garden, a hanging garden in a large garage space, which included plants, plastic containers, waters, and fiberoptic cables, allowed plants and artificial lights to coexist and coevolve based on people's movements. As visitors approached the installation, the light spectrum changed to enrich the energy provided to the plants' roots while illuminating the garage's dark space. The installation made viewers aware of the diversity of light we encounter in life: the lack of light, homogenous light in interior spaces, and overlighted spaces. One of the event's curators, Jutta Friedrichs describes[19]:

> As one walks closer to the Cyborg Garden by Zenovia Toloudi, the plants, one by one subtly light up. Like signals transmitted from underneath the pavement, feeding a constant stream of information into homes and workspaces, each plant is fed with light via an individual fiber optic cable welling up from an artificial source. The glowing tips illuminate unnoticed details of the plants and their roots, normally hidden. The sterile rows of cylindrical water vessels reminds one of a laboratory setting or specimen jars displayed in a natural history museum, preserving extinct

[18] How the notion of small operates as social device is presented in "Lilli-pot Spaces" essay, published by MAS Context. Visit the link: http://www.mascontext.com/issues/23-ordinary-fall-14/ordinary-lilli-pot-spaces-rendezvous-in-tokyo/.

[19] http://www.illuminusboston.org/project/cyborg-garden.

Fig. 14 Zenovia Toloudi / Studio Z, *Photodotes V: Cyborg Garden*. Boston, MA, 2012. Interaction Design: Spyridon Ampanavos. Installation as part of Illuminus Boston event at Fenway (*Source* © Photograph by Dimitris Papanikolaou)

> or endangered organisms. The plants seem in danger; detached from their natural environment, they have become dependent on human care. The visitor's proximity activates the life support mechanism, and light travels through the cables like nutrients through an IV drip, feeding the plants their essentials for survival. All twenty-five plants are connected to a central light and sensor network weaving together nature, technology and human spectators into one interdependent system.[20]

The capsule is an element which both presents the past (e.g., pots) and future (e.g., scientific petri-dishes), something reinforces the idea of *Technoecologies* playing between technophilia and technophobia.[21]

[20]There is a correction here, the final configuration of the installation included 20 plants. .

[21]In the essay, "The Capsule as Cyborg Bioarchitecture," I present four categories / scales of capsules and how they function as cyborg bioarchitectures. For more: Toloudi, Z., The Capsule as Cyborg Bioarchitecture (*Technoetic Arts Journal*), *14(*1–2): Complexism (Intellect Books, 2016), 95–104.

Vulnerability and Empathy

Cyborg Garden framed the need for design based on living bio-rhythms. The role of the user is integral to plants' existence, as humans, technology, and plants become one interdependent system: the users co-author the event as custodians watering and feeding plants, or as performer-spectators offering the light energy and nutrition through movements and interactions. Depending on human interaction, the plants in the *Photodotes* installations either flourish or die. Such an unpleasant encounter with their vulnerability cultivates empathy. In *Photodotes,* the plants' presence documents the ever-changing natural light through their growth and evolution. The metabolic materialized in the interdependent relationship between users and structures.[22] The role of humans, and who is taking care of these new types of spaces is crucial. This new architecture is envisioned through more democratic environments and non-hierarchical ways of working and collaborating.[23]

Publics Participation and User Engagement

The evidence and size of the ecological crisis we all experience requests to work beyond dystopia and to find ways to activate the public collectively, to reinforce the public participation, and the public imagination. Between utopia and dystopia, there is project *Silo(e)scapes* (Fig. 15).

Is the future of Mediterranean food a ruined landscape? The *Silo(e)scapes* art installation transforms the anxiety of such dystopia into the experience of a futuristic architecture. *Silo(e)scapes* envision a hybrid of a seed bank, a sharing economy, and a museum for Mediterranean plant species that may disappear. In the *Silo(e)scapes* techno-utopia, the threatened native seeds are stored in transparent silos/museum displays,

---

[22]The interaction between plants and people in the case of Cyborg Garden is analyzed in the essay: Toloudi, Z. and Ampanavos, S., "*On Interdependent Metabolic Structures: The Case of Cyborg Garden,*" Human Computer Interaction International Conference Proceedings (Springer, 2018).

[23]How this community operates is presented through the fictional essay: Toloudi, Z., "*Hacking Light,* Organs Everywhere," ed. Simone Ferracina, Vol. 5 (New York, NY, 2017), 140–147.

a
b

Fig. 15 a,b Zenovia Toloudi / Studio Z, *Silo(e)scapes* (interior view) Athens, Greece, 2017. Installation as part of Tomorrows: Urban Fictions for Possible Futures exhibition

which are also the columns of a communal architecture. *Silo(e)scapes* provide to its "community members" the preservation of local seeds' biodiversity and the protection of Mediterranean tastes, flavors, nutrients, and medicinal capacities that are threatened by environmental catastrophes and the increasing demand for control and standardization. *Silo(e)scapes* do not belong to private corporations. The "citizens" of *Silo(e)scapes* share the contents of the deposits. Self-sufficiency is a priority. So is freedom and security.

Spectators of *Silo(e)scapes* survey this doll-house metaphor of a futuristic microcosmos through a panopticon structure that expands in infinity. *Silo(e)scapes* function as a wearable room, a portal between reality and fantasy: Spectators insert their heads into a hole to observe the threatened species, the seed bank museum, and the sharing economy of Lilliputian citizens. The seed columns, a kaleidoscope of mirrors, and agrarian sounds construct a perceptible space which is neither real, nor a replica; it is rather artificial and illusive. *Silo(e)scapes* are both threatening and seductive. The theatrical and voyeuristic experience of *Silo(e)scapes* forms an apparatus that awakens memories, but also empowers spectators to disrupt the sequence of events causing the disappearance of these species (Fig. 16).

Fig. 16 Zenovia Toloudi / Studio Z, *Silo(e)scapes* (exterior view) Athens, Greece, 2017. Installation as part of Tomorrows: Urban Fictions for Possible Futures exhibition

In projects such as *Silo(e)scapes* visitors become the witnesses of the imaginary, but possible utopia. Now, they may identify through their public self, and through other opportunities and events they can work toward building more public-ness, whether it is structures, spaces, or resources. At the same time, *Technoecologies* projects being presented in a gallery setting becomes a space to learn from the users of this future architecture. In this case, it is about design with participation of users, not through the unrealistic and even failed participatory design processes, but through experiencing art.

Conclusion

This essay presented an example of how an exhibition and body or works at the intersection of art, architecture and humanities can explore concepts such as experiment and experience, metabolic aesthetics, ordinary and illusionary, empathy and vulnerability, public participation and user engagement. Working through tangible media (models and installations), with a grounded vision, and modes such as the aforementioned, *Technoecologies* exhibition shapes a future artificial environment, in which the living can be imagined as possible, positive, and even playful.

References

Bijutsukan, M. (2011), *Metabolism, the City of the Future: Dreams and Visions of Reconstruction in Postwar and Present-day Japan*. Tokyo: Mori Art Museum.

Bishop, C. *Installation Art: A Critical History*. London: Tate Publ. (2014).

Diller, Scofidio + Renfro, Incerti, G., Ricchi, D., and Simpson, D. (2007). *Diller + Scofidio (+ Renfro): The Ciliary Function; Works and Projects 1979–2007*. Milan: Skira.

Latour, B. (2003). Atmosphere, Atmosphere. In *Olafur Eliasson: The Weather Project*. London: New Tate Gallery, 29–41.

Obrist, H. (2001). Installations Are the Answer, What Is the Question? *Oxford Art Journal, 24*(2), 95–101.

Piene, O. *Otto Piene: Lichtballett, Hans Haacke 1967: Artist Talks*, MIT List Visual Arts Center website. listart.mit.edu, https://listart.mit.edu/files/audio/Piene_Haacke_102011.mp3. Accessed December 13, 2011.

Popper, F. (1975). *Art—Action and Participation*. New York: New Work University Press.

Sloterdijk, P. (2005). Atmospheric Politics. In Latour, B. and Weibel, P. *Making Things Public. Atmospheres of Democracy*. Cambridge. MA: The MIT Press, 944–951.

Toloudi, Z. *Architecture and Living Matter(s): From Art/Architectural Installations to Metabolic Aesthetics*, The Routledge Companion to Biology in Art and Architecture, ed. Charissa Terranova and Meredith Tromble. New York: Routledge Press, 197–217.

Toloudi, Z. (2013). Natural and Artificial Light as Energy: Experiments in Space. In *Proceedings of ACSA 101: New Constellations, New Ecologies*. Washington, DC: ASCA Press, 219–225.

Toloudi, Z. (2014). Ordinary Lilli-Pot Gardens: Rendezvous in Tokyo. In ed. I. Gil, *MAS Context: Ordinary*, Vol. 23. Chicago: MAS Studio, 130–147.

Toloudi, Z. (2015). *Metamaquette* Exhibition, Strauss Gallery, Dartmouth College. https://studioart.dartmouth.edu/news/2014/09/zenovia-toloudi-metamaquette. Accessed March 6, 2019.

Toloudi, Z. (2016). The Capsule as Cyborg Bioarchitecture. *Technoetic Arts Journal*, Vol. 14, Issue 1–2: Complexism (Intellect Books), 95–104.

Toloudi, Z. (2017). *Hacking Light*, Organs Everywhere, ed. Simone Ferracina, Vol. 5. New York, NY, 140–147.

Toloudi, Z. (2018a). *Technoecologies* Exhibition, Design Building gallery, UMass Amherst. http://www.umass.edu/architecture/event/technoecologies-zenovia-toloudistudio-z. Accessed March 6, 2019.

Toloudi, Z. (2018b).*Technoecologies* Exhibition, Storrs gallery, UNCC. https://inside.uncc.edu/news-features/2018-01-23/storrs-gallery-exhibit-%E2%80%98technoecologies%E2%80%99. Accessed March 6, 2019.

Toloudi, Z. (2019). *Metamaquettes: Between the Lab and the Site* Exhibition. https://the-bac.edu/experience-the-bac/news-and-events/events/metamaquettes-exhibition. Accessed March 6, 2019.

Toloudi, Z., and Ampanavos, S. (2018). *On Interdependent Metabolic Structures: The Case of Cyborg Garden*, Human Computer Interaction International Conference Proceedings. Springer.

Toloudi, Z., and Auten, G. (2018). *A Temporary Museum of Ideas in the Making* Exhibition, Strauss Gallery, Dartmouth College, https://studioart.dartmo

uth.edu/news/2018/01/temporary-museum-ideas-making. Accessed March 6, 2019.

Ursprung, P. (2002). *Herzog & De Meuron: Natural History*. Montréal: Canadian Centre for Architecture.

Meaningful Inefficiencies: Incorporating Play into Civic Design

Eric Gordon and Gabriel Mugar

Every generation, the indigenous peoples of the Shuswap region of British Columbia intentionally move their village. As the Canadian ethnographer Richard Kool described to psychologist Mihaly Csikszentmihalyi, the region is considered:

> … a rich place: rich in salmon and game, rich in below-ground food resources such as tubers and roots—a plentiful land. In this region, the people would live in permanent village sites and exploit the environs for needed resources. They had elaborate technologies for very effectively using the resources of the environment, and perceived their lives as

This chapter is adapted from Chapter 3 of Gordon, E. & Mugar, G. *Meaningful Inefficiencies: Civic Design in an Age of Digital Expediency* (Oxford University Press, 2020).

E. Gordon (✉)
Visual and Media Arts, Emerson College, Boston, MA, USA
e-mail: eric_gordon@emerson.edu

G. Mugar
IDEO Cambridge, Cambridge, MA, USA

V. Rapti and E. Gordon (eds.), *Ludics*,
https://doi.org/10.1007/978-981-15-7435-1_7

> being good and rich. Yet, the elders said, at times the world became too predictable and the challenge began to go out of life. Without challenge, life had no meaning. So the elders, in their wisdom, would decide that the entire village should move, those moves occurring every 25–30 years. The entire population would move to a different part of the Shuswap land there, they found challenge. There were new streams to figure out, new game trails to learn, new areas where the balsamroot would be plentiful. Now life would regain its meaning and be worth living. Everyone would feel rejuvenated and healthy. Incidentally, it also allowed exploited resources in one area to recover after years of harvesting…[1]

This is a meaningful inefficiency—the intentional cultivation of difficulty, confined within clear structure, for the purpose of meaning making. Even though there were clear environmental reasons, namely, the recovery of resources, for moving about the region, the elders told the story of renewing challenge so that life would be worth living. So, what would appear to be a hardship is in fact a kind of playfulness. Challenges are cultivated for the sake of challenge, with an understanding that the process of overcoming those challenges, not the result, is meaningful. John Dewey writes about the affordance of play in a democratic context: "Persons who play are not just doing something … they are *trying* to do or effect something, an attitude that involved anticipatory forecasts which stimulate their present responses."[2] Play, for Dewey, is directional and motivated. Whether the goal is to win a game, exist within an imaginary world, or simply to engage in an activity for its own sake (i.e., tossing a ball), play is presence structured by futures or other time-bound limitations. Public life is filled with future orientations—traveling to work, accessing services, even voting—but it typically is absent of presence, activities contained by futures, but which exist for their own sake.

In this chapter, we present play, or those cordoned off spaces that exist for their own sake, as a necessary component in the design of meaningful public processes. We begin by reviewing the philosophical treatment of

[1] Csikszentmihalyi & Csikszentmihalyi, *Optimal Experience: Psychological Studies of Flow in Consciousness* (Cambridge, UK: Cambridge University Press, 1992), 184.

[2] Dewey, *Democracy and Education* (Digireads.com Publishing, 1922), 195.

play and examine where it directly applies to civic life. We then explore a short case study of a project that sought to involve youth from underserved neighborhoods of Boston in the sourcing and writing of Pokéstops in the augmented reality game *Pokémon GO*. This project was an example of a private–public partnership designed as a meaningful inefficiency. We will discuss the difficulty in aligning goals across stakeholders and some of the challenges such design processes pose. Finally, we explore how public-sector and civil society organizations have put play into practice through gamification efforts, and we address some of the challenges with these approaches. We look closely at why people choose to use games and how some of the assumptions about the work games do provide a disconnect from the value of play.

Play and Limitations

The sociologist Pierre Bourdieu uses the metaphor of a game to describe how people interface with social systems in general. He begins by referencing the common phrase of having a "feel for the game" and he explains it as the "almost miraculous encounter between *habitus* and a field."[3] The field in this case is a playing field, or a board, the "magic circle" of a game—that discrete space that a player steps into in order to play.[4] And the *habitus* describes being in the world—all the normative assumptions and ingrained behaviors that define individuals and cultures. What Bourdieu is describing is that experience when naturalized practice butts up against systems. When one has a "feel for the game," it suggests that the game system has become natural for the player, or in the practice of playing the game, she no longer feels its artifice. Extending this metaphor, he states that in social fields, "which are the products of a long, slow process of automatization, and are therefore, so to speak, games 'in themselves' and not 'for themselves,' one does not

---

[3]Bourdieu, *The Logic of Practice* (Stanford, CA: Stanford University Press, 1990), 66.
[4]Huizinga, *Homo Ludens: A Study of the Play-element in Culture* (Boston, MA: Beacon Press, 1955).

embark on the game by a conscious act, one is born into the game, with the game."[5]

He continues, "the earlier a player enters the game and the less he is aware of the associated learning (…), the greater is his ignorance of all that is tacitly granted through his investment in the field and his interest in its very existence and perpetuation and in everything that is played for in it."[6] As a good sociologist, Bourdieu is not talking about games, he is talking about society. The game is a metaphor through which to understand the tacit acceptance of rules that govern daily life, and that lead to ideological complacency, and even oppression. Being in the game can be blinding. When the "feel for it" becomes too natural, then the player fails to see the artifice, or the structures that surround and support the process of play. By bringing play into the civic design process, the goal is to counteract the moments when the visibility of power structures fade into the background, operating as a means to bring the question of process and power as a key variable influencing the design of civic spaces.

The rules of the game are policed both by the players and by those looking at the game from the outside. In professional Baseball, for example, the players are on the field and fully committed to playing, but so too are the spectators committed to their play. They enforce the rules by debating who's the best, pouring over statistics and telling stories, all within the carefully limited context of the game. The anthropologist Norton Long describes how this process creates the conditions through which sense can be made of the situation.

> If we know the game being played is baseball and that X is a third baseman, by knowing his position and the game being played we can tell more about X's activities on the field than we could if we examined X as a psychologist or a psychiatrist. If such were not the case, X would belong in the mental ward rather than in a ballpark. The behavior of X is not some disembodied rationality but, rather, behavior within an organized

[5]Bourdieu, *The Logic of Practice*, 67.

[6]Ibid., 67.

> group activity that has goals, norms, strategies, and roles that give the very field and ground for rationality. Baseball structures the situation.[7]

Games provide context for understanding actions that individuals take within a given social context. Each action taken by the third baseman is structured by the formal rules of baseball (i.e., play will take place over nine innings, each inning is comprised of three outs, and each batter is limited to three strikes before getting an out); it is also structured by informal norms (the third baseman typically stands between third and second base, and if the ball is hit to him with no outs, he would typically throw across the field to first base). When one is observing a game, they are aware of some combination of formal rules and informal norms, but in all cases behavior is structured within limitations. So while games represent systems that constrain, they also represent systems that enable acceptable play. They provide opportunities, within a prescribed set of rules and norms, to play toward desirable outcomes. This goes back to John Dewey's forecasting, or the ability of play to be at once present and future oriented.

But this structural approach to play is not without its dangers. Bourdieu warns of the game becoming normalized, wherein one doesn't see the game as fabrication, but as naturalization. What if the baseball player didn't know that the rules of baseball were limited to the field? Would he be playing? Or simply allowing the rules to play out before him? Play, in this case, is different from the game. If the game does not have clear limits, then it becomes impossible to play within it. Games provide structure for play. But a game can cease to be a game when the structure fades either through disuse or active resistance. When a group of children are playing a game of "cops and robbers" in the playground and one child who is playing the robber says, "I am now a dolphin," and another says, "I am now a whale," the game rules change and play is redefined. While play is structured through limits, players can modify those limits, or simply step out of them. The philosopher Bernard Suits puts it this way: "To play a game is to attempt to achieve a specific state

[7]Quoted in Tsebelis, *Nested Games: Rational Choice in Comparative Politics* (Berkeley, CA: University of California Press, 1991), 33.

of affairs, using only means permitted by rules, where the rules prohibit the use of more efficient in favor of less efficient means, and where rules are accepted just because they make possible such an activity.... playing a game is the *voluntary* attempt to overcome unnecessary obstacles."[8]

Playing within a game is always voluntary. One must make the decision to step into the magic circle and accept the rules that structure play. However, for Bourdieu, when one develops a feel for the game, and is even perhaps born into it, the rules are accepted and not elected. In this case, the game is not a place for play, but a place where rules play out. The ability to understand that one is playing a game, is acting within a set of rules that are distinct from those governing everyday life, and importantly, that those rules are prohibiting the more efficient in favor of the less efficient means of achieving a state of affairs, are the system requirements for play. Meaningful inefficiencies are fields wherein one voluntarily steps so that they can play, and where the outcomes of such play are apparent but not primary.

The goal of meaningfully inefficient systems is for its occupants to make power and process in a particular context visible by confronting challenges that have become normalized, or invisible. When playing, one is both inside and outside. The poet Charles Baudelaire, writing of his experience on the Parisian sidewalk in the nineteenth century, described himself as a *flaneur*, both a part of and alienated from the crowd. As he watches the crowded sidewalk from inside a cafe, he is a spectator of urban play. But when he leaves the cafe, he is again a part of the crowd. While he doesn't use the term, the urban *flâneur* is playing, stepping into play (and its structuring limitations), but always capable of stepping out of it. *In play there is agency.* There is agency in the moment (Huizinga says that "all play means something"[9]), and in the player's ability to step outside. If the player were to feel manipulated, as if she was "being played," she can step out of the game, refuse to play, or demand a check on the rules. As a design strategy, meaningful inefficiencies structure play, but equally as important, they structure the ability for players (and spectators) to reflect on the rules and limits of a game. By defining

[8]Suits, *The Grasshopper: Games, Life, and Utopia* (New York: Broadview Press), 10.
[9]Huizinga, *Homo Ludens: A Study of the Play-element in Culture.*

the field and its constituent rules, one inevitably defines the conditions that create the experience of playing within it, and the possibilities of playing with it.

Consider the example of the Shuswap people again. By designating another field, defined by its rules and unnecessary obstacles, they are able to play toward achieving a certain state of affairs. Media theorist Ian Bogost further refines the conditions of play. "Play," he argues, "is the act of manipulating something that doesn't dictate all of its capacities in advance, but that *limits* its capacities through focus and exclusion."[10] In his book *Play Anything*, he uses the example of walking with his daughter in a mall while holding her hand. She is bored and dragging a bit, but then she starts playing a game where she tries to walk only on the cracks between the tiles. By self imposing obstacles on herself, she regains agency in the situation through her play. Play is a mechanism of overcoming structural limitations to achieve a goal. In this case, her goal changed from "I want to be home," to "I want to not step off the cracks." One might argue that this is an example of oppression, where the oppressed gives up on real structural change and cultivates false agency. But, while she remains captive by her father's walk through the mall, she now has agency within her self-imposed rule set to explore, experiment, fail, and discover. In fact, her play is comprised of actions—what Arendt would call "new beginnings"—that set other events into motion.

The play theorist Miguel Sicart calls this "playfulness," which is when people play in a context that is not "created or intended for play."[11] It is about the "appropriation of what should not be play" into something that takes on personal meaning for the player. Bogost's daughter is exhibiting playfulness in her appropriation of non play spaces, but in so doing she is crafting new spaces for play that are bounded, confined by rules, and self-imposed.

The design of civic spaces should always make room for play and accommodate playfulness. Civic spaces are play spaces. Instead of asking "how does one get from here to there?" the civic designer asks "how

[10]Bogost, *Play Anything: The Pleasure of Limits, the Uses of Boredom, and the Secret of Games* (New York: Basic Books, 2016), 92–93.

[11]Sicart, *Play Matters* (Cambridge: MIT Press, 2014), 27.

does one understand the practice of playing within limitations to achieve goals?" The end result is a system that can be played, or a system that presents opportunities to be shaped by the people within it—where they are allowed to *play within and with* the system itself, not just *play out* preconceived tasks.

Play and Freedom

Play is an outcome of particular systems designed with the appropriate structure and room to cultivate it. Bogost explains that to play is "to take something—anything—on its own terms, to treat it as if its existence were reasonable. The power of games lies not in their capacity to deliver rewards or enjoyment, but in the structured constraint of their design, which opens abundant possible spaces for play."[12] But play is not just the result of system design, it requires what Bernard Suits[13] calls a ludic, or playful, attitude.

Playing requires a suspension of disbelief and a voluntary stepping into the magic circle. Even in Bogost's example of his daughter being dragged through the mall, she was forced into the situation, but her decision to play was voluntary. Playing a game of baseball requires an acceptance of the rules and willingness to play within them; playing a fantasy game of princesses and dragons requires a playful attitude that both accepts limitations and desires to stretch their limits. Even driving home in traffic can be playful. When Eric (one of the authors) worked in Los Angeles in the 1990s, he lived on the east side and worked on the west side. Each day on the way to work, he would take a different route to beat his time to and from work. The activity was the same, but by transposing rules and obstacles (time) onto the situation, he was able to have some agency in an otherwise dismal situation. Even while physically occupying the same space, the game was a distinct field, in that he would determine prior to departing home or work that he was playing the game, accept that it was reasonable, and then operate within the rules. There

[12] Bogost, *Play Anything: The Pleasure of Limits, the Uses of Boredom, and the Secret of Games*, x.
[13] Suits, *The Grasshopper: Games, Life, and Utopia.*

was nothing at stake except the satisfaction of beating a previous time, but by providing permission to play, the field becomes a space of manipulation and discovery—of new paths in the environment and a constant reminder of the limitations of the game itself.

It is possible that the traffic game was simply an escape from reality, a binary between labor and playfulness.[14] It passed the time. It was fun. It was amusing and entertaining. But it was also frustrating and enervating, as it focused attention on the severity of the traffic, and its subtle variations from day to day. Play, according to Miguel Sicart[15] is not simply about fun—he prefers the term pleasurable. "The pleasures it creates are not always submissive to enjoyment, happiness, or positive traits," he says. "Play can be pleasurable when it hurts, offends, challenges and teases us, and even when we are not playing. Let's not talk about play as fun but as pleasurable, opening us to immense variations of pleasure in this world."[16] Pleasure provides a way of talking about play that is open to a range of human responses—whereas fun too easily degrades into frivolity, pleasure resonates with a wide variety of meaningful activities.

But who gets to play? Is the playful attitude a luxury, only available to those with existing mobility and freedom of choice? By extension, can one talk of pleasure in design when the real challenge is meeting people's basic needs and human rights? This is precisely why, we argue, play is important. Beyond the provision of services, the core requirement of good civic design is empowering people to take action within systems and holding institutions accountable for the rules they create. This is particularly important when the design process involves those typically excluded from systems. McDowell and Chinchilla[17] advocate for a frame of civic inclusion, which "requires that all individuals learn to engage with established organizational structures, and that institutions become adept in serving an increasingly heterogeneous membership."[18] This, of

---

[14]Arendt, *The Human Condition* (Chicago, IL: University of Chicago Press, 1998).

[15]Sicart, *Play Matters*.

[16]Ibid., 3.

[17]McDowell & Chinchilla, "Partnering with Communities and Institutions." In Gordon, E. & Mihailidis, P. (eds.) *Civic Media: Technology, Design, Practice* (Cambridge, MA: MIT Press, 2016).

[18]Ibid., 462.

course, presents a design challenge, which can be met by recommending that institutions "design from the margins." In other words, inclusion only happens when design processes (not just outcomes) include those who have been excluded. In this case, the design process, rather than providing an efficient solution, becomes a tool to motivate the attitudes and knowledge required for inclusion. Playfulness brings freedom to a system through choice—even when that system is oppressive—consider traffic in Los Angeles or being led through a mall by your father. bell hooks defines *oppression* simply as "*an absence of choice*" and *discrimination* and *exploitation* as being presented with fewer choices than those in dominating groups. Play can respond to oppression by offering choices where before there was none.

Bringing freedom through choice was at the heart of the Place/Setting project, a series of social art installations that one of the authors (Gabriel) collaborated on with the design firm French 2D. As academics and practitioners, the organizers found that the humanity of idea exchange was often lost to the formality of contexts like symposia, lectures, and conferences. Power dynamics and politics stifle conversations and the physical, social, and financial barriers to participation prevented access to a broader public that might want to hear the ideas. To address these challenges, Place/Setting experimented with the physical arrangements, atmosphere, and formats of spaces for conversations as people explore important social issues. In one version of Place/Setting, the organizers ran a workshop with students that were a week into a new program. The organizers asked the students to design dueling dinner parties. They were given tables and chairs and some conversation starters. How they chose to deploy these resources was up to them. One group tested out a triangular setup for the tables, while another group created a cozy campfire setting, using the tables as tents while they sat around in a circle. After the groups finished their dinner parties, they shared their approaches and results, reflecting on how playful experimentation with the physical and social structure of the conversation created varying levels of human connection.

There is always ambiguity in choice. Simone de Beauvoir argues that personal freedom emerges through ambiguity. Building off of Sartre's existentialism, wherein personal freedom rests in the movement from facticity, or that which is, to transcendence, or that which is not yet, de Beauvoir argues for an ethics of ambiguity, wherein one's freedom is not about the perpetual striving for transcendence, but about the recognition of the ambiguity between facticity and transcendence. de Beauvoir argues that "to attain his truth, man must not attempt to dispel the ambiguity of his being but, on the contrary, accept the task of realizing it."[19]

Ambiguity does not equate to lack of clarity. de Beauvoir argues that an ethics of ambiguity implies the acceptance of the task of realizing the ambiguity of one's being. So, not the pursuit of transcendence or the acceptance of facticity, but the acceptance that one will always strive to be comfortable in between these constructs. For example, an average waiter in Los Angeles is not merely the waiter (facticity), nor is he the actor (transcendence), but for him to be free, he must accept that he is always both. There is clarity in that ambiguity. Civic life often demands the embracing of ambiguity—as one might be neighbor, customer, renter, advocate, and visitor all at the same time. As opposed to pushing people into one primary role, it is the challenge of the civic designer to understand that people are multiple. Embracing of peoples' multiple identities and needs is a step in the direction of designing public contexts that embrace pluralism rather than operating on a rigid system of inclusion and process that, by design, exclude wide swaths of voices and concerns.

Perhaps the most important contribution of de Beauvoir to this discussion of play is her assertion that the pursuit of freedom is never individual. An individual's freedom necessarily impacts the freedom of others. For example, if backpacking around Europe is one person's realization of transcendence, all the people that retreat into their facticity to support her journey, are impacted. The ticket collector on the train, the people whose livelihoods are dependent on the tourist-oriented economies that support the traveler's comfort—these people are in some way impacted by the traveler's pursuit of her freedom. "Only the freedom of others," de Beauvoir says, "keeps each one of us from hardening in the absurdity of facticity."[20] For de Beauvoir, freedom is social, it is in and of the world, not a metaphysical pursuit one undergoes on their own. This

[19]de Beauvoir, *The Ethics of Ambiguity* (New York: Open Road Media, 2011), 12.
[20]Ibid., 77.

is a radical, and feminist, concept that places the pursuit of freedom not only within the constraints of a system that enables individual choice, but within a system where individual choice always impacts the choices of others. While playing a game of Baseball, the third baseman is free to play within the limits of the game. But if the second baseman was not free to do the same, then the third baseman would not be free. Simply put, one cannot be free to play a game that others are not free to play. This does not mean they need access to that game in the moment, but that the rules are transparent and accessible so that they are understood both by players and observers. Even a game of solitaire, while not open to other players in the moment, is understood by others as a game with rules that can be played. So, while one may not be able to play in the World Series, one is able to play a game of Baseball with friends. In short, for one to be free while playing, the structures of play need to be accessible, either in the moment or at a later time, to anyone who desires to play. The work of the civic designer then is to ensure that the context they design for is informed by an awareness of such rules and subsequently, reveals and makes visible such rules to future participants.

Gamification

The summation of what we have been arguing in this chapter is that play is the pre-condition for action-taking. And if civic life is the ability for people to take actions, then creating the structures for play is fundamental to civic design. And yet, what wins the big grants and press coverage are the tools, the machines that accelerate people's achieving of goals, and not the conditions under which goals are achieved. This is well encapsulated through the example of gamification, defined as "adding game elements to non-game contexts,"[21] or more specifically, the transformation of "non-recreational, tedious tasks, which are often driven by utilitarian motives, into enjoyable, self-purposeful and hence hedonistic

[21] Deterding, et al., "Gamification: Using Game Design Elements in Non-Game Contexts." In *Proceedings of the 2011 Annual Conference Extended Abstracts on Human Factors in Computing Systems* (2011), 2425–2428.

activities."[22] From workplace compliance[23] to physical activity,[24] the use of incentives like points and badges, offer a challenge to make seemingly boring activities meaningful.

Even though the term gamification has only recently become popular, there is a long history to game-based incentives. Some of the earliest examples come out of the Soviet Union. Soviet work games were designed to "re-conceptualize" work away from capitalist assumptions and provide a way of filling the void left by the absent game of capitalist markets. While direct individual competition was not desirable in the workplace, factories built systems to compete with each other, or groups within larger teams were given incentives such as badges and rankings, to motivate production.[25] On the contrary, by the 1980s, trends in management consulting in the United States turned to making the individual worker happy by making work fun. Emphasis was placed on individual productivity and satisfaction of the worker. What Nelson calls "funsultants" were brought into engage the employee with "elements that attempt to make workers feel like they have a stake and expressive role in their workplace."[26] While the difference between Socialist and Capitalist workplace games was subtle, with the former focusing on collective outputs and the latter on individual agency, each directed play to the service of labor. In the gamified workplace, in both the socialist and capitalist contexts, play was offered as an escape from labor.

The term gamification began as a description of advergames in the late 90s, or flash-based web games that contained sponsor messages. These banner ads were simple games that attracted user attention to an advertising message. They were by no means quality games, but they

---

[22]Thiel, et al., Playing (with) Democracy: A Review of Gamified Participation Approaches (*Journal of E-Democracy and Open Government, 8*[2], in print, 2016); Van der Heijden, User Acceptance of Hedonic Information Systems (*MIS Quarterly, 28*[4], 2004), 695–704; Hamari & Koivisto, Why Do People Use Gamification Services? (*International Journal of Information Management, 45*[4], 2015), 419–431.

[23]Nelson, *Soviet and American Precursors to the Gamification of Work, Proceeding of the 16th International Academic MindTrek Conference on—MindTrek' 12*, 23 (2012). https://doi.org/10.1145/2393132.2393138.

[24]Zuckerman & Gal-Az, 2014.

[25]Ibid.

[26]Ibid., 2.

used the structure of games to capture people's scarce attention. Since these early days, gamification has been widely celebrated as a motivation system in business, health care and government.[27] Through the addition of game elements, including points, badges, leaderboards, mayorships, and rewards, gamified systems have been applied to a range of tasks, from worker productivity, to diabetics taking their insulin, to exercise (i.e., Fitbit). As Walz and Deterding[28] point out in the preface to their edited volume *The Gameful World*, there is a robust debate as to the value of gamified systems. Jane McGonigal captured a popular audience with her TED talk and book *Reality is Broken*,[29] where she argued that games can repair this broken reality through maximizing individual potential. On the contrary, many critics see gamified systems as taking "the thing that is least essential to games and representing it as the core of the experience."[30] In other words, gamified systems tend to place extrinsic reward systems onto actions, such that the action is not done for its own sake, but only for the sake of the reward (i.e., points, badges, etc.). This can be quite effective with certain behaviors (Fitbit keeps track of personal exercise and rewards users for 'healthy' behaviors; or Duolingo, the language software, provides points and incentives for continuing to use the system). In the case of exercise or language learning, the motivation of individual pursuits have little bearing on the freedom or pursuits of others. And it should be pointed out that, while game elements are used in these systems, it is difficult to talk about them as playful. One does not play the Fitbit or Duolingo; these systems clarify incentives so users have less room to play. They are designed to be efficient, not inefficient, and they are goal oriented, not concerned with embracing ambiguity.

---

[27] McGonigal, *Reality Is Broken: Why Games Make Us Better and How They Can Change the World* (Penguin Press HC, The, 2011). Retrieved from http://www.amazon.com/Reality-Is-Broken-Better-Change/dp/1594202850.

[28] Walz & Deterding, *The Gameful World: Approaches, Issues, Applications* (Cambridge, MA: MIT Press, 2014).

[29] McGonigal, *Reality Is Broken: Why Games Make Us Better and How They Can Change the World.*

[30] Robertson, "Can't Play, Won't Play" (2010). https://kotaku.com/5686393/cant-play-wont-play. Retrieved November 3, 2018.

While gamified systems make good sense for certain contexts, when they enter into the civic realm, wherein play is the pre-condition for action-taking, they can be destructive. Gamified systems are transactional and predefined, preventing players from inventing new approaches to play or interacting with each other in any direct way. As a general rule they are not playful. As an extreme case, these systems resonate with the cultural critic Herbert Marcuse's critique of mass culture.[31] He warns against cultural systems that are set up to contain unpredictable human passions—such as love, fighting, awe, wonder—in order to maintain control over people. He calls this function of advanced capitalism "repressive desublimation." By sanctioning a controllable amount of "uncontrol," or allowing citizens to *feel* as if they are engaging in something free and real, they think that they are cathartically releasing parts of their inner natures—i.e., desublimating—but they are in fact just incorporating into their psyches the repressive designs of the entity allowing this desublimation to happen. When powerful institutions—from government to corporations—create "fun" processes for participation, they are ostensibly tokenizing or placating their citizens or users. They are looking for them to operate within distinct modes of behavior that meet the needs of the game designer. There are many potential examples of this, from *Commons*,[32] a location-based game that seeks to make reporting more gameful, to *Community PlanIt*,[33] a planning game where big ideas are shared to produce influence toward short term goals.[34] While neither of these systems are designed to placate, often as these tools are implemented, they become means of data collection or placation. Again, as one of the authors of this chapter is the creator of the *Community PlanIt* platform, we understand the value of the system in certain contexts, but we are also keenly aware of how implementation can remove the nuance required for the successful incorporation of

[31] Marcuse, *One-Dimensional Man: Studies in the Ideology of Advanced Industrial Societies*, 2nd ed. (Boston, MA: Beacon Press, 1991).

[32] 2011.

[33] 2011–2015.

[34] Gordon & Baldwin-Philippi, Playful Civic Learning: Enabling Lateral Trust and Reflection in Game-based Public Participation (*International Journal of Communication*, 2014). Retrieved from http://ijoc.org/index.php/ijoc/article/view/2195.

play in civic contexts. Game scholar Jesper Juul makes this point as it pertains to corporate structures. During the 2008 financial crisis, large banks and financial institutions made their organizations "too game-like by giving employees the clear goal of approving as many loans as possible and punishing naysayers with termination. This was a case where the design that works so well inside games can be disastrous outside games.... Games are not a pixie dust of motivation to be sprinkled on any subject."[35]

Our contribution to this debate is not to argue for or against gamified systems, or to lament, as many game scholars have,[36] the lack of quality games in applied contexts. For this chapter, we interviewed practitioners who have designed or applied games to organizational contexts. Often, these practitioners are interested in designing for play, and the game becomes a shorthand for that process. From a project manager at the San Francisco Public Utilities Commission, who was part of a team that created a game for engaging people in conversation about the local watershed: "We see that people who've gone through this gaming process have gone through an extreme experience of education of how a watershed works, how the sewer system works, and they've done it by learning not just from us, but from each other."[37] The focus on peer learning is important to understand how the priorities of the project allowed the definition of the game to emerge. When the project began, they were calling it a dialogue toolkit and then a charette. "It de facto became a game because people played it," according to the project manager. "And so the difference between just an exercise and a game is this notion of winning—or coming in and meeting your goals. And there's an evaluative criteria associated with it. That's the difference. Otherwise, it is really just a discussion or a dialogue and an exercise. And so the point

[35]Juul, "Video Games Make Us All Losers! Does Dying Over and Over in Modern Video Games Create a New Kind of Artistic Tragedy?" Excerpted from "The Art of Failure: An Essay on the Pain of Playing Video Games" (MIT Press, 2013), 10. Retrieved from https://www.salon.com/2013/07/13/video_games_make_us_all_losers/.

[36]Bogost, "Why Gamification Is Bullshit." In Walz, S. & Deterding, S. (eds.) *The Gameful World: Approaches, Issues, Applications* (Cambridge, MA: MIT Press, 2014); O'Donnell, Getting Played: Gamification, Bullshit, and the Rise of Algorithmic Surveillance (*Surveillance & Society, 12*[3]), 349–359. http://www.surveillance-and-society.org. ISSN: 1477-74872014.

[37]Anonymous, personal communication, 2014.

of calling it a game is, it makes it fun. And people had an amazingly fun time. There was a lot of laughing, and arguing, and people talking to people that have completely different skill sets from themselves. And so it sort of felt to me like a party. So, there's this aspect of playing, and fun, and having social interaction that's clearly a strong part of it."[38]

The point of calling it a game is that it "makes it fun." While this might be a slip of tongue, it is telling that the project manager specifically started calling it a game because she felt that it provided the context for having fun that other labels didn't offer. Throughout our interview with her, she continued to focus on how best to harness dialogue. The game was not a structure to create play, but in fact, it emerged post fact as a means of capturing and communicating the kind of play that was taking place in these interactions.

According to a serious game designer: "Games have to be fun. No matter how serious, no matter how important or how relevant, if somebody is not having a good time doing it, they're not going to play it. Sounds frivolous, especially if you're talking about serious games, as we are, but it has to be fun."[39] This commitment to fun was common across all the organizations with which we spoke. From designers to the people running the projects in the organizations, the common assumption about games is that they need to be fun and engaging. Fun, for most of the people we spoke to, had a very low bar. It was fun because it was not boring. It was fun because people were attracted to the novelty of the system and were transformed into willing players. The utility of fun is typically associated with keeping people in the system, keeping them engaged. It was never placed in association with a state of play or the freedom that such a state implied. Instead, fun was a means of holding people captive in a voluntary system.

In our conversation with a program director from the World Bank who was using a game to engage youth in community planning, the use of the word became a limiting factor in the project's life as most of his colleagues only thought of violent video games. "I think social games, social impact games, have gained a little bit more understanding

[38]Anonymous, personal communication, 2014.

[39]Anonymous, personal communication, 2014.

and traction, but still extremely limited. And the word gamification, from a business perspective, has kind of opened some space amongst a certain number of colleagues. But a lot still see it as non-serious and non-academic and kind of a fun extra thing to do as opposed to a way to really engage and motivate young people."[40]

Games applied in civic contexts are difficult to design. But it is far more difficult to design for play. For those looking for playful ways of engaging publics, the language of games and fun dominate the discourse. Through the framework of meaningful inefficiencies, we advocate for prioritizing play over the game that structures it. In the next section, we examine one of our own projects that sought to do just that in the context of a popular social game.

Participatory Pokémon GO

Pokémon GO became a global sensation when it was released in 2016 by the Bay Area game company Niantic. A record-breaking 45 million daily users worldwide were playing the game in the first months after release. As of summer 2018, the game still boasts five million daily users, with the numbers remaining steady since 2017. Pokémon GO is an augmented reality game, or a game that uses physical location as the game board where players navigate located data with their mobile phones. In Pokémon GO, players travel to physical locations to capture Pokémon (little fictional creatures) who appear on the map of where the player is standing. Also in the environment are Pokéstops, which are power stations where players collect necessary game resources, located at various "landmarks" in the environment. To play Pokémon GO, players need to move around. In fact, the game rewards movement explicitly by offering 5 kilometer and 10 kilometer Pokémon eggs that hatch only after traveling that distance.

[40]Anonymous, personal interview, 2014.

While augmented reality games have been around for over a decade,[41] they have largely been experimental or niche. Even Niantic's first game Ingress, while reaching 5 million active players at its peak, never quite became a household name. Pokémon GO represents the crossover moment where augmented reality entered the mainstream. The reason for this is complicated, but it likely has to do with a perfect storm of simple and engaging game mechanics combined with the rich narrative world of Pokémon that first captured the hearts of all those who grew up with Pokémon games or television, and then quickly spread to those who didn't.

During the peak of its popularity in 2016, we became interested in how the game represented Boston's neighborhoods, and how that corresponded to who was actually playing the game. During the summer of 2016, no matter what neighborhood you went into—rich, poor, black, white—there were hordes of (mostly) kids wandering the streets with their phones hunting for Pokémon. Players were recognizable through a familiar gait, which included steady oscillation between stopping and running, and the occasional cheer and high five to a stranger catching the same rare Pokémon. The game activated the sociability of city sidewalks—while each was engaged in their individual pursuit, there was collectivity and camaraderie that would suddenly and surprisingly emerge. As urbanist William Whyte said of urban spaces:

> What attracts people most, it would appear, is other people. If I belabor the point, it is because many urban spaces are being designed as though the opposite were true, and that what people liked best were the places they stay away from. People often do talk along such lines; this is why their responses to questionnaires can be so misleading. How many people would say they like to sit in the middle of a crowd? Instead they speak of getting away from it all, and use terms like "escape," "oasis," "retreat." What people do, however, reveals a different priority.[42]

---

[41] Gordon & de Souza e Silva, *Net Locality: Why Location Matters in a Networked World* (Boston, MA: Blackwell, 2011).

[42] Whyte, *Social Life of Small Urban Spaces* (New York: Project for Public Spaces, 2001), 19.

Pokémon GO allows people to escape while being with others. It captures precisely the expressed desires *and* actions that Whyte references. The sociologist Erving Goffman spoke of "getting away with going away," or the comfort that retreating into a device or a daydream brings when in uncomfortable social situations. While watching young people gather on sidewalks and parks, they would interact, but not be forced to interact. They were in public, but also easily able to go away to their device. This moving in and out of the play space was freedom—an embracing of ambiguity that allowed the player to be both inside and outside of the structures guiding play.

With all the interactions happening alongside the game from a truly diverse group of people, we began to wonder how the data in the game reflected the neighborhoods where players actually lived. Pokéstops are comprised of city landmarks, and recognized landmarks are unequally distributed. While players were coming from all over the city, a truly remarkable feat, the data that comprised the game board in the city of Boston was filled with "Poké deserts," or areas of the city with considerably fewer resources than others. Not surprisingly, these deserts existed in neighborhoods primarily occupied by people of color that lacked other resources as well, including access to healthy foods, adequately maintained parks and sidewalks.

We reached out to Niantic in the fall of 2016 to partner on a project we called Participatory Pokémon GO that would bring youth voices from these neighborhoods to source and better define Pokéstops in Boston. We launched the project in the summer 2017 with a series of workshops intended to enable youth to source new Pokéstops and to rewrite the descriptions of existing ones. Early conversations about the nature of the Participatory Pokémon GO project revealed that stakeholders were more interested in focusing on the representation of local history than the objectives of increasing the number of game locations. This new direction was well received by partners in the City and the Boston Public Schools, as well as key allies from grassroots organizations focused on youth development and preservation of local history. Responding to this feedback, we began suggesting an event where participants tour local historic locations and write historically relevant descriptions for PokéStops.

Initial outreach with community stakeholders involved conversations with offices at Boston's City Hall as well as offices at the Boston Public School headquarters. While the staff at the municipal level had a grasp of salient local issues and needs, it was not until we began engaging with organizations at the grassroots level that we were able to generate unified enthusiasm for the project amongst all stakeholders. We renamed the project AR (augmented reality) Stories, as interest from youth and partner organizations in Pokémon GO itself was not as high as we originally suspected it would be.

During the month of September we met and coordinated with a group of key stakeholders for the series of AR Stories workshops. We coordinated with 826, a national extracurricular writing program with a branch at one of Boston's premier exam schools in the Dudley Square neighborhood, as a way to engage students that had an interest in writing and research about the topic of local history. We also brought in the Roxbury Historical Society and the Hawthorne Youth and Community Center, one of Roxbury's oldest and most well respected youth service organizations, to support our work in identifying important historic locations for students to choose from in the creation of their itinerary.

Meetings with key community stakeholders at the grassroots level was not as straightforward as picking up the phone and cold calling people. Because many local grassroots organizations are wary of collaborating with large corporations and institutions of higher education given a history of extractive and one-sided collaborations, making connections was a product of reaching out to key gatekeepers to make introductions. Furthermore, conversations required extensive in-person meetings at the headquarters of the different organizations. By conducting frequent face-to-face meetings with stakeholders in the neighborhood where they work, we demonstrated a commitment to being in the community where the project would eventually take place.

In October we deployed two workshops that engaged students from colleges and high schools in the Boston area. Leading up to the first workshop, we worked with the Roxbury Historical Society to identify a wide range of locations that would benefit from having comprehensive and detailed information included in AR products by Niantic. With this list in hand, we conducted a workshop in early October with BPS students in the 826 Writing program that asked them to review this list and then generate a tour itinerary based on their favorite locations. The itinerary generated by students from this workshop framed our culminating workshop in late October. Leading up to this workshop, we worked with BPS students and the Hawthorne Youth and Community Center to generate a tour guide script based on the itinerary created by students in the previous workshop.

The second workshop started with the tour of historic locations, where attendees of the open house and workshop participants were invited to use Pokémon GO while they took part in the tour. After the tour, workshop participants conducted research and wrote new descriptions for locations they had just visited in the tour itinerary. In addition to the workshop, a table at the open house featured a poster of the locations that were modified or added from the summer program. Attendees were also invited to nominate new locations from the list generated by the Roxbury Historical Society. This event generated six new location descriptions as well as 18 nominations for new locations in Roxbury. In total, the workshops reached over 300 students and recreated 74 Pokéstop locations in Boston.

For this project to achieve local impact, even while boosted by the attraction of Pokémon GO, required investment in local context and an understanding of local barriers to implementation. To speak to the first point, the initial composition of stakeholders for the project were municipal government employees. While the administrators at the city government level as well as administrators of public schools were well positioned to understand the needs of their city, it was not until we started the deployment of the project and interacted with local historical societies and grassroots youth organizations focused on celebrating local culture and history that we began to better understand the nuance of digital equity we had originally set out to address.

Through early pilots of the project and extensive conversations with various stakeholders, we found that digital equity was perceived with urgency through a unique lens, not that of equity in the quantity of locations for game play, but through quality of how locations are represented. Picking up on this interest in how locations are represented, we conducted our own investigation and found that many Pokéstops, including those with historical significance, had little to no writing about them. This clear gap in historical representation revealed itself as a potential turning point in the project that was aligned with the interests of digital equity expressed by stakeholders (Fig. 1).

One of the Pokéstop descriptions that was rewritten in the process was "The Faces of Dudley" mural. This mural has, since its creation in 1995, become an important landmark for Black history and empowerment in Boston. However, the original description of the Pokéstop in the game was "BYCC mural, 1995." A group of local high school kids rewrote this description in the culminating workshop and ended up with the following: "This locally famous mural, created in 1995, was remodeled in 2015 to include more women. It has the faces of black activists that made a major contribution to the Roxbury/Dudley area, as it captures the essence of Dudley while emphasizing key black figures to promote pride within the community." This rewritten Pokéstop description is now public in the game.

Pokémon GO served as an important and necessary staging area for this expression, but we quickly learned that the project was not about the game—it was about creating conditions for freedom through play. It was about playfulness. The project sought to give young people influence over local data, because otherwise, the freedom of some players would impinge on the freedom of others. Presenting youth with the problem of

Fig. 1 Screenshot of faces of Dudley mural Pokéstop before and after the workshop

data and representation was an effective way of making them aware of the field and its limits. We worked through youth serving organizations to make this happen.

Throughout this project, we encountered tensions between scale and depth. Niantic, of course, was most interested in a city-wide event that captured attention and brought people to the game; the City of Boston and the Boston Public School district, were interested in generating goodwill, but as we drilled down into local needs and interest, the real value was in performing local control over the information that increasingly defines urban neighborhoods. It was not simply an invitation to play, it was an invitation to shape the playing field and the sorts of people who would feel welcome to play in the future.

AR Stories was designed as a meaningful inefficiency—one that invited play as a means of creating the conditions for action. It shed light on the complexity of data inequities in Boston, but not just through exposing, it shed light through enabling action. Sicart argues that play does something more for complex systems: while understanding systems is typically associated with "reduction and synthesis," play brings "action and performance" to systems.[43] Play enables action-taking, in the Arendtian sense, by allowing people to set things in motion through exploration, experimentation, and discovery. And importantly, that freedom of movement requires trust in the system occupied, trust in the other players, and a willingness to play. The case of AR Stories points to the work involved in designing systems in a civic context that people trust such that they are willing to allow themselves and others to play.

Conclusion

Meaningful inefficiencies create room for play. But as we have explained in this essay, the work of designing effective play spaces is complex and difficult. It is not just a matter of designing an attractive field or system, it requires creating the conditions where participants are comfortable and willing to play. This work is not glamorous, and is typically undervalued

---

[43] Sicart, *Play Matters*, 97.

or unrecognized. From taking the time to meet with groups to clarify individual and mutual goals, to involving stakeholders in every step of the design process, the actual work involved in creating meaningful inefficiencies is relational and time consuming.

Play is not an aesthetic state or a proximate experience to civic life, it is the fundamental condition in which people can explore, discover and create in the world—in other words, take action. But no matter how hard one tries, play makes people vulnerable because they submit to rules and allow themselves to be in a state other than the one they occupy normally. As such, play always contains a risk of failure. As Jack Halberstam writes in his book, *The Queer Art of Failure*, "under certain circumstances, failing, losing, forgetting, unmaking, undoing, unbecoming, not knowing may in fact offer more creative, more cooperative, more surprising ways of being in the world."[44] Failure, in the context of play, is twofold: failure of letting oneself play when the rules are not clear (threat of humiliation), and failure within the confines of rules (experimentation and failing safely). The work of building spaces for play is to assure that the former does not come into being and the latter always does. de Beauvoir puts this in the context of ethics. An act is ethical, she says, as long as one creates the conditions for another to pursue their freedom, which often involves the freedom to fail. Playing requires giving oneself over to the possibility of failure, and the sensitivity to others' failures; as such, to play means to be vulnerable. And as civic designers construct spaces for play, they need to do the work of building trust in the systems people inhabit, so even if a player fails, there are more opportunities to play. Good games, according to Juul, "promise us a fair chance of redeeming ourselves."[45]

---

[44]Halberstam, *The Queer Art of Failure* (Raleigh, NC: Duke University Press), 2.

[45]Juul, "Video Games Make Us All Losers! Does Dying Over and Over in Modern Video Games Create a New Kind of Artistic Tragedy?" Excerpted from "The Art of Failure: An Essay on the Pain of Playing Video Games" (MIT Press, 2013), 7. Retrieved from https://www.salon.com/2013/07/13/video_games_make_us_all_losers/.

References

Arendt, H. (1998). *The Human Condition.* Chicago, IL: University of Chicago Press.

Bogost, I. (2014). "Why Gamification Is Bullshit." In Walz, S. & Deterding, S. (eds.) *The Gameful World: Approaches, Issues, Applications.* Cambridge, MA: MIT Press.

Bogost, I. (2016). *Play Anything: The Pleasure of Limits, the Uses of Boredom, and the Secret of Games.* New York: Basic Books.

Bourdieu, P. (1990). *The Logic of Practice.* Stanford, CA: Stanford University Press.

Costikyan, G. (2013). *Uncertainty in Games.* Cambridge, MA: MIT Press.

Csikszentmihalyi, M., & Csikszentmihalyi, I.S. (1992). *Optimal Experience: Psychological Studies of Flow in Consciousness.* Cambridge, UK: Cambridge University Press.

de Beauvoir, S. (2011). *The Ethics of Ambiguity.* New York: Open Road Media.

Deterding, S., Dixon, D., Khaled, R., Nacke, L., Sicart, M., & O'hara, K. (2011). "Gamification: Using Game Design Elements in Non-Game Contexts." In *Proceedings of the 2011 Annual Conference Extended Abstracts on Human Factors in Computing Systems* (pp. 2425–2428).

Dewey, J. (1922). "Democracy and Education." Digireads.com Publishing. (pp. 195).

Gordon, E., & Baldwin-Philippi, J. (2014, February 26). "Playful Civic Learning: Enabling Lateral Trust and Reflection in Game-based Public Participation." *International Journal of Communication.* Retrieved from http://ijoc.org/index.php/ijoc/article/view/2195.

Gordon, E., & de Souza e Silva, A. (2011). *Net Locality: Why Location Matters in a Networked World.* Boston, MA: Blackwell.

Halberstam, J. (2011). *The Queer Art of Failure.* Raleigh, NC: Duke University Press.

Hamari, J., & Koivisto, J. (2015). Why Do People Use Gamification Services? *International Journal of Information Management, 45*(4), 419–431.

Huizinga, J. (1955). *Homo Ludens: A Study of the Play-element in Culture.* Boston, MA: Beacon Press.

Jenkins, H. (2008). *Convergence Culture: Where Old and New Media Collide.* New York: NYU Press.

Jenkins, H., & Shresthova, S. (2012). Up, Up, and Away! The Power and Potential of Fan Activism. *Transformative Works and Cultures,*

10. Retrieved from http://journal.transformativeworks.org/index.php/twc/article/view/435/305.

Juul, J. (July 13, 2013). Video Games Make Us All Losers! Does Dying Over and Over in Modern Video Games Create a New Kind of Artistic Tragedy? Excerpted from "The Art of Failure: An Essay on the Pain of Playing Video Games" (MIT Press, 2013). Retrieved from https://www.salon.com/2013/07/13/video_games_make_us_all_losers/.

Marcuse, H. (1991). *One-Dimensional Man: Studies in the Ideology of Advanced Industrial Societies* (2nd ed.). Boston, MA: Beacon Press.

McDowell C., & Chinchilla, M. (2016). "Partnering with Communities and Institutions." In Gordon, E. & Mihailidis, P. (eds.) *Civic Media: Technology, Design, Practice.* Cambridge, MA: MIT Press.

McGonigal, J. (2011). *Reality Is Broken: Why Games Make Us Better and How They Can Change the World*. Penguin Press HC, The. Retrieved from http://www.amazon.com/Reality-Is-Broken-Better-Change/dp/1594202850.

Nelson, M. J. (2012). Soviet and American Precursors to the Gamification of Work. *Proceeding of the 16th International Academic MindTrek Conference on—MindTrek' 12*, 23. https://doi.org/10.1145/2393132.2393138.

O'Donnell, C. (2014). "Getting Played: Gamification, Bullshit, and the Rise of Algorithmic Surveillance." *Surveillance & Society, 12*(3), 349–359. http://www.surveillance-and-society.org. ISSN: 1477-7487.

Robertson, M. (2010). "Can't Play, Won't Play." https://kotaku.com/5686393/cant-play-wont-play. Retrieved November 3, 2018.

Sicart, M. (2014). *Play Matters*. Cambridge, Cambridge: MIT Press.

Suits, B. (2005). *The Grasshopper: Games, Life, and Utopia.* New York: Broadview Press.

Sutton-Smith, B. (1997). *The Ambiguity of Play*. Cambridge: Harvard University Press.

Thiel, S.-K., Reisinger, M., Röderer, K., & Fröhlich, P. (2016). Playing (with) Democracy: A Review of Gamified Participation Approaches. *Journal of E-Democracy and Open Government*, *8*(2), in print.

Tsebelis, G. (1991). *Nested Games: Rational Choice in Comparative Politics.* Berkeley, CA: University of California Press.

Van der Heijden, H. (2004). User Acceptance of Hedonic Information Systems. *MIS Quarterly*, *28*(4), 695–704.

Walz, S., & Deterding, S. (eds.) (2014). *The Gameful World: Approaches, Issues, Applications.* Cambridge, MA: MIT Press.

Whyte, W. (2001). *Social Life of Small Urban Spaces.* New York: Project for Public Spaces.

Zuckerman, O., & Gal-Oz, A. (2014). Deconstructing Gamification: Evaluating the Effectiveness of Continuous Measurement, Virtual Rewards, and Social Comparison for Promoting Physical Activity. *Personal and Ubiquitous Computing*, *18*(7), 1705–1719. Retrieved from http://doi.org/10.1007/s00779-014-0783-2.

Playthings, Comedy & Laughter

"Let Us Laugh and Play": Laughter in Greek Lyric Poetry

Mary J. Yossi

Ancient Greek Lyric poetry shares with epic a common approach to various functions of laughter, adapting the relative vocabulary (*γέλως*, *γελῶ*, *γελοῖον* and their derivatives) to new cultural and historical contexts. The same functions that the main theories of laughter have proposed studying it as a sign of "the comic," i.e., interpreting laughter as an expression of superiority, or as a reaction to a contradiction or incoherence, or as an attempt to relieve tensions,[1] can be attested in the ancient Greek lyric texts that have come down to us. The texts themselves, though, offer as representations a much broader frame of

[1]For a bibliographical survey, see Mader, *Das Problem des Lachens*, 146–152, with a critical presentation of Bergson's, Freud's, Plessner's, Baums's and Helmer's views in pp. 83–88. Important bibliography in Desclos. *Le rire des Grecs*, 591–623. For a recent bibliography on ancient Greek laughter, see Halliwell, *Greek Laughter*, 553–602 and Yossi and Melista, *Exaisioi Gelwtes*, 1073–1142.

M. J. Yossi (✉)
National and Kapodistrian University of Athens, Athens, Greece
e-mail: maryosi@phil.uoa.gr

V. Rapti and E. Gordon (eds.), *Ludics*,
https://doi.org/10.1007/978-981-15-7435-1_8

references to this particularly human—according to Aristotle—[2] characteristic. G*elōs* (and *gelō*) usually imply a close connection to play and lightheartedness, as opposed to seriousness (*spoudē*). Although all three terms (*gelān*, *paizein*, and *spoudē*) appear in the *adespoton* elegiac fragment 12 GP (discussed below), the term *spoudē* (σπουδή), which will become later (mainly in Plato)[3] the standard opposite of "play" (παιδιά), is not found again in this sense[4] in the lyric fragments that have come down to us. Surprisingly enough, neither the words παιδιά ("play" or "playfulness") nor παίγνιον ("play" or "plaything") are attested in the remnants of archaic lyric poetry. Only in Stesichorus 232 *PMG* we find the hapax παιγμοσύνη, whose meaning, according to the context and the similar uses of the verb παίζειν ("to play"), is close to the εὐφροσύνη ("mirth") shared by the participants in a feast in honor of a god (here Apollo) or a symposium:

> *†μάλα† τοι μάλιστα*
> *παιγμοσύνας <τε> φιλεῖ μολπάς τ᾽Ἀπόλλων,*
> *κήδεα δὲ στοναχάς τ᾽ Ἀίδας ἔλαχε.*

The verb παίζειν ("to play") appears in epic[5] and lyric poetry mainly in connection with μολπή ("song") or μουσική (poetry and music) and ὀρχηθμόν ("danse") and all the examples indicate that it refers not simply to musical performance (playing at the *lyre* or the αὐλός, the pipe) but to choral performances, either formal (in a feast or a symposium)[6] or informal (for example, by a group of young girls, recalling the choruses of

[2] Aristotle, *De partibus animalium*, 673a 2–31. Aristotle, of course, is discussing here the function of the diaphragm, and γέλως is examined as a result of tickling (γαργαλισμός) to which man alone is susceptible because the thinness of his skin permits the easy transmission of heat that produces laughter (i.e., from the point of view of biology and medicine). On this Aristotelian passage, see Melista in Yossi and Melista, *Exaisioi Gelwtes*, passage 99, 798–811.

[3] See, for example, the famous platonic definition of μίμησις (mimetic art, and mainly mimetic poetry, i.e. tragedy) as παιδιά and not σπουδή in *Rep*. X 602b 6–10.

[4] A rare word in both epic and lyric vocabulary, with a variety of meanings (the most common among these is the meaning of σπουδῇ "in haste"). As the standard opposite of παιδιά (in Xenophon, Plato, etc.), it denotes the "serious engagement or pursuit" (see LSJ, s.v.).

[5] It is interesting to note that the word is absent from the *Iliad*.

[6] See Homer, *Od*. 23. 133 ff., *Hom. Hymn to Apollo*, 201–206, Hesiod, *Scutum*, 275–285, Pindar, *Ol*. 1, 16 and *Ol*. 13, 86.

Nymphs and most importantly of the Muses).[7] In rare instances *paizein* is associated with playing a game, as for example "playing at the ball"[8] or indicates the playfulness of a young girl who "leaps" (or "danses") with light steps.[9]

According to the above, we could say that "playing" (*παίζειν*) provides the general frame of mind within which laughter exhibits the various forms it takes (sympotic, derisory, erotic, ritual, etc.) as they appear in the examples discussed below considering parameters as literary genre and intertextuality, but also the occasion for their performance.

* * *

Theognis 1041–1042 & 1217–1218[10]

The approximately 1400 elegiac verses that constitute the *Theognideia*, the corpus of poetry attributed to Theognis, have always puzzled the scholars since, on the one hand, the collection includes poems or fragments not only by Theognis but also by the other elegiac poets (Tyrtaeus, Mimnermus, Solon, Euenus, etc.) and, on the other hand, the direct or indirect historical references found in it are chronologically so remote one from the other that exclude the possibility for the corpus to be the work of one and the same author. Moreover, the repetition of verses or couplets, the so-called dittographies (no less than 22)—with or without variations—presents us with one more problem closely linked to the

---

[7]Like Nausika and her maids in Homer, *Od.* 6. 99 ff. and 7. 290–291; see also, *Hom. Hymn* XXX, 15.

[8]See Hom. *Od.* 6. 100, Anacreon 358 *PMG.*

[9]*κοῦφά τε σκιρτῶσα παίζεις*, Anacreon 417, 7 *PMG* or *παρθενικαί τε χοροῖς…παίζουσι σκαίρουσαι*, *Hom. Hymn* XXX, 14–15.

[10]For an extended version of my discussion of Theognis's controversial couplets 1041–1042 & 1217–1218, see Yossi, "*δεῦρο σὺν αὐλητῆρι*", 99–106. The text cited below is from Young's critical edition. See also the editions—with or without commentary—by Van Groningen, *Théognis*, Gentili and Prato, *Poetae Elegiaci* I, Vetta, *Theognis*, West, *Iambi et Elegi Graeci* I, Ferrari, *Teognide*. See also De Martino and Vox, *Lirica Greca.*

discussion about the compilation, but also about the transmission of the corpus.[11]

The emphasis given in the last four decades to the socio-political institution of the *symposion*, shed light on the context in which archaic lyric poetry developed, suggesting a rather bold reorganization of our way of approaching it. The *symposion* became not only the place for the performance of Greek lyric poetry but also the occasion for its composition.[12]

While the sympotic character of Teognidean poetry had been recognized since the end of nineteenth century, the revival of the interest in it generated new and intriguing readings as well as a re-examination of old ones.[13] On another level, we should remark that this focus on the sympotic context of Theognis' elegies led us to abandon the "nostalgic"[14] quest for the author as the person who could guarantee the unity—or rather the "authentic meaning"—of the work.[15]

The two fragments we are going to discuss [a] 1041–1042 and [b] 1217–1218 are characteristic examples of sympotic poetry, in which the reference to *gelōs* (laughter) or related words (i.e., the adjective *geloios*—laughable, ridicule—and the verb *gelān*—to laugh) are used as strong sympotic indices.

Theognis' sympotic poetics have some *external* and some *internal* elements. The repetitions, for example, or the "dittographies" ("doublets" in Nagy's terms) belong to the "external" elements, whereas particular scenes, key-words, even *gnomai*, belong to the "internal," since even what

---

[11]See, Carrière, *Théognis de Mégare*, Peretti, *Teognide*, Young, "Borrowings and Self-adaptations in Theognis," 307–390, West, *Studies*, 40–64, Bowie, "The *Theognidea*," 53–66 etc.

[12]See especially, Rossi, "Il simposio greco arcaico," 41–50, Vetta, *Poesia e simposio*, Bowie, "Early Greek Elegy, Symposium and Public Festival", Fiqueira and Nagy, *Theognis of Megara*, Myrray, *Sympotica*, etc.

[13]Colesanti, "Dittografie," 459–495, for example, suggests the re-evaluation of Nietzsche's views on the corpus (in his 1867 study "Zur Geschichte der theognideischen Spruchsammlung"), who argued that the organizing principle of the *Theognideia* was the thematic structuring of the *syllogē* based on specific key-words. On the sympotic character of Theognis' poetry and its relation to the Attic *scholia*, see Reitzenstein, *Epigram und Skolion*, Carrière, *Théognis de Mégare*, etc.

[14]Scodel, "*Listening to Homer*," esp. 1–41.

[15]Nagy, "Theognis and Megara," 22–81.

we call "sympotic ethics"[16] when detached from its historical context assumes the character of a typical (and recurrent) motif, i.e., something equivalent to "sympotic ritual,"[17] if we move to the level of social practice.

Let us now turn to the couplets:

[α] Theognis 1041–1042

δεῦρο σὺν αὐλητῆρι· παρὰ κλαίοντι γελῶντες
πίνωμεν, κείνου κήδεσι τερπόμενοι.

Come over, with the piper! Let's drink beside one who weeps,
Laughing and taking pleasure at his grief.

[b] Theognis 1217–1218

Μήποτε πὰρ κλαίοντα καθεζόμενοι γελάσωμεν
τοῖς αὐτῶν ἀγαθοῖς, Κύρν", ἐπιτερπόμενοι.

Let's never laugh siting by one who weeps
Rejoicing at our own good fortune, Cyrnus.

There is perhaps no other instance in the Theognidean corpus of such a blatant contradiction. What the [a] urges us to do is found totally inappropriate in [b], in which—apart from the name of Cyrnus, which is considered as a kind of *sphragis,* or seal of authenticity—we find a typical reference to sympotic *decorum* that prohibits anyone to laugh when his next to him is for some reason in distress. The indifference to somebody else's sufferings is underlined in [b] by the mention of *τέρψις* (pleasure), which incites this untimely and insensitive laughter.

In [a], though, the sympotic laughter of [b] is transformed into a laughter of derision. Thus, although [a] follows faithfully, as far as the structure is concerned, [b] (*παρὰ κλαίοντι/ πὰρ κλαίοντα,/ γελῶντες,*

[16]See Bielohlawek, "Gastmahls- und Symposionslehren bei griechischen Dichtern," 11–30 [= Vetta, *Poesia e simposio,* 95–116], Slater, "Peace, the Symposium and the Poet," 205–214, Pellizer, "Morphology of Sympotic Entertainment," 177–184, etc.

[17]Schmitt Pantel, "Sacrificial Meal and *Symposion,*" 14–33.

τερπόμενοι/ ἐπιτερπόμενοι), couplet [a] introduces a different speaker from [b]'s.

The efforts to remedy this contradiction focused on either of these two couplets. Hartung and Bergk,[18] for example, were inclined to ascribe [a] not to Theognis but to Archilochus, because of its derisory content, but also because in the Theognidean corpus a number of couplets or longer fragments are identical with fragments assigned to other poets (i.e., to Solon, Xenophon, Mimnermus, etc.). West, on the other hand,[19] put in brackets the initial *μήποτε* ("never") of [b] to eliminate the contradiction. Given the peculiarity of the Theognidean corpus we will attempt an examination of the sympotic context to which both these couplets belong, and in which the practice of *repetitio cum variatione* is more than usual.

Fr. [b] corresponds—as van Groningen indicated—[20] to Chilon's dictum *τῷ δυστυχοῦντι μὴ ἐπιγέλα* ("do not laugh at somebody's distress").[21] In Theognis this laughter of derision, an aggressive gesture, is not limited to the domain of what is or is not a socially acceptable behavior, but enters the domain of political ethics, as other instances of doublets in the Theognidean corpus indicate.[22]

Viewed in the sympotic context, [b] conforms to the idea of *μεσότης* that Theognis proposes in several fragments, as a wise attitude that refrains somebody from excesses (in drinking, talking, or making indecent gestures).[23] This applies not only to pleasure, but to sorrow as well.[24]

---

[18] *apud* Van Groningen, *Théognis*, 388.

[19] *Iambi et Elegi Graeci* I, *ad loc.*

[20] Van Groningen, *Théognis*, 439.

[21] Diels and Kranz, *Die Fragmente der Vorsokratiker*, I, 63.

[22] See, for example, Theognis 53–60 "they deceive each other, laughing at each other, not being able to distinguish which advise is sound and which is wrong" and 1109–1114 "they deceive each other, laughing at each other, having no memory of who is high born or who is base –or low born," where we have this kind of repetition with some variation.

[23] See Pellizer, "Morphology of Sympotic Entertainment," 178–179, Vetta, *Poesia e simposio*, XXV–XLVI. For the notion pf sympotic *ethos* (and the related notions of συμποτικόν *τέλος*, *λόγος συμποτικός* and *νόμος συμποτικός*), cf. Plutarch, *Quaest. Conv.* 614a ff., 621c και 659e–660d, Plato, *Leg.* 636e ff, etc.

[24] See for example Theognis 655–656: "We all share your pain, Cyrnus, in your misfortune,/ but grief for another is short-lived" (trans. by G. Gerber] or Theognis 657–658, etc. An interesting description of the sympotic *decorum* is found in Theognis 309–312.

Ἐν μὲν συσσίτοισιν ἀνὴρ πεπνυμένος[25] *εἶναι.*
πάντα δέ μιν λήθειν ὡς ἀπεόντα δοκοῖ,
εἰς δὲ φέροι τὰ γελοῖα˙ θύρηφιν καρτερὸς εἴη
γινώσκων ὀργὴν ἥντιν' ἕκαστος ἔχει. (17)

At the symposion a man should be courteous
Seeming not to notice all that happens, as if he were absent,
While allowing for some innocuous jokes;
Once outside, though, let him be harsh in his judgment
Being aware of the temperament of each fellow.

We also encounter a detailed description of the sympotic *decorum* in the lengthy fragment 467–496 addressed to Semonides (usually attributed not to Theognis but to the poet Euenus) as well as in other fragments. In the context of sympotic poetics we have other examples too: the famous Xenophanes' fragment 1 W (known as the "sympotic elegy"), or the "violation" of the *decorum* in Alcaeus 332, 1 L-P: "now, let's get drunk, let's drink even by force, since the tyrant Myrsilos has been overthrown." Drunkenness (*μέθη*) is a disgrace to a wise and moderate symposiast; see, for example, Theognis' Onomacritos fragment 503–508 ("I have a hangover, Onomacritos, the wine has overpowered me…"].

A last example of laughter as an element of sympotic poetics is the fifth century B.C. elegiac *adespoton*, fr. 12 G.-P. = 27 W:

Χαίρετε, συμπόται ἄνδρες, ὁμήλικες ἐξ ἀγαθοῦ γὰρ
ἀρξάμενος τελέω τὸν λόγον εἰς ἀγαθόν.
Χρὴ δ' ὅταν εἰς τοιοῦτο συνέλθωμεν, φίλοι ἄνδρες,
πρᾶγμα, γελᾶν, παίζειν χρησαμένους ἀρετῇ
ἥδεσθαί τε συνῶντας ἐς ἀλλήλους τε φλυαρεῖν
καὶ σκώπτειν τοιαῦθ' οἷα γέλωτα φέρειν.
Ἡ δὲ σπουδὴ ἑπέσθω, ἀκούων μέν τε λεγόντων,

[25]The meaning of the homeric *πεπνυμένος* is much disputed. In the *Iliad* it usually characterizes Nestor and Menelaus, while in the *Odyssey* Telemachus and Odysseus himself. In all instances it denotes somebody's ability to persuasive and timely speaking, to use convincing arguments or simply tell the truth. Halliwell, *Greek Laughter*, 117–118 translates *πεπνυμένος* as "shrewdly sagacious", suggesting an ability to develop and retain good sense in severely testing circumstances". For the meaning of *γελοῖα*, cf. Archilochus 168 W. *Ἐρασμονίδη Χαρίλαε, χρῆμά τοι γελοῖον/ ἐρέω, πολὺ φίλταθ' ἑταίρων, τέρψεαι δ' ἀκούων*, ["Charilaus, son of Erasmon, by far the dearest of my companions, I'll tell you a droll thing, and you'll be delighted in hearing it."] and my discussion of it in Yossi and Melista, *Exaisioi Gelwtes*, 550–553.

ἐν μέρει˙ ἥδ'' ἀρετή συμποσίου πέλεται.
τοῦ δὲ ποταρχοῦντος πειθόμεθα˙ ταῦτα γὰρ ἐστὶν
ἔργ'' ἀνδρῶν ἀγαθῶν εὐλογίαν τε φέρει.

Greetings, fellow drinkers […]! I''ll give my speech a good beginning
And carry it through to a good conclusion too.
Whenever we gather together as friends for such an occasion,
We should laugh and play (while still upholding excellence)
And take pleasure in each other's company, and send up each other
With mockery of a kind that yields laughter.
But seriousness must be maintained as well. Let's listen to each other
Speaking in turn: that's a symposium's mark of excellence.
And let's follow the instructions of our drinking-master. This way of behaving
Belongs to good men and is apt to yield good repute.[26]

Let us now turn to fr. [a]: The reference to the piper (*αὐλητής*) introduces the notion of poetry (or song) [*ἀοιδῆς*]. A whole group of fragments links this reference to the pipe or the piper to poetry performed at the symposia, which produces the appropriate pleasure (*τέρψις*). Let us consider a few examples:

In his lengthy fragment addressed to Cyrnus (237–254) the poet, after presenting his art as the wings offered to Cyrnus "to fly with ease aloft the boundless sea and all the land," adds (237–254): "No meal or feast but thou'lt be there, couched "twixt the lips of many a guest, and lovely youths shall sing thee clear and well in orderly wise to the clear-voiced flute. […]"[27]

In ll. 531–534 the poet describes a scene of sympotic mirth (*εὐφροσύνη*) where "the tuneful lyre" accompanies "the pipe's delightful voice," while in the ritual context of ll. 757–764 the harp and the pipe sound the *ἱερὸν μέλος* which accompanies the libations and the joyful conversations of the symposiasts.[28]

---

[26]Trans. S. Halliwell, *Greek Laughter*, 114.

[27]Trans. J. Edmonds.

[28]See also Theognis 825–830, 939–942, 973–978, 1055–1058 & 1063–1068, paying attention to the relevant vocabulary: *αὐλός* (the pipe), *αὐλητήρ* the piper), *κῶμος* (revel), *τέρψις* or *τερπωλή* (pleasure), the Muses or the v. *ἀείδειν* (to sing)].

We previously referred to the view—now shared by all—[29] that elegy was a genre sung to the pipe. It is not necessary to suppose, as Cerri does,[30] that the mention of the piper in [a] linked to the participle "weeping" (*κλαίοντι*) implies the plaintive sound of the pipe (taking the participle as referring to the musical instrument, untimely sad and mournful for the light-spirited *symposion*). The speaker in [a] is accompanying the piper in a quite lighthearted mood, so that the parody of [b] introduced by [a] on the level of the context, expands to the level of form as well, with the use of a metrical formula that reminds us of the well-known Simonidean epigram "O Stranger, tell the Lakedaimonians that we lie here, faithful to their orders" [*τοῖς κείνων ῥήμασι πειθόμενοι*], which in the Theognidean fragment is transformed into *κείνου κήδεσι τερπόμενοι* "rejoicing in his grief."

We may, therefore, suppose that [b] is the model for the parody that [a] introduces, which within the context of the Theognidean corpus illustrates Theognis' sympotic poetics through the use of key-words indicating the genre of elegy sung to the sound of the pipe in order to produce the (moderate and not licentious) pleasure or *τέρψις*, always referring to sympotic ethics as well. The contradiction that the two fragments present could then be—as Carrière already suggested in 1948—to the practice of *responsio*, where a member of the *symposion* is replying to a fellow symposiast by altering (shifting) his words. Another way to remedy this contradiction would be to consider that our poet (if the two fragments are attributed to one and the same author) is here quoting somebody else's view, perhaps criticizing it for overstepping the measures of the sympotic *decorum*.

* * *

[29] Despite Campbell's arguments ("Flutes and Elegiac Couplets", 63–68), refuted by Bowie, "Early Greek Elegy, Symposium and Public Festival", 13–35 (esp. 22–27). See also Aloni, "Elegy," 170.

[30] "Frammento di teoria musicale e di ideologia simposiale," 20.

Semonides 7, 71–82 W

Semonides of Amorgos (seventh—or sixth, as Hubbart argued—[31] century B.C.) is the author of the 118 lines long poem of "blame" or *psogos* against women (as Stobaeus characterized it in his fifth century A.D. *Anthology*), known widely as *Iambos on Women* (fr. 7 W),[32] which, following an eastern tradition,[33] presents us with vivid zoomorphic portraits of various types of women: there is the swine-woman, the fox-woman, the bitch-woman, and after two non-zoomorphic types: the earth-woman and the sea-woman, there follow the donkey-woman, the weasel-woman, the mare-woman, the monkey-woman and, last, the bee-woman, the *coronis* of the species. A shorter list of women types (the swine-woman, the bitch-woman, the mare-woman, and the bee-woman) is preserved in Phocylides' fr. 2 W, probably based on Semonides' poem. Patterned on the Hesiodic poetic background[34] and the Aesopic fables,[35] these female types exhibit mainly their negative characteristics, except for the bee-woman who is depicted in the most favorable light. Of all

[31] Hubbart, "Elementary Psychology", 175–197.

[32] The term *iambos* does not indicate only the iambic metre but also "the function of the genre" as Nagy put it in his 1976 article "Iambos: Typologies of Invective and Praise," 191. Both meanings are found in Aristotle's *Poetics* 4, 1448b 30–1449a 28.

[33] See Pizzagalli (1934) 918–930, Meuli (1975) II, 739–754, Lloyd-Jones (1975) 21, Burkert (1992) 121–122, West (1997) 236–237, et al.

[34] The 'attack' on women has its origins in Pandora's myth, twice found in Hesiod's work (*Theogony* 570–602 and *Works and Days* 42–105). In Hesiod's *Theogony* (l. 585) Pandora is called "a beautiful evil" (*kalon kakon*).

[35] This zoomorphic presentation of people is also found in Archilochus' *ainoi* (frr. 174 and 185–187 W) where again serves as the means of invective [for Archilochus' *ainoi* see Karadagli, *Fabel und Ainos*, 6–52, Kakridis, *Come, Aphrodite*, 25–31, Brown, "Iambos," 50–66, van Dijk, *Fables*, 138–144, Konstantakos, *Akicharos*, 128–142, Carey, "Iambos", 158–160, etc. In Archilochus' fr. 172 W, closely linked to the *ainos* of fr. 174 W, we find a close parallel to Semonides' reference to this laughter of derision: "Old-Lukambes, what were you thinking of?/Who has deprived you of your good senses?/ Now, you've become the laughing stock of your fellow citizens." The target of this derisory laughter of the *astoi* [the people of the asty/city] is in this case Archilochus' would-be father-in-law Lykambes. As Steiner, *Fables and Frames*, 19, notes: "The mention of this wider public expands the circle of potential auditors and takes Archilochus's performance out of the confines of the dining room and into the public forum where political discourse occurs."

these types, only the monkey-woman provokes laughter, and ll. 71–82 of Semonides' *Iambos* illustrate how laughter works as a weapon of invective:

τὴν δ᾽ ἐκ πιθήκου· τοῦτο δὴ διακριδὸν
Ζεὺς ἀνδράσιν μέγιστον ὤπασεν κακόν.
αἴσχιστα μὲν πρόσωπα· τοιαύτη γυνὴ
εἶσιν δι᾽ ἄστεος πᾶσιν ἀνθρώποις γέλως·
ἐπ᾽ αὐχένα βραχεῖα· κινεῖται μόγις·
ἄπυγος, αὐτόκωλος. ἆ τάλας ἀνὴρ
ὅστις κακὸν τοιοῦτον ἀγκαλίζεται.
δήνεα δὲ πάντα καὶ τρόπους ἐπίσταται
ὥσπερ πίθηκος· οὐδέ οἱ γέλως μέλει·
οὐδ᾽ ἄν τιν᾽ εὖ ἔρξειεν, ἀλλὰ τοῦτ᾽ ὁρᾶι
καὶ τοῦτο πᾶσαν ἡμέρην βουλεύεται,
ὅκως τι κὼς μέγιστον ἔρξειεν κακόν.

Another is from a monkey. This is by far the worst evil
That Zeus gave to men. She has the ugliest face;
When such a woman goes through the town
Becomes the laughing stock of everyone.
Her neck is short, she moves limping,
She has no buttocks and is all legs.
Ah, wretched is the man who embraces such an evil.
She knows every scheme, just like a monkey.
She doesn't even care if people laugh at her!
She wouldn't do a favor to anyone;
Her only thought is how to plot
and do the greatest possible mischiefs.

There is a strong satiric element in the traditional "poetics of blame" that this passage employs with the detailed description of the monkey-woman's movements and attitude. It seems that the poet relies on the compliance of his (probably male) audience and this indicates that the poem was intended for performance in a *symposion*[36] and that the comic

[36]See Pellizer and Tedeschi, *Semonides*, xxvi–xxxiv, Stehle, *Performance*, 238, Osborne, "Use and abuse," 47–64, Carey, "Iambos", 160–162. For a wedding feast argued Schear, "Wives and their Husbands," 41–46 and de Martino–Vox, *Lirica greca* II, 686–686.

exaggeration in the depiction of a woman's defects would contribute to a strengthening of the bonds among the members of the *symposion* and to a relieving from the tensions that as members of a community would probably experience both in their *oikos* (household, family) and in the *polis* (the broader political community).[37]

Oikos and *polis* are actually the two poles of the criticism exercised by Semonides in his *Iambos on Women*. The *oikos*, a *par excellence* woman's space, usually reflects the orderly or disorderly state of the *polis*' affairs (i.e., the State's or the political community's affairs).[38] By turn, the *oikos*' disorderly state damages a man's public image, and that is why the harsh criticism on women turns out to be a criticism against the man as the head of his *oikos*, who thus becomes the target of his fellow symposiasts' derision.

In the case of the "monkey-woman" this laughter is also provoked by her ugliness. First, the ugliness of her appearance:

> She has the ugliest face;
> When such a woman goes through the town
> Becomes the laughing stock of everyone.
> Her neck is short, she moves limping,
> She has no buttocks and is all legs.

From the description of physical ugliness, Semonides then proceeds to the description of her character. An accumulation of negative terms in the superlative ("by far the worst," "the ugliest," "the greatest evil") reveals that this woman type has more negative characteristic than any other type. Moreover, the fact that she doesn't mind at all being the laughing stock of others is, according to Halliwell "a symptom of a deficient sense of honour or self-worth."[39]

This woman's comparison to a monkey is most interesting since the monkey (or ape) is the animal most akin to humans. In Galen (130 A.D. Pergamon–200 A.D. Rome), the monkey provokes laughter just because

---

[37] See Footnote 5 above, for the reference to Archilochus' fr. 172 W.

[38] Cf. Xenophon, *Oeconomicos* 8.3, 8.6, 8.11 etc. for the notion of *taxis* and *kosmos* in the city, the army, the household. Cf. Kostopoulos, "Xen. *Oecon.* 8.18–23" in Yossi and Melista, *Exaisioi Gelwtes*, passage 33, 290–292.

[39] *Greek Laughter*, 42.

he imitates man.[40] This peculiarity (as well as the ugliness of the animal) is particularly emphasized in Heraclitus's saying that "the most handsome of the monkeys is like the ugliest of men."[41] The same philosopher argues also that "the wisest man looks like a monkey in comparison to the wisdom and beauty and all the other virtues of the gods."[42] In the *Sayings of the Seven Wise Men* a monkey makes the Scythian Anacharsis laugh as a creature apt to provoke laughter (*geloion*) by nature (*physei*), while the professional clown they bring in to entertain the symposium of the Seven Wise Men does not succeed in it, as he tries to make all laugh by his skills *(epithdeusei*).[43] The connection of the monkey to a clown (or the Joker or the Fool) operates on two levels: On the first, the movements of the monkey (as the movements of the "monkey-woman"—in our fragment she moves awkwardly, limping in a way), which, according to Galen is due to the disharmony or disproportion of the animal"s members[44]—i.e., very long hands and legs, very spasmodic motion—is compared to the movements of a lame person whom the Joker imitates in order to provoke laughter.[45] On a second level, we should recall that in the Platonic myth of Er, at the end of the *Republic* (620c 2–3), the soul of Thersites, the notorious for his ugliness and his base character Homeric anti-hero, who is there called *gelotopoios* ("Joker" or "Fool"), chooses to be re-incarnated in the form of a monkey. Demosthenes too calls the sycophant (or slanderer) a "tragic monkey,"[46] while Plutarch[47] compares to a monkey the flatterer, a good-for-nothing fellow who puts

---

[40] See Melista on Galen's *De usu partibus* i 58, 13–60, 5 and i 194, 7–22 Helmreich (= 3. 79–82 and 264 Kühn) in Yossi and Melista, *Exaisioi Gelwtes*, passage 42, 327–338.

[41] fr. 82 D-K [= Plato, *Hippias Major* 289a 3]: *πιθήκων ὁ κάλλιστος αἰσχρὸς ἀνθρώπων γένει συμβάλλειν.*

[42] fr. 83 D-K [= Plato, *Hippias Major* 289b 4]: *ἀνθρώπων ὁ σοφώτατος πρὸς θεὸν πίθηκος φανεῖται καὶ σοφίαι καὶ κάλλει καὶ τοῖς ἄλλοις πᾶσιν.*

[43] 10.25: *Οἶδα καὶ Ἀνάχαρσιν τὸν Σκύθην ἐν συμποσίῳ γελωτοποιῶν εἰσαχθέντων ἀγέλαστον διαμείναντα, πιθήκου δ᾽ ἐπεισαχθέντος γελάσαντα φάναι ὡς οὗτος μὲν φύσει γελοῖός ἐστιν, ὁ δ᾽ ἄνθρωπος ἐπιτηδεύσει.*

[44] See Melista on Galen (Footnote 10 above).

[45] Galen, *De usu partibus* 3.264.18–3.265.1 Kühn: *ὡς ἄν τις καὶ ἄνθρωπος γελωτοποιῶν τε καὶ σκώπτων ἕτερον ἄνθρωπον χωλὸν ἵσταιτό τε καὶ βαδίζοι καὶ διαθέοι χωλεύων, οὕτω καὶ πίθηκος χρῆται τοῖς σκέλεσιν.*

[46] *On the Crown* 242.1–5.

[47] *How to tell a flatterer from a friend* 64E 7–11.

up with the derision and the insults coming from the others, showing the same lack of self-respect as Semonides' "monkey-woman."

Our fragment, nevertheless, distinguishes to some degree the ugly (*aischron*) from the base (*kakon*) since the laughter of the others is provoked by the woman's movements (a "locomotion" as Bain put it).[48] In our case we have the opposite of what we have in Galen, where the awkward movements of the monkey are due to his imperfect bodily structure (which again denotes an imperfect soul),[49] while the laughter he provokes comes from his attempt to imitate man.

The laughter at the "monkey-woman" is also a form of what Forsdyke[50] called "street theatre," a sort of social criticism "ritually" enacted in public space (see in our fragment the indication: "through the city"). And while the target is initially the woman (who doesn't even care a bit), the derision's ultimate target is the woman's poor husband.

Moreover, the scene depicted here (the "monkey-woman" walking awkwardly through the city) is the exact opposite not only of the good wife's movements within the *oikos* (the one who comes from the bee in Semonides' poem), but also of the famous scene on the walls of Troy[51] when Helen, that other (like Pandora) *kalon kakon* ("beautiful evil") walks through the gates and all the elders of Troy watch her in amazement.

* * *

Sappho 31 L-P

In Sappho's fr. 1 LP, the smiling Aphrodite, the goddess of Love, responds with amusement to the speaker's prayer to stand *once more* at her side and grant her what her heart desires. "Whom am I to persuade *this time* to

---

[48] Bain, "Semonides 7.75," 93–94.

[49] Melista on Galen in Yossi and Melista, *Exaisioi Gelwtes*, passage 42, 334 with Footnote 36.

[50] "Street Theatre," 3.

[51] Homer, *Iliad* 3, 134–160.

join you in *φιλότατα*?" ("friendship" or "love," with "amorous connotations" to use Page words[52]). The poetics of *eros*, that in this case use the term *μειδιαίσασα* ("smiling") as the most appropriate adjective for Aphrodite, introduces the charming (*ἰμέροεν*, "exciting desire") laughter of the girl in Sappho's fr. 31 LP as the center of her poetic composition.

φαίνεταί μοι κῆνος ἴσος θέοισιν
ἔμμεν' ὤνηρ, ὄττις ἐνάντιός τοι
ἰσδάνει καὶ πλάσιον ἆδυ φωνεί-
σας ὐπακούει

καὶ γελαίσας ἰμέροεν, τό μ' ἦ μὰν
καρδίαν ἐν στήθεσιν ἐπτόαισεν·
ὠς γὰρ ἔς σ' ἴδω βρόχε', ὤς με φώναι-
σ' οὐδ' ἒν ἔτ' εἴκει,

ἀλλ' ἄκαν μὲν γλῶσσα †ἔαγε†, λέπτον
δ' αὔτικα χρῶι πῦρ ὐπαδεδρόμηκεν,
ὀππάτεσσι δ' οὐδ' ἒν ὄρημμ', ἐπιρρόμ-
βεισι δ' ἄκουαι,

†έκαδε μ' ἴδρως ψῦχρος κακχέεται†, τρόμος δὲ
παῖσαν ἄγρει, χλωροτέρα δὲ ποίας
ἔμμι, τεθνάκην δ' ὀλίγω 'πιδεύης
φαίνομ' ἔμ' αὔται·

ἀλλὰ πὰν τόλματον ἐπεὶ †καὶ πένητα†

Equal to the gods he seems to me, that man
who sits opposite to you
and leaning over
listens to your sweet voice

and your charming laughter; that has made in truth
my heart within my breast to break.
For when I look at you, even for a moment,

[52]Page, *Sappho and Alcaeus*, 10.

I lose my speech,

My tongue is silent, a thin flame
runs suddenly beneath my skin,
my eyes see nothing,
my ears are humming,

a cold sweat covers me,
and I am trembling
paler than grass.
I feel I am about to die…

But one must endure everything, since †even a poor man…

The anonymity of all three *dramatis personae* of this lyric "drama"—the "equal-to-the-gods" man, the girl opposite to him, and the "speaker"—contributes to the broadening of the personal experience (of *eros*) to embrace all humans. The figure of the laughing girl is the luminous center of the "painting" created by the "speaker," a center to which converge the presence/absence of the man and the much revealing "speechlessness" of the "speaker." The dark periphery of this center is agitated by the *πάθη* described with medical precision as bodily sufferings.[53] The *tableau vivant* described by the lyric "I" comes to life thanks to the sweet voice and the erotic laughter of the girl. Her laughter is here accompanied by *ἵμερος* (desire): *ἔρως* and Aphrodite are not mentioned explicitly, but they are brought to the foreground by the expression *γελαίσασ' ἰμέροεν*.[54] In Hesiod's *Theogony*,[55] Aphrodite's companions are *ἔρως* and *ἵμερος*, and generally in archaic Greek lyric poetry the personified *Ἵμερος* forms together with *Ἔρως* and *Γέλως* the typical

[53]For a comprehensive approach to a much-discussed topic, see Ferrari, *Una mitra per Kleis*, 159–167.

[54]For the ritual-rhythmical dimension of the fragment, see Segal, "Eros and Incantation", 146–148. For the vocabulary of *eros* in Sappho, see Lanata, "Sul linguaggio amoroso di Saffo," 257–267, Winkler, "Double consciousness," etc.

[55]l. 201.

triad of the goddess' followers. The same triad appears in poem 57 of the *Anacreontea*,[56] where γελῶσα ("laughing") is the goddess herself.

As the source of poetic inspiration, the erotic laughter of the girl in Sappho 31 LP dictates the "centripetal" movement of the scene where the poetic "I" is lured into the abyss of love's passions.

* * *

Pindar, *Pythian* 10, 21–44

Pindar's *Pythian* 10, the oldest surviving epinician ode by the poet (performed on the occasion of Pythian Games of 498 B.C., when Pindar was only 20 years old), celebrates the victory of Hippocles in the boys' double race (*diaulos*). The ode was commissioned by Thorax (a friend or companion, *hetairos*, of the victor, according to the ancient Scholia 8a and 99a), lord of Larisa, and descendant of the Aleuades dynasty. The Aleuades of Thessaly, as the Heracleides of Sparta are all descendants of Heracles, who in his turn is the descendent of Perseus by his father Amphitryon's side. Thus, the mention of both dynasties at the beginning of the ode "Happy Lacedaemon, blessed Thessaly," as well as the mythological *exemplum* of the ode[57]—which refers to Perseus' travel to the Hyperboreans—is more than fitting. This mythological *exemplum* includes the reference to a hecatomb of asses—known mainly from later sources—[58] in honor of Apollo, a god particularly associated with the land of the Hyperboreans.[59] In the following passage,[60] the glory that Phricias (the father of the victorious boy) receives, although raises him to the heights of blessedness (*eudaimonia*), cannot be compared, of course,

[56]ll. 23–30.

[57]The Scholiast calls it an "absurd digression" (ἄλογος παρέκβασις). On the function of myth in Pindar's *Pyth.* 10, see Köhnken, *Die Funktion des Mythos*, 158–187.

[58]Callimachus, frr. 187 and 188 (ed. Schneider) and Simmias of Rhodes *apud* Antoninus Liberalis, *Metam.* 20 (ed. Martini).

[59]On the testimony of Hecataeus, see Diod. Sic. ii. 47, as well as fr. 5 (*F.H.G.* III, 387), Aelian, *Hist. anim.* xi, 1. See also Krappe," Ἀπόλλων Ὄνος," 223–234.

[60]*Pyth.* 10, 21–44.

to the fate of Perseus, who aided by Athena, reached the land of the Hyperboreans in a magical way (flying, as some suppose[61]), and attended their feasts and their sacrifices. Here is the story:

[…] θεὸς εἴη
ἀπήμων κέαρ: εὐδαίμων δὲ καὶ ὑμνητὸς οὗτος ἀνὴρ γίγνεται σοφοῖς,
ὃς ἂν χερσὶν ἢ ποδῶν ἀρετᾷ κρατήσαις
τὰ μέγιστ' ἀέθλων ἕλῃ τόλμᾳ τε καὶ σθένει,

καὶ ζώων ἔτι νεαρὸν
κατ' αἶσαν υἱὸν ἴδῃ τυχόντα στεφάνων Πυθίων.
ὁ χάλκεος οὐρανὸς οὔ ποτ' ἀμβατὸς αὐτῷ.
ὅσαις δὲ βροτὸν ἔθνος ἀγλαΐαις ἁπτόμεσθα, περαίνει πρὸς ἔσχατον
πλόον. ναυσὶ δ' οὔτε πεζὸς ἰὼν κεν εὕροις
ἐς Ὑπερβορέων ἀγῶνα θαυματὰν ὁδόν

παρ' οἷς ποτε Περσεὺς ἐδαίσατο λαγέτας,
δώματ' ἐσελθών,
κλειτὰς ὄνων ἑκατόμβας ἐπιτόσσαις θεῷ
ῥέζοντας: ὧν θαλίαις ἔμπεδον
εὐφαμίαις τε μάλιστ' Ἀπόλλων
χαίρει, γελᾷ θ' ὁρῶν ὕβριν ὀρθίαν κνωδάλων.

Μοῖσα δ' οὐκ ἀποδαμεῖ
τρόποις ἐπὶ σφετέροισι: παντᾷ, δὲ χοροὶ παρθένων
λυρᾶν τε βοαὶ καναχαί τ' αὐλῶν δονέονται:
δάφνᾳ τε χρυσέᾳ κόμας ἀναδήσαντες εἰλαπινάζοισιν εὐφρόνως
νόσοι δ' οὔτε γῆρας οὐλόμενον κέκραται
ἱερᾷ γενεᾷ: πόνων δὲ καὶ μαχᾶν ἄτερ

οἰκέοισι φυγόντες
ὑπέρδικον Νέμεσιν. […]

To be without grief
of heart is to be god; but blessed,
worthy the poet's song, is the man
who by excellence of hand and speed in his feet

[61] Barkhuizen, "Une note sur Pindare," 169–170.

takes by strength and daring the highest of prizes,

living yet, sees his son
in the turn of his youth reaping Pythian garlands.
He cannot walk in the brazen sky, but among
those goods that we of mortality attain to he goes
the whole way. Never on foot or ship could you find
the marvelous road to the feast of the- Hyperboreans.

Perseus came to them once, a leader of men,
entered their houses,
found them making hecatombs of asses
to Apollo, who in their joyance and favorable
speech rejoices, and smiles[62] to see
the rampant lust of the lewd beasts.

Never the Muse is absent
from their ways: lyres clash, and the flutes cry,
and everywhere maiden choruses whirling.
They bind their hair in golden laurel and take their holiday.
Neither disease nor bitter old age is mixed
in their sacred blood; far from labor and battle

they live; they escape Nemesis,
the over just.[63]

The blessedness of the Hyperboreans doesn't equal immortality,[64] but a privileged treatment from the part of the gods, comparable to that of the Ethiopians in Homer, who often host the gods in their feasts and sacrifices. They might offer hospitality to gods and semi-gods, but they are still mortals. They are situated at the limits of the world, at the border between myth and reality, there where poetry is also found,[65] since "the Muse is not absent from their customs." A poet's creation themselves, sharing the characteristics of Hesiod's "golden race," are connected in

[62]The Greek text has *γελᾷ* ('laughs') and not *μειδιᾷ* ('smiles') as Lattimore translates.

[63]Trans. by Richmond Lattimore.

[64]Brown, "The Hyperboreans," 95–107.

[65]Péron, "Le Pays des Hyperboréens," 68–71.

the poetic tradition with two heroes/semi-gods, Perseus and Heracles.[66] In our poem, Perseus returns from their mythical land carrying with him the "death of stone," the head of Medusa.[67]

The mythological example that frames the reference to the sacrifice of asses introduces the description of a divine Epiphany: Apollo, present in the sacrifice, rejoices with the offerings and laughs amused by the asses' ithyphallism,[68] a ritual element but also a proverbial asset of this particular animal.[69] The god's laughter reveals his approval for the sacrifice, but it also works as a reminder of the circle of death and rebirth in the physical world (where the "erect arrogance" of the sacrificial victim becomes the symbol of fertility).

The connection of Apollo to the sacrifice of asses is testified by an epigraph from Delphi[70] dated at 380 B.C., listing the asses among the *hiereia* (sacrificial victims) offered to the god. The ass, usually associated with Dionysus,[71] is known to cult practices already from the Mycenaean period,[72] but it has probably Near Eastern origins (the ass is a fertility daemon in Egyptian religion, associated with the goddess Taweret; in Egyptian cult practices, though, it is never sacrificed but participates in other fertility rites). The chthonic nature of the ass[73] explains its role in the Orphic-Dionysian tradition, where the sexual element is particularly prominent (in the *phallophoria* of the Dionysian procession, an effeminate Dionysus mounts an ass amidst erect phalluses). As in the asses'

---

[66]Cf. Pindar, *Ol.* 3, 18–32.

[67]The same myth is found in Pindar's *Pythian* 12, but without a reference to the Hyperboreans.

[68]See Hoffmann, "*ΥΒΡΙΝ ΟΡΘΙΑΝ ΚΝΩΔΑΛΩΝ*", 61–73 (esp. 63–64), Rose, *Sons of the Gods*, 181–182 ff.

[69]This anatomical detail connects the ass to the satyrs, as Lissarague, "The Sexual Life of Satyrs", 55 observes, and is particularly stressed to provoke laughter. For the depiction of asses or asses and satyrs on vases, see Hoffmann (Footnote 10 above) and Davies, "Asses and Rams," 169–183.

[70]Boeckh, *C.I.G.* I, 807 (l. 14), Cook, "Animal Worship", 81–102, Farnell, *The Works of Pindar*, on *Pyth.* 10 *ad loc*, etc.

[71]See Keuls, "The ass in the cult of Dionysus", 41–70.

[72]A Mycenean fresco's piece [now exhibit no. 2683 at Athens' National Archaeological Museum—see M. Tsountas, *Εφημερίς Αρχαιολογική* (1887) 160–161, ill. X] depicts a procession of "ass-headed daemons," now known as "Minoan daemons," associated with the Egyptian goddess Taweret. For onomorphic paintings of men in vases, see Davies, "Asses and Rams," 176–177, n. 18 (with bibliography).

[73]See Gildersleeve, *Pindar*, on *Pyth.* 10 *ad loc*.

hecatomb in honor of Apollo in our passage, or as in the sacrifice of asses in honor of the god Priapus (with whom the onomorphic or ass-looking Apollo Priapaeus is connected, according to Krappe[74]), violence (even sacrificial violence) is alleviated—as Burkert remarked—[75] by laughter. And what generates laughter is in this case—as in the case of the incident between Demeter and Baubo—[76]the sight of the genitals within the context of a ritual, in this case a sacrificial ritual.

* * *

Sympotic, derisory or aggressive, erotic and ritual are the aspects of laughter discussed in the above passages. These are not clear-cut distinctions (far less "categories") of ancient Greek lyric laughter: the sympotic *decorum* implies a moral "tint," while derision might become a means for harsh social or political criticism. The "erotic" laughter in Sappho defines in a way her poetics, while the ritual context of Apollo's laughter in Pindar's *Pythian* 10 indicates a "fluidity" between a sacrificial and a fertility rite, as well as the *euphrosyne* ("mirth") which usually accompanies a feast or a *symposion.*[77] All these aspects of lyric laughter resurface in later Greek literature either as *mimesis* (in Hellenistic literature) or as a means to illustrate an argument (in philosophy or oratory) or enhance the vividness of a narrative (in history). This *metapoiesis* of lyric laughter introduces the first theoretical approaches to the phenomenon from the

[74]"*Ἀπόλλων Ὄνος*", 223–234.

[75]*Homo Necans*, 68–72.

[76]On Baubo see Chronopoulos, "*Homeric Hymn to Demeter* 169–210," in Yossi and Melista, *Exaisioi Gelwtes*, passage 75, 613–632 (esp. 625–630).

[77]Another common word to describe this *euphoria* is *γηθοσύνη* (or the verb *γηθέω*), usually in instances where the gods are involved. In Theognis, 9–10, for example, the wide Earth and the deep Sea laugh and rejoice at the birth of Apollo *ἐγέλασσε δὲ Γαῖα πελώρη,/γήθησεν δὲ βαθὺς πόντος ἁλὸς πολιῆς* (see Yossi and Melista, *Exaisioi Gelwtes*, fr. 126, 1021–1024). In the *Homeric Hymn to Apollo* 205–206 the term used for this kind of 'mirth' and 'rejoicing' is *ἐπιτέρπονται* ("Golden-haired Leto and Zeus of wise counsel rejoice at their beloved son [Apollo] playing music and dancing among the immortal gods").

point of view of ethics, poetics, and rhetoric,[78] while more emphasis is now given to the notion of *γελοῖον* rather than *γέλως* itself.

Mary J. Yossi (Athens)

Select Bibliography

Aloni, Antonio. "Elegy. Forms, functions and communication," in *Budelmann* (2009): 168–188.

Bain, David M. "Semonides 7.75—The Locomotion of the Ape-Woman," *LCM* 8 (1983): 93–94.

Barkhuizen, John H. "Une note sur Pindare, *Pyth.* X, 28–31," *AClass* 12 (1969): 169–170.

Bielohlawek, K."Gastmahls- und Symposionslehren bei griechischen Dichtern. (Von Homer bis Theognissammlung und Kritias)," *WS* 58 (1940): 11–30 [= Vetta *Poesia e simposio*, 95–116].

Bowie, Ewen."The *Theognidea*: A Step Toards a Collection of Fragments?" in Most, *Collecting Fragments* (1977): 53–66.

Bowie, Ewen. "Early Greek Elegy, Symposium and Public Festival," *JHS* CVI (1986): 13–35.

Brown, Christopher. "The Hyperboreans and Nemesis in Pindar's Tenth Pythian," *Phoenix* 46, no. 2 (1992): 95–107.

Brown, Cristopher. "Iambos: Introduction, Archilochus, Semonides, Hipponax," στο Gerber (ed.), *A Companion to the Greek Lyric Poets* (1997): 11–88.

Budelmann, Felix, ed. *The Cambridge Companion to Greek Lyric*. Cambridge, 2009.

Burkert, Walter. *Homo Necans. The Anthropology of Ancient Greek Sacrificial Ritual and Myth.* Translation P. Bing. Berkeley, Los Angeles, and London, 1983.

Campbell, David. "Flutes and Elegiac Couplets," *JHS* 84 (1964): 63–68.

Carey, Chris. "Iambos," in Budelman. *The Cambridge Companion to Greek Lyric* (2009): 149–167.

---

[78]See Sections III (laughter and ethics), X (poetics and rhetoric of laughter) and XI (*geloion* as *atopon* in oratory and philosophy) in Yossi and Melista, *Exaisioi Gelwtes*, with discussion of selected passages.

Carrière, Jean. *Théognis de Mégare. Étude sur le recueil élégiaque attribué à ce poète*. Paris, 1948.
Cerri, Giovanni. "Frammento di teoria musicale e di ideologia simposiale in un distico di Teognide (v. 1041 sg.): il ruolo paradossale dell" auleta. La fonte probabile di G. Pascoli, *Solon* 13–15," *QUCC* 21–22 (1976): 25–38.
Chronopoulos, Stelios. "*Homeric Hymn to Demeter* 169–210," in Yossi and Melista (eds.), *Exaisioi Gelwtes*, passage 75 (2017): 613–632.
Colesanti, Giulio. "Dittografie e Scambi simposiali nel *corpus* Teognideo," *Athenaeum* 89, no. 2 (2001): 459–495.
Cook, Albert B. "Animal Worship in the Mycenean Age, 1. The Cult of the Ass," *JHS* 14 (1894): 81–102.
Davies, Mark. "Asses and Rams: Dionysiac Release in Aristophanes" *Wasps* and Attic Vase-Painting," *Mètis* 5, nos. 1–2 (1990): 169–183.
De Martino, Francesco and Vox, Onofrio, eds. *Lirica Greca*. Bari, 1996.
Desclos, Marie-Laurence, ed. *Le rire des Grecs. Anthropologie du rire en Grèce ancienne*. Grenoble, 2000.
Farnell, Lewis R. *The Works of Pindar*, vol. II: *Critical Commentary*. [London 1932], Amsterdam, 1965.
Ferrari, Franco. *Teognide. Elegie*. Milano, 1989.
Ferrari, Franco. *Una mitra per Kleis, Saffo e il suo publico*. Biblioteca di "Materiali e discussioni per l"analisi dei testi classici" 19. Pisa, 2007.
Fiqueira, Thomas and Nagy, Gregory, eds. *Theognis of Megara. Poetry and the* Polis. Baltimore and London, 1985.
Forsdyke, Sara. "Street Theatre and Popular Justice in Ancient Greece: Shaming, Stoning and Starving Offenders inside and outside the Courts," *Past and Present* 201, no. 1 (2008): 3–50.
Gentili, Bruno and Prato, C., eds. *Poetae Elegiaci* I. Leipzig, 1979.
Gerber, Douglas E., ed. *A Companion to the Greek Lyric Poets*. Leiden, 1997.
Gildersleeve, Basil K. *Pindar: The Olympian and Pythian Odes* [New York 1890], Amsterdam, 1965.
Halperin, David. M. Winkler John J. and Zeitlin, Froma I., eds. *Before Sexuality. The Construction of Erotic Experience in the Ancient Greek World*. Princeron, 1990.
Halliwell, Stephen. *Greek Laughter. A Study of Cultural Psychology from Homer to Early Christianity*. Cambridge and New York, 2008.
Hoffmann, Herbert. "ΥΒΡΙΝ ΟΡΘΙΑΝ ΚΝΩΔΑΛΩΝ," in *Antidoron. Festschrift für J. Thimme* (1983): 61–73.
Hubbard, Thomas K. "Elemental Psychology and the Date of Semonides of Amorgos." *AJP* 115, no. 2 (1994): 175–197.

Kakridis, Ioannis Th. "*Come, Aphrodite, Crowned with flowers*" (= *Έλα, Αφροδίτη, ανθοστεφανωμένη*), Athens, 1983.
Karadagli, Triantaphyllia. *Fabel und Ainos. Studien zu griechischen Fabel*, Köningstein, 1981.
Karamalengou, Eleni and Makrygianni, Eugenia, eds. *Αντιφίλησις. Studies on Classical, Byzantine and Modern Greek Literature in Honour of John-Theophanes A. Papademetriou*. Stuttgart, 2009.
Keuls, Eva C. "The Ass in the Cult of Dionysus as a Symbol of Toil and Suffering," in *Painter and Poet in Ancient Greece: Iconography and the Literary Arts*. Stuttgart/Leipzig (1997): 41–70.
Köhnken, Adolf. *Die Funktion des Mythos bei Pindar*. Berlin, 1971.
Konstantakos, Ioannis M. *Akicharos. The Story of Ahicar in Ancient Grrece* (= *Ἀκίχαρος. Ἡ* Διήγηση τοῦ Ἀχικάρ *στὴν Ἀρχαία Ἑλλάδα*), 2 vols. Athens, 2008.
Krappe, Alexander H. "*Απόλλων Όνος*," *CP* 42 (1947): 223–234.
Lanata, Guliana. "Sul linguaggio amoroso di Saffo," *QUCC* 2 (1966): 257–267.
Lattimore, Richmond. "Notes on Greek Poetry," *AJP* 65 (1944): 172–175.
Lattimore, Richmond. *Greek Lyrics*. Chicago 1960.[2]
Lissarague, Francois. "The Sexual Life of Satyrs," in Halperin et al. *Before Sexuality* (1990): 53–81.
Lloyd-Jones, Hugh. *Females of the Species. Semonides on Women*. London, 1975.
Melista, Alexandra. "Galen, *De usu partibus* I 58, 13–60 and I 194, 7–22 Helmreich," in Yossi and Melista, *Exaisioi Gelwtes*, passage 42, 327–338.
Melista, Alexandra. "Aristotle, *De partibus animalium* 673a 2–31," in Yossi and Melista, *Exaisioi Gelwtes*, passage 99 (2017): 798–811.
Meuli, Karl. *Gesammelte Schriften* I-II. Basel–Stuttgart, 1975.
Most, Glen W. *Collecting Fragments—Fragmenete sammeln*. Göttingen, 1997.
Myrray, Oswyn, ed. *Sympotica. A Symposium on the Symposion*. Oxford, 1990.
Nagy, Gregory. "Theognis and Megara: A Poet's Vision of his City," in Fiqueira and Nagy (eds.), *Theognis of Megara*, 222–281.
Page, Denys L. *Sappho and Alcaeus. An Introduction to the Study of Ancient Lesbian Poetry*. Oxford, 1955.
Pellizer, Aetius–Tedeschi, Ianuarius., eds. *Semonides. Testimonia et Fragmenta*. Roma, 1990.
Pellizer, Ezio. "Outlines of a Morphology of Sympotic Entertainment," in Murray (ed.) (1990): 177–184.
Peretti, Aurelio. *Teognide nella tradizione gnomologica*. Pisa, 1953.

Péron, Jacques. "Le Pays des Hyperboréens," in *Les images maritimes de Pindare*, Études et Commentaires 87, Paris (1974): 68–71.

Reitzenstein, Richard. *Epigram und Skolion*. Giessen, 1893.

Rose, Peter W. *Sons of the Gods, Children of Earth. Ideology and Literary Form in Ancient Greece*. Ithaca and London, 1992.

Rossi, Luigi. "Il simposio greco arcaico e classico come spettacolo a se stesso," στο *Spettacoli conviviali dall"antichità classica alle corte italiane del "400: Atti del VII convegno di studio*, Viterbo (1983): 41–50.

Schear L. "Semonides Fr. 7: Wives and their Husbands." *EMC* 28 (1984): 39–49.

Schmitt Pantel, Pauline. "Sacrificial Meal and *Symposion*: Two Models of Civic Institutions in the Archaic City?" in Murray (ed.) (1990): 14–33.

Scodel, Ruth. *Listening to Homer. Tradition, Narrative, and Audience*, Ann Arbor, 2002.

Segal, Charles. "¨Eros and Incantation¨: Sappho and Oral Poetry," *Arethusa* 7, no. 2 (1974): 139–160.

Skiadas, Aristoxenos D. *Archaic Lyric Poetry* (= *Αρχαϊκός Λυρισμός*). Athens, vol. 1. 1979 and vol. 2, 1981.

Slater, William J. "Peace, the Symposium and the Poet," *ICS* 1–2 (1981): 205–214.

Stehle, Eva Marie. *Performance and Gender in Ancient Greece*. Princeton, 1997.

Steiner, Deborah. "Fables and Frames: The Poetics and Politics of Animal Fables in Hesiod, Archilochus, and the Aesopica," *Arethusa* 45, no. 1 (2012): 1–41.

Steiner, Deborah. "Making Monkeys: Archilochus frr. 185–7 *in* Performance," in V. Cazatto, A. M. P. H. Lardinois, R. Martin and A.-E. Peponi (eds.), *The Look* of *Lyric*: *Greek Song* and the *Visual*. Leiden, 2014.

Van Dijk, Gert–Jan. *Αἶνοι, Λόγοι, Μῦθοι. Fables in Archaic, Classical, and Hellenistic Greek Literature*. Leiden, New York and Köln, 1997.

Van Groningen, Bernhard A. *Théognis: Le premier livre*. Amsterdam, 1966.

Vetta, Massimo. *Theognis: elegiarum liber secundus*. Roma, 1980.

Vetta, Massimo, ed. *Poesia e simposio nella Grecia antica*. Roma–Bari, 1995.[2]

West, Martin L. *Studies in Greek Elegy and Iambus*. Berlin, 1974.

West, Martin L. *Iambi et Elegi Graeci* I. Oxford, 1989.[2]

Winkler, John J. "Double consciousness in Sappho's Lyrics," in *The Constraints of Desire. The Anthropology of Sex and Gender in Ancient Greece*. New York (1990): 162–187.

Yossi, Mary J. "*δεῦρο σὺν αὐλητῆρι.* Sympotic Poetics in the Theognidean Corpus" [= «*δεῦρο σὺν αὐλητῆρι.* Συμποτική ποιητική στο Θεογνίδειο corpus»], in Karamalengou and Makrygianni (eds.) (2009): 99–106.
Yossi, Mary J. and Melista, Alexandra D. eds., *Exaisioi Gelwtes. Laughter in Ancient Greek Literature* [= *Εξαίσιοι Γέλωτες. Το γέλιο στην αρχαία ελληνική γραμματεία*], Athens, 2017.
Young, Douglas. *Theognis.* Lipsiae, 1961.
Young, Douglas. "Borrowings and Self-Adaptations in Theognis," in *Miscellanea Critica.* Leipzig (1964): 307–390.

Ludic Music in Ancient Greek and Roman Theater

Timothy J. Moore

It would be hard to overestimate the degree to which theater in ancient Greece and Rome was musical theater. Visual and literary evidence together reveal that virtually all theatrical performances of the ancient world, from the proto-tragedies and comedies of archaic Greece through the pantomimes of late antiquity, included accompaniment by a two-piped, double reed instrument, called *aulos* in Greek, *tibia* in Latin.[1] The instrument and its player, the *auletes* or *tibicen*, appear conspicuously

[1] Peter Wilson, The Musicians among the Actors, in *Greek and Roman Actors: Aspects of an Ancient Profession*, eds. Pat Easterling and Edith Hall (Cambridge: Cambridge University Press, 2002), 39–68.

T. J. Moore (✉)
Washington University, St. Louis, MO, USA
e-mail: tmoore26@wustl.edu

V. Rapti and E. Gordon (eds.), *Ludics*,
https://doi.org/10.1007/978-981-15-7435-1_9

in portrayals of every theatrical genre in nearly every period,[2] and they are mentioned repeatedly both within plays and when ancient authors describe theatrical performances. Long wistfully dismissed as something we can know practically nothing about, Greek and Roman theatrical music has come into its own in the last decades, participating in an exciting explosion of work on ancient music in general. Our expanded appreciation and knowledge of the music of the ancient theater allow us to discover in new ways the profoundly ludic aspect of much of that music.

Although almost no written melodies survive from ancient plays,[3] we can tell a great deal about ancient theatrical music from the meter of its verses. We know from various sources that one meter, the iambic trimeter, usually called the iambic senarius when referring to Latin plays of the Roman Republic, was as a rule spoken by actors without the accompaniment of the *aulos*/ *tibia*. When playwrights used other meters, actors usually sang or chanted while the *auletes*/*tibicen* played.[4] We can thus determine from the texts of our plays which parts of the plays were performed musically and which were not. Meter also tells us much about the rhythms performed on the ancient stage. Greek and Latin meters are quantitative: they are based on patterns of long and short syllables rather than, like most English meters, on patterns of stress. Because it took about twice as long to sing a short syllable as a long syllable, we are justified in treating a long syllable, marked "–," like our quarter note, and a short syllable, marked "⏑," like our eighth note. Using this equivalence, we can reproduce the basic rhythmic patterns of all ancient theatrical songs.

---

[2]Some examples of the *aulos*/*tibia* shown accompanying or associated with theatrical performances in ancient art: Taplin (2007, 30–31), figures 9, 10, and 12 (Greek tragedy and satyr play); Taplin (1993, 102–104 and plate 24.28) (Greek comedy); Moore (2012, 32), figure 1 (Roman comedy), Dunbabin (2016, 32), figure 2.12a (Roman imperial theater); Bieber (1961, 180), figure 629 (pantomime).

[3]Pöhlmann and West (2001) contains a few exceptions.

[4]Timothy J. Moore, "When Did the *Tibicen* Play? Meter and Musical Accompaniment in Roman Comedy" (*Transactions of the American Philological Association,* 2008), 138: 3–46.

Ancient theatrical music contributes in important ways to some of the most serious moments of ancient drama. To offer just one example, the music of Euripides' *Medea* begins as the title character, singing, or chanting a meter called anapests, laments her fate from off stage[5]:

> – –
>
> ἰώ,
>
> – – ˘ ˘ – ˘ ⏓ ˘ ˘ –
>
> δύστανος ἐγὼ μελέα τε πόνων,
>
> – – – – – ˘ ˘ – –
>
> ἰώ μοί μοι, πῶς ἂν ὀλοίμαν; (96-97)
>
> Oh! I'm so unhappy and wretched in my sufferings! Oh my pain, my pain! How might I perish?

In most Greek plays, members of the chorus start the music: that is, usually it is the chorus who first performs in a meter other than iambic trimeter. Euripides, as his career progressed, would more and more have characters other than the chorus begin plays' music, but the practice appears to have been quite rare when *Medea* was first produced in 431BCE[6]; and there is no parallel for the introduction of music by a character who is off stage, as Medea is.

The strikingly unusual nature of this first music would encourage spectators to recall it as other characters echo Medea's anapests throughout the play: first the nurse delivers anapests (99), and then the chorus, both at their first entrance (131) and in three of their choral interludes (357, 759, 1081). Finally, Jason begins the last music of the play with more anapests, as he curses Medea for killing his children:

---

[5]Donald J. Mastronarde, *Euripides Medea* (Cambridge: Cambridge University Press, ed. 2002).

[6]A character other than the chorus performs the first meters other than iambic trimeter in Euripides' *Alcestis*, *Andromache*, *Electra*, *Hecuba*, *Helen*, *Hippolytus*, *Ion*, *Iphigenia at Aulis*, *Orestes*, *Phoenissae*, and *Troades*; in Sophocles' *Electra*; and in *Prometheus Bound* attributed to Aeschylus. All these plays except *Alcestis* and perhaps *Prometheus Bound* were first produced after *Medea*.

– ⏑ ⏑ –– ⏑⏑ –⏑ ⏑ –

ἀλλά σ' Ἐρινὺς ὀλέσειε τέκνων

⏑⏑ – ⏑ ⏑ –

φονία τε Δίκη. (1389-1390)

But may the Fury of your children and bloody Justice destroy you!

The basic building block of anapestic meters is the anapest: ⏑ ⏑ –, equivalent to two eighth notes followed by a quarter note. A long syllable can substitute for the two short syllables, yielding – – , and the initial pattern can be reversed, yielding – ⏑ ⏑. On very rare occasions the basic unit consists of four consecutive short syllables: ⏑⏑⏑⏑. Regardless of which variation is used, every basic musical unit—an anapest or its equivalent—will be equivalent to a 2/4 measure in our time: all units are of the same length, and all units can be divided into even halves. Such steadiness, while taken for granted in most modern Western music, was rare in ancient theatrical music. Almost every other meter used on the ancient Greek and Roman stage has basic units that cannot be divided into even halves and that vary in length. Typical, for example, is the cretic, a meter we will encounter often in this essay: –⏑–. This basic unit, equivalent to two quarter notes and an eighth note, cannot be divided into even halves; and since playwrights sometimes substituted a long syllable for the central short syllable, yielding – – –, passages in cretics regularly contain units of different lengths.

Jacqueline Dangel has observed of anapests used by the Roman playwright Seneca that their steadiness lends itself to a feeling of inexorability.[7] The same is true of anapests in Greek drama: the rhythm, continuing without variations in the size or divisibility of basic units, reinforces a sense that the action of the play is moving unwaveringly

[7]Jacqueline Dangel, "Sénèque, *poeta fabricator*: Lyrique chorale et évidence tragique." In *Le poète architecte: Arts métriques et art poétique latins*, ed. Jacqueline Dangel (Louvain: Peeters, 2001), 214–216.

toward its conclusion. The repeated anapests in this play thus underline the terrifying progress of Medea's successful quest for vengeance as it leads to the deaths of Jason's new bride and father-in-law and even her own children.

For all its serious possibilities, however, ancient theatrical music is inherently ludic, for it introduces to the theatrical performance, itself a ludic phenomenon, a further element of playfulness, beyond what is required for the presentation of a plot. In what follows I will look briefly at three moments of Greek theatrical music where its ludic element is most conspicuous. Two involve the first music of a play, where music provides the most effective possible jolt, thrusting the audience and the characters into a world of play. In the third, the silliest of music crowns a profoundly ludic theatrical scene. I will then provide a closer analysis of the music of Plautus' *Mostellaria*, where the playfulness of ancient theatrical music reaches one of its highest peaks.

It is no surprise to find that the music of Greek comedy is playful. In Aristophanes' *Frogs* the combination of music and play gains special thematic significance. When the play begins, the god Dionysus is on his way to the underworld to bring back to earth the now-dead tragic playwright Euripides. As he rows across a lake into Hades, he is serenaded by a chorus of frogs, who begin as follows[8]:

[8]Jeffrey Henderson, *Aristophanes: Frogs, Assemblywomen, Wealth* (Cambridge: Harvard University Press, ed. 2002).

⏑ ⏑ ⏑ – ⏑ – ⏑ –

Βρεκεκεκὲξ κοὰξ κοάξ,

⏑ ⏑ ⏑ – ⏑ – ⏑ –

βρεκεκεκὲξ κοὰξ κοάξ·

– – ⏑ – – ⏑ ⏑

λιμναῖα κρηνῶν τέκνα,

⏑ – ⏑ – – ⏑ –

ξύναυλον ὕμνων βοὰν

– – ⏑ – – ⏑ ⏑ –

φθεγξώμεθ', εὔγηρυν ἐμὰν

⏑ – – ⏑ – ⏑ –

ἀοιδάν, κοὰξ κοάξ (209-214).

Brekekekex koax koax

Brekekekex koax koax

Let us, the marshy children of the springs,

sing a shout of hymns along with the *aulos*,

my sweet-sounding song, koax koax.

This opening chorus is unique in several ways. First, all the other extant plays of Aristophanes start their music not with lyrics, but with one of the meters that have become known as "recitative" meters: trochaic tetrameters, iambic tetrameters, or so-called "marching anapests." Most scholars have assumed that when these meters were performed the mode of vocal utterance was closer to what we would call chanting than to what we would call song.[9] Aristophanes' frogs, on the other hand, sing lyric meters, which most scholars have assumed were performed in a manner close to or equivalent to what we would call song. This distinction between song and chant may not be as clear-cut as most have assumed; but we can be sure that the lyrics were rhythmically more complex than the so-called recitative meters, and it is likely that their melodic complexity was also greater.

[9] Pickard-Cambridge (1968, 156–165).

Second, the music of most Aristophanic plays begins as a character, a member of the chorus, or the entire chorus stirs the chorus to action: to search for the criminal Dikaiopolis in *Acharnians* (204), for example, or to come and find out about Chremylus' plans in *Wealth* (253). Here the frogs do not urge themselves to do anything, but simply rejoice in being frogs, celebrating, as they do, the joy they bring through their music. They boast that they are dear to the Muses, to Pan who plays the panpipes, and to Apollo who plays the lyre (229–234). They also, uniquely, turn out not to be "the" chorus of the play at all: they are never heard again after this song.

Finally, the frog's singing leads to a bizarre contest between Dionysus and the chorus. Complaining about the pain caused by his rowing, Dionysus asks the frogs to stop singing, in meters distinct from those used by the frogs. When they refuse to stop, he claims that he can out sing them, and he ends the song by picking up the frogs' meter and singing his own "brekekekex koax koax" (267).[10]

The unusual features of this chorus result in large part from the scene's determined sense of play. On the face of it, nothing could be more somber than Hades; and Dionysus, for all the farce of the play's first scenes, is nevertheless on a serious quest: to retrieve Euripides, whom he thinks can save a very troubled Athens. He remains serious as the song begins. Rowing earnestly and with much complaining, he finds the frogs' frivolity unacceptable. But then he is himself drawn into the frogs' playful musical world. He competes with them on their own terms, picking up their rhythms and even their words, and probably their melodies as well. He claims ultimately to have won the contest with the frogs (268), and indeed the frogs stop singing after Dionysus' final "brekekekex koax koax." But in fact, the frogs have not been defeated. Before their song began, Charon told Dionysus that the frogs would help Dionysus row to Hades (205–206). They stop now not because Dionysus has bested them, but because Dionysus has reached the other side of their lake, and they have accomplished their purpose. With their emphatically unserious song, they have made clear to Dionysus and to the audience

[10]On the metrical competition, see Zimmermann (1985, 155–168) and Parker (1997, 456–466).

that Aristophanes' Hades will be not Homer's gloomy afterlife, but a place of fun.[11]

One could argue that satyr play is all about the ludic. As the fourth play in the tetralogy a tragic playwright would produce as one day's fare in a theatrical festival, the satyr play gives playwright, performers, and audience an opportunity to play after the seriousness of the three tragedies that preceded it. And indeed, we find some conspicuously ludic music in the remains of this genre. The fragments of Sophocles' *Ichneutai* offer another good example of a play's initial music propelling the audience and characters into the world of play. *Ichneutai*'s music begins as the chorus of satyrs enters searching for Apollo's stolen cattle: Apollo has promised their father, Silenus, that he will reward them with freedom if they find them. They begin as follows[12]:

˘ ˘˘

ἴθ' ἄγε δ[. .]

˘ ˘ –

πόδα βά[. .]

˘ ˘ ˘

ἀπαπαπ[. .]

– – ˘ –

ὢ ὤ, σέ τοι [. .]

˘ ˘˘ –

ἔπιθι κλωπ[..] (64-68)

Come on, go…

Your foot and your step…

Apapap…!

Oh! Oh! You…

Go... the thief…

---

[11]On the importance of the frogs to the play's comic tone, cf. Campbell (1984). For other explanations of the frogs and their song, see, e.g., Moorton (1989, 311–317) (the frogs contribute to Dionysus' initiation) and Corbel-Morana (2012, 235–239) (the frogs' song is a parody of contemporary dithyramb).

[12]Stefan Radt, "*Tragicorum Graecorum Fragmenta*" (Göttingen: Vandenhoeck & Ruprecht, ed. 1977), *Vol. 4: Sophocles.*

Much of the satyrs' song, like these opening verses, is fragmentary; but the papyrus eventually yields some full verses:

˘ ˘˘ ˘˘ ˘ ˘˘ ˘˘ –

ξὺν ἅμα θεὸς ὁ φίλος ἀνέτω

˘ – ˘ – – ˘– – ˘

πόνους, προφήνας ἀρίζηλα

˘ – ˘ ˘ – ˘ ˘

χρυσοῦ πα[ρ]αδείγματα. (76-78)

At the same time let the dear god let loose

our toils, he who has displayed

such clear examples of gold.

These last verses, and almost certainly most, if not all, of the fragmentary verses that precede it, include an exceptionally erratic meter called dochmiacs. Dochmiacs are the most emotional of Greek dramatic meters, used frequently at moments such as Cassandra's raving in Aeschylus' *Agamemnon* (1072–1177), Creon's laments after the death of Haemon in Sophocles' *Antigone* (1261–1346), and the chorus responding to Medea's murder of her children in Euripides (1251–1292). Dochmiacs are, as A. M. Dale has pointed out, peculiarly tragic (1968, 113). Here the satyrs, cavorting about in their lewd costumes, overwhelmed by the prospect of a reward from Apollo, are far removed from tragedy. The contrast between music and context makes the playful inversion of tragic seriousness as emphatic as it can be.[13]

Another exceptionally ludic genre was the mime, where farce consistently triumphed over any seriousness. Almost no theatrical mimes survive from the ancient world, but in the fragments of one mime from the Roman empire preserved on papyrus we can see well how music contributed to mime's playfulness (the mime is called the "Charition mime" after its leading character). The mime is a parody of Euripides' *Iphigenia among the Taurians*, in which several Greek characters escape from a group of Indians. They do so by getting the Indian king and his

[13]On the contrast between this chorus of searching satyrs and the searching choruses of tragedy, see Zagagi (1999, 188–194).

entourage drunk. The words of the papyrus are supplemented by several kinds of marks, most of which are almost certainly cues for musical instruments: an *aulos*, *crotala* (hand clappers), and a *tympanon*.[14] The instrumental interjections reach a climax as the drunk Indians indulge in a wild dance accompanied by gibberish meant to sound like an Indian language, transliterated here along with the stage directions[15]:

> KING: Zabede. (*crotala; sound from aulos*) Zabiligidoumba.
>
> INDIANS: Aba oun [...]
>
> KING: Panoumbretikatemanousambretououeni.
>
> INDIANS: Panoumbretikatemanousambretououeni.
>
> Panoumbretikatemanouambretououeni.
>
> Olusadizapardapiskoupiskatemanareiman [...]
>
> ridaou. (*crotala; sound from aulos*) oupatei ... a. (*crotala*; *sound from tibia; five crashes from tympanon*) (82-87).

This highly musical scene has been explained as a religious ritual[16]; and indeed, the combination of *aulos*, *tympanon*, and *crotala* is reminiscent of the music of Dionysian cult. Whatever its religious significance to the Indians, however, the dominant effect of this scene of wild drunken dance and nonsensical song on the audience must have been one of play.

Roman comedy was, in terms of the total percentage of performance time dedicated to accompanied song or chant, more musical than most Greek theater, and its music was decidedly ludic. Plautus' *Mostellaria* offers us ancient theatrical music at its most playful.

Mostellaria has a remarkably simple plot. Theopropides, a merchant, is off on a business trip to Egypt. While he has been gone, his young son, Philolaches, has been spending his father's money, partying night and day and buying for himself his enslaved girlfriend, Philematium. Philolaches' slave, Tranio, encourages him in this behavior. The first part of the play leads to a party on stage with Philolaches, Philematium, and their friends

---

14A round flat drum; cf. Skulimowska (1966).

15Stefania Santelia, "*Charition Liberata*" (Bari: Levante, 1991), *P. Oxy. 413*.

16Santelia, "*Charition Liberata*," 34–37.

Callidamates and Delphium. That party comes to an abrupt end when Tranio enters from the harbor with news that Theopoprides has returned home unexpectedly. Faced with this impending disaster, Tranio comes up with a plan. He persuades the returning Theopropides that the house is haunted, and he should flee. Things get complicated, however, when Theopropides and Tranio encounter a moneylender, Misargyrides, who demands interest on the money Philolaches borrowed to buy his girlfriend. Always ready to improvise, Tranio persuades Theopropides that Philolaches borrowed the money to buy the house of their next-door neighbor, Simo. He then persuades Simo that Theopropides is thinking about buying a house like Simo's and leads the two duped old men on a tour of Simo's house. The ruse can only last so long: after a pair of slaves coming to fetch Callidamates tell Theopropides the truth, Tranio takes refuge on an altar. Callidamates, as a kind of *adulescens ex machina*, saves the day when he promises to pay Philolaches' debts and persuades Theopropides to forgive both his son and his slave.

The plot summary alone suggests the degree to which *Mostellaria*, perhaps more than any other extant ancient drama, is about play for its own sake. Musical patterns reinforce the play's decidedly ludic nature. To see that ludic music in action, we will do best to begin with Roman comedy's basic tools for producing musical variety.

The key building block of Roman Comedy's music is the default meter of Roman comedy, the trochaic septenarius. This meter, which was either sung or chanted to the accompaniment of the *tibia*, might be called the meter of movement. Throughout Roman comedy, it tends to be used for progress of the plot. Here it is used in the last lines of the play, as Tranio receives a most undeserved reprieve from punishment[17]:

[17]Text and metrical analyses from Questa (1995) for polymetric passages; text from Leo (1896) for passages in other meters.

– ⏑ –– ⏑ ⏑ – – – – ⏑⏑ ⏑⏑– – ⏑–

TR. quid gravaris? quasi non cras iam commeream aliam noxiam:

⏑⏑⏑ – ⏑ – ⏑ – – ⏑⏑ ⏑ – – – ⏑ –

ibi utrumque, et hoc et illud, poteris ulcisci probe.

⏑⏑ – – ⏑ ⏑ ⏑ – – – – ⏑ –– – ⏑–

CALL. sine te exorem. TH.: age abi, abi impune. em huic habeto gratiam.

– – – – – ⏑ – – – ⏑ – – – ⏑ ⏑

spectatores, fabula haec est acta, vos plausum date. (1178-1181)

TRANIO: Why do you hesitate? As if I won't do something else to deserve punishment tomorrow. Then you can punish me beautifully for both crimes, this one and that one.

CALLIDAMATES: Let me win you over.

THEOPROPIDES: All right, go, go free. There: consider this a favor to him. Spectators, our play is over. Give us your applause.

The most conspicuous way playwrights varied musically from the trochaic septenarius was to write verses where there would be no music at all. They accomplished that, as we have seen, by writing iambic senarii, like these first lines of *Mostellaria*:

– – ⏑– – – ⏑ – – – ⏑⏑

exi e culina sis foras, mastigia,

– – – ⏑⏑ – – ⏑ – – –⏑–

qui mi inter patinas exhibes argutias. (1-2)

Get out of the kitchen, you jailbird, showing off your cleverness to me among the dishes.

The second method of variation is a move to another accompanied meter besides trochaic septenarius. Plautus uses many of these other meters, but two are especially important in *Mostellaria*. One is bacchiacs, a meter built on repetitions of a short syllable followed by two long syllables (⏑– –). As in almost all meters of Roman comedy, playwrights often substituted two short syllables for one long syllable, and sometimes they replaced the single short syllable with a long syllable. Bacchiacs are known as a rising meter: the repeated movement from the short syllable to the two long syllables gives an impression of a slight struggle to move forward, as here:

– – – – – – ˘ – – ˘ – –

auscultate, argumenta dum dico ad hanc rem: ba4

˘ – – ˘ – – ˘ – – – – –

simul gnaruris vos volo esse hanc rem mecum. (99-100)

Listen, while I tell you my arguments on this matter: I want you to be aware of this matter along with me.

The second is cretics, in which, as we saw above, the repeated pattern is a short syllable in between two long syllables (–˘–). Cretics are a falling meter. The position of the short syllable between the two long ones gives the impression of a continual falling and getting back up, as here:

˘ ˘˘ – – ˘ – – ˘ – ˘ –

melius anno hoc mihi non fuit domi, cr2crcol

– ˘ – – ˘ – – ˘ – ˘ –

nec quod una esca me iuverit magis. (690-691)

I've not had a better meal at home in more than a year,

nor one that pleased me more.

In combining these three types of musical building blocks—accompanied trochaic septenarii, other accompanied meters, and unaccompanied iambic senarii—Plautus tends to use what I call "ABC progression": more often than not, iambic senarii (A) come first, followed by one or more accompanied meters other than trochaic septenarii (B), followed by trochaic septenarii (C). Almost all plays start this way, and then the pattern is repeated with variations as the play continues. The iambic senarii often provide essential information: thus, for example, prologues are always in iambic senarii. The accompanied meters other than trochaic septenarii tend to be the plays' most ludic moments, as characters revel in self-presentation, emotion, or pure silliness. A switch to trochaic septenarii tends to suggest that after such a diversion the plot is ready to progress again (cf. Moore 2012, 253–255).

Another way the Roman comic playwrights varied their musical performance was to change between stichic and polymetric passages. In stichic passages, the same meter is repeated from line to line, as in the following passage, from a dialogue between Philematium and her maid Scapha, in a stichic meter called iambic septenarius:

– – – – – – ᵕ – – – – ᵕ ᵕ ᵕ – –

PHIL. iam pridem ecastor frigida non lavi magis lubenter

– – – ᵕ ᵕ – ᵕ ᵕ – – ᵕ ᵕ – ᵕ – ᵕ – –

nec quom me melius, mea Scapha, rear esse deficatam.

– – – – ᵕ – ᵕ – ᵕ ᵕ – – – – – ᵕ

SCA. eventus rebus omnibus, velut horno messis magna

ᵕ ᵕ ᵕ ᵕ ᵕ – ᵕ – ᵕ – – ᵕ ᵕ – – ᵕ – –

fuit. PHILE. quid ea messis attinet ad meam lavationem? (157-160)

PHILEMATIUM: Really, Scapha, it's been a long time since I had a better cold bath or have felt myself to be so well cleaned up.

SCAPHA: There's an outcome for everything, just as there is a great harvest this year.

PHILE.: What does this year's harvest have to with my bath?

In polymetric passages like the following exchange between two slaves near the end of *Mostellaria*, the meter changes from verse to verse. The abbreviations after each verse stand for different metrical forms:

⏑⏑ – ⏑– – – ⏑⏑ ⏑⏑ – ⏑⏑ – –

PIN. tace sis, faber, qui cudere soles plumbeos nummos. versreiz

– ⏑– – – ⏑⏑ – ⏑⏑ ⏑⏑ – –

PHA. non potes tu cogere me, ut tibi male dicam. tr4^colreiz

– – ⏑– – – ⏑ – – – ⏑⏑ ⏑ – –

novit erus me. PIN. suam quidem pol culcitulam oportet. ia4ith

– – ⏑⏑ – ⏑⏑ – – – ⏑ ⏑ – ⏑⏑ – – – ⏑⏑ –

PHA. si sobrius sis, male non dicas. tibi obtemperem, cum tu mi nequeas? an8

(892-896)

PINACIUM: Shut up, please, you counterfeit coin maker.

PHANISCUS: You can't force me to insult you. My master knows me.

PI.: He sure ought to know his little pillow.

PH.: If you were sober, you wouldn't insult me.

PI.: Why should I follow your wishes, when you can't follow mine?

Our evidence suggests that meter played an important role in what melodies were performed as well as what rhythms were used. It is quite likely, therefore, that in stichic passages both melody and rhythm were largely the same from verse to verse.[18] The frequent changes of rhythm and melody in polymetric songs would ratchet up their potential ludic effect.

Plautus also produced musical variety by varying the degree of regularity in his accompanied verses. Almost all the meters of Roman comedy allow stunning metrical freedom. Compare the following two cretic verses, for example, both from a song of Philolaches early in *Mostellaria*:

[18]For an attempt to approximate what the melody and rhythm of a scene written in a stichic meter might have sounded like, see James et al. (2012).

– ˘ – – ˘ – – ˘ – – ˘ –

nunc simul res, fides, fama, virtus decus (144) cr4

Now at the same time my property, my good credit, my reputation, my virtue, and my glory…

and

– ˘ ˘ ˘ ˘ – – ˘ ˘ ˘ – ˘ –

tigna putrefacit, perdit operam fabri (112) crcol cr2

Rots the timbers, destroys the work of the builder.

The first is a completely regular variation of a meter called a cretic quaternarius: four repetitions of a short syllable in between two long syllables. In the second verse, the second long syllable of the first and third cretics have been resolved into two shorts, and the second cretic is truncated, producing what is called a cretic colon (the verse is thus called a cretic colon followed by a cretic dipody). The two verses would sound very different when performed. The first would produce a predictable musical pattern, the second a series of jarring changes in pace and an unexpected abbreviation of one of the musical units. Greater irregularity in rhythm can reflect more intense emotion or general chaos, but it can also produce an elevated sense of play, as characters respond to the standard metrical patterns with insouciance.

Table 1 charts some of these musical building blocks in *Mostellaria*. It reveals that the play is in many ways typical of Plautus' oeuvre, but with a more ludic bent.

The *tibicen* thus played for about two-thirds of *Mostellaria* when it was first performed: everywhere except when the actors delivered iambic

Table 1 Musical patterns in Plautus' *Mostellaria*

	All plays of Plautus	*Mostellaria*
Iambic senarii	33.46%	34.6%
Polymetric	14.3%	17.52%
Meter changes per play	average play: 96.3 (19.6 verses per change)	169 (6.92 verses per change)
ABC pattern followed	64%	69%
Bacchiacs	2.18%	4.15%
Cretics	2.01%	6.42%

senarii. In just under a fifth of the play, actors sang polymetric songs, in which rhythms and melodies changed frequently. That percentage is slightly above the average, and as a whole *Mostellaria* has considerably more changes of meter than an average Plautine play. As is typical, about two-thirds of the major metrical changes in *Mostellaria* follow the ABC pattern, but bacchiacs and cretics are significantly more common in *Mostellaria* than they are in most Plautine plays.

A review of these musical building blocks in action reveals still more how they contribute to the play's ludic nature. Table 2 shows the play's basic musical structure.

The play begins with some essential exposition: in chastising Tranio for aiding and abetting their young master's profligacy, the country slave Grumio describes all that has happened since Theopropides left, thus revealing the background to the play (1–83). As is to be expected when so much important information is being relayed, this passage is without music.

The next scene, however, tells us nothing that we need to know to understand the plot. Philolaches enters, remorseful, proposing that a young man is like a house. Just as a house thrives under good owners, Philolaches himself thrived under the tutelage of his parents but fell to ruin when left to his own devices (84–156). This scene is pure play. Philolaches' moralizing is hardly to be taken seriously, and one gets the distinct impression that he doth protest too much, enjoying the pleasures of his downfall along with his pompous imitation of a persuasive speech in the courts or the rhetorical schools. The song thus suits very well the first "B" moment in the ABC progression, the first accompanied meters that are not trochaic septenarii. Rhythms—and probably melodies as well—change with abandon here: there are 46 meter changes in 73 verses, an average of one meter change every 1.59 verses.

Table 2 Plautus, *Mostellaria*: metrical structure

Iambic senarii (A)	**Accompanied meters besides trochaic septenarii (B)**[a]	*Trochaic septenarii (C)*
1–83: Grumio and Tranio		
	84–153 (bacchiacs and cretics dominate): Philolaches monody	
		154–156: Philolaches concludes monody
	157–247 (iambic septenarii): Philematium and Scapha overheard by Philolaches	
		248–312: Philematium and Scapha overheard by Philolaches; Philematium and Philolaches
	313–347 (bacchiacs and cretics dominate): Callidamates and Delphium; Callidamates, Philolaches, Philematium and Delphium	
		348–408: Tranio monody; Tranio, Callidamates, Philolaches, Philematium, and Delphium
409–689: Tranio monologue; Tranio and Theopropides; Tranio, Theopropides and Misargyrides		
	690–746 (cretics dominate): Simo monody; Simo and Tranio	
747–782: Simo and Tranio		

(continued)

Table 2 (continued)

Iambic senarii (A)	**Accompanied meters besides trochaic septenarii (B)**[a]	*Trochaic septenarii (C)*
	783–804 (bacchiacs dominate): Tranio and Theopropides	
		805–857: Tranio, Theopropides and Simo
	858–903 (no meter dominates): Phaniscus monody; Phaniscus and Pinacium	
		904–992: Tranio and Theopropides; Theopropides, Phaniscus and Pinacium
993–1040: Theopropides and Simo		
		1041–1181: Tranio monody; Theopropides and Tranio; Theopropides, Tranio, and Callidamates

[a]Includes some isolated trochaic septenarii

Among those changes, the most conspicuous are two moves from bacchiacs to cretics. Bacchiacs and iambics, another rising meter, dominate the opening of the song, as Philolaches explains how a house thrives under good owners, as in the following passage:

– –   – –   – –   ˘ –   – ˘– –

aedes quom extemplo sunt paratae, expolitae, ba4

– –   ˘   – ˘   –   –

factae probe examussim, ia4^

– –   ˘   –   – –   ˘ –   ˘˘ –   –   –   –   –   ˘ –

laudant fabrum atque aedis probant, sibi quisque inde exemplum expetunt. ia8

(101-103)

As soon as the house is well built and polished up, and made completely according to rule, they praise the builder and approve of the building; everyone seeks an example from it for himself.

When new owners take over and the house falls to ruin, however, cretics replace the rising meters, and the music seems to fall along with the house:

–   – – –   ˘ –   –   – –   ˘ –

atque illud saepe fit: tempestas venit, cr2crcol

–   – –   – ˘– –   ˘ –   ˘–

confringit tegulas imbricesque: ibi

˘ ˘   ˘ –   –˘ –   –   ˘   ˘˘–   ˘ –

dominus indiligens reddere alias nevolt; cr4

˘ ˘ –   –   –   ˘–   ˘ ˘ ˘ –   –   ˘–

venit imber, perlavit parietes, perpluont, crcolcr2

– ˘   ˘   ˘˘ –   –   ˘ ˘ ˘ –   ˘ –

tigna putrefacit, perdit operam fabri:

– ˘–   – ˘   –   – ˘   – ˘ –

nequior factus iam est usus aedium. (108-113) cr2crcol

And that's what often happens: a storm comes, it breaks the roof covers and tiles: then the lazy master doesn't want to put up others; the rain comes in, it soaks the walls, they let the rain through, it rots the beams and destroys the work of the builder. The use of the house has been made more worthless.

Then, Philolaches repeats the same pattern for the youth. Bacchiacs dominate his account of the well-raised youth, as here:

– – – ⏑ – – ⏑ – – ⏑ – –

primumdum parentes fabri liberum sunt: ba4

– – – – – – ⏑ – – ⏑ – –

ei fundamentum substruont liberorum;

– – – ⏑ – – ⏑ – – ⏑ – –

extollunt, parant sedulo in firmitatem. (120-122)

First of all, the parents are the builders of children: they lay a foundation for their children. They raise them up, and they carefully prepare them for solidity.

But as the youth, namely, Philolaches himself, falls into depravity, cretics take over[19]:

– – – – ⏑ – – – – – ⏕

venit ignavia, ea mi tempestas fuit, cr4

– – –⏑– – ⏑ – – ⏑ –

mi adventu suo grandinem imbrem attulit; crcolcr2

– ⏑ – – ⏑– – – – – ⏑ –

haec verecundiam mi et virtutis modum cr4

– – – – – – – – –⏑–

deturbavit detexitque a me ilico; cr2crcol

– – – ⏑⏑⏑ – – ⏑– ⏑–

postilla optigere me neglegens fui. (137-141)

Idleness came: that was my storm. That brought hail and rain with its arrival. Straightaway that disturbed my sense of shame and the moderation of my virtue and denuded me of them. Afterwards I was too lazy to cover myself up.

Philolaches thus associates bacchiacs with the earnest—the good homeowner and the virtuous youth—and cretics with those who value pleasure over the practical: the lazy homeowner and himself. This pattern will become a leitmotif throughout the play, as cretics repeatedly bring a crescendo in the play's emphasis on pure fun.

19On the pattern of cretics following bacchiacs in this song, see Duckworth (1952, 372) and Moore (2012, 196).

Philolaches concludes his song with three trochaic septenarii:

– ⏑ – ⏑ – – ⏑⏑– – ⏑⏑ – ⏑⏑– ⏑ –

parsimonia et duritia discipulinae aliis eram,

– ⏑ – – – ⏑ – – – – – – – ⏑–

optumi quique expetebant a me doctrinam sibi;

– – – ⏑⏑– – – – – – ⏑⏑– – ⏑ –

nunc, postquam nihili sum, id vero meopte ingenio repperi. (154-156)

In my frugality and my toughness, I served as a model for others. All the best people sought to learn from me. But now that I am worthless I have found it is from my own nature.

The music thus hints that the pure playfulness is over now, and the plot will proceed. But Plautus has fooled us. After just three verses, Philematium enters (157). Breaking the usual entrance patterns of Roman comedy, she enters unannounced; and she also breaks the usual ABC pattern, for the meter changes to iambic septenarii. What follows is a long scene in which Philolaches eavesdrops on Philematium conversing with her slave Scapha. Nothing happens here to advance the plot, even when the meter does finally change to trochaic septenarii midway through the scene (248). The change to trochaic septenarii does suggest a kind of movement, but only of the most frivolous kind: Philematium asks Scapha for her mirror, for she wishes to prepare her appearance for Philolaches.

Near the end of the scene, Philolaches stops eavesdropping and reveals himself to Philematium. It looks as if now something will really happen (293). But again, we are deceived. After just twenty more verses, Philolaches' friend Callidamates enters, very drunk, with his girlfriend Delphium, and the ABC pattern is broken again (313). Callidamates' drunken entrance is a musical tour de force. The meter changes 25 times in 37 verses, an average of once every 1.48 verses. Many of these verses are irregular to a remarkable degree.

Callidamates' song repeats Philolaches' pattern of bacchiacs moving to cretics. The very irregular bacchiacs that dominate Callidamates' first verses underline not building, as Philolaches' did, but the drunken man's struggle to move forward:

– – – ⏑ – – ⏑ – ⏑⏑⏑ –

CA. adversum veniri mihi ad Philolachem ba2bacol

⏑ – – ⏑ – – ⏑ – ⏑ – –

volo temperi. audi, em tibi imperatum est.

– ⏑ – ⏑– | – – – – ⏑ –

nam illi ubi fui, inde effugi foras, cr2crcol

⏑⏑ ⏑⏑ ⏑ ⏑ – –– – – – ⏑ – –

ita me ibi male convivi sermonisque taesumst. ba4

– – – – – – | – ⏑ ⏑ ⏑ ––

nunc comissatum ibo ad Philolachetem, ba2bacol

⏑⏑ – ⏑ ⏑ – ⏑⏑– | – ⏑ ⏑ – ⏑⏑–

ubi nos hilari ingenio et lepide accipient.

– – ⏑⏑ ⏑⏑– – ⏑⏑–⏑

ecquid tibi videor mammamadere? (313-319) ba3

I want somebody to come and get me at Philolaches' house in a timely manner.

Listen, that's an order. When I was there, I took off from there, I was so bored with the party and the conversation. Now I'll go party at Philolaches', where they'll receive us with fun and pleasure. Do you think maybe I'm a little d-d-d-drunk?

Then a switch to cretics, which underlined a metaphorical fall in Philolaches' song, here accompanies a literal fall:

– ⏑ – – ⏑ –

DE. semper istoc modo... cr2

– ⏑ ⏑ – – ⏑ – – ⏑ – – –

CA. duce me amabo. DE. cave ne cadas, asta... cr2crcol

⏑ ⏑ ⏑ – – ⏑ – – ⏑ – – –

cave modo, ne prius in via accumbas, cr2crcol

– ⏑ – – ⏑ – – ⏑ – – ⏑ –

quam illi, ubi lectus est stratus, concumbimus. cr4

⏑⏑ ⏑⏑ ⏑ ⏑ ⏑ –

CA. sine, sine cadere me. (320, 324, 326-8) crcol

DELPHIUM: It's always like this...

CALLIDAMATES: Please lead me.

DE. Watch that you don't fall. Stand up... Watch out, now, so you don't fall down in the street, before we get to recline there, where there's a couch laid out for us.

CA. Just let me fall.

In more polymetric verses, the friends join and begin to party; but they are rudely interrupted by Tranio, who returns from the harbor with bad news: Theopropides has returned from abroad. Here the real action of the play finally does begin, and Tranio performs trochaic septenarii (348).

In the midst of his own and the partiers' panic, Tranio comes up with a plan, and he has everyone hide inside the house. The trochaic septenarii end with this exchange:

PHILO. in tuam custodem meque et meas spes trado, Tranio— tr7

TR. pluma haud interest, patronus an cliens probior siet. (406-408)

PHILOLACHES: Tranio, I hand over myself and my hopes to you—

TRANIO: It doesn't make a bit of difference whether the patron or the client is better.

What follows is the longest continuous passage of iambic senarii in Roman comedy (409–689). Tranio first persuades Theopropides that the house is haunted, so he must not enter it. Then, in response to the inopportune entrance of the moneylender Misargyrides, demanding interest on his loan, Tranio concocts the story that Philolaches borrowed money to buy the unhaunted house of his neighbor. The long stretch without music allows the audience to concentrate on the intricacies of the deception; at the same time it sets the play's two major blocking characters, Theopropides and Misargyrides, apart from the rollicking playfulness we have seen so far.

Conspicuous play returns with the entrance of the neighbor and alleged seller, Simo. Simo is escaping from his wife, who wants sex after feeding him a nice lunch. Simo uses the same cretics that underlined playfulness earlier, but he introduces an additional element of play by replacing some cretics with thymelici, in which three short syllables replace the usual single short syllable of a cretic (– ⏑ ⏑ –). Each thymelicus comes at the end of a cretic verse. We expect a continuation of the cretics, and the addition of the extra short syllables produces a humorous surprise, which augments Simo's comic dismissal of his wife's advances:

– ⏑ – – ⏑– – ⏑ – ⏑ –
prandium uxor mihi perbonum dedit, cr2crcol
– – – – ⏑ – – ⏑ ⏑⏑ –
nunc dormitum iubet me ire: minime. cr2thy
– – – – ⏑ – – ⏑ – ⏑–
non mihi forte visum ilico fuit, cr2crcol
⏑ ⏑ ⏑ – – ⏑– – ⏑ – ⏑ –
melius qum prandium quam solet dedit: cr2crcol
⏑ ⏑⏑ – ⏑ ⏑⏑ – – ⏑⏑ ⏑–
voluit in cubiculum abducere me anus. cr2thy
– ⏑– – ⏑ – – ⏑ ⏑ ⏑ ⏑
non bonust somnus de prandio: apage!… (692-697) cr2thy

My wife has given me a very fine lunch. Now she bids me go to bed. No way! That didn't seem at all by chance to me, when my wife gave me a lunch better than she usually does: that old woman wanted to get me into bed. Sleep after lunch is not good. Away with it!...

Tranio then greets Simo, and the two converse in more polymetric verses dominated by cretics. The accompanied section ends with this exchange:

TR. … genua obsecro ia8
ne indicium ero facias meo. SI. e me, ne quid metuas, nil sciet.
TR. patrone, salve. SI. nil moror mi istius modi clientis. ia7
TR. nunc hoc quod ad te noster me misit senex— (743-747) ia6

TRANIO: I beg you at your knees: please don't tell my master.
SIMO: Don't worry. He won't learn anything from me.
TR.: Hail, my patron!
SI.: I don't care for any clients like you.
(*switch to iambic senarii*)
TR.: Now, as to what my old master sent me to you for.

With its reference to a patron and a client, the play's second move from musical to non-musical performance thus echoes its first one: the dialogue between Philolaches and Tranio noted above (406–408). Musical and verbal echoes thus combine to echo the movement from Tranio's first plan, the initial deception of Theopropides, to his second plan, the deception of Simo. The move is also accompanied by another break in the ABC pattern, the first such break in which iambic senarii succeed meters besides trochaic septenarii.

The ABC pattern returns as Tranio goes back to Theopropides, telling him that they must pretend Philolaches has not purchased Simo's house, in order to assuage Simo's remorse at selling (783). Tranio and Theopropides use primarily bacchiacs, echoing the bacchiacs Philolaches used of a youth under the control of his parents and contrasting with the cretics used by other characters. The bacchaics also serve well to underline what Theopropides sees as Tranio's slowness, as they earlier underlined the difficulty in moving of the drunk Callidamates:

˘ ˘ – – ˘ – – ⏓ – ˘ – –

TH. quid illic, opsecro, tam diu destitisti? ba4

˘ – – ⏓ – ˘ – – ˘ – –

TR. seni non erat otium, id sum opperitus.

– – – ˘ – – ˘ – – ˘ – –

TH. antiquum optines hoc tuum, tardus ut sis. (787-789)

TH. What on earth took you so long?

TR. The old man was busy: I had to wait.

TH. You haven't changed: you've always been slow.

Now the preliminaries are done, and the meter changes to trochaic septenarii, as Tranio leads Simo and Theopropides on a tour of the front of Simo's house, hilariously deceiving both of them (805–857). When the three have entered the house, Callidamates' slaves Phaniscus and Pinacium arrive to fetch their master home from Philolaches' house (858). Musical patterns reflect the fact that these two will derail Tranio's plot: Plautus again breaks the ABC pattern, and for the first time a polymetric section does not begin with bacchiacs or cretics, but rather with iambic and anapestic verses.

The playfulness does not stop, though. Phaniscus is a variation of the stock "good slave": he boasts about how loyal he is to his master. One of the ironies of Plautine comedy is that such "good slaves," who would seem to be bulwarks of propriety, produce some of Plautus' most exuberant music. This scene thus has an extraordinary metrical variety, matching or even exceeding the play's earlier polymetric songs in pure musical fun.[20] The ratio of verses to metrical changes is the smallest of any song in the play (1.33),[21] and the degree of irregularity and the variety of different meters find no parallels elsewhere in the play and few elsewhere in Plautus. No meter ever becomes dominant, but the cretics

[20] For a metrical analysis of this song, see Moore (2012, 295–300).

[21] There are 36 changes of meter in 48 verses.

that have played such an important role so far in the play do come to the fore in a short section near the end of Phaniscus' monody:

⏑ ⏑ ⏑ – – ⏑ – – ⏑ ⏑⏑– ⏑ –

bene merens hoc preti inde abstuli. abii foras; cr4

–⏑ – ⏑ ⏑ – ⏑ – –⏑ – – –

solus nunc eo advorsum ero ex plurimis servis. glcrcol

– ⏑⏑ – ⏑– ⏑| ⏑ ⏑ – – ⏑–

hoc die crastini quom erus resciverit, cr4

–⏑ – – – ⏑ ⏑–

mane castigabit eos wil

– ⏑ – – ⏑⏑–

bubulis exuviis. (877-882a) ith

That's the reward I got for doing good. I went out. Now I alone, out of all those slaves, am going to meet my master. When the master learns about this tomorrow, he'll punish them in the morning with the hides of cattle.

The bouncy cretics underline well Phaniscus' cheerful self-satisfaction. Sung by this ardent rule-keeper, they also echo ironically the earlier cretics that were so closely associated with the breaking of rules.

Tranio is blithely unaware of the disaster to come, and as he reenters with Theopropides they perform the same trochaic septenarii with which they left (904). The trochaic septenarii continue after Tranio leaves and Theopropides meets Phaniscus and Pinacium. When they have told Theopropides the truth and leave, the music suddenly stops:

TH. puere, iamne abis? PH. libertas paenulast tergo tuo: tr7
mihi, nisi ut erum metuam et curem, nihil est qui tergum tegam.—

TH. perii hercle, quid opust verbis? ut verba audio, ia6
non equidem in Aegyptum hinc modo vectus fui,
sed etiam in terras solas orasque ultumas
sum circumvectus, ita ubi nunc sim nescio. (991-996)

THEOPROPIDES: Boy, where are you going?
PHANISCUS: Freedom is a cloak for your back. For my back, unless I fear and pay attention to my master there's no cover.
(*switch to iambic senarii*)
TH.: Oh no! What can I say? From what I'm hearing, I didn't sail at all to Egypt, but I've sailed around into deserted lands and farthest shores: I've no idea where I am.

As happens elsewhere in Roman comedy, the switch to unaccompanied iambic senarii underlines Theopropides' shock. At the same time, it helps make clear that for Tranio the gig is up. The music remains off as Simo and Theopropides plot to catch and punish Tranio (997–1040). The first and second plans, presented without music, have now been replaced by a third plan, also unaccompanied. This time the plan is made not by Tranio but against him.

Tranio still has no idea what is happening, and he reenters with the same trochaic septenarii he used in his two last scenes (1041). With his entrance he brings the play's last music, and its final break from the ABC pattern, the only time in the play trochaic septenarii replace iambic senarii without an intervening passage in another accompanied meter. He thus continues to demonstrate the musical power he has shown throughout the play. That power reflects his control over the plot, as he sits on an altar and manages to escape punishment, in spite of mocking Theopropides right to the end.

As the deathly serious anapests of Euripides' *Medea* demonstrate, it would be a gross exaggeration to claim that ancient theater's music was just for fun. The ludic potential of that music, however, is undeniable. By adding an unusual song early in his *Frogs*, Aristophanes guaranteed his audience would appreciate that his version of the underworld is far from serious. The opening song of Sophocles' satyr play *Ichneutai* played an important role in the relief it brought from the seriousness of the three tragedies that preceded it. Even more ludic would be the farcical burlesque of a tragic plot in the Charition mime. Here an exuberant combination of song or chant, dance, and instruments brings the climax of the fun. *Mostellaria* offers a sustained emphasis on its own ludic nature, reinforced throughout by Plautus' musical choices. Music on the Greek and Roman stage could carry audiences into a realm of playfulness that would be impossible in drama that was merely spoken.

Works Cited

Bieber, Margarete. 1961. *The History of the Greek and Roman Theater*. 2nd edition. Princeton, NJ: Princeton University Press.

Campbell, David A. 1984. "The Frogs in the *Frogs*." *Journal of Hellenic Studies* 104: 163–165.

Corbel-Morana, Cécile. 2012. *Le Bestiaire d'Aristophane*. Paris: Les Belles Lettres.

Dale, A.M. 1968. *The Lyric Metres of Greek Drama*. 2nd edition. Cambridge, UK: Cambridge University Press.

Dangel, Jacqueline. 2001. "Sénèque, *poeta fabricator*: Lyrique chorale et évidence tragique," in *Le poète architecte: Arts métriques et art poétique latins*, ed. Jacqueline Dangel. Louvain: Peeters: 185–292.

Duckworth, George E. 1952. *The Nature of Roman Comedy*. Princeton, NJ: Princeton University Press.

Dunbabin, Katherine M.D. 2016. *Theater and Spectacle in the Art of the Roman Empire*. Ithaca, NY: Cornell University Press.

Henderson, Jeffrey (ed.). 2002. *Aristophanes: Frogs, Assemblywomen, Wealth*. Cambridge, MA: Harvard University Press.

James, Sharon L., et al. 2012. "Plautus *Truculentus* 775–853: Version 2, Performed in Latin." Online video. Accessed March 3, 2018. https://www.youtube.com/watch?v=8CCpYeqzBgA.

Leo, Friedrich (ed.). 1896. *Plauti Comoediae. Vol. 2*. Berlin: Weidmann.

Mastronarde, Donald J. (ed.). 2002. *Euripides. Medea*. Cambridge, UK: Cambridge University Press.

Moore, Timothy J. 2008. "When Did the *Tibicen* Play? Meter and Musical Accompaniment in Roman Comedy." *Transactions of the American Philological Association* 138: 3–46.

Moore, Timothy J. 2012. *Music in Roman Comedy*. Cambridge: Cambridge University Press.

Moorton, Richard F. 1989. "Rites of Passage in Aristophanes' *Frogs*." *Classical Journal* 84: 308–324.

Parker, L.P.E. 1997. *The Songs of Aristophanes*. Oxford: Clarendon.

Pickard-Cambridge, Arthur. 1968. *The Dramatic Festivals of Athens*. 2nd edition, revised by John Gould and D.M. Lewis. Oxford: Clarendon.

Pöhlmann, Egert, and Martin L. West (eds.). 2001. *Documents of Ancient Greek Music: The Extant Melodies and Fragments*. Oxford: Clarendon.

Questa, Cesare (ed.). 1995. *Titi Macci Plauti cantica*. Urbino: QuattroVenti.

Radt, Stefan (ed.). 1977. *Tragicorum Graecorum Fragmenta. Vol. 4: Sophocles*. Göttingen: Vandenhoeck & Ruprecht.

Santelia, Stefania. 1991. *Charition Liberata (P. Oxy. 413)*. Bari: Levante.

Skulimowska, Zofia. 1966. "Les instruments de musique dans le mime scénique grec en Égypte," in *Mélanges offerts à Kazimierz Michałowski*. Warsaw: Państwowe Wydawnictwo Naukowe: 175–179.

Taplin, Oliver. 1993. *Comic Angels and Other Approaches to Greek Drama Through Vase-Paintings*. Oxford: Clarendon.

Taplin, Oliver. 2007. *Pots and Plays: Interactions Between Tragedy and Greek Vase-painting of the Fourth Century B.C.* Los Angeles: The J. Paul Getty Museum.

Wilson, Peter. 2002. "The Musicians among the Actors," in *Greek and Roman Actors: Aspects of an Ancient Profession*, eds. Pat Easterling and Edith Hall. Cambridge: Cambridge University Press: 39–68.

Zagagi, Netta. 1999. "Comic Patterns in Sophocles' *Ichneutae*," in *Sophocles Revisited: Essays Presented to Sir Hugh Lloyd-Jones*, ed. Jasper Griffin. Oxford: Oxford University Press: 177–218.

Zimmermann, Bernhard. 1985. *Untersuchungen zur Form und dramatischen Technik der Aristophanischen Komödien. Band 1: Parodos und Amoibaion*. 2nd edition. Königstein: Hain.

Did Christ Laugh? Umberto Eco's Question and Saint John Chrysostom's Response

Chrysostomos A. Stamoulis

At first I did not understand why William involved himself in this debate, and indeed with a man who did not seem to love such topics; but George's answer showed me how smart my teacher was. "On that day we did not talk about comedy, but about the appropriateness of laughter," said George sullenly. And I remembered quite clearly that just the day before, when Venansios mentioned that debate, George claimed that he did not remember. "Oh," William said casually. "I thought you were talking about the lies of poets and cunning riddles [...]". "We were talking about laughter," George said caustically. "The comedies were written by pagans in order to instigate laughter amongst the pagans, and they acted wrongly. Our Lord Jesus Christ never recounted comedies or fables, but transparent parables which allegorically teach us how to gain paradise, and so it should be." "I wonder," said William, "why

C. A. Stamoulis (✉)
School of Theology, Aristotle University
of Thessaloniki, Thessaloniki, Greece
e-mail: stamchr@theo.auth.gr

V. Rapti and E. Gordon (eds.), *Ludics*,
https://doi.org/10.1007/978-981-15-7435-1_10

do you object so strongly to the thought that maybe Jesus laughed. I believe laughter is a good medicine, like baths; It heals juices and other diseases of the body, particularly melancholy". "Baths are a good thing," George said, "and Aquinas himself recommends them to fight sadness, which can become a nasty passion when it is not employed to fight evil; only courage can drive it away. Baths restore the balance of the juices. Laughter shakes the body, deforms facial lines; it makes man look like a monkey." "Monkeys do not laugh; laughter is a unique characteristic of man, a sign of rationality," William said. "The point of human rationality is reason, and through reason we can blaspheme God. That which makes man unique is not necessarily always *true*. Laughter is a sign of stupidity. He who laughs does not believe in the object of his laughter, but neither does he hate it. Therefore the Rule says: *The tenth degree of humility is for a person to not be acquiescent and ready to laugh; for it is in the scriptures: the moron raises his voice in laughter*" [...] "Laughter is characteristic of an idiot. Laughter promotes doubting [...] By laughing the ignorant merely states implicitly that *Deus non est* [...] But you know that Christ did not laugh?" [...] "I'm not sure."[1]

Dear friends, we are in an era where the body's value is besieged in many ways. Or even better, I might say that humanity in its entirety is under attack. And I'm now convinced that such a "sin" (and here we are referring to the ontological astochia of missing the mark, as opposed to merely a transgression of some impersonal ethical code) starts from a distorted understanding of the incarnation. An understanding that does not allow Christ to be a real human, leading to a domino-effect absolute degradation, to the point of disappearance, of God himself. For what kind of God would he be if, upon taking on human nature, he would first force the human person to abandon all elements which constitute his/her humanness? A practice followed by ancient heretics, such as Nestorius and Apollinarius (leading moralistic thinkers) who, though located on opposite extremes of heretical Christologies, agree perfectly in their anthropological views.[2] An agreement which is built on the altar of

[1]Umberto Eco, *The Name of the Rose*, trans. E. Kallifatide (Athens: Hellenic Letter, 1999), 236–242.

[2]George Martzelos, *The Christology of Basil of Seleuceia and Its Ecumenical Significance* (Thessaloniki: P. Pournaras, 1990).

absolute rejection upon which, without any sense of the tragedy of the matter, human nature is sacrificed. And this sacrifice continues today (as a recurring "mystery") by new moralistic thinkers, who cannot and do not want to understand that Man is not the result of an accident. In this way, though, Man as "unclean" and "polluted" either remains far from God (vindicating the philosophical doctrine, "The divine and human nature cannot be mixed,"[3] accepted by Nestorius and his followers in the history of Christianity) or, in order to arrive at an encounter, is forced to abandon part of his physical existence, and therefore, being deficient and weak, disappears upon his encounter with the creator, in the creators' vast and inhuman greatness (as in the case of Monophysitism).[4] So we can comfortably talk about the apotheosis of man (when man is swallowed up entirely by God), but we cannot speak of his deification (when the human nature is preserved). We can also defend the preservation of God's "dignity," but fail completely to discuss the revocation of Man's ontological loneliness, namely the abrogation of his non-existence, as Gregory the Theologian remarked. ["*What is not assumed cannot be healed; Only what is united with God can be saved*"].[5]

However, accepting such a reality is what allows the formulation of questions like: Did Christ laugh or not? Or even to come to the conclusion with certainty that *Christ never laughed*. Of course, such a statement immediately goes to the heart of biblical[6] and patristic

[3]Plato, *Symposium* (Chicago: University of Chicago Press, 2001), 202c–203a.

[4]The Monophysites, as also precisely the Nestorians, believed that sin constitutes an ontological characteristic of the "fallen" human nature. For this reason they avoided confessing the homoousion nature of Christ—"according to our humanity"—a principle of Orthodox theology, fearing perhaps that in this way "by extension the body of Christ would be considered sinful and profane." (Martzelos G, 172–173). Most classical of all is the case of Eutychios, who, while referring to this theme, would say: "Until now I did not say that the body of the Lord and our God is homoousios with us… because while I confess it to be the body of God […] I have not called the body of God a body of man […] fearing until this moment to say it, because I knew the Lord to be our God" (*Mansi* VI, 741εξ.).

[5]Gregory the Theologian, *Epistle 101, To Cledonius against Apollinarius*, *PG* 37, 181C–184A.

[6]It is clear that in the Bible there is no information telling us that Christ laughed. By the same token, there is no information indicating that Christ did not laugh. However, there are indications to the laughter of God. See, for example, *Psalm* 2:4 and *Proverbs* 1:26, where these are related to the destruction of the impious, as well as other very interesting comments about the place of laughter in the lives of people, but also in their eschatological destiny (most classical of all: *Eccl* 2:2; 3:4; *Gen* 18:9–15; *Jam* 4:9; *Lk* 6:21–25. See Webster G., *Laughter in the Bible*"

theology,[7] according to which (in its entirety and without exception, and in contrast to the gods of Homer[8] or to the Jesus of the apocryphal and Gnostic texts,[9] Christ never laughed.[10] The question that immediately arises from such a finding is clear: Why did Christ not laugh? Is this a weakness of his human nature? Does Christ possess

(St. Louis: The Bethany Press), 1960. This was a reality that raised serious questions in patristic theology and nourished the related dialogue, in which other people, besides theologians, took part primarily among men of letters, such as for example Umberto Eco, *The Name of the Rose*, and Bountelier, *Curiosités Esthetiqués, L' Arte Romantique et Autres Oeuvres Critiques* (Paris: Garnier Freres, 1971). The laughter of God, of course, was sometimes considered malevolent, as in the case of an intolerant and punishing God, and sometimes benevolent, as in the case of a reconciling and loving God who forgives. With extreme sensitivity this problem appears in Hesse E., *Narcissus and Chrysostom*, translated into Greek by Kondyles Fontas (Athens: Kastaniotes, 1989), 244, and especially in Kazantzakis N., *The Life of Alexis Zorbas* (Athens: Kazantzakis, 2007), 117, where the following delightful remarks are written: "Lately Zorba would light the fire quickly, cook, we would eat and then disappear on the road to the village. After some time, he would return in a sullen mood. 'Where were you wandering again, Zorba?' I would ask him. 'Curse them all, boss'," and change the conversation. One night upon returning, he asked me with a sense of urgency: 'Does God exist, or not? What do you say, boss? And if he exists – anything can happen – how do you imagine him to be?' I just simply raised my shoulders and didn't say anything. 'Now, don't laugh, but I imagine God to be just like me. Only much taller, much stronger, more fool hardy; and immortal. He sits on soft sheepskins in ease, and his hut is the sky. It's not made with scrap metals like ours but with clouds. He holds in his right hand not a sword, not a scale – such tools are for killers and grocers; God holds a large sponge filled with water, like a rain cloud. To his right is Paradise and to his left is Hell. Here comes the ill-fated soul, all naked, having lost its body and trembling. God looks upon it and laughs under his mustache, pretending to be bogeyman. 'Come here,' he says to her, 'you coursed soul!' He begins the interrogation. The soul falls down at the feet of God. 'O my God!' she cries out. 'I have sinned!' And she begins to innumerate all her sins, one after another, without end. And God grows weary and yawns. 'Stop!' he shouts. 'You have deafened me!' He then stretches out his arm with the sponge and with one stroke wipes off all the sins. 'Get yourself over to Paradise!' he gestures. 'Peter, take in this poor soul also!'."

[7]Most characteristic is the reference of Clement of Alexandria, who, in his Pedagogue, dedicates a whole chapter on laughter with the title "*On Laughter*," *PG* 8 445C–452A. See the related reference in Grosso A. M., Clemente Alessandrino, "*A. Rostagni: il cristiano come l 'uomos che sa sordridere, Quaderni Diparimento di Filologia, Linguistica e Traditione*," Classica 17, 2001, 19–242.

[8]Jean Rudhart, *Rires et sourires divins. Essais sur la sensibilitè religieuse des Grecs premiers chrétiens. In Revue de théologie et de philosophie* (1992), 124.

[9]The disciples said to him, 'Lord, why do you laugh over our prayer of thanksgiving? We have done whatever is appropriate.' He answered and said to them, 'I do not laugh at you. You did not do this on account of your will, but because it is that through which your God will be glorified' (Rudolf Kascher, Marvin Mayer, Gregor Vurst, translated by Eleni Asteriou, Tina Theou, Billy Kouris, Maria Mavromataki, Elina Sinopoulou 2006).

[10]Teodor Baconsky, *Les rire des Pères. Essai sur le rire dans la patristique grecque* (Paris: Desclée de Brouwer, 1996).

an incomplete human nature? Or maybe laughter is sinful? Does this mean, therefore, that in Christ we have the revelation of the only true human nature which does not know how to laugh, should not laugh, and cannot laugh? Or, maybe, finally, we find ourselves facing the dramatic unfolding of the plan of the Divine Economy, the illumination of which necessitates the emergence of only those elements which promote the revelation of the ultimate purpose of the Incarnation, which is none other than the salvation of people by the passion and the Cross of Christ.

I believe that the answer lies in the third case. Without this, of course, meaning that here, as well as in other areas and themes of Christian theology, there were not excesses and extremes (like those already described, and like those described by Umberto Eco), which led to the depreciation of human nature in yet another escape from "the here and now"—from the only true land on which the battle of the eschaton takes place. However, the choice of St. John Chrysostom, who was regarded as "the toughest opponent of laughter among the Church Fathers" to support the view that in Christian theology "laughter came from hell," is most unfortunate. And I say this because it is clear that the saint from Antioch, who is misunderstood more than anyone else, both outside of the Church, and within it, though he remains faithful to the biblical theology that does not show Christ laughing (and how could it be otherwise with a precise interpreter of Scriptures?), never on any occasion denies the naturalness of laughter or its necessity for the proper functioning of human societies. Chrysostom's reproach is against a culture of sensuality and greed—which is seemingly followed without caution, regret and shame[11] even by members of the ecclesiastical body; the result of which, among others, is that inappropriate laughter, which does not even stop at the time of common prayer,[12] dishonoring thus Christ

[11]Constantine P. Cavafy, *The Walls in the Poems* (Thessaloniki: Metope., n.d. 1897–1933), 23.

[12]"And the amazing thing, at the same time as prayer, there was no ceasing of much laughter…Tell me, O woman, you cover your head (for prayer) and sitting in church you laugh? You came to confess your sins, bowing before God to beseech him and to make your plea over those transgressions that condemn you and you do this with laughter?", Chrysostom, *Interpretation of the Epistle to the Hebrews*, 121–122.

himself, the precious content of the Eucharist, as well as the Church, and in this way leading the Church to absolute exile.[13]

In the center of the city now, as Chrysostom says, having surrendered their bodies and souls to the devil's power, the greedy and the prostitutes are dancing together.[14]

I would say, therefore, that the attitude of the saint in this case, is nothing more and nothing less than an eruption of pain for the people's loss of the poetic measure (people in general and of the ecclesial community in particular), which allows a person the measure of grounded abiding, to the measure of Christ, who "cried when he saw Jerusalem, and was disturbed when he considered the traitor, and wept when Lazarus was about to resurrect."[15] And with it also a cry of the saint against a way, called civilization, which in its totalitarianism deprives the Church even from the ability to place Christ in a new manger (just as humble as the old one), in a corner of the city.[16]

And this sorrow and indignation is reflected by Chrysostom in his Interpretation of Hebrews (that "gave" him many pages of reference in

[13]"Always this overturn, this put down; laughter has become our possession and culture and amusement; nothing is stable, nothing firm. I say this not only to the men in public life, but also to those I am presuming; for the Church is replete with laughter. If someone says a joke, laughter occurs directly to those sitting about; and the amazing thing is that many do not cease laughing even at the time of prayer. Everywhere the devil is dancing, having so dressed all and in control of all; Christ is dishonored; no part of the Church is without it." John Chrysostom, *Interpretation of the Epistle to the Hebrews*, 121.

[14]Here then stands the greedy man, not in a house, but at the center of the city, giving over to the devil, not his body, but his soul, and as if joining himself with and entering into a prostitute, he fulfills all of his desire and then goes out; and this the entire city sees, not just two or three men. And this is particular to the prostitutes, the silver belongs to the giver (John Chrysostom, *Interpretation of the Epistle to the Hebrews*, 121).

[15]John Chrysostom, *Interpretation of the Epistle to the Hebrews*, 122.

[16]There is some confusion in the use of these coming from the fact that in the Greek reality, especially on the level of legal terminology, the "public" is usually identified with the "state" [...] The "state" and everything belonging to the "state" is also connected to the legal exercise of state power. To the degree that the "public" is identified with the "state," it too is connected with exercise of power and authority. Thus, the understanding of what is public is confused with what is "common," belonging to the realm of the community, because in this case it must be disconnected from the idea of exercising state power. On the other hand, when the idea of "private" is properly understood, then this is not antithetical to the "public," but only to the "state." Such an understanding, however, presupposes the differentiation of the "public" from the "state," as noted above (John Petrou, *Multiculturalisme and Religious Freedom*, Thessaloniki: Paratiritis, 2003, 211).

the history of culture): "Do you not hear Paul saying that filthiness, silly talk, and levity should be taken from you? After filthiness, he puts liveliness. Do you still laugh? What is silly talk? It is the kind of talk that brings nothing useful. And do you continue to laugh even though you are a monastic, even though you are a crucifier of passions and a mourner? Tell me. Have you heard of Christ doing so? No. He never did that. On the contrary oftentimes he was sad."[17]

I am sure that even before the ink dried that formed the final words of the Antiochian father, some will have already raised their hand with questions for me. And I think that despite their hurriedness, they are right. Further explanation is needed. Okay, Christ did not laugh. We said that the purpose of biblical and ecclesiastical writers is the revelation of the urgency of salvation. But is this enough to convert at once the Orthodox Church into an unsmiling commonwealth in a country of absolute sadness and gloom? That is, in other and simpler words, are laughing and happy people not real members of the body of the Church? Have they no hope of salvation?

Allow me to say that this is not the case. Not only because Chrysostom himself says it (his words will be quoted below), but because, long before Chrysostom, the Biblical texts and especially the Gospels have said it. I will limit myself to only two examples, which may not show us that Christ laughed, but suggest (if nothing else) that in his private moments, which are usually to be found at the margins of the central biblical history struggling to reveal the state of the mystery of the divine Economy, he revealed an existence which was open, joyful, full of a thirst for life. To such an extent, in fact, that it constitutes a counter-example to the absolute asceticism introduced in the case of John the Baptist. The evangelist Matthew suggests this very point, commenting on the reaction of Jesus' generation toward him, but also toward John. Let us listen to him:

> To what can I compare this generation? They are like children sitting in the marketplaces and calling out to others: "We played the pipe for you, and you did not dance; we sang a dirge, and you did not mourn." For

[17]John Chrysostom, *Interpretation of the Epistle to the Hebrews*, 122.

> John came neither eating nor drinking, and they say, "He has a demon" The Son of Man came eating and drinking, and they say, "Here is a glutton and a drunkard, a friend of tax collectors and sinners." But wisdom is proved right by her deeds. Then Jesus began to denounce the towns in which most of his miracles had been performed, because they did not repent. "Woe to you, Chorazin! Woe to you, Bethsaida! For if the miracles that were performed in you had been performed in Tyre and Sidon, they would have repented long ago in sackcloth and ashes. But I tell you, it will be more bearable for Tyre and Sidon on the day of judgment than for you. And you, Capernaum, will you be lifted to the heavens? No, you will go down to Hades. For if the miracles that were performed in you had been performed in Sodom, it would have remained to this day. But I tell you that it will be more bearable for Sodom on the day of judgment than for you."[18]

I will not make any comments. The evangelist, with this the absolutely subversive text, says it all. Almost the same can be said of what John suggests, with the description of the wedding at Cana. The purity, of course, and the intensity of the text is not the same as that of Matthew.[19] But, without a doubt, the whole description of such a festival (which is usually exhausted by the revelation of Christ's messianic identity and the eschatological interpretation of the miracle of changing water into wine), allows us to see, from afar but clearly enough, that true life *before* death is not a reality that conflicts with the eschatological truth of man.[20] As long as one does not believe that the End of Times is a "pure reality," set apart from the "here and now," calling man to a denial of the his total way of existence, forgetting that this way of existence belongs to the very good creation of the good God, the God of unconditional love.

It is time to return to Chrysostom, who, I must say, was definitely influenced in his treatment of the subject by references to eschatological laughter found in the Book of Job, the Gospel of Luke,[21] and the Letter

[18] *Mt* 11:16–24.

[19] *Jn* 2:1–12.

[20] See Chrysostomos A. Stamoulis, *Theotokos and Orthodox Doctrine. Study in the Doctrine of St. Cyrill of Alexandria*, 227–233.

[21] *Lk* 6:21–25.

of James.[22] However, Chrysostom's position did not lead him in any way to those bizarre anti-humanistic attitudes (about which we have already spoken), but instead it led him to the heart of the event of the incarnation, wherein shines the mystery of the crucifixion's contradiction and ambiguity.

So without hesitation, now, I could say that what bothers the prophet of ecumenical love is inopportune and measureless laughter, which distances man from Godly mourning—the confusion, in other words, of biblical time (kairos),[23] which engenders a laughter empty of sorrow, empty of memory, an empty laughter, unable to find that "one thing needful."[24] In contrast to this bankruptcy, Chrysostom, revealing once again philanthropy as a measure of precise existence that assumes responsibility, points out prophetically,[25] with the view in other words that defines the form of life after the great event[26] that laughter and desire are not by nature bad.[27] Laughter is, moreover, that which allows the flourishing of the mystery of friendship and community, essential for the resurrection of the human soul, according to Thomas Eliot.[28] As long as one knows the poetic measure which madly denies both the Luciferian, absolute introversion that insists on ignoring Heaven, and the ecstatic, complete openness, which cuts ties between the human person

---

[22] *Jam* 4:9.

[23] "For everything there is a season, and a time for a every matter under the sun: a time to be born, and a time to die; a time to plant, and a time to pluck up what is planted; a time to kill, and time to heal; a time to break down, and a time to build up; a time to weep, and a time to laugh; a time to mourn, and a time to dance; a time to cast away stones, and a time to gather stones together; a time to embrace, and a time to refrain from embracing; a time to seek, and a time to lose; a time to keep and a time to cast away; a time to rend, and a time to sew; a time to keep silence, and time to speak; a time to love, and time to hate; a time for war, and a time for peace" (*Ec* 3:1–8).

[24] *Lk* 10:42.

[25] On the Prophetic glance see Chrysostomos A. Stamoulis, *The Art of Theology and the Theology of the Art. Theology and Art* (114).

[26] "And that strange happiness you sometimes feel, even when all things around you have become ashes—perhaps that is God" (Leivadites T., 247).

[27] John Chrysostom, *Interpretation of the Epistle to the Hebrews*, 122.

[28] "You don't know what my friends mean to me/ And how, how strange and rare it is to find/ In a life made up so much, so much of remnants/... To discover some friend who has those qualities/ To have and to offer/ Those qualities on which the friendship is founded/ What significance is there in me telling you all these things -/ Without these friendships – life is a cauchemar!" (a bad dream) (Eliot T. S., 27).

and mother Earth.[29] A reality that presents joy, as a reality mixed with sorrow and pain which moves beyond theories of purity and fleshless idolatry of "types and forms."[30] As a reality firmly oriented toward the liturgical summation which, refusing to accept any pietistic and moralistic scandalization, verifies that Sunday (the Lord's day), as the feast

---

[29]At the end of this enquiry. I do not know if Rudhardt is right when he says that "Greek laughter signifies an adhesion to the world, while Christianity leads one away from this world." I am not even sure if present and future scholars would still dare to proffer so general an opinion given our so various early Christian sources. One thing, however, is clear for me now: Christianity that laughed certainly existed and did not escape from the world. At least not from the scholarly world (Claire Clivaze, 28).

[30]The greatest commemoration of the Church takes place at the heart of the Mystery of the Holy Eucharist. That is why I do not understand why there is so much ritualism over the day when Memorials may be offered. What is the "inappropriate" or "sinful" element (see introductory remarks on the subject of the Kollyvades in Papoulides K. (1991). *The Kollyvades Movement*. Athens: Apostolike Diaconia. I am of the opinion that the only reasons that hold up to their restrictive transfer from the day of Sunday to the day of Saturday are those of practicality. Thus, I have a feeling that the Church contributes in her own way to the exaggeration of the culture of oblivion. The exaggeration of a way, in a manner of speaking, of burying its dead all the more deeply, it no longer understands what it means to commemorate. (On the commemorations in the Holy Eucharist, see Priestmonk Gregory, *The Holy Liturgy, Commentary* (Athens: Synaxi, 1982), pp. 30, 35–36, 92–93, 116–119, 311–314, 318–319. From such a perspective, a similar contribution is also made by the way most of our contemporary churches are being built in our area, including the way they are "filled" with all those "unrelated" things that, in their non-esthetic and distasteful exaggeration, tend to distance rather than reveal, each day more and more, the mystery of the Incarnation of the Logos of God, the mystery of the reasonable worship. It is the manner by which the Christological memory and commemorations can flourish upon earth. Images of such a forgotten way are given to us in the writings of Nikos Gabriel Pentzikes: "Thessalonica is filled with such brilliant churches of that period […] We already mentioned specifics about the houses and the virtually homey dimensions of the church of this period. We also mentioned the fact that externally they resemble display cabinets of jewelry or antiques. Greatly contributing to this end is the wall-formation and the awareness of the construction material as if the stones and the bricks are elements of the organic formulation of a body. Many times, as one looks from the outside the arched windows, it appears as if one sees a human being. There! And you show the eyes. There! There in the cross between the eyebrows upon the nose. Twins or just simple, the windows seem to be children of the Church, who, regardless of her magnitude or if she is full of people or not, it is a complete world […] With the cross as the basic motif or the name of Jesus Christ and Jesus Christ is victorious… Outside of the church, as you wander around, you feel a sense of respect, which the body inspires as a vessel of the mystery of life […] the body conceals all the wealth of the star-filled sky that reflects the glory of the Lord God [… By building the churches of today, with their wall-formations and the treatment of their surfaces and levels, as well as their iconography and decoration, we demonstrate that we do not allow our soul to become aware or be inspired by the material and its geometric formulation, nor the themes depicted upon it, thus destroying with the mind every place where there could be, even in a naïve demonstration, the yearning and the authenticity of a deep sigh," *Toward Attending Church* (Thessaloniki, Agrotikes Synetairistikes Ekdoseis, 1986), 33–40.

par excellence, although dominated by the resurrection is somehow, as the Greek composer Tsitsanis would say, cloudy.[31] A day, forcing you to "count those who are absent"[32] and slowly but surely, by commemorating all of the departed brethren and the cross that the members of the church body carry, opening yourself to the transformative anticipation of light. To that fulfillment of heaven, earth, and the realm under the earth through the risen Christ; The Sunday of Sundays, the Feast of Feasts, which promises the healing of wounds left on people by the temporal

---

[31]It appears that Fr. Philotheos Faros agrees with Tsitsanis, while Pentzikes totally disagrees. I have the feeling that the two approaches, existential to the extreme, are not by necessity in contradiction. In each case, I like to believe that the cloudiness of Sunday is removed in the end by the mystery of liturgical communication, the Holy eucharist, which as an inaugurated eschatology has already entered into the present time. Its ultimate fulfillment, however, the catholic resurrection and encounter, is something that the Church, at the present time, can only anticipate and hope for. See N.G. Pentzikes, *Consolation for the City and Prefecture of Drama*, Athens: Agra, 1986, where he observes: "They found the old man, with the multitude of sins like a mountain on his hunched back, singing, thanking God and all the Saints, glorifying their sacred names, and dancing on the hollow, between the height where the Sacred Cemetery of the city of Drama lies, and the opposite side, where there is a humble and popular café. In the shop they were playing the famous record of Tsitsanis, Cloudy Sunday. I had asked that they change that record, saying that it was Sunday and it cannot be cloudy, but always, in the ebb and flow of the days, it is the sunny and glorious day of God, when another sun, more powerful than the one we see shedding light upon us, one that, from time to time and often frequently, is hidden. Once you realize this Sun's Light even once, it will never go out." Fr. Ph. Faros, *Circumstances and Choices. Autobiography* (Athens: Armos, 2005), 88–89: "My father left early in the morning and returned drunk in order to sit at the festive table. Before eating our final bite, father would begin his earthquake that developed into a pandemonium of shouts, tears, threats and many other similarly frightful things. These experiences were the primary reason why during the rest of my life the festive days and even on Sundays I always had a sense of melancholy. Tsitsanis spoke to my heart with his song: "Cloudy Sunday you resemble my heart that is always cloudy." Some "pious" people, of course, were scandalized by Tsitsanis who spoke like this about Sunday, the day of the Resurrection of the Lord. The Resurrection of the Lord however is not some "theological" chit chat, but a life experience that begins with the Holy Eucharist and is completed and realized to become a joy and a communion and a way of life. In recent years, when some of us have started having an essential relationship among ourselves on the day of Sunday with the Divine Liturgy in church and continue this relationship in a climate of fellowship outside of the church, reaching its zenith with a common meal that lasts until late into the afternoon, I experience Sunday as the joyful day of the Resurrection of the Lord."

[32]"Feast day wounds/ force you to count those absent/ empty places at the table/ even when someone else is sitting there" (Koumourou Sonia, 2000).

separation from God.[33] The singer of divine love, being changed to the deepest core of his being from such a perspective, notes the following:

> But (one says) what harm is there in laughter? There is no harm in laughter; the harm is when it is beyond measure, and out of season. Laughter has been implanted in us, that when we see our friends after a long time, we may laugh; that when we see any persons downcast and fearful, we may relieve them by our smile; not that we should burst out violently and be always laughing. Laughter has been implanted in our soul, that the soul may sometimes be refreshed, not that it may be quite relaxed. For carnal desire also is implanted in us, and yet it is not by any means necessary that because it is implanted in us, therefore we should use it, or use it immoderately: but we should hold it in subjection, and not say, Because it is implanted in us, let us use it [...] Therefore it is a time for tears [...] Let us mourn therefore, beloved, let us mourn in order that we may laugh indeed, that we may rejoice indeed in the time of unmixed joy. For with this joy [here] grief is altogether mingled: and never is it possible to find it pure. But that is simple and undeceiving joy: it has nothing treacherous, nor any admixture. In that joy let us delight ourselves (John Chrysostom, 123–124).

Suggested Reading

Baconsky T. (1996). *Les rire des Pères. Essai sur le rire dans la patristique grecque.* Paris: Desclée de Brouwer.

Cavafy C. (n.d.). *The Walls in the Poems* (1897–1933). Thessalonica: Metope.

Eco U. (1999). *The Name of the Rose*, trans. E. Kallifatide. Athens: Hellenic Leter (pp. 236–242).

Gregory the Theologian. *Epistle 101, To Cledonius Against Apollinarius, PG* 37 (181C–184A).

John Chrysostom. *Interpretation of the Epistle to the Hebrews 15*, PG 63.

[33]"Now all things are filled with light—heaven and earth and the places beneath the earth; let all creation celebrate the Feast, the resurrection of Christ, upon which it is founded" (Matsoukas N. A., 553).

Martzelos G. (1990). *The Christology of Basil of Seleuceia and Its Ecumenical Significance*. Thessalonica: P. Pournaras.
Minois G. (2000). *Histoire du rire et du la derision*. Paris: Fayard.
Rudhart J. (1992). *Rires et sourires divins. Essais sur la sensibilitè religieuse des Grecs premiers chrétiens. In Revue de théologie et de philosophie.*
Stamoulis Ch. (2000). *The Art of Theology and the Theology of Art. Theology and Art*. Thessaloniki: Palimpseston.
Stamoulis Ch. (2003). *Theotokos and Orthodox Doctrine. Study in the Teaching of St. Cyril of Alexandria*. Thessaloniki: Palimpseston.
Stamoulis Ch. (2004). *The Human Nature of Christ and Sin in the Antiochian Theologians of the Fifth Century. An Exercise in Self-Consciousness*. Thessaloniki: Palimpseston.
Webster G. (1960). *Laughter in the Bible*. St. Louis: The Bethany Press.

Comedy, Physicality, and Ludic Dance Gestures: The Comic in Ballet and Tai Chi?

Jonathon Robinson-Appels

How does the comic present itself in disciplined forms of body training, whether in ballet within the Western tradition, or Tai Chi within the Asian tradition? Are both of these forms of training founded on ascetic, aesthetic, or medical principles, or a combination thereof? How do their practice, performance, and presentation express ludic sensibilities and gestures? That is, what happens to the ludic in formal systems such as ballet and Tai Chi? The concern here is to understand the physical nature of the ludic, how the comic is embedded in bodily actions and gestures, and in what ways comedy may or may not appear in the bodily practices of ballet and Tai Chi. How is it that ballet gestures and ballet meaning often become theatricalized, and even caricatured, when comic repartee is expressed?

In this essay the terms ludic and comic will occasionally be exchanged. Yet the ludic remains the physicalized precondition of the comic and pure

J. Robinson-Appels (✉)
Columbia University, New York, NY, USA
e-mail: jr2168@columbia.edu

V. Rapti and E. Gordon (eds.), *Ludics*,
https://doi.org/10.1007/978-981-15-7435-1_11

comedy cannot occur without some form of immediate bodily accident; this is the essence of the ludic. This ludic sensibility is what breaks the temporality of the moment. Huizinga speaks often of the structured and ordered nature of play, such as when he is discussing the action of drama, and the practice of rituals. He understands how play is materialized through participatory action:

> The rite is a *dromenon* which means "something acted", an act, action. That which is enacted, or the stuff of the action, is a *drama*, which again means act, action represented on a stage. Such action may occur as a performance or a contest. The rite, or "ritual act" represents a cosmic happening, an event in the natural process…The rite produces the effect which is then not so much *shown figuratively* as *actually reproduced* in the action. The function of the rite, therefore, is far from being merely imitative; it causes the worshipers to participate in the sacred happening itself. As the Greeks would say, "it is *methectic* rather than *mimetic*". It is "a helping-out of the action".[1]

Huizinga refers to two studies on religion (by Harrison and Marett) to make his point concerning the substantially active and expressed dedication to play. Yet within the "helping-out of the action" that he refers to is something unexpected. The committed activity of play produces an unimagined or unintended consequence, which is less "tense" in its structure than non-play activities. (Huizinga also writes in *Homo Ludens* of the tense nature of play.) But where is ballet, and where is Tai Chi, in the oscillation between play and tension?

To speak of tension in relation to forms of body training is also to ask about stress and illness. Let us now refer specifically to physical comedy, a type of physicalized enactment and a type of instantiation which, in *Anatomy of an Illness*, journalist Norman Cousins argues can cure illness and physical deterioration. (His notion of an individual cure is similar to the Ancient Greek use of theatrical catharsis as a form of social medicine.) Cousins' definition of the comic as a form of cure must include physical gesture, which is created in the marriage

---

[1]Johan Huizinga, *Homo Ludens: A Study of the Play-Element in Culture* (Boston: Beacon, 1962), 14–15.

between the gestures of the patient and those of the comedian. Cousins prescribed physicalized comic actions to treat his life-threatening illness. Specifically, he employed Marx Brothers films, and the Candid Camera series by Allen Funt (the filming of live spoofs on unsuspecting individuals), which were able to produce (in a methectic manner, as Huizinga argues) voluminous bodily laughter. As Cousins writes, laughter was "affecting my body chemistry" and "would enhance the system's ability to fight the inflammation."[2] Cousins' mentor in this endeavor, Dr. Albert Schweitzer, "employed humor as a form of equatorial therapy, a way of reducing the temperatures and the humidity and the tensions. His use of humor, in fact, was so artistic that one had the feeling he almost regarded it as a musical instrument."[3] While the work of Schweitzer and Cousins on laughter as a healing art has not in recent decades been widely considered, we can understand how the physical presence offered by music, dance, and Tai Chi has practical and profound effects.

Cousins argues throughout *Anatomy of an Illness* for the oral and enacted transmission of jokes and humorous stories. Curiously, many of Cousins' readers often requested his medical advice. He speaks of the time when he asked one of his "patients" to narrate a few funny stories to him, since she had not yet enacted those humorous vignettes in a social context. Cousins discusses how it was essential, as well, that her family be included when she physically acted out her comic narratives. He notices that while she is recounting these comic stories the concerned faces of her family were transformed. Their physiognomies "were no longer morose and furrowed but open and expectant" as they imagined what lay ahead within the patient's healing cycle.[4] In this way Cousins observes that physical humor has an environmental effect, as well as individual success.

When discussing the limitations of Western medical science, and the general absence of "warmth of human contact," he speaks also of his own healing process, "A warm smile and an outstretched hand were valued even above the offerings of modern science, but the latter were

[2]Norman Cousins, *Anatomy of an Illness as Perceived by the Patient* (New York: W. W. Norton, 2005), 44.

[3]Ibid., 91–2.

[4]Ibid., 166.

far more accessible than the former."[5] Cousins argues for a physicalized comic sensibility: these lithe sensations can be found in their purest ludic forms through the exchange of aesthetic gestures, that is, gestures which are formed through formal processes, but subject to interruption and accident, to the vagaries and joys of life.

Consider, also, physical comedy in relation to sports, in particular the experience of a Rutgers University African-American football player who has explained the threefold distinction between his activities as a "player" of the sport, how he dances when he goes to a club on the weekend, and how he plays with toy games when visiting his nephew. In all cases he was curious about his commitment to the experience of the physicality and intention of ludic gestures. Because he did not understand football to be a "comic game," he often lost the agility that he so easily found in the other two expressions. Similarly, Jeroen Hofmans, former principal dancer of New York City Ballet, found himself unable to rehearse (even with freshly created choreography) because of the reified and compartmentalized nature of the rehearsal studio where he had trained for ballet since age six. By introducing a beach ball, which was flung toward him at various moments as he received newly shaped choreography, he was able to lose the memory of the rehearsal studio. Instead he found the ludic and comic action in playing with his intertwined gestures (which were responses to the thrown ball), rather than in the prescribed history of his ballet training (Note #1).

To more completely understand the physical nature of the ludic, we will work with phenomenological philosopher Maurice Merleau-Ponty's discussion of the gesture. Gestures have in themselves the action of the body form out of which they are composed. Furthermore, their actions have a rhythm. Merleau-Ponty describes emotions and gestures: "One can see what there is in common between the gesture and its meaning, for example in the case of emotional expression and the emotions themselves: the smile, the relaxed face, gaiety of gesture really have in them

[5] Ibid., 172–3.

the rhythm of action."[6] We can even say that the gesture leans out of the body, bringing the body alongside.

Yet, Merleau-Ponty sees the body, and not the gesture, as enigmatic. He speaks of "the enigmatic nature of our own body."[7] The body becomes a shape of the gesture. For, as Merleau-Ponty writes, "It is the body which points out, and which speaks."[8] Indeed, the gesture heralds the future because it links the past and the history of the body on the one hand, and on the other, the motive present. The gesture is thus meaning making meaning. But Merleau-Ponty does not provide imagery for the gesture as the vehicle of the body moving interpretively ahead of itself. Merleau-Ponty instead describes the gesture by its contour, "The gesture which I witness outlines an intentional object."[9] What is this object? How does the ludic reside near this intended object? Does the ludic, through its force of action, transform the object to a subject?

Let us now pose a larger question as to whether there is something inherently tragic about ballet and Tai Chi, such as an existential sense of mortality. If it is true that theatre itself, with the Ancient Greek dance chorus as an historical ancestor of ballet, descended from dirge-like processions which processed down the Greek hillsides, then perhaps this will help clarify why the comic is so difficult to present in ballet (that is, without it fully falling into a caricatured or theatricalized status). In other words, the ballet has tragic procession both in its history, and its intent. Stephanie Crouch, a graduate of the School of Richmond Ballet, narrates an example which distills this argument: "When the male dancers had to learn to be en pointe when playing the stepsisters in *Cinderella*, they commented that it was a particularly difficult role, because they first had to learn how to be en pointe correctly, before they could perform it incorrectly and then be funny. So ballet has to be itself correct, and even not funny, in order to make fun of itself." Perhaps Crouch means that ballet has first to be learned as a materialized, tragic, and formal tradition before it can be made comic.

---

[6]Maurice Merleau-Ponty, *Phenomenology of Perception*. Trans. Colin Smith (New York: Routledge, 1966), 186.

[7]Ibid., 197.

[8]Ibid.

[9]Ibid., 185.

Another example is Jerome Robbins' "The Concert," which is closer to a theatre piece precisely because it attempts the comic. Gestures are amplified for their comic effects, and movement for movement's sake is diminished. Robbins' ballet is a comedy, but is it really a ballet? Is there something in the nature of ballet and ballet training that hesitates when confronted with the possibility of receiving playful action, built and improvised as ludic action is outside the ballet studio? The solos of Polina Semionova and Herman Cornejo, while interpretively fine, rich, delicately nuanced, and majestic, would not be construed as playful. It can be argued that in both ballet and Tai Chi the playful is initially seen as an intrusion on the form.

Former Pennsylvania Ballet dancer Elinor Hitt introduces the question of pantomime, a broad language situated between the performative discourses of theatre and dance, which is another disciplined form where the ludic can be examined. She refers to pantomime as "an overdetermined set of simple balletic gestures" which present the narrative of a ballet story. Hitt is precise: "when the dancer must mime, the dancing ceases altogether." She discusses a section in the nineteenth century ballet *Coppélia* in which the principal dancer and character experience frustration. As she writes:

> While the modern audience may or may not find humor in the theatricality of this display, there's no humor in the dancing itself. There can be lightness in her jumps and power in her turns, but the technical executions must stop for the pantomime to begin. There is a clear divide between dance steps and comic gesture, and, in its rigid 19th Century fashion there is little room for permeability between the two performative languages.[10]

While we will not consider pantomime in any detail here, we can see that Hitt understands that dancing steps themselves are usually performed outside the characteristics of ludic action. In this sense the ludic has difficulty finding physicalized form within ballet steps and ballet performances (Fig. 1).

---

[10]Elinor Hitt, Interview with Jonathon Robinson-Appels. Personal Interview. March 28, 2018.

Fig. 1 Elinor Hitt moving from the tragic, and toward the ludic gesture, personal archive

But what of the relation to another formal body training process, that of Tai Chi? Huizinga, in his discussion of play and order, which is associated with both social and individual structure and composure, speaks of the Chinese music and dance traditions as bringing us closer to form: "According to ancient Chinese lore the purpose of music and the dance is to keep the world in its right course".[11] Why are movement practices such as dance and Tai Chi often considered ascetic? Is it that the pleasure emanating from them is focused on the development of the forms of energy cultivation and circulation? The ancient tradition of body, emotion, and energy (Chi) sculpting can be clearly found in Tai Chi. Adison Martin, Tai Chi and Qi Gong master, has demonstrated how the facial features of Tai Chi training do not immediately reveal "the inner smile" which is part of the Tai Chi relaxed jaw and overall body composure. (This relaxed smile is to be distinguished from the sometimes real,

[11] Huizinga, *Homo Ludens: A Study of the Play-Element in Culture*, 14.

and sometimes artificial, wide-open smile often seen in American ballet performances.) He offers a description of how to find the muscularity and emotional state which will produce an inner smile:

> Many of us regularly train our muscles through exercises such as running and weightlifting, to develop our legs, arms, and torso. But how many of us neglect developing our smile? There are many ancient teachings that talk about the inner smile. And all have one thing in common: persistence.
>
> Out of the many techniques that exist, what would I suggest one do on a daily basis? To start, for the beginner – just sit. It only needs to be for a brief moment, to begin with. Close your eyes and think of something that brings you joy. And in that moment, just experience how your face receives pleasure. The subtle muscle flex that leads to the curl of the lips…don't rush it. Allow it to happen as you focus on what makes you happy. Over time you will come up with other things that make you happy, and you will start to realize all the joyous moments you've had in your life. Be gentle with yourself, and that will translate to inner harmony (Fig. 2).[12]

The training of the inner smile, as Martin describes, is part of the Tai Chi tradition, though its relation to the external, outer smile of the balletic tradition is not always clear. In ballet training there is often a series of corrections that are meant to generate some form of an external smile. While Tai Chi and ballet may be similar in their sensing of, reception to, and interpretation of the tragic, their approach to the gesture of the smile would seem to be opposing.

We do not know why so few comedies survived from Ancient Greece, and why so many more tragedies did survive. Is there something reified in the writing down, and in the transmission, of the tragic? Is the comic always more ephemeral, and less easy to hold to the page, and to the stage? But we can note that the fluid, cyclical, and transmutative nature of the Yin Yang symbol  has a balance that is unlike the disequilibrium, and sharp contrast we see between tragedy and comedy  in the West. Why this historical disjuncture between East and West?

[12]Adison Martin. Interview with Jonathon Robinson-Appels. Personal Interview.

Fig. 2 Adison Martin contemplating the inner smile, personal archive

Let us consider anthropologist Gregory Bateson's essay, "A Theory of Play and Fantasy" as we look at the relationship between play and the comic. Bateson considers, "a more complex form of play; the game which is constructed not upon the premise 'This is play' but rather around the question 'Is this play?'"[13] Unlike those physical comedies filled with ludic gestures, the tragic would seem to be something that does not ask about itself, but rather about mortality. Bateson offers an extended analysis of the physicality of how animals play:

> Paradox is doubly present in the signals which are exchanged within the context of play, fantasy, threat, etc. Not only does the playful nip not denote what would be denoted by the bite for which it stands, but, in addition, the bite itself is fictional. Not only do the playing animals not quite mean what they are saying but, also, they are usually communicating about something, which does not exist. At the human level, this leads to a vast variety of complications and inversions in the fields of play, fantasy, and art. Conjurers and painters of the *trompe l'oeil* school concentrate upon acquiring a virtuosity whose only reward is reached after the viewer detects that he has been deceived and is forced to smile or marvel at the skill of the deceiver.[14]

But is the smile of the viewer not a deception, nor forced, but rather a true valuation? In the West we might not automatically see the smile as part of the ascetic tradition of training (such as Martin practices). We often see the smile simply as an irregularity because it falls out of what is preconceived. What is the relation between play, the ludic gesture, and the smile? What is the intent, meaning, and signal being exchanged? Bateson continues with his definition of play: "We face then two peculiarities of play: (a) that the messages or signals exchanged in play are in a certain sense untrue or not meant; and (b) that that which is denoted by these signals is nonexistent."[15] How can we understand the physicality of the ludic gesture when play often includes what Bateson refers to as the "nonexistent"?

---

[13]Gregory Bateson, *Steps to an Ecology of Mind* (Chicago: University of Chicago, 2000), 182.
[14]Ibid.
[15]Ibid., 183.

Bateson introduces, in the same essay, several additional categories for understanding play which will help expand our understanding of the actions of the ludic: "Very brief analysis of childhood behavior shows that such combinations as histrionic play, bluff, playful threat, teasing play in response to threats, histrionic threat, and so on form together a single total complex of phenomena."[16] Is what exists within the histrionics of play, the physical acting out of play, even if it is a bluff, or something "nonexistent," as Bateson outlines, is this acting out nevertheless always a kind of launching pad for the physicality of the ludic gesture?

As we consider the playful, let us look again more closely at the smile. Philosopher Wittgenstein speaks of the Mona Lisa smile. Recent remarks by art historian Silvano Vinceti suggest that the model for the Mona Lisa painting, the sketches underneath, are of one of Da Vinci's boy lovers, repainted entirely to become what we now know to be the fully embodied Mona Lisa portrait. What is that smile of, if not the cyclical or oppositional nature of gender, the Yin and Yang? As Wittgenstein writes in *Philosophical Investigations*, "When we speak of the enigmatic smile of the Mona Lisa, that may well mean that we ask ourselves: In what situation, in what story, might one smile like that?"[17] But what is the story of Mona Lisa, and what is the story of the smile, internal or not? (Note #2). When is the smile also a gesture? What aspect of the ludic produces the smile?

Perhaps Proust's rare description of a dancer will help here (he seldom refers to dancers, rather to actors and to music itself). Proust's dancer "with smiling lips" describes patterns which he also physically produces through aesthetic bodily patterns:

> I was delighted to observe, in the thick of a crowd of journalists or men of fashion, admirers of the actresses, who were greeting one another, talking, smoking, as though at a party in town, a young man in a black velvet cap and hortensia-coloured skirt, his cheeks chalked in red like a page from a Watteau album, who with smiling lips and eyes raised to the ceiling,

---

[16]Ibid., 181.

[17]Ludwig Wittgenstein, *Remarks on the Philosophy of Psychology*, Volume I. Ed. G.E.M. Anscombe and G.H. von Wright, Trans G.E.M. Anscombe (Chicago: University of Chicago, 1988), 75.

> describing graceful patterns with the palms of his hands and springing lightly into the air, seemed so entirely of another species from the sensible people in everyday clothes in the midst of whom he was pursuing like a madman the course of his ecstatic dream, so alien to the preoccupations of their life, so anterior to the habits of their civilization, so enfranchised from the laws of nature, that it was as restful and refreshing a spectacle as watching a butterfly straying through a crowd to follow with one's eyes, between the flats, the natural arabesques traced by his winged, capricious, painted curvetings.[18]

The dancer is understood in the social context to be ludic (silly, extemporaneous, inefficient, capricious, unnecessary to the serious business of journalists or "men of fashion"). Yet the fulfillment of his duties as a dancer is as serious (similar to the seriousness with which children play, as Bateson notes elsewhere in the same essay), attentive, and committed, as the practice of a Tai Chi master. This seriousness of approach is in dialogue with the tragic.

We have sketched in this essay how the ludic is embodied in the gestures of the body, indeed how the body itself is a ludic gesture when it is not materialized as being a body-by-itself, or a body for efficiency or labor, or a sign of mortality. Is the ludic body a place that asks the comic to be taken seriously, to deter us from our goals and the disembodied dreams of our aspirations? Certainly the mortal nature of the body clarifies (in some cultures) its tragic form. The body practices of ballet and Tai Chi, serious, ascetic, aesthetic, and sensate-articulate are, as always, akin to the freshness of the breath of the moment. A shift in weight and perspective allows the improvisational nature of the earth's axis to be felt at any moment, thus a kind of spring (as with Proust's dance figure) which is the primordial foundation of the ludic gesture; the ludic gesture then produces the comic. Even if ludic gestures are not obvious in both ballet and Tai Chi, and even less obvious in the training practices of both, they nevertheless manifest themselves through the spring and cushion (Fig. 3), the feeling of the ground underneath, allowing the trained ascetic body to feel less arduous. Yet, surprisingly,

[18] Marcel Proust, *Remembrance of Things Past*, Volume II. Trans. C.K. Scott Moncrieff and Terence Kilmartin (New York: Vintage, 1982), 180.

Fig. 3 The spring, cushion, and buoyancy: Company Appels, Princeton University, April 23, 2007, personal archive, Photo Credit: Gene Schiavone

within the codependent environment of audience and ballet dancers on stage, and also the onlookers and those practicing Tai Chi on ground, the tragic can seem to disappear. How is this transmutative circulation of the energy of the performers relayed to others? Again, it is through the spring and cushion of ludic action, the possibility and hope of ludic action.

To continue our review of what has been considered in this essay, we can say that there is not a particular ludic gesture per se, for once a gesture is spoken, enacted, or written, it is subject to a process of reification or improvisation dependent on its trajectory and climate. We have seen that the dimension of physical training is a precondition of the ludic (what Martin calls persistence); such training produces a receptivity to the fluid pathways of the comic. Two training examples particularly illustrated in this essay are the traditions of ballet and Tai Chi. The training process itself is akin to the tragic through its use of renunciation, historical anamnesis, and the devotion to form. Yet this formation of the physical body also creates a field of sensate receptivity to the conditions of the improvisatory in which the ludic gesture can then give way to the comic.

We have seen how epicentral the ludic is for Huizinga's theories of social organization and interaction, and in Bateson how the ludic is essential to the play activities of animals. The journalist Cousins has shown that it is the physical and bodily enacting of the ludic that is a precondition of the comic sensibility, and this enacting offers the capacity to reverse the tragic existential nature of illness. For it is the ludic that questions the training requirements of our bodies, and calibrates the dimensions of the misapplication of training which form illnesses. Merleau-Ponty has demonstrated the physical dimension of the gesture, its emanation from the body and how gestures "outline an intentional object." As well, ludic gestures interrogate the reality-fabric of the world, testing to see what is there through touch. Within the sensation of touch is the realization of how the world is being made around oneself. This interrogation of the real through touch easily dismisses the assumptions of the reality-fabric of the world and introduces the ludic as a response to the presumed logic of the real.

To clarify again, the ludic is the physical form of the comic, the comic is then enacted, spoken, gestured, or written. Despite the tragic element found within ballet and Tai Chi training, there is produced a field of potentiality for the rarely seen appearance of the ludic gesture within the training of the body, and next its manifestation as the comic, appearing as they can on a rather barren plain.

Within the training and performing traditions of ballet and Tai Chi we can see that the smile, as is true with the Mona Lisa smile, is an enigmatic gesture in which both the tragic and the comic are interpreted. The physical action of producing a smile is a ludic operation filled with both hope and trepidation, and is deployed upon the domains of the tragic and the comic. The comic, again, is a byproduct of the ludic gesture, the result of a ludic action, the aftereffect, the afterglow, of a committed physical gesture which has been enacted.

(Note #1:)

We can ask at another time why professional ballet dancers usually dance with less extension and less abandon when at a club involved in social dancing. After all, they do not want to exhaust their bodies for the work of class and rehearsal the following day. Yet this reduction and abbreviation of movement within the social dance context of club dancing is often understood initially as less expressive, even though it is often fully felt and even has a large degree of improvisation within the relaxed comic sensibility found in its deployment.

(Note #2:)

One should consider carefully the many uses of repetitive imagery of the Mona Lisa in Warhol's works.

Bibliography

Bateson, Gregory. *Steps to an Ecology of Mind*. Chicago: University of Chicago, 2000.

Cousins, Norman. *Anatomy of an Illness as Perceived by the Patient*. New York: W. W. Norton, 2005.

Crouch, Stephanie. Interview.

Hitt, Elinor. Paper.

Huizinga, Johan. *Homo Ludens: A Study of the Play-Element in Culture*. Boston: Beacon, 1962.

Martin, Adison. Interview.

Merleau-Ponty, Maurice. *Phenomenology of Perception*. Trans Colin Smith. New York: Routledge, 1966.

Proust, Marcel. *Remembrance of Things Past*, Volume II. Trans C.K. Scott Moncrieff and Terence Kilmartin. New York: Vintage, 1982.

Wittgenstein, Ludwig. *Remarks on the Philosophy of Psychology*, Volume I. Ed. G.E.M. Anscombe and G.H. von Wright, Trans G.E.M. Anscombe. Chicago: University of Chicago, 1988.

Toys, Childhood, and Material Culture in Byzantium

Brigitte Pitarakis

Public games were at the center of social life during late antiquity until around the late seventh century, when home and the church became the two axes of Byzantine social life, resulting in a turning inward. As now, toys and games at that time closely reflected the society in which they emerged. Circus races, animal combat, and hunts were activities that captivated the imagination of children, as did the religious and secular rituals, biblical stories, and classical mythology they encountered at home and in school.

Material evidence of Byzantine toys is severely lacking. The same paucity applies to Byzantine written sources, where references to childhood and children at play are scarce. That said, studies related to

B. Pitarakis (✉)
Centre national de la recherche scientifique, Paris, France

V. Rapti and E. Gordon (eds.), *Ludics*,
https://doi.org/10.1007/978-981-15-7435-1_12

Fig. 1 *Toy in the Shape of a Rider and Two Horses on Wheels*, fourth century AD, Wood 14.2 cm (5 9/16 in.), The J. Paul Getty Museum, Getty Villa, Pacific Palisades, CA, inv, 82.AI.76.22 (Digital image courtesy of the Getty's Open Content Program)

Fig. 2 Bone doll with a body made of rags, eighth or ninth century AD, Egypt. H. 11 cm; W. 8 cm. Benaki Museum, Athens, inv. 10390 (*Source* © Benaki Museum)

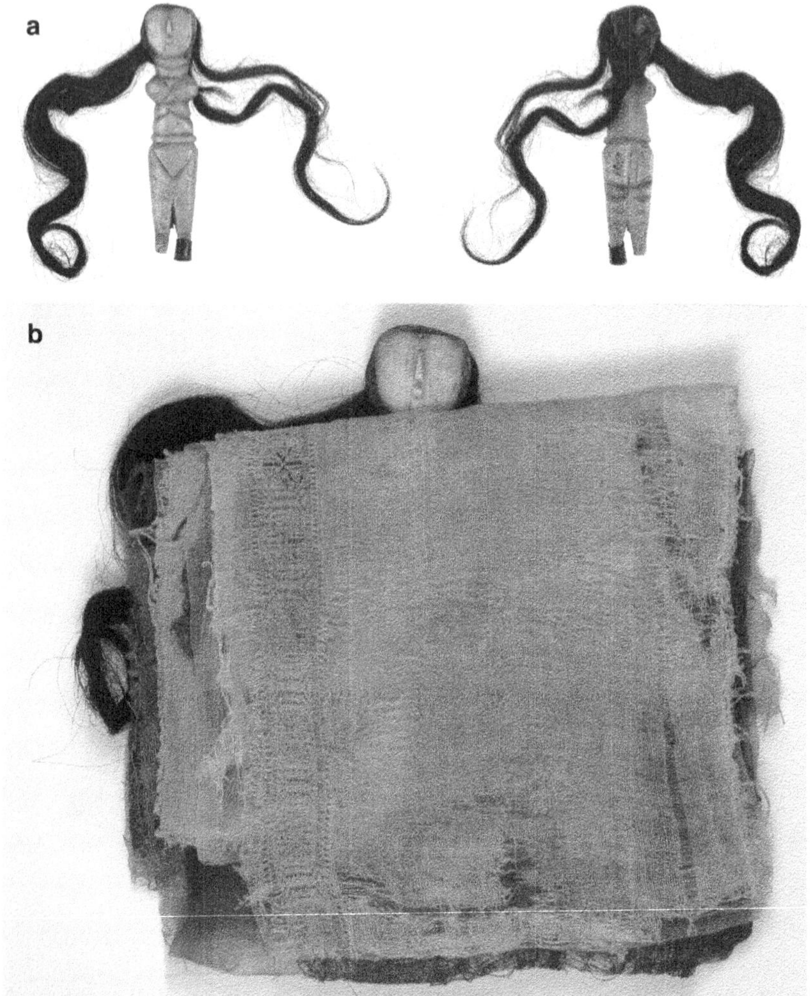

Fig. 3 Bone doll Fatimid period (909–1171), Egypt. Benaki Museum, Athens, inv. 10737. **a**. Naked bone figurine, front and back views. H. 13.5 cm; W. 3 cm. **b**. Bone doll dressed in fourteen layers of tunics (*Source* © Benaki Museum)

a
b

Fig. 4 Miniature wooden boat found during the excavations of the Theodosian harbor (Theodosios I, r. 379–395) of Yenikapı, Marmaray Excavations, Istanbul, 2008. Late fifth or sixth century AD (?). Length 17.2 cm; Width 7.1 cm. Istanbul Archaeological Museum, inv. MRY'08-9060. **a**. side view **b**. view from above (*Source* © Istanbul Archaeological Museums)

Byzantine childhood and adolescence in recent years through interdisciplinary research offers rich evidence for a contextualization of available objects.[1]

The commonly accepted average ages for the end of childhood are around twelve for girls and fourteen for boys. It is within this scope that this chapter covers late antiquity to the Palaiologan era, taking into consideration that the physical development of children also relates to changes in cultural and gender identity.[2] Major categories and types of toys are examined according to their function and the age groups for which they were intended. Substitutes for crafted toys devised by children and as well as collective games are discussed along with toys and games within the context of children's cognitive development. This approach allows drawing parallels with the mechanisms of secular and religious ritual and artistic patterns in Byzantium.

Children's Toys in Late Antiquity and Byzantium: Material Evidence

The archaeology of Egypt is the main source providing context for the study of material culture of children in Byzantium. Available materials also come from late antique levels of classical cities, including Athens, exhibiting continuity with earlier Roman production. Archaeological excavations in Istanbul in recent years have also brought to light rich evidence of Byzantine material culture, including objects identified as toys.

[1]Hennessy, *Images of Children in Byzantium* (Farnham and Burlington, VT: Ashgate, 2008); Papaconstantinou and Talbot, *Becoming Byzantine: Children and Childhood in Byzantium* (Washington, DC: Dumbarton Oaks Research Library and Collection, 2009); Horn and Phenix, *Children in Late Antique Christianity*, Studien und Texte zu Antike und Christentum 58. (Tübingen: Mohr Siebeck, 2009); Ariantzi, *Coming of Age in Byzantium: Adolescence and Society*, Millenium Studies 69 (Berlin and Boston: De Gruyter, 2018).

[2]Bourbou, *Health and Disease in Byzantine Crete (7th–12th Centuries AD)*, Medicine in the Medieval Mediterranean (Farnham and Burlington, VT: Ashgate, 2010), 101.

Audible Toys

Rattles are universally among the first toy provided to an infant. They are intended to calm the child when he or she is upset, by lulling and amusing. They are also supposed to avert evil spirits. Unsurprisingly, rattles have taken various forms over time. There were small spherical bells (*crepundia* or πλαταγή) strung on a thread and suspended on the body of a child or on a cradle in addition to larger rattles made of clay, wood, or bronze that toddlers or adults could shake by hand.

The miniature from the lively episode of Joseph and Potiphar's wife[3] in the sixth-century Vienna Genesis[4] includes a woman standing next to a cradle holding a rattle above the child.[5] This rattle offers a simplified version of a krotalon serving as a musical instrument.[6]

Children of all ages have entertained a privileged bond with animals, so to appeal visually to an infant and amuse him, clay rattles were often shaped like domesticated animals and painted in bright colors. They produced sound through the clattering of small pebbles or seeds placed inside them. Such examples are well known from productions of coroplasts in Athens beginning in the late third century and apparently continuing into the fifth century. Maltese lapdogs and roosters feature among the most popular shapes for rattles from this period.

In early childhood, whistles were often a child's primary toy, which would be carried along during outdoor activities. Usually made of clay, whistles, like other categories of toys, were also often made in the shape of animals. A production of clay whistles formed on a potter's wheel and dated to the tenth or eleventh century was found during restoration work and excavations conducted from 1994 to 2001 in Istanbul in the environs of the Great Palace of Constantinople and the Boukoleon Palace

---

[3]Genesis 39:9.

[4]Vienna Österreichische Nationalbibliothek, theol. gr. 31, fol. 16r.

[5]Zimmermann, *Die Wiener Genesis im Rahmen der antiken Buchmalerei: Ikonographie, Darstellung, Illustrationsverfahren und Aussageeintention* (Wiesbaden: Reichert Verlag, 2003), 155–60, Fig. 31.

[6]Santrot et al., *Au fil du Nil: couleurs de l'Égypte chrétienne*, Exhibition catalogue (Paris: Samogy éditions d'art; Nantes: Conseil général de Loire-Atlantique [musée Dobrée], 2001), 158, no. 117.

harbor. The finds included zoomorphic and goblet-shaped whistles that produced the sound of a bird when filled with water.[7]

Besides tooting whistles, children also played musical instruments such as the flute. Examples of flutes carved from bone are found often in the archaeological record, but the gender and age of their owners cannot be determined.[8] Playing of the flute was sometimes accompanied by singing and dancing.

Toys and Motor Skill Development

Once a baby could crawl or walk, he or she might receive a toy on wheels to push or pull. These play things often took the shape of animals. Horses are the most popular type, but birds are also attested. Horses fashioned from clay, wood, or even bone were mounted on wheels and equipped with a hole in their muzzle through which to insert a thread for pulling it. They were painted in bright colors to attract and hold a child's attention. Toddlers of both genders could with pull toys.

Clay finds from the Athenian Agora include several examples of horses on wheels dated to the fourth century and of terracotta wheels alone. During excavations conducted for the construction of the Athenian metropolitan railway, archaeologists found a handsome horse on wheels made of painted clay from the same period.[9] Such clay horses were usually made of two symmetrical halves pressed in double-sided molds. Two such molds attributed to the early Christian period are in the Hessisches Puppenmuseum, in Hanau-Wilhelmsbad, Germany.[10] Fragmented clay horses with a pierced muzzle, indicating their design as pull toys, were found together with other clay artifacts from the fourth to sixth

[7]Baran Çelik, *Byzantine Palaces in Istanbul*, Exhibition catalogue (Istanbul: Zero Books, 2010), 42, no. 44; 47–48, nos. 56–58; 82, nos. 138–139.

[8]Ayalon, *The Assemblage of Bone and Ivory Artifacts from Caesarea Maritima, Israel, 1st–13th Centuries CE*, BAR International Series 1457 (Oxford: Archaeopress, 2005), 69–70.

[9]Pitarakis, "The Material Culture of Childhood in Byzantium" (In Papaconstantinou and Talbot, 2009), 222–24.

[10]Andres, *Die Antiken Sammlung, Hessisches Puppenmuseum Hanau-Wilhelmsbad: Griechische, Römische, Altorientalische Puppen und Verwandtes* (Hanau: Hessisches Puppenmuseum, 2000), 223.

century during excavations of the necropolis at Bawit in Egypt during 1901–1902.[11] Egyptian archaeology has also provided a rich variety of wooden pull toys in the shape of a horse on wheels, including some examples with a rider.[12] The different pieces of wood were assembled with pegs, and the surface usually highlighted with color. Red was a preferred color for such toys.

The ball is another universally enjoyed plaything from the very first stages in life through adolescence and into adulthood.[13] Children of both gender juggled small colorful, hard balls, which intentionally or not, developed their motor skills. Small balls were among the accessories accompanying dolls yielded by archaeologists in Egypt. The variety of balls included versions made from interlaced bands of fabric, wool, or painted leather secured with cords and stuffed with straw, animal hair, rushes, and other organic materials. Simpler versions were also made from bundles of rugs sewn or tied together. The trigon was a common juggling game during Roman antiquity, played with small hard balls. It probably involved three people standing in positions creating a triangle and passing the ball by catching it with the right hand and throwing it with the left.[14]

Dolls

The doll—the most universal and most common plaything among girls—was not exclusively a symbol of childhood in ancient societies. Dolls also had associations with religious rituals and magic. Female figurines of ivory, bone, or clay are among the most common finds from the archaeological record. A significant number of them were equipped with articulated limbs, the feature that led to their conventional labeling

[11] Palanque, "Notes sur quelques jouets coptes en terre cuite" (*Bulletin de l'Institut Français d'Archéologie Orientale*, 1903), 101, pl. II.4.

[12] See (Fig. 1).

[13] Pitarakis, "The Material Culture of Childhood in Byzantium," 233–34.

[14] Andres, *Die Antiken Sammlung, Hessisches Puppenmuseum Hanau-Wilhelmsbad: Griechische, Römische, Altorientalische Puppen und Verwandtes* (Hanau: Hessisches Puppenmuseum, 2000), 195.

as dolls.[15] Dolls with sophisticated grooming kits and wardrobes are attested in elite burials from second-century Rome[16] and fourth- and fifth-century burials in Egypt.[17]

The practice of burying a little girl with a doll did not fall into eclipse in the medieval period. The body of a child in a burial excavated during 1905/1906 at Saqqara, northeast of the Fayyum oasis, had a bronze cross on the left arm and a small rag doll in one hand. The burial dated to between the seventh and ninth centuries.[18]

Along with numerous rag dolls that can be dated through the textiles used in their construction,[19] a wide production of bone dolls, usually called Coptic dolls, can be traced from the time immediately after the Arab conquest, that is, from the late seventh century to the eleventh century.[20] Recent studies devoted to this material permit illustrating the

[15]Merker, *Corinth XVIII, Part 4, The Sanctuary of Demeter and Kore: Terracotta Figurines of the Classical, Hellenistic, and Roman Periods* (Princeton: American School of Classical Studies at Athens, 2000), 48–59; Baird, *The Inner Lives of Ancient Houses: An Archaeology of Dura Europos* (Oxford: Oxford University Press, 2014), 180–81.

[16]D'Ambra, "Beauty and the Roman Female Portrait," In *Art and Rhetoric in Roman Culture*, edited by Jaś Elsner and Michel Meyer (Cambridge: Cambridge University Press, 2014), 155–80; Hautala, "Why Did the Ancient Romans Put Toys in Their Children's Graves? Interpretations from the Era of Antiquarianism to 20th Century Anthropology," In *Agents and Objects: Children in Pre-Modern Europe*, edited by Katariina Mustakallio and Jussi Hanska (Rome: Institutum Romanum Finlandiae, 2015), 179–99; Newby, "The Grottarossa Doll and Her Mistress: Hope and Consolation in a Roman Tomb," In *The Materiality of Mourning: Cross-Disciplinary Perspectives*, edited by Zahra Newby and Ruth E. Toulson (Oxford: Routledge, 2019), 77–102.

[17]Janssen, "Soft Toys from Egypt," In *Archaeological Research in Roman Egypt: The Proceedings of the Seventeenth Classical Colloquium of the Department of Greek and Roman Antiquities, British Museum, held on 1–4 December, 1993*, edited by Donald M. Bailey, JRA Supplementary Series 19 (Ann Arbor, MI: Journal of Roman Studies, 1996), 231–39.

[18]Quibell, *Excavations at Saqqara (1905–1906)* (Cairo: Imprimerie de l'Institut français d'archéologie orientale, 1907), 12, pl. 38, no. 4; Fluck, "Ägyptische Puppen aus römischer bis früharabischer Zeit," In *Gedenkschrift Ulrike Horak (P. Horak)*, edited by Rosario Pintaudi, Papyrologica Florentina 34 (Florence: Edizioni Gonnelli, 2004), 389; Johnson, "Textile and Papyrus Figurines from Karanis" (*Bulletin of the University of Michigan Museums of Art and Archaeology* 15: 49–64, 2003), 59. https://quod.lib.umich.edu/b/bulletinfront/0054307.0015.103?view=text;rgn=main.

[19]Pitarakis, "The Material Culture of Childhood in Byzantium," 247.

[20]Evans and Ratliff, *Byzantium and Islam: Age of Transition, 7th–9th Century* (New York: Metropolitan Museum of Art, 2012), 193–94, nos. 134–135; Fluck, "Ägyptische Puppen aus römischer bis früharabischer Zeit," In *Gedenkschrift Ulrike Horak (P. Horak)*, edited by Rosario Pintaudi, Papyrologica Florentina 34 (Florence: Edizioni Gonnelli, 2004), 9–12; Török, *Coptic Antiquities, Vol. 1. Stone Sculpture, Bronze Objects; Ceramic Coffin Lids and Vessels; Terracotta Statuettes, Bone, Wood, and Glass Artefacts* (Rome: L'Erma di Bretschneider, 1993), 59–64.

broader geographical distribution of this trend throughout Palestine[21] and in eastern Anatolia during the Abbassid period.[22] The find spots from Palestine often include domestic contexts in major urban centers and city dumps, which have encouraged their identification as toy dolls.

Two main types of bone dolls can be distinguished. One is that of an elongated figurine, inspired by earlier pre-Islamic productions made from a single piece of bone, with triangular structuring around the pelvis, highlighting the reproductive power of females. The breasts are indicated through carving. A pair of drilled holes at shoulder level allow the insertion of arms with pegs. The legs are not articulated. The facial features are sculpted in the round and sometimes painted. The dolls often sport elaborate wigs of wool or human hair attached with bitumen or clay. The second type of doll has a head made of bone with a sharp triangular protrusion at the bottom that allows it to be stuck into the soft rags constituting the doll's body.[23]

A wardrobe, jewelry, and footwear accompanied these bone dolls. In some instances, the dolls also had small balls made from rag, testifying to their primary function as toys. Some took the shape of sophisticated women with long hair and luxurious garments. One such impressive example at the Benaki Museum wears fourteen layers of tunics made in different materials, including linen, wool, cotton, silk, and hemp.[24] Two of the tunics have luxurious strips of brocaded silk.[25] This outstanding piece was perhaps intended to prepare the girl who owned it for her new role as bride and may have been offered as a dowry gift, as in the case of bride dolls from nineteenth-century Greece.[26]

---

[21] Shatil, "Bone Figurines of the Early Islamic Period: The 'So-Called' Coptic Dolls from Palestine and Egypt," In *Close to Bone: Current Studies in Bone Technologies*, edited by Selena Vitesović (Belgrade: Institute of Archaeology, 2016), 296–314; Ayalon, *The Assemblage of Bone and Ivory Artifacts from Caesarea Maritima, Israel, 1st–13th Centuries CE*, BAR International Series 1457 (Oxford: Archaeopress, 2005), 80–85.

[22] Özyar et al., "Recent Fieldwork at Tarsus-Gözlukkule: The Medieval Layers," In *The Archaeology of Anatolia, Vol. 2. Recent Discoveries (2015–2016)*, edited by Sharon R. Steadman and Gregory Mc Mahon (Cambridge: Cambridge University Press, 2017), 214–15.

[23] See (Fig. 2).

[24] See (Fig. 3).

[25] Pitarakis, "The Material Culture of Childhood in Byzantium," 243–46.

[26] Argyriadi, "The Influences of Christian Ritual and Tradition on Children's Play: Religious Toys and Games" (*Εθνογραφικά* 9: 1993), 215.

The doll is historically a vector of humans psychological and cultural development, especially girls. It plays a role in forming gender and social identities. Recent discussions around the function of dolls from the Roman period tend to position them as toys invested with an educational purpose, primarily for preparing little girls for future roles as wives and mothers.[27] The size of dolls and their features can be modeled to allow a child to carry it, take it in her arms, feed it, dress and undress it, and have it perform hygiene rituals that she likely observes her mother doing. The dresses, accessories, and hair can transform it into the double of the little girl who owns it or people she sees in her life.

Spinning and weaving were the two major women's occupations in Byzantine households. Fashioning dresses for a doll's wardrobe and making rag dolls were probably the best pedagogical tools for teaching these skills to young girls. Through play, girls could be inculcated with the experience of motherhood. Testimony in a passage from the *Life* of Agatha by the patriarch Methodios[28] speaks of teenage girls "striving to breastfeed even figuratively in their childish play."[29]

The doll's role in imitating life situations during play has encouraged examination through the application of interpretations drawn from anthropological theory with regard to objects or images having power of action and agency. As in the case of idols, the doll assumes agency in the hands of a girl at play. What makes it an animate object are not only its inherent human features, such as jointed limbs, but the life a girl imparts it through dressing, adorning, feeding, and carrying her. The doll becomes a projected, idealized portrait of the girl who owns her.

The metaphors of marriage applied to death in Greek mythology and the Christian faith provide interesting clues for uncovering the message of dolls offered as grave goods. In the pagan context of accompanying the child in the rites of passage to adulthood, the doll offers auspicious

---

[27]Dolansky, "Playing with Gender: Girls, Dolls, and Adult Ideals in the Roman World" (*Classical Antiquity* 31, no. 2, October 2012), 256–92.

[28]Methodios, *Enkomion of St. Agatha (BHG* 38*)*, Mioni, Elpidio, ed. 1950, "L'Encomio di S. Agata: Di Metodio Patriarca di Constantinopoli," In *Mélanges Paul Peeters II, Analecta Bollandiana*, 788/800–847, 58–93.

[29]Ibid., 58–93; Krausmüller, "Divine Sex: Patriarch Methodios' Concept of Virginity," In *Desire and Denial in Byzantium: Papers from the Thirty-First Symposium of Byzantine Studies*, University of Sussex, Brighton, March, 1997, ed. Liz James (Aldershot: Ashgate, 1999), 62.

company for the child's journey to its last abode. From the Christian perspective, the doll, emphasizing the identity and status of the deceased as an unmarried virgin, was probably imbued with a spiritual message. One may suggest that it was intended to protect the child on its journey to the Judgment Seat, which in the Christian exegesis equates to the bridal chamber, where Christ the Bridegroom awaits the souls of the deceased.[30]

Education, Play, and Preparation for Adult Roles

As can be seen above, playful methods of teaching to make learning effective and enjoyable were not unknown to the ancients. The writings of the church fathers also provide interesting evidence. Parents from the upper echelons of society could afford to buy luxury items for their offspring. Among this set, learning the alphabet with letters made of boxwood or ivory was perceived as an enjoyable game. Jerome offers advice to four-year-old Paula's mother for her daughter's education. By encouraging the little girl to say the letters, her mother could turn play into learning. Jerome also advises the mother to entice her toward greater progress with a reward, namely, little gifts that delight the child.[31] Another letter, addressed to the mother of Pacatula, includes a list of rewards—a bright bunch of flowers, a glittering bauble, an enchanting doll—for encouraging the rapid performance of tasks.[32]

The link between play and education lay at the core of the formation of Christian identity and the intellectual consciousness of children. John Chrysostom's observations on the tempering of the passions of a young boy with regard to damage done to his writing implements offer an

[30]Clark, "The Celibate Bridegroom and His Virginal Brides: Metaphor and the Marriage of Jesus in Early Christian Ascetic Exegesis" (*Church History* 77, no. 1, March 2008), 1–25.

[31]Jerome, *Epistulae*, Hilberg, I., ed. 1910–1918, Sancti Eusebii Hieronymi Epistulae, 3 vols. CSEL 54–56, 107.4.2–3; Katz, "Educating Paula: A Proposed Curriculum for Raising a 4th-Century Christian Infant," In *Constructions of Childhood in Ancient Greece and in Italy*, edited by Ada Cohen and Jeremy B. Rutter, Hesperia Supplement 41 (Princeton: ASCSA Publications, 2007), 121–22.

[32]Jerome, *Epistulae*, Hilberg, I., ed. 1910–1918, Sancti Eusebii Hieronymi Epistulae, 3 vols. CSEL 54–56, 128.1.

instructive example: "If the boy has tablets fashioned of fine wood, clean and without stain, held together by bronze chains, and silver pencils and other boyish possessions, and his servant loses or breaks them, and the boy refrains from anger, he has displayed already all the marks of the philosophic mind."[33] The corpus of writing tablets and papyri from Egypt includes many examples of writing exercises involving the letters of the alphabet along with extracts from Psalms.[34]

Games of Skill and Chance

According to the testimony of the church father John Chrysostom, boys carried around sets of toys called *athyrmata* (ἀθύρματα), which they would play with their peers. These included knucklebones (*astragaloi*), marbles, nuts, gaming pieces for board games, hoops, and balls.[35] Especially appealing to boys were spinning tops (στρόμβος, βέμβιξ) made of wood or clay that turned on a peg or were spun by means of a cord or a stick.

Boys and girls alike enjoyed playing with knucklebones from the ankle joints of young calves, sheep, or goats. Imitations of astragaloi could also be crafted from a great variety of materials, including metal, marble, ivory, wood, glass, and terracotta. The simplest and perhaps most common game played with them was comparable to the modern game of jackstones. Five knucklebones were simultaneously tossed in the air with the goal of catching as many as possible on the back of one's hand. Knucklebones were also used like dice in games involving throwing. Each side has a different morphology—concave and convex

---

[33]Chrysostom, Laistner, Max L. V., trans. (1952) 1967, "An Address on Vainglory and The Right Way for Parents to Bring Up Their Children," In *Christianity and Pagan Culture in the Late Roman Empire, Together with an English Translation of John Chrysostom's Address on Vainglory and The Right Way for Parents to Bring Up Their Children*, Reprint (Ithaca, NY: Cornell University Press); Greek text and French translation by Anne-Marie Malingrey, *Sur la vaine gloire et l'éducation des enfants,* Sources chrétiennes 188 (Paris: Cerf, 1972), 73.

[34]Pitarakis, "Les images d'écoliers dans l'art byzantin: Origines et significations" (*Cahiers archéologiques*, 2011–2012), 93, n. 50; Fournet, "Nouveaux textes scolaires grecs et coptes" (*Bulletin de l'Institut français d'archéologie orientale* 101, 2001), 160–62.

[35]Chrysostom, *On Vainglory*, 58:486 and 59:386.

for the broader sides, flat and indented for the narrow ones—each representing a different numerical value. Usually astragaloi were thrown in sets of four or five and their values determined according to their upper face after they stopped rolling.[36]

Youths also played popular board games. A "board" could be scratched on any available material as well as on the ground and in sand. Several types of gameboards incised on benches, paving slabs, or reused bricks and tiles have come to light during archaeological work in Anatolia[37] and Greece.[38] Reconstructing them assisted with the restitution of multiple types of marbles, flat round board counters in terracotta, ivory, bone, and stone that were yielded in the same contexts. Two main types of boards were identified: those involving incised lines and diagrams and others using parallel rows of pits.

More research synthesizing work on gameboards from the Byzantine era still awaits. Knowledge about the types of games that were played remains fairly vague. It is commonly accepted that popular games from the Roman period continued well into late antiquity and the medieval period. Nine Men's Morris and Twelve Men's Morris are among the most popular strategy games played in late antiquity.[39]

Toy Substitutes: "Go Outside and Play"

Crafted toys from organized productions help create social interactions between children and the adult world. Presented as gifts to a child, such toys often had an educative purpose while retaining the concepts of

[36]Ayalon, *The Assemblage of Bone and Ivory Artifacts from Caesarea Maritima, Israel, 1st–13th Centuries CE*, BAR International Series 1457 (Oxford: Archaeopress, 2005), 71.

[37]Witte, "Toys, Game Pieces, and Boards, 1988–2005," In *Amorium Reports*, Vol. 3. *The Lower City Enclosure: Finds Reports and Technical Studies*, edited by Christopher S. Lightfoot and Eric A. Ivison (Istanbul: Amorium Excavations Project, 2012), 277–96; Roueché, "Late Roman and Byzantine Game Boards at Aphrodisias," In Finkel (2007), 100–105.

[38]Vroom, "Playing Games in the Valley of the Muses: A Medieval Board Game Found in Boeotia, Greece" (*Pharos* 7, 1999), 93–110; Papanikola-Bakirtzi, *Everyday Life in Byzantium*, Exhibition Catalogue (Athens: Hellenic Ministry of Culture, 2002), 206–207, nos. 233–234.

[39]Bell and Roueché, "Graeco-Roman Pavement Signs and Game Boards," In Finkel (2007), 106–109.

amusement and pastime inherent to toys. Such toys contribute to the cognitive development of children. As memory and imagination develop, a child invests objects with symbolic meanings, such that any object in his or her environment can become a plaything. Growing awareness of external events and of the thoughts, feelings, and beliefs of others then leads to play becoming a way of interacting with the outside world, entering the domain of animals and familiar and unfamiliar humans. During these various stages, the child devises multiple substitutes for toys, many of which do not leave material traces.

Child's Play and the Natural Environment

A universal characteristic of children is their ability to devise scores of collective outdoor games involving interaction with the immediate environment. Written and visual sources from Byzantium offer many instances of children playing on the shore of a river or a lake, fishing, climbing trees, picking fruit in trees, creating tree swings using rope, running, hiding, dancing, playing music, among other things. These activities do not entail the production of material culture but offer rich testimony to the central role of play in childrens' lives. As a child develops sufficiently to apply abstract meaning to material objects, he or she can use those objects as substitutes for a person or an animal. For instance, βιτάλιν, a well-attested game in Byzantium, involves using a stick as a substitute for a horse in order to mimic the act of riding and engaging with a real horse.[40]

The Byzantines reared birds not only for food but also for sport, hunting, and other purposes. Birds played an important role in the urban landscape, with peacocks, partridges, and geese being commonly placed in private gardens and public spaces as decoration. Catching birds as play was part of the daily life of Byzantine children, who were also hired to herd sheep or fowl. Pets played an important role in their lives as well.[41]

---

[40]Dirk C. Hessling and Hubert Pernot, *Poèmes prodromiques en grec vulgaire* (Amsterdam: Johannes Müller, 1910), 2.26.

[41]Bradley, "The Sentimental Education of the Roman Child: The Role of Pet Keeping" (*Latomus: Revue d'études latines* 57, No. 3, 1998), 523–57.

There were also instances of exotic animals, such as for example a giraffe offered around 1261 as a diplomatic gift from the sultan of Egypt, being walked around the agora of Constantinople for the amusement of the public.[42]

Birds' capacity to fly free from earthly bonds influenced their symbolic use in sacred settings. In the *Infancy Gospel of Thomas*,[43] one finds many elements drawn from real life in the episode of the five-year-old Jesus giving life to twelve sparrows that he shaped from soft clay while playing at the ford of a brook.[44]

The anecdote about the young patriarch Theophylact, who ascended to the patriarchal throne at the age of sixteen, bears interesting witness to the attachment of young boys from the court to their horses. In one instance, as Theophylact officiated in Hagia Sophia, he was told that his favorite mare had foaled. He hastily finished the service and ran to the stable. After satisfying himself that everything had been done for the comfort of the mare and foal, he returned to the cathedral and his place in the procession.[45]

It was an expectation that the Byzantine emperor master horsemanship, partaking in it as physical exercise and for hunting, activities highlighted in imperial panegyrics. One learns, for instance, that between the ages of eight and thirteen the future Andronikos II was leading the hounds and hunting hares and birds. He also excelled at discus throwing, jumping, and horse riding. Polo, a game of choice, allowed adolescent princes to test their horsemanship, and exercises simulating events on the battlefield were part of the young princes' education and play.[46]

---

[42]Ševčenko, "Wild Animals in the Byzantine Park," In *Byzantine Garden Culture*, edited by Antony Robert Littlewood, Henry Maguire, and Joachim Wolschke-Bulmahn (Washington, DC: Dumbarton Oaks Research Library and Collection, 2002), 78.

[43]Reider, *The Childhood of Jesus: Decoding the Apocryphal Infancy Gospel of Thomas* (Eugene, Oregon: Cascade Books, 2009), 2:2–4.

[44]Ibid., 86–102.

[45]McCabe, *Byzantine Encyclopaedia of Horse Medicine: The Sources, Compilation, and Transmission of the Hippiatrica* (Oxford: Oxford University Press 2007), 278.

[46]Angelov, "Emperors and Patriarchs as Ideal Children and Adolescents: Literary Conventions and Cultural Expectations," In Papaconstantinou and Talbot (2009), 109–11.

The Body as a Source of Play

A child crawling or taking its first steps toward a parent is a delightful moment as well as one introducing the child instinctively to the world of play. The need to develop motor skills, accompanied by a surplus of energy and motion, makes a child's body a source of play. Running, jumping, and twirling are among the various movements made by children at play, sometimes animated by laughter. Experimenting with the use of sound and motion leads them to mimic the actions and noises made by animals and other people as entertainment.

A vivid testimony from the *Life of Simeon the Holy Fool*[47] finds the holy man walking in the streets of Emesa, Syria, when he comes across some young girls dancing while singing satirical songs. To punish the girls, who are making fun of him, he makes them cross-eyed. To then relieve them of this affliction, he asks them to let him kiss their eyes.[48] In another passage, Simeon encounters some youths outside the city playing *lysoporta*,[49] which is equivalent to the American game red rover and is still played around the eastern Mediterranean.[50]

Sometimes boys organized into teams to play sequences of outdoor games. The playing of marbles or knucklebones, for instance, would be followed by a game involving physical strength, such as wrestling. The image of boys wrestling is common in iconography from the Palaiologan era, which is characterized by a growing taste for genre scenes. This motif was invested with a metaphorical meaning in religious iconography, however.

In *Address on Vainglory and The Right Way For Parents to Bring Up Their Children*, John Chrysostom extols to parents that among the members of

[47]Written ca. 642–649.

[48]Greek text with French translation Festugière, André Jean, and Lennart Rydén, eds. 1974, *Léontios de Néapolis, Vie de Syméon le fou et Vie de Jean de Chypre* (Paris: Librairie orientaliste Paul Geuthne, 1974), 91–92; Krueger, *Simeon the Holy Fool: Leontius's Life and the Late Antique City* (London: University of California Press, 1996), 41.

[49]Festugière, *Léontios de Néapolis, Vie de Syméon le fou et Vie de Jean de Chypre*, ch. 15; Krueger, *Simeon the Holy Fool: Leontius's Life and the Late Antique City*, 154.

[50]Aerts, "Emesa in der vita Simeonis Sali von Leontios von Neapolis," In *From Late Antiquity to Early Byzantium*, edited by Vladimir Vavrinék (Prague: Academia, 1985), 114–15.

the household, their boys especially should exercise and practice controlling their passions. Just as wrestlers train with their friends before a contest so that when they have triumphed against them they can go on to become invincible against other opponents, so must boys must be trained in the home.[51]

References to children's games in Byzantine literature show them in dangerous situations involving falls and various other kinds of accidents. Children fall out of buildings while playing when their curiosity leads them to crawl onto the window ledge. They also fall into boiling cauldrons and wells.[52] The *Infancy Gospel of Thomas*[53] includes an episode about a child engaged in a game on the roof of a house. The child falls off the roof and dies. Little Jesus resurrects the child. Another interesting example comes from the *Life* of Elias the Spelaiotes, a tenth-century southern Italian saint. Elias had crushed his fingers as a result of a childhood fall. An ignorant and inexperienced doctor places them in a wooden splint (*narthex*) and bounds them so tightly that in eight days all Elias's fingers fall off. As a result, the boy who received the surname Monocheir ("One Hand") decides to retreat from the world.[54]

Exploration of the skeletal remains of children in bioarchaeology can shed interesting light on children's lives in Byzantium. A picture from child skeletal groups of fracture patterns, muscular trauma, and infections due to fractures would serve as a valuable complement to the above discussion on accidents during play, although fractures may also be the result of violence against children or of child labor in difficult conditions.[55] The bones of infants and children are small and brittle, however, and more prone to physical and chemical changes after death than in

---

[51] Chrysostom, *On Vainglory*, ch. 68.

[52] Abrahamse, "Images of Childhood in Early Byzantine Hagiography" (*Journal of Psychohistory* 6 (4), 1979), 507; Moffatt, "The Byzantine Child" (*Social Research* 53: 1986), 707; Holman, "Sick Children and Healing Saints: Medical Treatment of the Child in Christian Antiquity," In Horn and Phenix (2009), 161–62.

[53] Reider, *The Childhood of Jesus: Decoding the Apocryphal Infancy Gospel of Thomas*, 9:1.

[54] Kazhdan, "The Image of the Medical Doctor in Byzantine Literature of the Tenth to Twelfth Centuries" (*DOP* 38 *Symposium on Byzantine Medicine*: 1984), 48; Skinner, *Health and Medicine in Early Medieval Southern Italy* (Leiden and New York: E.J. Brill, 1997), 94.

[55] Bourbou, *Health and Disease in Byzantine Crete (7th–12th Centuries AD)*. Medicine in the Medieval Mediterranean, 110.

the case of adults, so access to children's bones is more difficult. Worth mentioning is the example of a male youth who suffered from infection caused by a fracture. He was discovered among the eleventh- to thirteenth-century skeletal groups during excavations of the Church of St. Nicholas in Myra.[56] The ratio of infant death in these groups was found to be relatively low.[57]

Performance, Fantasy, and Parody: From Children's Play to Social Ritual and Artistic Production

Did Byzantines view children as miniature adults? Close observation of written and visual sources in conjunction with children's material culture tend to challenge this view, which has often been put forward following the controversial thesis of Philippe Ariès that medieval society had no concept of childhood.[58] Byzantines were aware that children had worlds of their own involving specific needs and behaviors. The feelings adults expressed toward children were different from those expressed toward other adults. One important element to take into consideration, however, is the distinction between an ordinary child and the ideal child. Maturity was expected of the ideal child, henceforth the motif of the *puer senex*, adult child. On the other hand, purity and the absence of sexual desire, essential characteristics of childhood in the eyes of early Christian thinkers, were the two driving forces fashioning the image of the ideal adult invested with solid hopes for entry into the eternal kingdom of God.

---

[56]Erdal, "Demre Aziz Nikolaos Topluluğundaki Travmaların Paleoepidemyolojik Analizi / Paleoepidemiology of Trauma in Saint Nicholas Church's Population from Demre," *Edebiyat Fakültesi Dergisi/Journal of Faculty of Letters* 26, no. 2 (Aralık / December): (in Turkish with English abstract), 2009a, 102–103. Many thanks to F. Arzu Demirel for her guidance on issues related to bioarchaeology in Anatolia.

[57]Erdal, "Demre Aziz Nikolaos Kilisesi Geç Bizans ve Yakınçağ İnsanlarının Yaşam Biçimleri," *Adalya* 12 (in Turkish with English abstract), 2009b, 365, 372.

[58]Brubaker, "Looking at the Byzantine Family," In Brubaker and Tougher (2013), 118; Brubaker, "Images of Byzantine Adolescents," In Ariantzi (2018), 144.

Toys, Enactment, and Illusion: A Glimpse into the Social Ritual and Artistic Production

Through the performative character of play, a toy acquires significance and power of agency. A similar relationship exists between a ritual object and the person using it in the performance of a ritual. In addition to the common feature of toys and ritual objects such as the bone figurines and clay animals tending to be small in size, they also share the further characteristic of possessing the power of agency. It is often difficult, however, to differentiate these categories through the archaeological record.

A miniature wooden boat equipped with a hole for pulling it by a string came to light in 2008 during excavations of the Theodosian port of Yenikapı in Istanbul.[59] It offers an amusing contrast to the numerous shipwrecks discovered during the same excavations.[60] An unequivocal identification of this object's initial function is difficult. It may have served as a toy, but one could plausibly also argue for its alternative function as a votive offering for protection while navigating the Mediterranean.

In exploring the possible meanings of the miniature boat, one may perhaps consider the Navigium Isidis, also known as the Carrus Navalis, or Greek Ploiaphesia (πλοιαφέσια), an important annual festival of the pagan world that survived into the fifth and sixth centuries.[61] During the celebration, a wheeled boat (*carrus navalis*) carrying wooden statues of Isis and her son, Horus/Harpocrates, was included in a procession as an allegoric representation of the forces of chaos challenging the creation and re-creation of the universe. The boat served as the model

---

[59] See (Fig. 4).

[60] Kızıltan and Baran Çelik, *Stories from the Hidden Harbor. Shipwrecks of Yenikapı* (Istanbul: Istanbul Archaeological Museums Press, 2013), 123, no. 67; Gökçay, "Yenikapı Ahşap Buluntularından Seçmeler / Selected Finds from Yenikapı," In İstanbul Arkeoloji Müzeleri 1. Marmaray Metro Kurtarma Kazıları Sempozyum Bildiriler Kitabı 5–6 Mayıs 2008 / Istanbul Archaeological Museums. Proceedings of the 1st Symposium of Marmaray-Metro Salvage Excavations. 5–6 May 2008, edited by Ufuk Kocabaş and Zeynep Kızıltan (Istanbul: Directorate of Istanbul Archaeological Museums, 2010), 152, no. 21.

[61] John Lydos, Wünsch, Richard, ed. 1898, *De mensibus*, Leipzig: B. G. Teubner,
Hooker Mischa, trans., *John Lydus, "On the Months" / "De Mensibus,"* Translated with Introduction and Annotation by Mischa Hooker, 2nd ed. (Internet Archive, Roger-Pearse Open Access, 2017), IV.45.

for the production of small-scale versions intended for private worship by members of the religious cult.

With the obvious intention of ridiculing pagan rituals, Lactantius, adviser to Constantine I and tutor to his son, observed that the ritual of the washing of the statues and adorning them with clothes and offering them food resembled the play of a little girl with her dolls. The only difference, he asserted, was their size. He grounded his argument in a quote from the Roman poet Persius, who spoke about the dolls that a girl had dedicated to Venus.[62] In the pagan statues that Constantine I had brought to Constantinople to adorn the city, the historian Eusebius, in his turn, saw toys for the laughter and amusement of the public.[63]

The fourth-century comparisons between pagan statues and toys bring to mind a much later testimony referencing the cult of icons during the iconoclast crisis. The first episode in the story concerns a visit by the daughters of the imperial couple Theodora and Theophilos to their maternal grandmother, Theoktiste, who introduces them to worshiping icons. One learns that during the visit of her five granddaughters, Theoktiste would greet them with gifts before privately taking them aside and instructing them to worship icons that she kept in a chest. When Theophilos hears about this and interrogates his daughters, the young Pulcheria, speaks of her grandmother's kindnesses and the multitude of fruits that she offered them. She also recounts worshiping the images, thinking and stating in her innocence that Theoktiste had dolls in a chest that she pressed upon the heads and faces of the girls after she and her sister had kissed them. In the next chapter of the same text, when the court jester Denderis discovers Empress Theodora worshiping an icon,

[62]Lactantius, Anthony Bowen and Peter Garnsey, eds. and trans., *Lactantius: Divine Institutes*, Translated Texts for Historians 40 (Liverpool: Liverpool University Press, 2003), 2.4.13; Hautala, "Why Did the Ancient Romans Put Toys in Their Children's Graves? Interpretations from the Era of Antiquarianism to 20th Century Anthropology," In *Agents and Objects: Children in Pre-Modern Europe*, edited by Katariina Mustakallio and Jussi Hanska (Rome: Institutum Romanum Finlandiae, 2015), 191.

[63]Cameron, Averil, and Hall, Stuart G., ed. and trans., *Eusebius: Life of Constantine*, Clarendon Ancient History Series (Oxford: Clarendon Press, 1999), 143.

the empress tries to fool him by claiming that she is actually playing with dolls.[64]

Byzantine parents were encouraged to take their children of all ages to church. Testimonies about children's church attendance offer interesting insight on the inclination of children to play everywhere and under all circumstances. It appears that children brought marbles to church, played with nuts, and wrote graffiti on the walls.[65] Impressed by the theatricality of the sacraments, they keenly reenacted the church ritual as play. Children reenacting the liturgy is a recurring feature in the beneficial tales literature.

In the collection known as the *Spiritual Meadow*, by John Moschos, from circa 600, these games are often presented as prophetic because their performers later come to occupy the highest positions in the church hierarchy, including the patriarchal throne. Such was the case of Athanasios, the future patriarch of Alexandria who had played at baptizing his friends on the beach.[66] Preceding the story of Athanasios is an evocative tale about a group of boys from a village near Apamea, in Syria, who celebrate the Eucharist as play. A flat rock served as the altar on which they placed bread and a jug of wine, representing the chalice. The boy pretending to be the priest pronounced the words of consecration. As they prepared to divide the bread, a miraculous fire burst from the heavens and consumes everything around the boys.[67] For the purposes of the beneficial tales, the play of the children was presented as a divine omen. Their sacrilegious behavior was forgiven because of their innocence and was used to put them on the path of God.

---

[64]Featherstone, Michael J., and Signes-Codoñer, Juan ed. and trans., *Chronographiae quae Theophanis Continuati nomine fertur Libri I-IV*, CFHB 53 (Boston and Berlin: Walter de Gruyter, 2015), III.5–6.

[65]Chevallier Caseau, "Childhood in Byzantine Saints' Lives," In Papaconstantinou and Talbot (2009), 150; "La place des enfants dans les églises d'orient (IIIe–Xe siècles)," In *Famille, violence et christianisation au Moyen Âge: Mélanges offerts à Michel Rouche*, edited by Martin Aurell and Thomas Deswarte (Paris: Presses de l'Université Paris Sorbonne, 2005), 19–22.

[66]Moschos, Wortley, John, trans., *The Spiritual Meadow* (Kalamazoo: Cistercian Publications, 1992), no. 197; PG 87:3084.

[67]Moschos, *The Spiritual Meadow*, no. 197; Duffy, "Playing at Ritual: Variations on a Theme in Byzantine Religious Tales," In *Greek Ritual Poetics*, edited by Dimitrios Yatromanolakis and Panagiotis Roilos (Cambridge, MA, and London: Center for Hellenic Studies, Trustees for Harvard University, and Foundation of the Hellenic World, 2004), 203–4.

When such realities were parodied by adults, they did not result in similar indulgence. Their origin was not divine, but demonic. Emperor Michael III[68] and members from his court mocked the liturgy in celebrating the Mysteries by performing the chants with a lyre and offered communion by filling the golden pearl-encrusted vessels with vinegar and mustard. Offended by the fake liturgies staged by a mock clergy, Theodora, the pious mother of the emperor, made clear to him that he had removed himself from the providence and hand of God.[69]

Fantasy and Reality on Stage: Children and Putti on Artistic Media

The Roman tradition of images of children and putti performing adult activities was also preserved during late antiquity. The mosaic pavements from Villa Casale, near Piazza Armerina, in south-central Sicily date to the first decades of the fourth century. The mosaics in the villa's private apartments include a parody of a circus game played by children riding chariots driven by birds.[70] Another section of pavement at the villa features a hunt by children modeled after compositions of gladiatorial combat, *venatio*, involving tame animals, such as a goat, a rooster, hares, geese, that is, animals that were sometimes kept as pets by children at the time. The images on the pavements are subject to various interpretations, including viewing them as part of children's education, as highlighting the private sphere, and as an attempt to illustrate the superiority of hunting to combat in an arena.[71]

The Villa Casale compositions find close comparison in the vestibule of the Great Palace of Constantinople dated to the first half of the sixth century. The mosaic of youths spinning hoops at the turning points of the Hippodrome is among the most frequently illustrated in studies

[68] r. 842–867.

[69] *Theophanes Continuatus, Theophanes Continuati Libri I–IV*, 38–39.

[70] Hennessy, *Images of Children in Byzantium* (Farnham and Burlington, VT: Ashgate Publishing Limited, 2008), 48–49, Fig. 4.

[71] Vendries, "L'enfant et le coq: Une allusion à la gladiature sur la mosaïque des enfants 'chasseurs' de Piazza Armerina" (*Antiquité Tardive* 15, 2007), 159–79.

devoted to children's games in Byzantium. The image is not of a real game, but is a parody in which the original setting of the Hippodrome has been transformed into a theater stage. The pavement also includes several bucolic scenes with children interacting with pets and exotic animals.[72]

The Hippodrome continued to present spectacles that fascinated children during the middle Byzantine period, when it became a stage for equestrian demonstrations, acrobatic performances, juggling, and so on. Children were among the fervent spectators at jestings and other events. Praise for children deemed exemplary for their maturity and seriousness in hagiographic literature often included that they did not participate in jesting and spectacles that delighted their peers.[73] Such performances were frequently held at the palace. Around 1200, according to the historian Niketas Choniates, a noble's child at the Blachernai Palace kicked the buttocks of the eunuch who was orchestrating the performances.[74]

Conclusion

As a privileged category of material culture, toys can assist in exploring the relationship between agency and object biography, two topics popular in the fields of social anthropology and ethnography.[75] The acquisition and offering of toys to a child create new chains of social interaction and links between generations. The power of agency inherent to toys also implies that any object in a child's environment can be transformed into a toy through phantasy and the capacity for abstraction.

The examination of the interactions of a child with nature and animals while playing and social interactions with the adult world and with other children show that child's play and toys also served as vehicles in the

---

[72]Hennessy, *Images of Children in Byzantium*, 53–57.

[73]Moffatt, "The Byzantine Child" (*Social Research* 53, 1986), 706.

[74]*V*an Dieten, Jan Louis, ed., *Nicetae Choniatae Historia*, CFHB 11, 1–2 (Berlin: De Gruyter, 1975), 508.

[75]Gell, *Art and Agency: A New Anthropological Theory* (Oxford: Oxford University Press, 1998); Hoskins, "Agency, Biography and Objects," In *Handbook of Material Culture*, edited by Christopher Tilley, Webb Keane, Susanne Küchler, Michael Rowlands, and Patricia Spyer (London: Sage, 2006), 74–84.

quest of knowledge of God. Abstraction and phantasm, the two central elements in children's play, also regulate exchanges between the sensible and the intelligible in all aspects of secular and religious life in Byzantium. The universe of children's play thus offers a valuable tool for a new reading of Byzantine artistic production.

References

Primary Sources

Eusebius, *Life.*

Cameron, Averil, and Hall, Stuart G., ed. and trans. 1999. *Eusebius: Life of Constantine*. Clarendon Ancient History Series. Oxford: Clarendon Press.

Infancy Gospel of Thomas.

Reider, Asgaard. 2009. *The Childhood of Jesus: Decoding the Apocryphal Infancy Gospel of Thomas*. Eugene, OR: Cascade Books.

Jerome, *Epistulae.*

Hilberg, I., ed. 1910–1918. *Sancti Eusebii Hieronymi Epistulae*, 3 vols. CSEL 54–56.

John Chrysostom, *On Vainglory.*

Laistner, Max L. V., trans. (1952) 1967. "An Address on Vainglory and The Right Way for Parents to Bring Up Their Children." In *Christianity and Pagan Culture in the Late Roman Empire, Together with an English Translation of John Chrysostom's Address on Vainglory and The Right Way for Parents to Bring Up Their Children*, 75–122. Reprint, Ithaca, NY: Cornell University Press; Greek text and French translation by Anne-Marie Malingrey, *Sur la vaine gloire et l'éducation des enfants* (Sources chrétiennes 188). Paris: Éditions du Cerf, 1972.

John Lydos, *De Mensibus.*

Wünsch, Richard (ed.). 1898. *De mensibus*. Leipzig: B. G. Teubner.

Hooker Mischa, trans. 2017. *John Lydus, "On the Months" / "De Mensibus."* Translated with Introduction and Annotation by Mischa Hooker. 2nd ed. Internet Archive. Roger-Pearse Open Access.

John Moschos, *The Spiritual Meadow.*

Wortley, John, trans. 1992. *The Spiritual Meadow*. Kalamazoo: Cistercian Publications.

Simeon the Fool.
Krueger, Derek, 1996. *Simeon the Holy Fool: Leontius's Life and the Late Antique City*. London: University of California Press; Greek text with French translation Festugière, André Jean, and Lennart Rydén, eds. 1974. *Léontios de Néapolis, Vie de Syméon le fou et Vie de Jean de Chypre*. Paris: Librairie orientaliste Paul Geuthner.
Lactantius, *Divine Institutes.*
Anthony Bowen, and Peter Garnsey, eds. and trans. 2003. *Lactantius: Divine Institutes*. Translated Texts for Historians 40. Liverpool: Liverpool University Press.
Niketas Choniates, *Historia.*
Van Dieten, Jan Louis, ed. 1975. *Nicetae Choniatae Historia.* CFHB 11, 1–2. Berlin: De Gruyter.
Prodromic Poems.
Hesseling, Dirk C., and Hubert Pernot. 1910. *Poèmes prodromiques en grec vulgaire*. Amsterdam: Johannes Müller.
Methodios, *Enkomion of St. Agatha (BHG 38).*
Mioni, Elpidio, ed. 1950. "L'Encomio di S. Agata: Di Metodio Patriarca di Constantinopoli." In *Mélanges Paul Peeters II, Analecta Bollandiana* 68: 58–93.
Theophanes Continuatus, *Theophanes Continuati Libri I–IV.*
Featherstone, Michael J., and Signes-Codoñer, Juan ed. and trans. 2015. *Chronographiae quae Theophanis Continuati nomine fertur Libri I-IV*. CFHB 53. Boston and Berlin: Walter de Gruyter.

Secondary Literature

Abrahamse, Dorothy. 1979. "Images of Childhood in Early Byzantine Hagiography." *Journal of Psychohistory* 6 (4): 497–517.
Aerts, Willem J. 1985. "Emesa in der vita Simeonis Sali von Leontios von Neapolis." In *From Late Antiquity to Early Byzantium*, edited by Vladimir Vavrinék, 113–16. Prague: Academia.
Andres, Mirjam. 2000. *Die Antiken Sammlung, Hessisches Puppenmuseum Hanau-Wilhelmsbad: Griechische, Römische, Altorientalische Puppen und Verwandtes*. Hanau: Hessisches Puppenmuseum.
Angelov, Dimiter G. 2009. "Emperors and Patriarchs as Ideal Children and Adolescents: Literary Conventions and Cultural Expectations." In Papaconstantinou and Talbot 2009, 85–125.

Argyriadi, Maria. 1993. "The Influences of Christian Ritual and Tradition on Children's Play: Religious Toys and Games." *Εθνογραφικά* 9: 213–22.

Ariantzi, Despoina, ed. 2018. *Coming of Age in Byzantium: Adolescence and Society*. Millenium Studies 69. Berlin and Boston: De Gruyter.

Ayalon, Etan. 2005. *The Assemblage of Bone and Ivory Artifacts from Caesarea Maritima, Israel, 1st–13th Centuries CE*. BAR International Series 1457. Oxford: Archaeopress.

Baird, Jennifer A. 2014. *The Inner Lives of Ancient Houses: An Archaeology of Dura Europos*. Oxford: Oxford University Press.

Baran Çelik, Gülbahar, ed. 2010. *Byzantine Palaces in Istanbul*. Exhibition catalogue. Istanbul: Zerobooks.

Bell, Robert Charles, and Charlotte M. Roueché. 2007. "Graeco-Roman Pavement Signs and Game Boards." In Finkel 2007, 106–109.

Bourbou, Chrysa. 2010. *Health and Disease in Byzantine Crete (7th–12th Centuries AD)*. Medicine in the Medieval Mediterranean. Farnham and Burlington, VT: Ashgate.

Bradley, Keith R. 1998. "The Sentimental Education of the Roman Child: The Role of Pet Keeping." *Latomus: Revue d'études latines* 57, no. 3: 523–57.

Brubaker, Leslie. 2013. "Looking at the Byzantine Family." In Brubaker and Tougher 2013, 177–206.

Brubaker, Leslie. 2018. "Images of Byzantine Adolescents." In Ariantzi 2018, 141–74.

Brubaker, Leslie, and Shaun Tougher, eds. 2013. *Approaches to the Byzantine Family*. Birmingham Byzantine and Ottoman Studies. London and New York: Routledge, Taylor and Francis Group.

Calament, Florence. 2005. *La révélation d'Antinoé par Albert Gayet. Histoire, archéologie, muséographie*, 2 vols. Bibliothèque des études coptes 18/1. Cairo: Institut français d'archéologie orientale.

Chevallier Caseau, Béatrice. 2005. "La place des enfants dans les églises d'orient (IIIe–Xe siècles)." In *Famille, violence et christianisation au Moyen Âge: Mélanges offerts à Michel Rouche*, edited by Martin Aurell and Thomas Deswarte, 15–27. Paris: Presses de l'Université Paris Sorbonne.

Chevallier Caseau, Béatrice. 2009. "Childhood in Byzantine Saints' Lives." In Papaconstantinou and Talbot 2009, 127–66.

Clark, Elizabeth A. 2008. "The Celibate Bridegroom and His Virginal Brides: Metaphor and the Marriage of Jesus in Early Christian Ascetic Exegesis." *Church History* 77, no. 1 (March): 1–25.

D'Ambra, Eve. 2014. "Beauty and the Roman Female Portrait." In *Art and Rhetoric in Roman Culture*, edited by Jaś Elsner and Michel Meyer. Cambridge: Cambridge University Press, 155–80.

Dolansky, Fanny. 2012. "Playing with Gender: Girls, Dolls, and Adult Ideals in the Roman World." *Classical Antiquity* 31, no. 2 (October): 256–92.

Duffy, John. 2004. "Playing at Ritual: Variations on a Theme in Byzantine Religious Tales." In *Greek Ritual Poetics*, edited by Dimitrios Yatromanolakis and Panagiotis Roilos, 203–4. Cambridge, MA, and London: Center for Hellenic Studies, Trustees for Harvard University, and Foundation of the Hellenic World.

Erdal, Ömür Dilek. 2009a. "Demre Aziz Nikolaos Topluluğundaki Travmaların Paleoepidemyolojik Analizi / Paleoepidemiology of Trauma in Saint Nicholas Church's Population from Demre." *Edebiyat Fakültesi Dergisi/Journal of Faculty of Letters* 26, no. 2 (Aralık/ December): 97–113 (in Turkish with English abstract).

Erdal, Ömür Dilek. 2009b. "Demre Aziz Nikolaos Kilisesi Geç Bizans ve Yakınçağ İnsanlarının Yaşam Biçimleri." *Adalya* 12: 361–88 (in Turkish with English abstract).

Evans, Helen C., and Bradley Ratliff, eds. 2012. *Byzantium and Islam: Age of Transition, 7th–9th Century.* New York: Metropolitan Museum of Art.

Finkel, Irving L. (ed.). 2007. *Ancient Board Games in Perspective: Papers from the 1990 British Museum Symposium, with Additional Contributions*. London: British Museum Press.

Fluck, Cäcilia. 2004. "Ägyptische Puppen aus römischer bis früharabischer Zeit." In *Gedenkschrift Ulrike Horak (P. Horak)*, edited by Rosario Pintaudi, 385–400. Papyrologica Florentina 34. Florence: Edizioni Gonnelli.

Fournet, Jean-Luc. 2001. "Nouveaux textes scolaires grecs et coptes." *Bulletin de l'Institut français d'archéologie orientale* 101: 159–81.

Gell, Alfred. 1998. *Art and Agency: A New Anthropological Theory*. Oxford: Oxford University Press.

Gökçay, Metin M. 2010. "Yenikapı Ahşap Buluntularından Seçmeler / Selected Finds from Yenikapı." In *İstanbul Arkeoloji Müzeleri 1. Marmaray Metro Kurtarma Kazıları Sempozyum Bildiriler Kitabı 5–6 Mayıs 2008 / Istanbul Archaeological Museums. Proceedings of the 1st Symposium of Marmaray-Metro Salvage Excavations. 5–6 May 2008*, edited by Ufuk Kocabaş and Zeynep Kızıltan, 135–52. Istanbul: Directorate of Istanbul Archaeological Museums.

Hautala, Svetlana. 2015. "Why Did the Ancient Romans Put Toys in Their Children's Graves? Interpretations from the Era of Antiquarianism to 20th Century Anthropology." In *Agents and Objects: Children in Pre-Modern*

Europe, edited by Katariina Mustakallio and Jussi Hanska, 179–99. Rome: Institutum Romanum Finlandiae.

Hennessy, Cecily. 2008. *Images of Children in Byzantium*. Farnham and Burlington, VT: Ashgate.

Hennessy, Cecily. 2013. "The Byzantine Child: Picturing Complex Family Dynamics." In Brubaker and Tougher 2013, 207–32.

Holman, Susan R. 2009. "Sick Children and Healing Saints: Medical Treatment of the Child in Christian Antiquity." In Horn and Phenix 2009, 143–70.

Horn, Cornelia B., and Robert R. Phenix Jr. eds. 2009. *Children in Late Antique Christianity*. Studien und Texte zu Antike und Christentum 58. Tübingen: Mohr Siebeck.

Hoskins, J. 2006. "Agency, Biography and Objects." In *Handbook of Material Culture*, edited by Christopher Tilley, Webb Keane, Susanne Küchler, Michael Rowlands, and Patricia Spyer, 74–84. London: Sage.

Janssen, R. 1996. "Soft Toys from Egypt." In *Archaeological Research in Roman Egypt: The Proceedings of the Seventeenth Classical Colloquium of the Department of Greek and Roman Antiquities, British Museum, held on 1–4 December, 1993*, edited by Donald M. Bailey, 231–39. JRA Supplementary Series 19. Ann Arbor, MI: Journal of Roman Studies.

Johnson, Karen. 2003. "Textile and Papyrus Figurines from Karanis." *Bulletin of the University of Michigan Museums of Art and Archaeology* 15: 49–64.

Katz, Phyllis B. 2007. "Educating Paula: A Proposed Curriculum for Raising a 4th-Century Christian Infant." In *Constructions of Childhood in Ancient Greece and in Italy*, edited by Ada Cohen and Jeremy B. Rutter, 115–27. Hesperia Supplement 41. Princeton: ASCSA Publications.

Kazhdan, Alexander. 1984. "The Image of the Medical Doctor in Byzantine Literature of the Tenth to Twelfth Centuries." *DOP* 38 (*Symposium on Byzantine Medicine*): 43–51.

Kızıltan, Zeynep, and Gülbahar Baran Çelik (eds.). 2013. *Stories from the Hidden Harbor. Shipwrecks of Yenikapı*. Istanbul: Istanbul Archaeological Museums Press.

Krausmüller, Dirk. 1999. "Divine Sex: Patriarch Methodios' Concept of Virginity." In *Desire and Denial in Byzantium: Papers from the Thirty-First Symposium of Byzantine Studies, University of Sussex, Brighton, March, 1997*, edited by Liz James, 57–65. Aldershot: Ashgate Publishing.

McCabe, Anne. 2007. *Byzantine Encyclopaedia of Horse Medicine: The Sources, Compilation, and Transmission of the Hippiatrica*. Oxford: Oxford University Press.

Merker, Gloria S. 2000. *Corinth XVIII,* part 4. *The Sanctuary of Demeter and Kore: Terracotta Figurines of the Classical, Hellenistic, and Roman Periods.* Princeton: American School of Classical Studies at Athens.

Moffatt, Ann. 1986. "The Byzantine Child." *Social Research* 53: 705–23.

Newby, Z. 2019. "The Grottarossa Doll and Her Mistress: Hope and Consolation in a Roman Tomb." In *The Materiality of Mourning: Cross-Disciplinary Perspectives,* edited by Zahra Newby and Ruth E. Toulson, 77–102. Oxford: Routledge.

Özyar, Aslı, Elif Ünlü, Oya Pancaroğlu, and Agnès Vokaer. 2017. "Recent Fieldwork at Tarsus-Gözlukkule: The Medieval Layers." In *The Archaeology of Anatolia,* vol. 2. *Recent Discoveries (2015–2016*), edited by Sharon R. Steadman and Gregory Mc Mahon, 200–229. Cambridge: Cambridge University Press.

Palanque, Charles. 1903. "Notes sur quelques jouets coptes en terre cuite." *Bulletin de L'Institut Français d'Archéologie Orientale* 3: 97–103.

Papaconstantinou, Arietta, and Alice-Mary Talbot. 2009. *Becoming Byzantine: Children and Childhood in Byzantium.* Washington, DC: Dumbarton Oaks Research Library and Collection.

Papaioannou, Stratis. 2013. *Michael Psellos: Rhetoric and Authorship in Byzantium.* New York: Cambridge University Press.

Papanikola-Bakirtzi, Demetra. 2002. *Everyday Life in Byzantium,* Exhibition catalogue. Athens: Hellenic Ministry of Culture.

Pitarakis, Brigitte. 2009. "The Material Culture of Childhood in Byzantium." In Papaconstantinou and Talbot 2009, 167–251.

Pitarakis, Brigitte. 2011–2012. "Les images d'écoliers dans l'art byzantin: Origines et significations." *Cahiers archéologiques* 54: 83–98.

Quibell, James Edward. 1907. *Excavations at Saqqara (1905–1906).* Cairo: Imprimerie de l'Institut français d'archéologie orientale.

Roueché, Charlotte M. 2007. "Late Roman and Byzantine Game Boards at Aphrodisias." In Finkel 2007, 100–105.

Santrot, Marie-Hélène, Rutshowscaya, Marie-Hélène, Bénazeth, Dominique, Giroire, Cécile, eds. 2001. *Au fil du Nil: couleurs de l'Égypte chrétienne.* Exhibition catalogue. Paris: Samogy éditions d'art; Nantes: Conseil général de Loire-Atlantique (musée Dobrée).

Ševčenko, Nancy P. 2002. "Wild Animals in the Byzantine Park." In *Byzantine Garden Culture,* edited by Antony Robert Littlewood, Henry Maguire, and Joachim Wolschke-Bulmahn, 69–86. Washington, DC: Dumbarton Oaks Research Library and Collection.

Shatil, Ariel. 2016. "Bone Figurines of the Early Islamic Period: The 'So-Called' Coptic Dolls from Palestine and Egypt." In *Close to Bone: Current Studies in Bone Technologies*, edited by Selena Vitesović, 296–314. Belgrade: Institute of Archaeology.

Skinner, Patricia. 1997. *Health and Medicine in Early Medieval Southern Italy*. Leiden and New York: E.J. Brill.

Török, Laszlo. 1993. *Coptic Antiquities*, vol. 1. *Stone Sculpture, Bronze Objects; Ceramic Coffin Lids and Vessels; Terracotta Statuettes, Bone, Wood, and Glass Artefacts*. Rome: L'Erma di Bretschneider.

Vendries, Christophe. 2007. L'enfant et le coq: Une allusion à la gladiature sur la mosaïque des enfants 'chasseurs' de Piazza Armerina. *Antiquité Tardive* 15: 159–179.

Vroom, Joanita. 1999. Playing Games in the Valley of the Muses: A Medieval Board Game Found in Boeotia, Greece. *Pharos* 7: 93–110.

Witte, Johanna. 2012. "Toys, Game Pieces, and Boards, 1988–2005." In *Amorium Reports*, vol. 3. *The Lower City Enclosure: Finds Reports and Technical Studies*, edited by Christopher S. Lightfoot and Eric A. Ivison, 277–96. Istanbul: Amorium Excavations Project.

Zimmermann, Barbara. 2003. *Die Wiener Genesis im Rahmen der antiken Buchmalerei: Ikonographie, Darstellung, Illustrationsverfahren und Aussageeintention*. Wiesbaden: Reichert Verlag.

Language & Poetics of Play

"How to Catch a Falling Knife:" Poetic Play as the Practice of Negative Capability

Sarah Green

John Keats wrote to his brothers in 1817: *[…] at once it struck me, what quality went to form a Man of Achievement especially in Literature & which Shakespeare possessed so enormously—I mean Negative Capability, that is when man is capable of being in uncertainties, Mysteries, doubts, without any irritable reaching* [….][1] Here in a most uncertain time in America in 2019, development of the capability to function—even thrive—within uncertainty has never been more crucial for the creative writer. Two questions arise: What habits of mind and/or art allowed a gravely ill Keats to maintain the negative capability needed to write in spite of his personal "mysteries and doubts"? What can the rest of us learn from his practice?

[1]John Keats, "Selections from Keats's Letters by John Keats," Poetry Foundation. Accessed February 17, 2019. https://www.poetryfoundation.org/articles/69384/selections-from-keatss-letters.

S. Green (✉)
St. Cloud State University, St. Cloud, MN, USA
e-mail: sgreen@stcloudstate.edu

V. Rapti and E. Gordon (eds.), *Ludics*,
https://doi.org/10.1007/978-981-15-7435-1_13

In considering this question, I found myself looking closely at his poem "When I Have Fears That I May Cease to Be"; a poem that presumably offers autobiographical insight into Keats' strategy for staving off the anxiety of uncertainty.

As I read the poem's narrative of Keats' process, and also reflected on my own process as a creative writer, I was put in mind of Diane Ackerman's book *Deep Play*,[2] in which she describes the actively sought psychological framework of play: "One enters into an alternate reality with its own rules, values, and expectations [...] One chooses to ... wipe the mental slate clean, chooses to be naive and wholly open to the world, as one once was as a child." Ackerman's description of play certainly seemed akin to Keats' description of negative capability; the two states as described share a sort of steely vulnerability, a focused flow. What emerged from this investigation was a hypothesis that the act of choosing and beginning to engage in the play of poetic form and technique sets a momentum in motion whereby negative capability can be sustained for the duration of that play; the play of the poem holds the writer in thrall.

To demonstrate this process, in addition to closely reading the Keats poem I mentioned earlier, I will be looking at poems by Daniel B. Johnson, Alice Fulton, Frank O'Hara that "catch" poetic play in action while simultaneously referring explicitly to doubt and/or anxiety. In some cases, the poems narratively describe the process of a character engaging in play as a method of negative capability; in all cases they enact that process.

WHEN I HAVE FEARS THAT I MAY CEASE TO BE

When I have fears that I may cease to be
Before my pen has gleaned my teeming brain,
Before high-pilèd books, in charactery,
Hold like rich garners the full ripened grain;
When I behold, upon the night's starred face,
Huge cloudy symbols of a high romance,
And think that I may never live to trace
Their shadows with the magic hand of chance;
And when I feel, fair creature of an hour,

---

[2]Diane Ackerman, *Deep Play* (New York: Random House International, 2000), 20–21.

That I shall never look upon thee more,
Never have relish in the faery power
Of unreflecting love—then on the shore
Of the wide world I stand alone, and think
Till love and fame to nothingness do sink.[3]

Anxiety looms over Keats—the writer and the speaker— in this sonnet. And who can blame him? What if he doesn't get to experience grand romance? What if he isn't able to see all of his ideas through to fruition? What if he dies before he can write several books of poetry?

The sonnet's solution—to "think/til love and fame to nothingness do sink," that is, to become powerfully contemplative until the mind stills and the grasping at worldly goals settles—might not seem directly related to play. This poem is filled with anxiety, sorrow, and stoicism. But play is here in the artifact of the poem itself with its diamond-cut rhyme scheme and meter, the sumptuous music of "glean," "garner," and "grain," the mirroring turn from the sky's "starred face" to the beloved's countenance; the flirtation of *fair creature*'s direct address. Formal virtuosity demands a focus and flow at odds with rumination and despair, and I'm thinking beyond Keats now. Athletes and artists and all performers must find a way to "stay in the pocket" of the beat, or the suspended knife, without thinking about what will happen next. My dancer friend Mandoline Whittlesey had a teacher who called this pocket "the tiny future."

"With a great poet the sense of Beauty overcomes every other consideration, or rather obliterates all consideration," Keats went on to say in his 1817 letter.[4] One way to stay in the "flow" of play in the creative process is to let beauty—found beauty, or the appealing puzzle of producing it—entrance us more than the fact of its impermanence. One can imagine the beauty of language and the puzzle of the sonnet form as a sort of refuge for Keats, in addition to the slight swagger of courtship the poem also contains. It must have been, in part, an appetite for beauty that

[3]John Keats, "When I Have Fears That I May Cease to Be by John Keats," Poetry Foundation. Accessed February 17, 2019. https://www.poetryfoundation.org/poems/44488/when-i-have-fears-that-i-may-cease-to-be.

[4]John Keats, "Selections from Keats's Letters by John Keats," Poetry Foundation. Accessed February 17, 2019. https://www.poetryfoundation.org/articles/69384/selections-from-keatss-letters.

invited him into this particular act of poetic play. Perhaps the magnetism of beauty coaxes the player out of his or her caution, and into the dance? Perhaps then the trick is to avoid becoming overly attached to the hope of beauty's sustained presence? (I will consider this particular angle further in the section of this paper where I discuss my poem "July Linden.")

Beauty isn't the only poetic mechanism by which negative capability can be attained. Daniel B. Johnson's poem "To Catch a Falling Knife"[5] instead uses the adrenaline of narrative danger to focus and arrest the speaker (and reader) in a space that is so magnetic as to collapse time into the immediate moment. "Temple your hands / palm to palm / and hold them out. / Let slice / between your thumbs / the day's last / light." Here, the image of a person being poised to catch a possible knife offers a metaphor for the flexible and alert state of a singer mid-performance or a writer mid-revision: tense yet electric, vigilant yet relaxed. This imagined stance is the flow state of deep play; the poem is a kind of *ars poetica*, reflecting on writing. The poem walks its talk; it embodies play at a line level.

Let's look first at the *ars poetica* angle. Where is the knife, we might ask, in the act of writing? While it's true that most American writers these days aren't placing ourselves physically in harm's way to pursue our craft—indeed, some of my writer friends scoff at the idea of a poem being "risk taking"—the creative writer is still vulnerable. One still must engage with certain fears. The potential fears are many: fear of not finding the right language, of running out of inspiration, of running out of time. Obsolescence; isolation; encounters with shadowy selves… the list is long.

Ironically—and I think the poem illustrates this irony well— the more we attend to our fears as writers, the more likely they are to come true. "You have to believe / there is no knife." We have to suspend our worries enough to focus on making something. This suspension is not the same thing as denial. "Let slice/between your thumbs / the day's last/light," Johnson also says. Here is where play comes into the process as I see it. On one hand, Johnson is telling us to believe there is nothing to fear; on

[5]Daniel Johnson, *How to Catch a Falling Knife* (Farmington, ME: Alice James Books, 2010), 37.

the other hand, he seems to encourage us to retain an awareness of our limitations. That charged simultaneity of real limitations on one hand and limit-defying activity on the other carves out a kind of athletic arena, an arena within which the game can happen.

Jeremy Bentham,[6] who coined the phrase "deep play," described it as any activity in which "the stakes are so high that… it is irrational for anyone to engage in it at all, since the marginal utility of what you stand to win is grossly outweighed by the disutility of what you stand to lose." If the person trying to catch the knife really believed there was *no* knife, there would also be no pleasure in trying. The threat brings the shiver of adrenaline and the unlikeliness of success—for a contrary person—fires up stubborn trying. That "believe there is no knife" advice is itself meant playfully, not literally; one could call this agnosticism. To remain engaged in the game, to "catch a falling knife," we must as Johnson says, "double-doubt / the knife: its rosewood handle / doubt and doubt / its stone-ground blade."

Let's savor the playful music there of "double-doubt"; it sounds like a child's *I double-dog dare ya.* Or else. To win the good, to catch the knife, we really have to trade one doubt for another, this poem seems to say. We have to stop doubting ourselves and doubt the worrisome outcome instead. And isn't there play in that? Because it takes both imagination and a mischievous defiance—a gambler's spirit—to act like we don't know the odds.

It's interesting to look more closely at this villain, the knife, as depicted by Johnson. What are the mindsets Johnson associates with the end of play and the severing of generativity? We can find them here. "You must believe there is no knife":

> or singing down
> the knife will come
> cleaving ring from pinky
> finger, light from
> dark and what you believe,
> once and for all,
> from what you don't.

[6]Jeremy Bentham, quoted in Diane Ackerman, *Deep Play* (New York: Random House International, 2000), 18.

In other words, once we remember the knife—once we observe, from the tightrope, how far away the ground is—we lose our access to the habits of mind that facilitate play. What are those habits? I think for this speaker the space of play is a space of non-duality. In contrast, the poem characterizes the "cleaving" of absolute thinking, the separation of "light from dark" as an irreversible puncture.

There's one more text I'd like to place in the lineage of serious play, and that's Alice Fulton's poem "Fix."[7] This love poem catalogues various natural dangers—earthquakes, the Alaskan pipeline, UV rays, melting polar ice— as well as personal dangers—the forfeiting of opportunities to play the field, the loss of privacy and autonomy—as backdrop to the speaker's devotion to her chosen "you." These are the stakes. Fulton's speaker navigates these fears, like Keats, through mindfulness ("count my breaths from here to Zen") and Fulton's signature brisk musical wordplay.

"There is no caring less," the poem repeats, although "the cosmos owns our luck" and "catastrophe is everywhere." Although the speaker "can find no shade." She endures negative capability as she contemplates the tenuousness—"it's *if* and *and* and *but,*" she says—of the world as we know it continuing. Unlike Keats' ideal Man of Achievement, Fulton's speaker *does* intermittently reach after facts and reason, and facts and reason lead her to conclude that her "presence here is extra." She is "waiting for a major quake." But attachment to her beloved overrides these fears and keeps returning as her main preoccupation. Romantic love, in other words, becomes the Beauty that for her "obliterates all consideration" as Keats puts it.

"There is no caring less / for you," begins Fulton's poem. "I fix on music in the weeds, / count cricket beats to tell the temp." Play is an accomplice in this obliteration of fear by love; the play of poetry and the play of flirtation as they function separately and cooperatively. There's the play of iambic pentameter: "for *you.* I *fix* on *music* in the *weeds";* and later trimeter: "Sept*em*ber *does* its *best.*" "With*out* the *moon* the *earth.*" There's the play of the title, "Fix," and its use as both noun and verb: to fixate or focus, and to solve. (Focus here *is* the solution). There's the

[7]Alice Fulton, "Poetry: Alice Fulton, 'Fix'," *The Atlantic*. April 29, 2010. Accessed February 17, 2019. https://www.theatlantic.com/entertainment/archive/2010/04/poetry-alice-fulton-fix/39669/.

play of diction: "temp" for temperature, saying "from here to Zen" to mean "from A-Z." The sexy/sly play of "I know [under] what conditions space and time could oscillate [for me]," i.e., in the earth-shaking presence of the beloved. There's the play of syntax: "there is no caring less for you for me"; the play of unreliability: "I have to stop myself from writing 'sovereign,'" claims the speaker, nevertheless writing it. And, of course, the performance of this wit and music in direct address to a lover function as overture or seduction; overall play, then, of courtship. In Fulton's deft hands the catalog of possible apocalypse becomes an almost-aphrodisiac.

So far, I have argued that the beauty created by the play of poetic form is part of what sweeps the poet up into the mode of negative capability. But Frank O'Hara's poem "Today"[8] is much less formal: "Oh! Kangaroos, sequins, chocolate sodas!" it begins. What does one do with O'Hara's subsequent jumble of "pearls, / harmonicas, jujubes, and aspirins"? Where is the beauty in his random items? O'Hara seems to anticipate this question when he insists, of those kangaroos et al.: "You really are beautiful!" Is the reader convinced? It seems O'Hara is less concerned with convincing readers of the aesthetic virtues of kangaroos than he is interested in inviting readers to (a) enjoy the pleasure of the sounds he is listing and (b) enjoy the energetic surprise of the juxtapositions. "You" is a sweeping collective address; the beauty here lies in that adrenaline rush of particulars arranged for maximum novelty.

It's interesting that O'Hara refers to his unusual list as "all the stuff they've always talked about" and adds "these things are with us every day." In the introduction to *Homo Ludens*, one of Huizinga's defining features of play is that it is a "stepping out of 'real life'"—yet, this supposedly "every day" catalog is full of mischief and energy. What to make of this contradiction? The fact is that while we may speak of "harmonicas" or "aspirins" every day, we rarely speak of them directly one after the other. The surprise of O'Hara's disjunctive list is arresting; we hear these words, and experience their meanings, as if for the first time.

---

[8]Frank O'Hara, *Collected Poems of Frank O'Hara* (Oakland: University of California Press, 1995), 15.

O'Hara seems to want to make it clear that language retains its integrity outside of narrative syntax, and/or that words can be meaningful at rest without being put to their expected use(s). Play does have depth. "They *do* have meaning," O'Hara says of these words, as if there's been a claim to the contrary. Perhaps we've taken jujubes for granted. By estranging concrete nouns from their usual schemas and "timing" their appearance unpredictably, O'Hara increases the reader's appreciation, both for those items' singular pleasures and for the joy of opening ourselves to chance. Unlike the other poems we looked at, in which a speaker plays against a backdrop of tension and we look on, this poem invites us to enter negative capability ourselves. When we read O'Hara's poem, however resistant or sympathetic we are to its landscape, we are playing.

Here's one of the poems from my first book, *Earth Science*.[9]

July Linden

At first I thought it was
a grape arbor or a guest's jasmine shampoo.
I would walk around barefoot
after a glass of wine
on the sidewalk, holding up a leaf
and sniffing— not this, not that,
it was not my house, I was only feeding
a couple's fish and sleeping lightly
on the woman's side. The man's end table
held spectacles and vitamins, hers
a goofy stuffed monster, Portuguese books
on tape, and I never fully closed
the blinds at night, the better to see
old starry neighborhoods I'd missed.
The better to eavesdrop
on a swaying couple in the parking lot—
shadowy heart to heart,
I will never....sweatshirt to sweatshirt,
Don't say that...one friend leaning against a car
reading his phone. *You have to get your life together*...

[9]Sarah Elizabeth Green, *Earth Science* (Atlanta, GA: 421 Atlanta, 2016), 3–4.

Neighbors yelling *It's 3 am!*

That city tree
coming in like a tide, like a piece of music
or embroidery, then sailing off, I still didn't know
it was a tree. It started to unlock me,
I started to leave the porch door open while
I slept through firecrackers almost but not quite
blowing off teens' hands, and someone could have
climbed the balcony and stabbed me
for whatever reason
people stab women sometimes,
but they had better things to do,
like watch TV. Feeling a need
to check the door, halfway through the night,
I finally didn't trip over my shoes in the hall
because I could see, the moon was full,
and the fish that had been sick got better
and started eating more, even built the foam nest
male bettas make when they're happy.
So I bragged about that, feeling responsible.

And the owner replied, from Brazil, *Cute,*
but it's sad, too, isn't it. He thinks he lives in an ocean.
He thinks he's changing his life.

In "July Linden" the intoxicating fragrance of a flowering tree in summertime acts as the instigator of play, simultaneously beckoning and eluding the speaker, who is housesitting in a neighborhood she's not used to. Her response to the pleasure and mystery of the scent—rather than just enjoying the unknown of it—is to want to physically trace it to its origin, and learn its name. Keats might call this an "irritable reaching after facts," although I wouldn't say this speaker's irritated—perhaps intrigued. What is the purpose of such investigating? Likely this "I" (okay, this "me") wants to track down a source to secure future hits of the same pleasure.

But her playful opponent, what or whomever it is—the tree itself, or fate, or some mischievous mid-summer fairy—doesn't make it easy. The near/far, intermittent fragrance continues to disarm and lure her outside of her comfort zone, with some pleasing side effects. We watch her crack the night blinds to let stars in. Beauty held playfully at bay has provoked curiosity that itself changes from being frantic and ego-centered (the *I* setting out to pin down knowledge) to being looser and more inflected with wonderment. Strangely, the wonderment seems to wrap the speaker up in the very dance of Beauty itself, leaving it unnecessary to look for it. Perhaps this is what Keats meant when he said "beauty obliterates every consideration."

But this openness to the outside world doesn't come without jarring intrusions, like the loud drunk teenagers outside keeping the speaker up late one evening. The speaker turns an affectionate sense of humor toward these fellow travelers, perhaps recognizing her own vulnerability in theirs. Their desire to change appeals to her too: "*I will never*….sweatshirt to sweatshirt, / *Don't say that*…one friend leaning against a car reading / his phone. *You have to get your life together…*" (These were real people, by the way. Two sort of slow-dancing, one off to the side. I should have said "crouched on a car hood," because that's what that last one was doing.)

Although she's being kept awake, she's on the side of the teens now; it's other neighbors who are "yelling *it's 3 AM*. She continues to surrender to the immediacy of the sensation, letting go of needing to know and to control. "That city tree coming in / like a tide, like a piece of music / or embroidery, then sailing off, I still didn't know/it was a tree. It started to unlock me, / I started to leave the porch door open…". She's entered into a game with unknown rules.

The source of the fragrance is no longer a fixation, and the poem stops talking about it; it seems the speaker has begun embodying the Playful Abiding of July Linden™ instead of seeking the tree as an object separate from herself. In this mode, she casts off her anxiety (fears of violent intruders) and clumsiness (stumbling over shoes). She even verges on overconfident in her new approach to living: there's a catalog of everything that's improving, including the fish she's responsible for pet-sitting.

The fish is getting better, and the sign of his health is that he's building a spit-bubble nest in a corner of his tank—spit-bubbles intended to make a cozy home for future offspring. To the extent that there's a bit of craft and panache in addition to instinct involved in this activity, one could consider the betta fish himself to be playing. The poem next sets up a sort of tragicomic interspecies-parallel between the speaker and the fish, starting with the speaker feeling proud of her hand in the pet's recovery:

> so I bragged about that, feeling responsible.
> And the owner replied, from Brazil, *Sweet,*
> *but it's sad, too, isn't it. He thinks he lives in an ocean.*
> He thinks he's changing his life.

This is a complicated moment. This abstract, over-the-telephone, disembodied "owner" weighs in with some condescension toward the clueless fish who doesn't realize the fruitlessness of his work/play. But that's not the final stance of "July Linden." Instead, the poem levels judgment against the illusion that one has ever arrived at the final epiphany or transformation. It's not the fish that the poem is critiquing; it may not actually be sad that he's building a purposeless nest. Rather, it's the last line—out of italics, so not voiced by the owner but presumably by the speaker— "he thinks he's changing his life." This line is meant to be read as the speaker projecting a realization: "I only think I'm changing my life." Perhaps there's hope there, too—if we want there to be. If the epiphany can't last forever, that might also mean the knife is still in the air. Everything's still possible.

I would now like to discuss a second poem of mine that uses play to work toward negative capability. I began composing the first lines of what would become "Hotel Winter" out loud when I was driving at night on a curving, snowy road in Lexington, Massachusetts, with almost no streetlights. As I peered through the dark, wishing I could see farther ahead of me than a few dozen feet, the first line came to me: "The dark is a way of moving." It occurs to me now that this line echoes Auden's observation about poetry, that it is "a way of happening," but I wasn't thinking about that then. Rather, I entered a space of "what if." What if it made no sense to bring to night driving the same expectations—a certain degree of control and of clarity—that I brought to driving in daylight? What if darkness was not an obstacle, not just an absence of light or an obstacle to knowing through seeing, but instead its own valid realm with its own fullness and presence?

This new idea—darkness or lack of clarity as a realm or stage in its own right, not just the failure to progress— provoked my curiosity. It was still stressful not to be able to see my surroundings well, but I became interested in gleaning the rules and shapes of this new "country." That curiosity became embedded in the form; Joni Mitchell calls her tunings "chords of inquiry" and that's what this poem's syntax felt like. In the process of trying out provisional declarations about this place I called "Hotel Winter," I engaged in linguistic games with the page through alliteration, cadence, rhyme, and parallel structure.

HOTEL WINTER[10]
By Sarah Green

The dark is a way of moving.
The wait is a place.
Zero filled me with its virile

nothings. Sweet, I know— zero—
the dark's a weight. The weight's
a place to let your truck run

off the road, uphill
where other wheels have gone
before you. The move's the way

station. The stay's one night,
the dark's sable, the dark's a stall
for a stallion named zero

[10]Green, *Earth Science*, 38.

with a moving mane.
There is no wait in vain.

One form of play in the poem is in the game of echoing "W" words. *Way, wait, weight, where, wheels* (and *winter* if you count the title). On top of the alliteration I added the homonym/rhyme play of *wait* and *weight*: narratively the uncertainty of waiting was feeling heavy; waiting was adding weight to the speaker's experience. I started to play with paradox: one could be filled with nothing(s); one could wait in motion. I repeated "the wait is a place" but changed it to "weight"; half the time I would write these pronouncements down as an exercise before knowing yet how I could prove them true. I thought about weigh stations for trucks; I thought about signs for side paths for trucks that can't slow down. The gravity of waiting, I thought, is a place where your imagination can go dangerously wild; but it's also not too dangerous—it has a path, however rough. You're not alone.

In my family we can't help making snarky asides and puns; we're Irish; this home culture has taught me to be quick with associations, competitive even. The line "Sweet, I know" presupposes a listener making such an aside—*nothings? As in Sweet Nothings?*—and the speaker getting there ahead of them. Conveniently "know" rhymes with "zero." Suddenly the abstraction of absence as presence becomes a kind of edgy lover whispering in the speaker's ear.

Later that glimmer of eros comes back with "the stay's one night" (there is a hotel in the title after all); waiting in uncertainty—negative capability in other words—could be reframed as a one-night stand. "Stay" allows for the poem's latter half alliteration and assonance to surface: *station, stay, sable, stall, stallion.* It was really the word play that led to the meaning and drama in this section and not the other way around. What had been "the dark is a way of moving" turned to "the move's the way/station"; "station" led me to "stay"; "stay" to hotel. The poem felt like a Rubik's cube at this point, spinning. I had set myself some repeating tasks; "the dark is a ___"; "the wait is a ____"; now I had other definitions spiraling off from them. "The move's a ____"; "The stay is x." Robert Frost has said that a poem should ride like a piece of ice on a hot stove "on its own melting" and the poem felt as if it was doing that here; the tightly interlocking games I'd set up for myself earlier in the piece created a momentum that started to almost write itself.

Because of the pattern of defining the dark: "the dark is": I defined it as "sable" which was almost a bratty thing to do when the reader's expecting a more contrary definition after what's come before. Okay the dark is an adjective for black, but "sable" sounds like "stable"—and now we obviously need a horse. What I am grateful for here is the serendipity of "stall," how it's both a noun and a verb. "Stall" works like a proof for "the wait is a place." And forms half of the word "stallion." Let's name that horse "Zero." Let's make his mane move because that brings us back to the beginning of the poem: "The dark is a way of moving."

As many poem endings do, this poem turns to iambs when it gets serious in its last line. "There is no wait in vain." It was the rhyme that triggered the idea here; I had "mane." "Vain" showed up as the word that fit, of course, because of its sound and its colloquial association with "waiting." We all know that there are plenty of times waiting is completely in vain so the assertion is itself a playful one, but sincerely meant. The idea is that there is no wait in vain if the wait as a space is deeply surrendered to on its own terms. That surrender is Keats' negative capability itself: being capable of being in uncertainty. The beauty and play of the musicality and puns of the poems' drafting arrested the writer long enough to withstand the dark of that winter.

I began this paper by asking what habit allowed John Keats to—to use Emily Dickinson's words—"dwell in possibility." I contend that poetic play is an imaginative arena within which writers (and readers) build our capacity for negative capability on and off of the page. To make my case, I have explored how Daniel B. Johnson's poem "To Catch a Falling Knife" instructs its readers in the playful suspension of disbelief in the midst of risk. I have observed how sonic play and seductive wit become a refuge for the speaker of Alice Fulton's poem "Fix" despite her apocalyptic worries. I have linked both of these poems to Keats' concept of "negative capability," and in turn, framed Frank O'Hara's disjunctive immediacy as an act of artistic defiance against the "death" of societal constraints around definitions of the beautiful. Why does any of this matter right now in our particular civic moment? The development of negative capability with its dead-serious focus and resolute insistence on imagining is a crucial exercise in independent thinking and alternate-future-envisioning—and poets can model that mode for us, that concentration-as-resistance. If we are to believe that another world is possible, then we need negative capability, and poetry can—will always—help us practice that.

Works Cited

Ackerman, Diane. 2000. *Deep Play*. New York: Random House International.

Fulton, Alice. "Poetry: Alice Fulton, 'Fix'." *The Atlantic*. April 29, 2010. Accessed February 17, 2019. https://www.theatlantic.com/entertainment/archive/2010/04/poetry-alice-fulton-fix/39669/.

Green, Sarah Elizabeth. *Earth Science*. Atlanta, GA: 421 Atlanta, 2016.

Johnson, Daniel. 2010. *How to Catch a Falling Knife*. Farmington, ME: Alice James Books.

Keats, John. "Selections from Keats's Letters by John Keats." Poetry Foundation. Accessed February 17, 2019. https://www.poetryfoundation.org/articles/69384/selections-from-keatss-letters.

Keats, John. "When I Have Fears That I May Cease to Be by John Keats." Poetry Foundation. Accessed February 17, 2019. https://www.poetryfoundation.org/poems/44488/when-i-have-fears-that-i-may-cease-to-be.

O'Hara, Frank. 1995. *The Collected Poems of Frank O'Hara*. Oakland: University of California Press.

The Ludic Impulse in Post-Postmodern Fiction

Danuta Fjellestad

The Gameful World: Approaches, Issues, Applications opens with Eric Zimmerman's "Manifesto."[1] In thirteen theses Zimmerman[2] tells us that:

1. Games are ancient.
2. Digital technology has given games a new relevance.
3. The twentieth century was the century of information.
4. In our Ludic Century, information has been put at play.
5. In the twentieth century, the moving image was the dominant cultural form.

[1]Zimmerman's essay comes directly after the introduction by the editors, Steffen P. Walz and Sebastian Deterding..

[2]Eric Zimmerman, *Narrative, Interactivity, Play, and Game: Four Naughty Concepts in Need of Discipline*, 19–22.

D. Fjellestad (✉)
Uppsala University, Uppsala, Sweden

V. Rapti and E. Gordon (eds.), *Ludics*,
https://doi.org/10.1007/978-981-15-7435-1_14

6. The Ludic Century is an era of games.
7. We live in a world of systems.
8. There is a need to be playful.
9. We should think like designers.
10. Games are a literacy.
11. Gaming literacy can address our problems.
12. In the Ludic Century, everyone will be a game designer.
13. Games are beautiful. They do not need to be justified.

It is in the nature of a manifesto, as Galia Yanoshevsky in her meta-study of the genre shows, to make assertions rather than present carefully chiseled arguments; to mix description with prophecy and prescription; to assume a polemical tone; to announce newness and produce rupture with what has been. Zimmerman follows these genre conventions, combining insights with highly contestable statements. Above all, his "Manifesto" seems to set the agenda for the rest of *The Gameful World*: to offer a comprehensive analysis of the current state of "gamification"[3] or "ludification"[4] of culture, or, if you wish, of the ludic turn.[5] Yet, surprisingly enough, none of the essays takes up literature, as if it were not part of the gameful world or, for that matter, of the post-postmodern culture with which the "ludic turn" coincides.[6] This erasure of literature is even more bewildering if one considers the fact that the concepts of play and game have been of great significance to literary studies for quite a long time.[7]

---

[3]Sebastian Deterding, Rilla Khaled, Lennart E. Nacke, and Dan Dixon, "Gamification: Toward a Definition," *CHI2011 Gamification Workshop Proceedings* (Vancouver, Canada, 2011).

[4]Joost Raessens, "Playful Identities, or the Ludification of Culture" (*Games and Culture: A Journal of Interactive Media*, 2006), 1 (1): 52–57.

[5]Joost Raessens, *Homo Ludens 2.0. The Ludic Turn in Media Theory* (Utrecht: Utrecht University, lecture November 19, 2010).

[6]There is no shortage of proposals as to how to name the current historical and cultural moment. Eshelman (2008), for instance, promotes the notion of "performatism" and Kirby (2009), "digimodernism." Like Kirby, a number of critics attempt to revalorize the concept of modernism by adding a variety of prefixes. Thus we hear about "Altermodern" (Bourriaud 2009), "Remodernism" (Evans 2000), "Hypermodernism" (Lipovetsky 2005), "cosmodernism" (Moraru 2011), "Automodernity" (Samuels 2009) or "Metamodernism" (Vermeulen and van den Akker 2010).

[7]To give but one example: Ihab Hassan's oft-reproduced—if controversial— chart of differences between modernism and postmodernism lists "play" as a characteristic aspect of postmodernism.

This essay is an attempt to (re)claim a place for literature in the ludic turn. My examination of the ludic impulse in post-postmodern literature is anchored in some broad queries and reflections: What specific work can the concepts of play and game do in literary studies? Are play and game mostly useful as loose metaphors or can they be precise analytical concepts? What interpretive venues do they open? What do they make us see and understand? How, if at all, can they help us understand literature in a historicizing perspective? Aware of the impossibility to adequately address any of these questions in a brief essay, my focus here is necessarily selective: I show how the ludic impulse reveals itself in post-postmodern literature and discuss to what ends the ludic is set in motion. I argue, first, that while the verbal structures of linear discourse continue to be the object of a playful assault in post-postmodern literature just as they were in postmodernism, the scale, intensity, and timbre now differ. Second, I propose that the ludic impulse in post-postmodern literature surfaces the strongest in attempts to re-conceptualize the format of the codex: the gaming elements are recast from the diegetic level, the level of the story, onto the material machine or platform for telling stories, the book. To put it differently: the postmodern loosening of narrative conventions finds its Siamese twin in the loosening of the bound volume. Here tactility, as I will show, is of primary importance.

Terminological Considerations

Risking overlap with other essays in this volume, I would still like to remind us that the word "ludic" began to circulate broadly in the 1960s, although its primary source, Johan Huizinga's *Homo Ludens: A Study of the Play-Element in Culture*, was, in fact, published more than two decades earlier, in 1938.[8] Originally written in Dutch, it was eventually

In a (playful) attempt to map the characteristics of what goes under the umbrella term of post-postmodernism, I and my co-author propose the category of "game": Fjellestad and Engberg, "Toward a Concept of Post-Postmodernism or Lady Gaga's Reconfigurations of Madonna" (*Reconstruction: Studies in Contemporary Culture*, 2013), 12 (4).

[8]As virtually all critics writing on play point out, play has been an issue discussed by philosophers since Heraclitus. One of the most often cited statements about play is Schiller's, *On*

translated into a number of languages, with the English translation out in the United Kingdom in 1949 and in the US in 1950. For Huizinga, play is "a primary category of life,"[9] it constitutes the foundation of culture and civilization. He defines play as a free activity standing quite consciously outside "ordinary" life as being "not serious," but at the same time absorbing the player intensely and utterly. It is an activity connected with no material interest, and no profit can be gained by it. It proceeds within its own proper boundaries of time and space according to fixed rules and in an orderly manner. It promotes the formation of social groupings which tend to surround themselves with secrecy and to stress their difference from the common world by disguise or other means.[10]

According to Huizinga, then, playful activities are characterized by being separate from everyday life in terms of place and time, by being voluntary, uncertain in outcome, unproductive, and governed by rules. Not surprisingly, all of these characteristics have been vehemently debated by scholars ever since Huizinga's pioneering work became available. Perhaps the most significant engagement is Roger Caillois's *Les jeux et les hommes* (1958), translated into English as *Man, Play, and Games* and published in 1961. Though there is no need to give an account of Caillois's critique of Huizinga's theory of play, one point should be brought up: Caillois's distinction between *paidia* and *ludus*. *Paidia* refers to "free play," improvisation, carefree gaiety and laughter, and spontaneous, impulsive, joyous, and uncontrolled fantasy; *Ludus*, on the other hand, is a rule-governed form of play that often involves specific skills and mastery. This distinction lies at the core of all the other attempts to differentiate between play and game, both terms simultaneously asking for and resisting "discipline."[11]

Huizinga's work not only inaugurated the anthropology of play, but also inspired a number of other disciplines. Play has been used as a

the Aesthetic Education of Man, Translated with an introduction by Reginald Snell (New York: Dover Publications, 2004), 80, assertion that "Man plays only when he is in the full sense of the word a man, and he is only wholly Man when he is playing."

[9]Johan Huizinga, *Homo Ludens: A Study of the Play-Element in Culture* (Boston: Beacon Press, 1962), 3.

[10]Huizinga, *Homo Ludens: A Study of the Play-Element in Culture*, 13.

[11]Zimmerman, "Narrative, Interactivity, Play, and Game: Four Naughty Concepts in Need of Discipline."

model to think about "learning procedures, social interaction, personal expressivity, cultural formation and transformation, as well as a wide range of activities that involve the creation and reception of works of art, simulation, dissimulation, risk-taking, strategic thinking, tactical decision making, structural experimentation, the testing or trying out of ideas."[12] Indeed, it would be difficult to find an area of life that has escaped the touch of ludus.[13]

However, for literary scholars interested in the ludic it is undoubtedly the publication of a special issue of *Yale French Studies* in 1968 on "Game, Play, Literature" that is of primary importance. The most significant contribution was Jacques Ehrmann's[14] essay "Homo Ludens Revisited" in which he subjected both Huizinga's and Caillois's texts to a systematic critique for the logic of binarisms that informs their arguments. The same year saw the publication in English of Bakhtin's *Rabelais and his World*. And just two years prior to this another significant landmark had seen the light of the day: Jacques Derrida delivered a lecture (in French) titled "Structure, Sign, and Play in the Discourse of Human Sciences" at Johns Hopkins University. His thought became available to broader English-speaking audiences when it was published in *Writing and Difference*.[15] These texts vigorously ushered the concept of play (and its twin, game) into literary criticism and theory. Both concepts were promptly disseminated, their popularity amounting to something like a "ludification" of literary studies. The broad appeal of the game/play rhetoric in literary criticism is clearly signaled by titles such as *The Games of Poetics: Ludic Criticism and Postmodern Fiction*,[16] *The Games*

---

[12]Rawdon R. Wilson, *In Palamedes' Shadow: Explorations in Play, Game, and Narrative Theory* (Boston: Northeastern University Press, 1990), 28.

[13]Even the genre of self-help books takes advantage of it. Jane McGonigal (2015), for instance, appropriates the language of games to spread the all too familiar message of personal care techniques, such as drinking a lot of water or cultivating one's social networks. In her 2012 TED talk, she claimed that games can boost resilience and help overcome traumatic experiences.

[14]Jacques Ehrmann, "Homo Ludens Revisited" (*Yale French Studies*, 1968), 41, 31–57.

[15]Jacques Derrida, "Structure, Sign, and Play in the Discourse of Human Sciences," in *Writing and Difference*, translated with an introduction and additional notes by Alan Bass (Chicago: University of Chicago Press, 1978), 278–293.

[16]Ruth E. Burke, *The Games of Poetics: Ludic Criticism and Postmodern Fiction* (New York: Peter Lang, 1994).

of Fiction,[17] *The Ludic and Labyrinthine Text,*[18] *Games Authors Play,*[19] *Postmodern Gaming*[20] or *Explorations in Play, Game, and Narrative Theory.*[21]

That literary criticism has been interested in the ludic is of course not surprising; after all, play and game are fairly common themes and motifs in literature. The game of chess is important in, for instance, Lewis Carroll's *Through the Looking Glass,*[22] T. S. Eliot's *Waste Land,*[23] and Vladimir Nabokov's *Speak, Memory.*[24] Sports games are so prevalent that we can speak of a whole sub-genre: in Robert Coover's *The Universal Baseball Association, Inc, J. Henry Waugh, Prop.,*[25] baseball plays a central role, while David Foster Wallace's *Infinite Jest*[26] puts tennis at the center. And then there is a slew of recent popular novels that focus on video games, like *Ready Player One*[27] by Ernest Cline. Apart from being a thematic preoccupation, games—language games—are also occasionally used as structuring devices. The case of *Alice's Adventures in Wonderland* is known even to those who have not read the novel. Perhaps less known are experiments such as Walter Abish's *Alphabetical Africa,*[28] whose first sentence reads: "Ages ago, Alex, Allen, and Alva arrived at Antibes." The novel is a lipogram: only words starting with "a" are included in the first chapter; in the second there are words starting with "a" and "b," and so

---

[17]David Gascoigne, *The Games of Fiction: Georges Perec and Modern French Ludic Narrative* (Oxford: Peter Lang, 2006).

[18]Julian Wolfreys Gibson, *Peter Ackroyd: The Ludic and Labyrinthine Text*, with a foreword by Peter Nicholls (Houndsmills: Macmillan, 2000).

[19]Peter Hutchinson, *Games Authors Play* (London: Methuen, 1983).

[20]Timan Küchler, 1994. *Postmodern Gaming: Heidegger, Duchamps, Derrida* (New York: Peter Lang, 1994).

[21]Rawdon R. Wilson, *In Palamedes' Shadow: Explorations in Play, Game, and Narrative Theory.*

[22]Lewis Carroll, *Through the Looking-Glass and What Alice Found There* (London: The Folio Society, 1871).

[23]Thomas Stearns Eliot, *The Waste Land* (New York: Horace Liveright, 1922).

[24]Vladimir Nabakov, *Speak, Memory: An Autobiography Revisited* (New York: G. P. Putnam's Sons, 1930).

[25]Robert Coover, *The Universal Baseball Association, Inc., J. Henry Waugh, Prop.* (Plume, Penguin Books, 1968).

[26]David Foster Wallace, *Infinite Jest* (Boston: Little, Brown and Company, 1996).

[27]Ernest Cline, *Ready Player One (*New York: Crown Publishers, 2011).

[28]Walter Abish, *Alphabetical Africa* (New York: New Directions, 1974).

on until the whole alphabet is used, at which point Abish works backward toward the beginning of the alphabet by eliminating the letter "z." The plot of another lipogrammatic novel, *Ella Minnow Pea* by Mark Dunn,[29] is predicated on the progressive banning of the use of various letters as the tiles of each letter fall off of a statute of Nevin Nollop, an alleged creator of the well-known pangram "The quick brown fox jumps over the lazy dog."

For the most part, however, critics and theorists working under the more or less explicit patronage of Huizinga, Caillois, Derrida, or Bakhtin are interested in play as "endemic in the operation of language,"[30] while the concept of game is used as a metaphor to describe the dynamics between the author and the reader. In fact, no lesser a writer than Nabokov himself encouraged this line of thinking when he compared the writer to a master chess-player who creates "delusive opening moves, false scents, specious lines of play, astutely and lovingly prepared to lead the would-be solver astray."[31] To violate the rules of literary conventions in order to surprise (and perhaps delight) the reader is for the writer "one of the many joys" of the literary game, another writer, Jorge Luis Borges, has claimed.[32]

While in one sense the "ludic" may be inherent to all literature, some critics argue for the recognition of a special category of "ludic texts." David Gascoigne,[33] for instance, proposes that the word "ludic" be used as a generic term to refer to "texts in which the 'rules' of textual production and operation are sufficiently unusual to become noticeable in features of the text itself," something which raises the question of how to distinguish between experimental and ludic texts. Of course there is a significant nuance of difference in the connotation between the terms "experimental" and "ludic." In literary studies, the term "experimental," as the editors of *The Routledge Companion to Experimental*

---

[29] Mark Dunn, *Ella Minnow Pea* (San Francesco: MacAdam/Cage Publishing, 2001).

[30] Brian Edwards, *Theories of Play and Postmodern Fiction*. New York: Garland Publishing, 1998), 17.

[31] Vladimir Nabokov, *Speak, Memory: An Autobiography Revisited* (New York: G. P. Putnam's Sons, 1970), 290.

[32] Hutchinson, *Games Authors Play*, viii.

[33] Gascoigne, *The Games of Fiction: Georges Perec and Modern French Ludic Narrative*, 17.

Literature point out, is used in reference to unconventional and cutting-edge literature that has the qualities "of shock and affront, iconoclasm and difficulty."[34] The ludic, on the other hand, evokes connotations of fun, humor, pleasure, and lightheartedness. Yet the categories of humor or pleasure are themselves far from clear. So rather than to get further into the definitional quagmire I would like to propose that instead of thinking about ludic literature as a special category, we should speak about the ludic *impulse* in experimental literature, an impulse to amuse and delight rather than shock and frustrate.

Permutations of the Ludic Impulse

In order to elucidate a couple of the ludic impulses in post-postmodern fiction, in what follows I make brief references to its predecessor, the postmodern novel.[35] One of the most cited postmodern experiments is Raymond Federman's *Double or Nothing*,[36] a novel which situates itself in the realm of the ludic by virtue of its title, a phrase from gambling. At the narrative core we find a typical metafictional device: the first person, called "the recorder," records the efforts of the second person (called "the inventor") who intends to lock himself up in a room for 365 days to tell a story about a third one (the protagonist), a young Polish Jew who comes to America from post-WW II Europe. At some point a fourth person, the author, also makes an appearance. This structural skeleton is provided at the opening of the novel called "This is not the beginning." Appropriating the conventions of concrete poetry and the calligram, Federman visually structures the narrative so as to impede and obstruct reading: page after page text fragments are presented in a broad variety of layouts, derailing acts of interpretation. Varied as the arrangement of

34Quoted in JoeBray, Alison Gibbons, and Brian McHale, eds., Introduction in *The Routledge Companion to Experimental Literature* (London: Routledge, 2012), 2.

35It should be noted, however, that the ludic impulse informs literary texts in virtually all historical periods. For instance, playing with the conventions of page layout can be traced back to Laurence Sterne's *Tristram Shandy* (1759–1767).

36Raymond Federman, *Double or Nothing: A Real Fictitious Discourse* (Athens, OH: Swallow Press, 1971).

text is, it has a rather austere aura, especially in comparison with its post-postmodern cousin, Steve Tomasula's[37] *VAS: An Opera in Flatland*. This novel's main character, called Square, is about to undergo a vasectomy, demanded by his wife Circle, who has gone through many problems linked to pregnancy, of which the most traumatizing one was an abortion when the fetus was discovered to have some anomaly. As the names of the two main characters suggest, the novel abounds in word play. But what is most striking is the visually rich design: the story is told through an assemblage of various materials (diagrams, maps, photographs, etc.) that the protagonist Square finds as he does his research into genetics, procreation, gender, and all manner of medical and social issues while pondering his pending vasectomy. Many images are in full color, a broad variety of fonts are used, some pages can be folded out. There is a certain sense of lushness to the book, *VAS* resonating at times with the aesthetics of a scrapbook, an aesthetics associated with the familiar, the personal, and the everyday. Even though there are some self-reflexive elements (like authorial asides), the text tells a story rather than telling us about the difficulty of telling a story. The text may look challenging, but it does not request the type of mental acrobatics Federman's novel does.

Postmodern and post-postmodern fictions share not only an interest in (playful) violation of the conventional layout but also in the fun of reading. However, while postmodern experimental fictions aim to *block* the pleasure of reading (*pace* Barthes!), especially reading for the plot, and to create anxiety and irritation, confusion and annoyance, post-postmodern fiction tends to *celebrate* readerly competence. The first tends to verbally harangue, ridicule, offend, and tease the reader. Take this narratorial outburst in John Barth's "Life-Story":[38] "The reader! You, dogged, uninsultable, print-oriented bastard, it's you I'm addressing, who else, from inside this monstrous fiction." Or this from William H. Gass's *Willie Masters' Lonesome Wife* (1968, n. p.): "Now that I've got you alone down here, you bastard, don't you think I'm letting you get away easily, not sir, not you brother." In contradistinction to such explicit tirades,

[37] Steve Tomasula, *VAS: An Opera in Flatland* (Chicago: University of Chicago Press, 2002).

[38] John Barth, "Life-Story" in *Lost in the Funhouse: Fiction for Print, Tape, Live Voices* (New York: Doubleday, 1968), 123.

many post-postmodern novels tacitly bestow praise on readers as being highly competent co-players; they may be made fun of, but it is done gently and amiably, something *S.* by J. J. Abrams and Doug Dorst[39] can serve as a prime example of this. *S.* turns out to be but a slip-case for a hardbound book with the title *Ship of Theseus*, written by one V. M. Starka, a fictional writer purportedly of the first half of the twentieth century. The core story is that of an amnesiac man, known only as S. Searching for a mysterious woman referred to as Sola (aka Szalómé or Samar), S. finds himself on a ghostly unnamed ship that takes him to various places of conflict which appear to take place in different historical times. The mysterious and enigmatic author of *Ship of Theseus*, Starka, is an object of another story that unfolds through the comments of the (fictional) translator and editor of the novel, F. X. Caldeira. The third story layer is that of two readers of *Ship of Theseus*, Jennifer (Jen) Hayward and Eric Hush, both students at the (fictional) Pollard State University, who collaborate on resolving the mysteries surrounding both Starka and Caldeira. Jen and Eric are model readers on the diegetic level, the first a "naïve" but shrewd undergraduate, the other an expelled Ph.D. student who has been studying *Ship of Theseus* since his teenage years. The pages of Starka's novel are filled with handwritten marginal comments made by Jen and Eric. Their exchanges testify to their intellectual acumen and detective powers; the book's margins become the site of (book) lovers' discourse which eventually morphs into erotic intimacy. If the multitude of marginal comments and the variety of colors in which they are penned may initially strike the reader as somewhat baffling, the fun of tracing the love story and cracking the color code of the message soon takes over.[40]

---

[39]J. J. Abrams and Doug Dorst, *S.* (New York: Mulholland Books, 2013).

[40]The earliest notes are in faint gray pencil; they trace Eric's first response to the book. Jen's first comments are in blue; Eric's response to them is in black. The second round of reading is signaled by Jen's use of orange and Eric's of green colors, the third by Jen's purple and Eric's red. The final, fourth set of comments is made in black.

Denaturalizing the Codex

S. is also a good example of the ludic impulse that is much more common in today's fiction than in its postmodern predecessor: playing with the very format of the codex. Here we can find a whole spectrum of strategies: whereas Abrams and Dorst's book unbounds the codex rather modestly, Eric Zimmerman and Robert Coover radically transform it into a deck of game cards. *S.*—at least initially— emphasizes containment: *Ship of Theseus* can be accessed only after the reader has broken the seal (featuring the names J. J. Abrams and Doug Dorst and images of a monkey and a sailing ship) that protects the cardboard slipcase within which the hardbound book is tucked. The volume itself is a hardcover book mimicking a much-used library book from 1947. But tucked within the pages of *Ship of Theseus* the reader will find over twenty inserts that can be pulled out of the volume: postcards, copies of documents, handwritten letters on differently colored paper, pages from the Pollard State University student newspaper and other newspaper clippings, a paper napkin from the university coffee shop with a detailed campus map drawn on it in ink, etc. All these items are tangible, physical objects with all the optical and tactile qualities of real life things. Indeed, I want to propose that creating rich tactile experiences is perhaps the most distinct feature of the ludic impulse in post-postmodern experimental fiction. It is at its clearest when the codex is reformatted as a deck of game cards.[41]

[41] Scenes of card games are not infrequent in literature. One of the better known examples may be found in Charles Dickens's *Great Expectations*: the rich but demented Miss Havisham invites the poor country boy Pip to her house to play cards with her charge, the beautiful Estella. The card game is an occasion to humiliate Pip, as Estella taunts him and comments "He calls the knaves Jacks, this boy!" (901). Or who does not remember the closing scene in *Alice in Wonderland* in which, in response to her disdainful comment "Who cares for you? ... You're nothing but a pack of cards," the cards rise up into the air and come flying upon her (110). Italo Calvino's *Castle of Crossed Destinies* (1973) resonates with the scene in Lewis Carroll's book in the combination of narrative with images. Calvino has chosen two different packs of Tarot cards as the central device for his by now classic postmodern novel. Reproduced in various constellations in the margins of the novel, the cards are the means for the group of speechless medieval characters to tell their stories. Or, to be more precise, the sequence in which each character puts on the table Tarot cards is interpreted by the nameless narrator as telling a more or less coherent and more or less unambiguous story.

While relatively rare, such "interactive"[42] or "shuffle"[43] fictions are prime examples of the "gamification" of the codex.[44] "Life in the Garden: A Deck of Stories," written by Eric Zimmerman and designed by Nancy Nowacek,[45] presents itself as a set of 54 cards inside a box the size of a standard deck of cards. Apart from the cards, the box contains a tiny cardboard book cover, the inside left-hand page featuring the sentence "Adam, Eve, and the serpent lived in the garden," and the right-hand "The End." Each of the loose cards has a short text—most often one or two sentences—printed on one side; the reversed side exhibits hand-drawn images in blue ink. In a fashion familiar from many video games, the reader/player is given instructions printed on the box as to what he/she is to do: "Shuffle the pages. Without looking, select five pages and place them between the covers of the book. Then read the story." A suggestion for variations of the game follows: "Try three pages for a brief parable or seven for an epic tale. The possibilities, as they say, are endless." The setting invariably that of the mythic Garden of Eden, the set of the main characters limited (Eve, Adam, the serpent, and God, if an occasional personification of the earth, the sun, or the sky is ignored), the stories that emerge from combinations of the modular texts focus on a fairly narrow number of activities, motifs, and themes: sleeping, dreaming, laughter, the passing of time, sexuality, jealousy. The layout of textual fragments prompts the reader to activate the conventions of reading poetry, in particular free verse, so that the descriptive sentences acquire the condensation and intensity of metaphoric and lyric expressions. Since "lexias" are printed on physically separate pages, the reader's task of filling the narrative gaps is intensified, the Iserian "game of the

[42]Katherine N. Hayles, Nick Montfort, "Interactive Fiction," in *The Routledge to Experimental Literature*, edited by Joe Bray, Alison Gibbons, and Brian McHale (London: Routledge, 2012).

[43]Zuzana Husárová, Nick Montfort, "Shuffle Literature and the Hand of Fate" (*Electronic Book Review*, May 8th, 2012). http://electronicbookreview.com/essay/shuffle-literature-and-the-hand-of-fate/.

[44]Hayles and Montfort (2012, 452) define print interactive fiction as fiction that "requires the user to make choices [which] affect how the narrative proceeds in a literal (not merely interpretive) sense."

[45]Eric Zimmerman, *Life in the Garden: A Deck of Stories* (New York: Razorfish Subnetwork, 1999).

imagination"[46] animated as much by the "unwritten" parts of the text as mobilized by the physical act of selecting and arranging cards. Let me give two examples of what may emerge from five randomly assembled cards. The first set has resulted in the following sequence:

(1) Once Adam found
a piece of fruit
that had fallen
on the ground.

He picked it up
threw it into the sky
and to his astonishment
it never returned
to the earth.

(2) And Eve wondered
how it was all possible.

(3) The serpent just smiled.

(4) God was not pleased.

(5) Adam refused to speak.

The second sequence of cards has brought together the following lexias:

(1) From time to time,
while the two lovers slept
at night under the fruit tree,
the serpent
would slip between them
to enjoy their warmth
and envy their affection
and it wishes

[46]Wolfgang Iser, "The Reading Process: A Phenomenological Approach" (*New Literary History*, 1972), 280.

that it had the courage
to bite them both
and make them bleed.

(2) And the sun was angry.

(3) Things continued
in this fashion
for a very long time.

(4) And high above
the moon
and the sun
chased each other
around
and around the earth
like giddy lovers.

(5) God said nothing.

Framed by "Adam, Eve, and the serpent lived in the garden" and "The End," the text fragments make the reader infer links between them and supply what is not there. Yet textual gaps drawing the reader into creation of meaning turn out to be sites fertile with uncertainty and ambiguity. Is the sun angry because, unlike the lovers, it can only chase (and be chased by) the moon but never have the type of intimate contact with that Eve and Adam have? Why is God not pleased? Is the object of his displeasure the serpent's smile, Adam's throwing of the fruit or the fruit's disobedience of the laws of gravity? Is Adam's refusal to speak an act of disobedience toward God? Is there a relation between God's and Adam's silence? What logical or causal relations might the gaps imply? Discussing the creation of "Life in the Garden" Zimmerman[47] claims that whatever cards are selected, when put together they produce a "coherent narrative experience." But his assertion is problematic, I find: what "Life in the Garden" does is instead to make the reader aware of the compelling and

47 Zimmerman, *Life in the Garden: A Deck of Stories.*

even coercive force of the conventions of coherence. As the controlling voice of the narrator recedes, the hands of the reader take over the control of the arrangement of the narrative, but as a result the reader is faced with more puzzles and riddles.

While narrative gaps play a less prominent role in Robert Coover's "Heart Suit," they remain sites that breed (potentially endless) creativity. Originally published in *McSweeney*'s issue 16,[48] the text was republished the same year in the collection of short stories *The Child Again*. The main theme of this story is the discovery by the King of Hearts that his favorite tarts have been stolen. Taken as "an assault upon the very raison d'être of the kingdom itself" (n. pag.), the theft leads to an investigation, suspicion having fallen on eight persons "close to the royal family." These are specified as the King's Viceroy, known for his "lust for the King's power"; the Lord High Chamberlain, "cruel and conniving"; the Royal Chaplain, "with his scandalous weakness for sensual pleasures"; the King's Jester, "who likes to rhyme hearts and tarts with upstarts, farts, and private parts"; the Cook, a person jealous of his domain; the Flautist, an "unscrupulous aesthete"; the White Knight, an outsider to the kingdom; and the Knave of Hearts, "a thieving rascal and disdainful of the higher powers."

This archetypal story of crime and punishment is told in a strikingly innovative fashion, the narrative printed on one side of a set of fifteen cards, oversized and made of plastic-coated heavy paper.[49] The cover card starts with an instruction: "The thirteen heart cards may be shuffled and read in any order, with this card first and the joker last." The text on each of the subsequent thirteen cards starts and ends with an ellipsis. The final line names one of the suspects in the criminal investigation, the ellipsis that follows functioning as a transition to any other card. For instance, the last line on card number two reads: "The King's Royal Chaplain, the Holy Father…." When followed by card number three, the sentence will continue with "… is the thief who actually stole the tray of tarts, but he stole the cards, not out of avarice or hunger, but to save the Queen's

[48]Robert Coover, "Heart Suit," in *A Child Again* (San Francisco: McSweeney's Books, 2005).

[49]The cards are inserted in a sleeve attached to the back of the cover of *A Child Again*. It is not listed in the table of contents, which further stresses the story's teasing unbounding of the codex.

life—or, if not to save it, to give it shape and meaning, his theft of the tarts immortalizing the making of them and she who made them." When instead it is followed by the Queen of Hearts card, the line will continue thus: "…, masked as it were by his own bobbing derrière, is making love to the Queen of Hearts on the pastry board, when the King of Hearts passes through the pantry in search of the missing tarts, presumed stolen, for which, as ever, he suffers a passionate craving, more especially when they are nowhere to be found." This design of each chunk of the text beginning and ending in mid-sentence secures a sense of narrative flow irrespective of the order in which the cards are read. Also irrespective of the order of reading, the ending is always the same: although one of the culprits has been hanged, and the King is momentarily relieved at the closure, a second tray of tarts goes missing, making the monarch start a new round of investigation. As the reader is told toward the end of the story, "Death is the inevitable punchline for the joke called life. It's always the same joke, all that matters is the telling."

Given the unconventional physical format of narrative delivery, the reader is likely to focus—at least initially—on the tactile experience of handling the cards and enjoying the type of amusement a card game elicits, the fun element overshadowing serious interpretive efforts, not least because the basic story echoes a familiar nursery rhyme, published anonymously in 1782:

> The Queen of Hearts she made some tarts on a summer's day;
> The Knave of Hearts he stole the tarts and took them clean away.
> The King of Hearts called for the tarts and beat the Knave full sore
> The Knave of Hearts brought back the tarts and vowed he'd steal no more.

However, the lightheartedness of a nursery rhyme about stolen tarts gains a much darker and more ominous tone if the theft is linked to such archetypal themes as absolute power, betrayal, rivalry, sexual jealousies, and the criminal system. Serious concerns like class inequality, the whims of jurisprudence, or double sexual standards are woven into the game fabric of "Heart Suit." Moreover, depending on how the reader shuffles the cards, the outcomes—who is interrogated first, who is second, what one learns about the queen, and who is sent to the scaffolds—will vary, making the reader, in a way, complicit in the grim outcome of the King's investigation.

The reader familiar with postmodern experimental literature will, undoubtedly, see the fictions by Zimmerman and Coover resonate with B.S. Johnson's *The Unfortunates*[50] or Marc Saporta's *Composition No. 1*.[51] There is, however, a significant difference between the two sets of "shuffle" fiction: while Johnson and Saporta unbound the codex but adhere to the conventional book format, Coover and Zimmerman vigorously denaturalize the format by mimicking a cultural artifact that is powerfully associated with ludic activities.[52]

Also Chris Ware's *Building Stories*[53] activates the frame of play by appropriating the cultural commodity of a large cardboard box typical of assembly toys for story-telling purposes. *Building Stories* comes as a rectangular box (42 × 29 × 4.5 cm, four times the size of an average book) that contains fourteen printed comics of diverse formats and tactile qualities. There are, among the fourteen pieces, a four-page broadsheet, a fifty-two-page wordless landscape booklet, a double-sided zigzag folded booklet, a single poster, folded in half, a cloth-bound book. The fourteen comics may be assembled and read in any order; there are no titles, no page numbers, and no authorial instructions. The board-book provides information about the time and place of the main events: 23 September 2000, a three-floor, 98-year-old Chicago apartment building. The physically individual stories are all about the inhabitants of this building, the box functioning as a proxy of the house. The title slyly indicates that the

[50]B.S. Johnson, *The Unfortunates* (London: Picador, 1999), first published in 1969.

[51]Marc Saporta, *Composition No. 1* (1962, English edition 1963).

[52]The text of *The Unfortunates* is printed on both sides of pages the size of a typical Penguin paperback, each of the 27 chapters individually bound and placed in a box. The reader is required to compose her individual narrative order by shuffling all but the chapters marked "First" and "Last." Saporta's novel consists of 150 unnumbered loose sheets of A5 paper, printed on one side with varying amount of text to a page. The pages are contained within a box. The instruction printed on the inside front cover of the box reads: "The reader is requested to shuffle these pages like a deck of cards; to cut, if he likes, with his left hand, as at a fortuneteller's." Yet the size and the thinness of the pages makes this type of shuffling impossible; the reader can, at best, re-arrange the order of the pages, rather cautiously at that, lest the pages get torn.

[53]Chris Ware, *Building Stories* (New York: Pantheon Graphic Library, 2012).

stories about the random encounters between the characters, the unpredictability with which their memories erupt, the fortuitous circumstances of their lives in the building are both echoed and magnified by the accidental order in which the various booklets that the box contains may be accessed and read by the reader. The physical format of the book, in a word, is far from gratuitous: it works in tandem with the themes, issues, and concerns of the narrative. In effect, the reader physically *experiences* this graphic novel as much as she *reads* it. To put it in another way, *Building Stories* is designed to actively involve the reader's body as well as her intellectual faculties. Little wonder, then, that critics like Hillary Chute and Patrick Jagoda[54] have called Ware's creation "a manifesto for the book as a material object" that simultaneously promotes "forms of decision making, spatial navigation, narrative architecture, and interactive play that are common to new media forms such as video games."

Ergodic Ludicity

As I hope to have made clear, the distinction between postmodern and post-postmodern fiction is not one between the absence and presence of the ludic impulse, but one between their different textures and modalities. Whereas postmodern playfulness is linked to a gratification of intellectual labor of grappling with radical aesthetic innovation that aims at irritating and confusing the reader, post-postmodern ludic impulse appears to be more immediately sensuous and visceral, less effortful, at times almost frivolous. However, coaxing the reader with playfulness, post-postmodern fiction surreptitiously confronts her with anxiety and gravity of issues such as social injustice or loneliness.

This difference in intensity, scale, and modality of the ludic impulse may, at least partly, be explained by the fact that post-postmodern fiction is enabled by computational media that make it possible to mass produce books that include color, images, foldout pages or can be printed in unusual formats. The ludic impulse in a post-postmodern fiction book is

[54]Hillary Chute and Patrick Jagoda, *Special Issue: Comics & Media* (*Critical Inquiry*, 2014), 7.

particularly clear in the cases that meaningfully engage the reader's touch to build a narrative, as is the case with *Building Stories* or "Heart Suit." The reader's hands are not only involved in (co)construing the narrative; they provide a variety of tactile experiences, the richness of which far exceeds the smooth and pragmatic clicking or touching the computer screen.

The video game scholar Astrid Ensslin[55] proposes that we distinguish between "cognitive" and "ergodic" ludicity. Cognitive ludicity, she explains, "involves mostly cognitive reading strategies"; they include activities such as solving whodunit riddles, or detecting intertextual associations, or, I would add, cracking the code of reading a given text. For Ensslin, who is interested in video games, "ergodic ludicity" involves "not only cognitive but corporeal, kinetic interaction with the hardware and software or a computational system." I would like to appropriate Ensslin's terms to argue that while postmodern fiction is high on cognitive ludicity, post-postmodern is high on ergodic ludicity. In post-postmodernism we witness a recasting or a transmission of the gaming element from the diagetic level, the level of the story, onto the material machine or platform for telling stories, the book. Books as objects morph, change shape, mimic other artifacts, surprise by their very looks, and challenge the reader when it comes to handling them in a most literal sense.

Obviously, this "ludification" of the codex can be related to a recent "material turn" in contemporary culture. This turn, which has been theorized by scholars such as Bill Brown[56] or Katherine N. Hayles,[57] implies an increasing interest in the material aspects of life, a turn toward things rather than texts. Yet for literature to shift attention from the ideational content to the materiality of the codex is somewhat risky, since design ingenuity may be a distraction that overshadows the book's content.

55 Astrid Ensslin, *Literary Gaming* (Cambridge, MA: MIT Press, 2014), 11.

56 Bill Brown, "The Matter of Materialism: Literary Mediations," in *Material Powers: Cultural Studies, History and the Material Turn*, edited by Tony Bennett and Patrick Joyce (London: Routledge, 2010), 60–78.

57 Katherine N. Hayles, "The Future of Literature: Complex Surfaces of Electronic Texts and Print Books," in *The Changing Book: Transitions in Design, Production and Preservation*, edited by Nancy E. Kraft and Holly Martin Huffman (New York: Routledge, 2008), 85–114.

Striving to appeal to readers by augmenting its ergodic ludicity, the codex may as much renew itself as further its cultural marginalization. In the meantime, though, post-postmodern fiction is fun to read.

References

Abish, Walter. 1974. *Alphabetical Africa.* New York: New Directions.

Abrams, J. J., and Doug Dorst. 2013. *S.* New York: Mulholland Books.

Barth, John. 1968. "Life-Story." In *Lost in the Funhouse: Fiction for Print, Tape, Live Voices*, 113–126. New York: Doubleday.

Bourriaud, Nicolas, 2009. "Altermodern." In *Altermodern: Tate Triennial*, edited by Nicolas Bourriaud. London: Tate.

Bray, Joe, Alison Gibbons, and Brian McHale, eds. 2012. Introduction. In *The Routledge Companion to Experimental Literature*, 1–18. London: Routledge.

Brown, Bill. 2010. "The Matter of Materialism: Literary Mediations." In *Material Powers: Cultural Studies, History and the Material Turn*, edited by Tony Bennett and Patrick Joyce, 60–78. London: Routledge.

Burke, Ruth E. 1994. *The Games of Poetics: Ludic Criticism and Postmodern Fiction.* New York: Peter Lang.

Caillois, Roger. 2001. *Man, Play, and Games.* 1958. Chicago: University of Chicago Press.

Calvino, Italo. (1973) 1977. *The Castle of Crosssed Destinies.* Translated by William Weaver. New York: Harcourt Brace and Company.

Caroll, Lewis. 1961. *Alice's Adventures in Wonderland*. London: The Folio Society.

Caroll, Lewis. 1962. *Through the Looking-Glass and What Alice Found There.* London: The Folio Society.

Chute, Hillary, and Patrick Jagoda. 2014. "Special Issue: Comics & Media." *Critical Inquiry* 40 (3): 1–10.

Cline, Ernest. 2011. *Ready Player One*. New York: Crown Publishers.

Coover, Robert. 2005. "Heart Suit." In *A Child Again.* San Francisco: McSweeney's Books.

Coover, Robert. 1971. "*The Universal Baseball Association, Inc., J. Henry Waugh, Prop.*" Plume, Penguin Books (originally published in 1968).

Derrida, Jacques. 1978. "Structure, Sign, and Play in the Discourse of Human Sciences." In *Writing and Difference*, translated with an introduction and additional notes by Alan Bass, 278–293. Chicago: University of Chicago Press.

Deterding, Sebastian, R. Khaled, L. E. Nacke, and D. Dixon. 2011. "Gamification: Toward a Definition." *CHI2011 Gamification Workshop Proceedings*. Vancouver.

Dickens, Charles. (1861) 1965. *Great Expectations*. Edited by Agnus Calder. Harmondsworth: Penguin.

Dunn, Mark. 2001. *Ella Minnow Pea*. San Francesco: MacAdam/Cage Publishing.

Edwards, Brian. 1998. *Theories of Play and Postmodern Fiction*. New York: Garland Publishing.

Ehrmann, Jacques. 1968. "Homo Ludens Revisited." *Yale French Studies* 41: 31–57.

Eliot, Thomas Stearns. 1922. *The Waste Land*. New York: Horace Liveright.

Ensslin, Astrid. 2014. *Literary Gaming*. Cambridge, MA: MIT Press.

Eshelman, Raoul. 2008. *Performatism or The End of Postmodernism*. Aurora, CO: Davis Group Publishers.

Evans, Katherine. 2000. *The Stuckists: The First Remodernist Art Group*. London: Victoria Press.

Federman, Raymond. 1971. *Double or Nothing: A Real Fictitious Discourse*. Athens, OH: Swallow Press.

Fjellestad, Danuta, and Maria Engberg. 2013. "Toward a Concept of Post-Postmodernism or Lady Gaga's Reconfigurations of Madonna." *Reconstruction: Studies in Contemporary Culture* 12 (4).

Gascoigne, David. 2006. *The Games of Fiction: Georges Perec and Modern French Ludic Narrative*. Oxford: Peter Lang.

Gass, William H. 1968. *Willie Masters' Lonesome Wife. TriQuarterly Supplement Number Two.*

Gibson, Jeremy, and Julian Wolfreys. 2000. *Peter Ackroyd: The Ludic and Labyrinthine Text, with a foreword by Peter Nicholls*. Houndsmills: Macmillan.

Hayles, N. Katherine. 2008. "The Future of Literature: Complex Surfaces of Electronic Texts and Print Books." In *The Changing Book: Transitions in Design, Production and Preservation*, edited by Nancy E. Kraft and Holly Martin Huffman, 85–114. New York: Routledge.

Hayles, N. Katherine, and Nick Montfort. 2012. Interactive Fiction. In *The Routledge to Experimental Literature*, edited by Joe Bray, Alison Gibbons, and Brian McHale, 452–466. London: Routledge.

Husárová, Zuzana, and Nick Montfort. 2012. "Shuffle Literature and the Hand of Fate. " *Electronic Book Review.* 8 May. http://electronicbookreview.com/essay/shuffle-literature-and-the-hand-of-fate/.

Hutchinson, Peter. 1983. *Games Authors Play*. London: Methuen.

Huizinga, Johan. 1962. *Homo Ludens: A Study of the Play-Element in Culture*. Boston: Beacon Press.

Iser, Wolfgang. 1972. "The Reading Process: A Phenomenological Approach." *New Literary History* 3 (2): 279–99.

Johnson, B.S. 1999. *The Unfortunates*. London: Picador. First published in 1969.

Kirby, Alan. 2009. *Digimodernism: How New Technologies Dismantle the Postmodern and Reconfigure our Culture*. New York: Continuum.

Küchler, Timan. 1994. *Postmodern Gaming: Heidegger, Duchamps, Derrida*. New York: Peter Lang.

Lipovetsky, Gilles, and Sébastian Charles. 2005. *Hypermodern Times*. Translated by Andrew Brown. Cambridge: Polity.

McGonigal, Jane. 2015. *SuperBetter: A Revolutionary Approach to Getting Stronger, Happier, Braver, and More Resilient—Powered by the Science of Games*. New York: Penguin.

Moraru, Christian. 2011. *Cosmodernism: American Narrative, Late Globalization, and the New Cultural Imaginary*. Ann Arbor: University of Michigan Press.

Nabokov, Vladimir. 1970. *Speak, Memory: An Autobiography Revisited*. New York: G. P. Putnam's Sons.

Raessens, Joost. 2006. "Playful Identities, or the Ludification of Culture." *Games and Culture: A Journal of Interactive Media* 1 (1): 52–7.

Raessens, Joost. 2010. *Homo Ludens 2.0: The Ludic Turn in Media Theory*. Lecture at Universiteit Utrecht, November 19. Web.

Samuels, Robert. 2009. *New Media, Cultural Studies, and Critical Theory after Postmodernism: Automodernity from Zizek to Laclau*. New York: Palgrave Macmillan.

Saporta, Mark. 1962. *Composition No. 1*. English edition 1963.

Schiller, Friedrich. (1795) 2004. *On the Aesthetic Education of Man*. Translated with an introduction by Reginald Snell. New York: Dover Publications.

Tomasula, Steve. 2002. *VAS: An Opera in Flatland*. Chicago: University of Chicago Press.

Vermeulen, Timotheus, and Robin van den Akker. 2010. "Notes on Metamodernism." *Journal of Aesthetics and Culture* 2.

Wallace, David Foster. 1996. *Infinite Jest*. Boston: Little, Brown and Company.

Walz, Steffen P., and Sebastian Deterding, eds. 2014. *The Gameful World: Approaches, Issues, Applications*. Cambridge, MA: MIT Press.
Ware, Chris. 2012. *Building Stories*. New York: Pantheon Graphic Library.
Wilson, R.Rawdon. 1990. *In Palamedes' Shadow: Explorations in Play, Game, and Narrative Theory*. Boston: Northeastern University Press.
Yanoshevsky, Galia. 2009. Three Decades of Writing on Manifesto: The Making of a Genre. *Poetics Today* 30 (2): 257–286.
Zimmerman, Eric. 1999. *Life in the Garden: A Deck of Stories*. New York: Razorfish Subnetwork.
Zimmerman, Eric. 2004. "Narrative, Interactivity, Play, and Game: Four Naughty Concepts in Need of Discipline." In *First Person: New Media as Story, Performance, and Game*, edited by Noah Wardrip-Fruin and Pat Harrigan, 154–164. Cambridge, MA: MIT Press, 2004.
Zimmerman, Eric. 2007. Creating a Meaning-Machine: The Deck of Stories Called *Life in the Garden*. In *Second Person: Role Playing and Story in Games and Playable Media*, edited by Pat Harrigan and Noah Wardrip-Fruin, 81–84. Cambridge, MA: MIT Press.
Zimmerman, Eric. 2014. Manifesto for a Ludic Century. In *The Gameful World: Approaches, Issues, Applications*, edited by Steffen P. Walz and Sebastian Deterding, 19–22. Cambridge, MA: MIT Press.

Games Translators Play in French-Canadian Theatre

Nicole Nolette

In her 2013 book *Against World Literature: On the Politics of Untranslatability*, Emily Apter denounces the recent "translational turn" in the humanities and more specifically, the boom of World Literature in a mostly American-based Comparative Literature. Against what she reads as the "market-driven notions of readability and universal appeal" behind World Literature, she counters with Untranslatables, or words that stop for a few moments the bulldozer of immediate communication, "words that are continually retranslated, mistranslated, transferred

This research was supported by the Social Sciences and Humanities Research Council of Canada. The author would like to thank the Council for its continued support. An earlier version of this piece was published in French as sections of *Jouer la traduction. Théâtre et hétérolinguisme au Canada francophone*. The author would like to thank the University of Ottawa Press for all permissions.

N. Nolette (✉)
French Studies, University of Waterloo, Waterloo, ON, Canada
e-mail: nicole.nolette@uwaterloo.ca

V. Rapti and E. Gordon (eds.), *Ludics*,
https://doi.org/10.1007/978-981-15-7435-1_15

from language to language, or especially resistant to substitution,"[1] or "a linguistic form of creative failure with homeopathic uses."[2] Apter's work solicits a profound ambivalence at the junction of Comparative Literature and Translation Studies. On the one hand, the "linguistic forms of creative failure" that attract her attention are typically of greater interest to translation scholars than to comparatists. On the other, as David Damrosch has noted in his review of Apter's book, *Against World Literature* is very selective about its use of theory from Translation Studies scholars, focusing almost exclusively on Jacques Derrida's theories of translation:

> Apart from a string citation in a single footnote, *Against World Literature* nowhere discusses or even mentions such seminal figures in the "cultural turn" of contemporary translation studies as Susan Bassnett, André Lefevere, Gideon Toury, Harish Trivedi, or Lawrence Venuti, even though from the 1980s onward these theorists revolutionized a previously formalist field to address issues of power, inequality, and the thorniness of language."[3]

I would go further: not only does Apter not discuss these scholars and their work, but she engages with the philosophy of translation by focusing on what could seem to be its anomalies (that is to say, "linguistic forms of creative failure") as Untranslatables without connecting them to the related concept of translatability, or with what "translation" could mean apart from easy transferability across systems. This article considers Apter's and Derrida's insistence that something should "stop" or "halt" translation temporarily to remind readers of the occurrence of a transfer, while also joining Damrosch, and many others, in their counterargument that pragmatically, translation happens, and that it is much more interesting to observe the circulation of translations and its interruptions than to erect new dogmas of Untranslatability. Incidentally,

---

[1]Apter, *Against World Literature: On the Politics of Untranslatability* (London; New York: Verso, 2013), cover.

[2]Apter, ibid., 21.

[3]Damrosch, "Against World Literature: On the Politics of Untranslatability by Emily Apter (Review)" (*Comparative Literature Studies* 2014), 51 (3): 504.

play and games help us understand how to avoid such dogmas. In what follows, I will bring together translation and play as connecting theories, then examine some manifestations that such connections bring to light in a corpus of bilingual French-Canadian theatre.

My work on world-literary circulation and translation has featured smaller geographies, nodding toward Michael Cronin's[4] invocation of the principle of fractal geometry, to claim that complexity on a large scale yields an equal complexity on a small scale. In accordance, I explore bilingual French-English theatre in parts of Canada like Acadie, Ontario, and Western Canada, where French is spoken by 2–30% of the population and where English is, if not the official language, then the one most frequently used. In the theatre produced in these regions, bilingualism is a common practice, so much so that its ubiquity is a distinguishing trait from its neighbor in Québec where French is the language of the majority:

> What is clear is that the question of how bilingualism is managed, as a reflection of an exacerbated coexistence of French and English, is a remarkable characteristic of literary production by minority Francophones in Canada. The management of bilingualism goes well beyond the question of works translated from one language to another; rather, it tends to be about writing translatability and untranslatability into the form and the narrative or performative content of literary works.[5]

In other words, French-Canadian writers tell and stage different stories of diglossia and bilingualism, play the game of literature by multiplying the ways translation figures in the form and contents of literature. To reference Eric Berne's *Games People Play*[6] and Peter Hutchison's

[4]Cronin, "Identité, Transmission et l'interculturel: Pour une politique de micro-cosmopolitisme." In *Des Cultures en contact : Visions de l'Amérique du Nord francophone*, edited by Jean Morency, Hélène Destrempes, Denise Merkle, and Martin Pâquet (Québec: Éditions Nota bene, 2005), 17–31.

[5]Paré, "Vers un discours de l'irrémédiable : les cultures francophones minoritaires au Canada," In *Francophonies minoritaires au Canada : L'État des lieux*, edited by Joseph Yvon Thériault (Moncton: Éditions d'Acadie, 1999), 509. Unless otherwise noted, all translations are my own.

[6]Berne, *Games People Play: The Psychology of Human Relationships* (New York: Ballantine Books, 1964).

Games Authors Play,[7] intertwined with theory from play and translation studies, the following are some of the games translators play both within French-Canadian drama and outside the borders of the communities its performances traditionally serve.

Playfully Defining Translation

But how can we associate translation with play, or define translation through play? Translation Studies scholar Maria Tymoczko[8] suggests that we start by conceptualizing translation as a cluster, the way that Wittgenstein instructs us to get rid of definitions on the basis that understanding a term depends on addressing its use in language. Conveniently, Wittgenstein illustrates what he means by identifying games such as board-games, card-games, ball-games, Olympic games. He says:

> What is common to them all? – Don't say: "There *must* be something common, or they would not be called 'games'" – but *look and see* whether there is anything common to all. — For if you look at them you will not see anything that is common to *all*, but similarities, relationships, and a whole series of them at that. To repeat: don't think, but look![9]

Among the analogies visible between certain "games" (but not all!), Wittgenstein finds pleasure, competition, interaction with other players, rules, etc.,—all similarities that can be spotted or lost depending on the objects chosen, constituting "a complicated network of similarities overlapping and crisscrossing: sometimes overall similarities, sometimes similarities of detail."[10] Since the common element of the network is found among its analogies, or "family resemblances,"[11] between the

---

[7]Hutchinson, *Games Authors Play* (London; New York: Methuen, 1983).

[8]Wittgenstein, *Philosophische Untersuchungen = Philosophical Investigations*, translated by G. E. M. Anscombe, P. M. S. Hacker, and Joachim. Schulte. Rev. 4th ed. (Chichester, West Sussex, UK; Wiley-Blackwell, 2009).

[9]Wittgenstein, *Philosophische Untersuchungen = Philosophical Investigations*, 66.

[10]Ibid.

[11]Ibid., 67.

objects accommodated, its limits must remain blurry. Wittgenstein's reflection allows us not only to identify games by seeing them, but also to conceive them together without imposing a forced coherence to this set. This is also the case for translation, for which a conceptualization after the fact could consider the games translators play as well as their enlarged family network. Gideon Toury[12] quoting Wittgenstein, already suggested in 1980 that translation should be an open concept, described retrospectively. Following Toury's intellectual heritage, Maria Tymoczko's[13] use of Wittgenstein's cluster-concepts proposes to enable a better understanding of translation, an enlargement of translation to non-Western approaches, and the empowerment of practising translators. Such "family resemblances" are also observable in the strategies of playful translation in bilingual French-Canadian theatre and its translation in the double perspective of play between languages and play on stage. This double ludic perspective incites a differentiated reception according to the linguistic profile of spectators.

Playful approaches to translation may seem counterintuitive in the immediate, as the tendency is to highlight the loss inherent to all translation—*traddutore traditore*. Yet some translation scholars and practitioners choose the rhetoric of creative spaces enabled by the act of translation. For Michael Cronin,[14] the concept of play could participate in advances in translation theory and pedagogy based on "the cognitive possibilities of translation and its contribution to aesthetic renewal." However, translation projects that could be claimed as playful are often named negatively, as if that dimension was already contradictory to the very notion of translation. Jacques Brault's project of "non-translation" in *Poèmes des quatre côtés* is one such example. Brault is all at once a translator and poet: he "eliminates the titles and sources of the poems he translates."[15] These references only reappear in the last pages of the book.

[12]Toury, *In Search of a Theory of Translation.* Meaning & Art 2. Tel Aviv: Porter Institute for Poetics and Semiotics, Tel Aviv University, 1980), 17–18.

[13]Tymoczko, *Enlarging Translation, Empowering Translators* (Manchester, UK; Kinderhook, NY: St. Jerome Pub, 2007), 83–90.

[14]Cronin, "Keeping One's Distance: Translation and the Play of Possibility" (1995), 242.

[15]Simon, *Translating Montreal: Episodes in the Life of a Divided City* (Montreal: McGill-Queen's University Press, 2006), 137.

In this way, Brault's "non-translation" negates the usual subordination of the translator. For Sherry Simon, this process of "non-translation" is not only negative: the poetic self-reflection that emanates from the translation of other poetry "opens out into a rich metaphor for the difficulties and promises of all elocution."[16] So do other Québécois projects identified by Simon as "perversions of translation"[17]: Gail Scott's "comma of translation," Agnes Whitfield's "translations without originals," Nicole Brossard's "pseudotranslation" and contiguous creative work with translators and collaborators, as well as Erin Mouré's "trans*e*lation" all figure as "perversions" of a conception of translation as anchored in equivalence or in clarification. Simon's acts of "perversion" come across in stylistic figures, in textual strategies that inhabit the space between writing and translating where contiguous languages interweave. They are not, as they are in the theatre translation research of Annie Brisset[18] or Sirkku Aaltonen,[19] a form of rebellion against a foreign source or text.

Finally, the notion of playing with translation could recall the theories of Jiří Levý[20] or Dinda L. Gorlée,[21] whose works are inspired in great part by semiotics and game theory as it was first put forward by mathematician John von Neumann and economist Oskar Morgenstern.[22] Yet as opposed to these game theories of translation, the questions of optimizing gain, minimizing loss, and passing on to translators a

---

[16]Ibid.

[17]Ibid., 119–161.

[18]Brisset, *Sociocritique de La Traduction: Théâtre et Altérité Au Québec (1968–1988)* (L'Univers Des Discours, Longueuil, Québec: Le Préambule, 1990), 107.

[19]Aaltonen, *Time-Sharing on Stage: Drama Translation in Theatre and Society*, Topics in Translation 17 (Clevedon, England; Buffalo, NY: Multilingual Matters, 2000), 73.

[20]Levý, "Translation as a Decision Process," in *To Honor Roman Jakobson, Essays on the Occasion of His Seventieth Birthday, 11 October 1966*, 1171–82, Janua Linguarum 31–33 (The Hague; Paris: Mouton, 1967).

[21]Gorlée, *Semiotics and the Problem of Translation: With Special Reference to the Semiotics of Charles S. Peirce* (Amsterdam; Atlanta, GA: Rodopi, 1994).

[22]Von Neumann and Morgenstern, *Theory of Games and Economic Behavior*, 60th anniversary ed. Princeton Classic Editions (Princeton, NJ; Woodstock: Princeton University Press, 2007 [1967]).

certain pessimism regarding their work are of less importance for French-Canadian theatre. Mathieu Guidère[23] rightly criticizes these theories for their "lack of a ludic dimension (play, precisely). Evidently, a preoccupation with strategy makes illusory the pleasure any translator or reader can derive from an eventual 'play on translation.'" And yet, doesn't the dynamism of "perverted" translation and its stage manifestations enhance this form of pleasure in a translator as a player? Paul Ricoeur[24] acknowledges that "it is this mourning for absolute translation that produces the happiness associated with translating." Though this happiness associated with translating makes playful translation a favorable ground for high and low comedy, humor, parody and irony, it is not a priori attributable to a single one of these concepts. Their close links with playful translation, however, means that it will be important to *look and see*, just as Wittgenstein proposed, to find the affinities that bind them to French-Canadian texts, translations and performances.

Playful Translation and the Supplement

As it manifests in bilingual French-Canadian theatre, playful translation falls within this happiness associated with translating, be it between languages or across the possibilities of the stage. This pleasure appears in the form of a supplement particular to bilingual creators and spectators, one that recalls the concept of the same name by Jacques Derrida. For Derrida,[25] who uses the supplement to examine Plato and Jean-Jacques Rousseau, the concept is firstly the result of an addition: "the supplement adds itself, it is a surplus, a plenitude enriching another plenitude, the *fullest measure* of presence. It cumulates and accumulates presence." But to this first meaning of the supplement, a second one superimposes

---

[23] Guidère, *Introduction à la traductologie: penser la traduction: hier, aujourd'hui, demain*, Traducto (Bruxelles: De Boeck, 2008), 74–75.

[24] Ricoeur, *On Translation*, translated by Eileen Brennan, Thinking in Action (London: Routledge, 2006), 10. http://catdir.loc.gov/catdir/toc/ecip0612/2006013346.html.

[25] Derrida, *Of Grammatology*, Corrected ed. (Baltimore: Johns Hopkins University Press, 1998), 144. http://catdir.loc.gov/catdir/bios/jhu052/98129525.html.

itself—that of *replacement*: "it intervenes or insinuates itself *in-the-place-of*; if it fills, it is as if one fills a void. [...] Compensatory [*suppléant*] and vicarious, the supplement is an adjunct, a subaltern instance which *takes-(the)-place* [tient-lieu]."[26] As a surplus or as a replacement, the supplement is always *outside*—that is what distinguishes it from the complement—which means that it adds on to an entity that was already believed to be complete, revealing both a gap in the original and a surplus that can be tacked onto it.

Homi Bhabha confirms the usefulness of Derrida's concept in his postcolonial reading of the multilingual poem "Missing Person" by Adil Jussawalla.

> A-'s a giggle now
> but on it Osiris, Ra.
> An अ' an er… a cough.
> once spoking your valleys with light.
> But the a's here to stay.
> On it St Pancras station
> The Indian and African railways
> That's why you learn it today.
> …
> 'Get back to your language,' they say.[27]

The supplement is crafted around the "a," already as Bhabha notes the first letter of the Roman alphabet and an indefinite article in English, a sign of grammar and of the language of the British empire. The "a" is quickly translated by the first letter of the Hindi alphabet, "अ'," preceded by its own indefinite article and followed by a phonetic transliteration, "an er"—so that the verse "An अ' an er… a cough" holds a transliteration, an ellipse and an intratextual translation. This ellipse becomes the delay of translation for the postcolonial subject, an exasperating but exhilarating delay: "like a schematic, post-structuralist joke."[28] This "joke" is not futile—it is the playground on which the postcolonial subject can

---

[26]Ibid., 145.

[27]Quoted in Bhabha, *The Location of Culture* (Routledge Classics. London; New York: Routledge, 2004), 82.

[28]Ibid., 84.

write to establish themselves within time. Bhabha's supplement opens up a space for the play for cultural translation and divergent linguistic iterations. Yet these metonymic divergences are often minimal, and accessory to the English-language text. Catherine Leclerc[29] takes notice of this, and adds that markers of difference for Bhabha are always placed under trusteeship by the dominant language, as if the hybridity claimed paradoxically implied a parallel linguistic assimilation. Playful translation, in its multiple incarnations, draws from multilingualism to different degrees, sometimes well beyond the accessory function found by Bhabha. The distribution of playful translation, already active in a bilingual text, can heighten or diminish in subsequent translations.

The play of translation proposed is therefore not only the affirmation of a principle of play and freedom of creation: it is also the manifestation of the supplement in systems of non-equivalence and non-redundancy. Consequently, it is also a play on different receptions. In this sense, Rainier Grutman[30] holds that what differentiates a bilingual text from a diglossic one is that in the first, "the appearance of the foreign language is pertinent and non-redundant," so that the implicit reader is also bilingual. Diglossic texts, on the other hand, constantly use redundancy to reinforce a "double codification: bilingual (or identity building) and unilingual (exoticizing)." While diglossia is often linked with identity both in texts and in the work of theoreticians, bilingualism seems to go beyond identity, but only for an elite. Sherry Simon[31] addresses this issue, stating: "It is much easier to accept linguistic hybridity that comes from play than that which comes from imposed (social) situations of diglossic bilingualism." Yet the production and reception of diglossic aesthetics don't necessarily divide into identity politics or exotic readings, and that a close reading of texts and performances that come from situations of great social diglossia can reveal as many games of non-redundancy as identity politics.

---

[29]Leclerc, *Des Langues en partage?: Cohabitation du français et de l'anglais en littérature contemporaine* (Montréal: XYZ éditeur, 2010), 86.

[30]Grutman, "La Textualisation de la diglossie dans les littératures francophones," In *Des Cultures en contact: Visions de l'Amérique du Nord francophone*," edited by Jean Morency, Hélène Destrempes, Denise Merkle, and Martin Pâquet (Québec: Nota Bene, 2005), 217.

[31]Simon, *Le Trafic des langues: Traduction et culture dans la littérature québécoise*, 112.

As opposed to "normal" wordplay, bilingual wordplay replaces the signaling of difference within a single language by that of formal similarities made possible by the contact of two languages. On the one hand, sociolinguists posit that bilingual punning "points up the ways in which the borders of languages can become fluid when they come in contact with each other."[32] On the other, the larger the asymmetry between these languages, the more blockages there are to this fluidity—which tends to reinforce ideologies of untranslatability—but also the more opportunities for political counter-discourses. In this sense, the language play of French-Canadian theatre is not that of modernist poetry. Rather, it is mobilized in the uneven transition between identity and post-identity theatre, between particularism and the desire for universalism.

These games and their politics intersect in unexpected ways through their bilingual and unilingual receptions, a hypothesis also present in the work of Doris Sommer[33] on bilingual aesthetics. Sommer detects that "the games of inclusion and exclusion (what linguists call "gatekeeping") produce artful effects that depend on a range of possible receptions." In this sense, unilingual metropolitan readers are target readers of diglossic literatures, as "[a] 'target' audience can mean the target of exclusion or confusion."[34] These "self-authorized readers"[35] readers who only wish to find exoticism in minority literatures are thus confronted or rebutted by these texts, on purpose. Playful translation considers these different receptions as a game of inclusion and exclusion that delimits the players from the befuddled. On the one hand, the differential effect of non-redundancy could induce a smile of superiority among those bilingual readers who understand the ironic parallel. On the other, spectators without access to both readings will at times be momentarily excluded, at times partake in the bonding laughter of shared experience.

---

[32]Hedrick, *Spik In Glyph? Translation, Wordplay, and Resistance in Chicano Bilingual Poetry* (*The Translator* 2 (2): 141–60, 1996), 146.

[33]Sommer, *Bilingual Aesthetics: A New Sentimental Education* (Public Planet books, Durham: Duke University Press, 2004), 64.

[34]Ibid., xviii.

[35]Ibid., 191.

The Translatability of Playful Translation

If the literary intervention of translation in bilingual and diglossic texts takes its ludic aspect from non-redundancy, the translation of these texts reinvents a multiplicity of possible readings and readers. Here again, a conversation on untranslatability emerges from playful puns and multilingualism. In their entries on "Translation Theory" and "Translatability'" in the *Dictionary of Translation Studies*, Mark Shuttleworth and Moira Cowie[36] give the example of wordplay as the utmost limit of translatability. Nevertheless, as Dirk Delabastita[37] indicates with nuance, "the term 'untranslatability' here sums up, not in the most precise of ways, what is in itself an incontestable fact, namely that wordplay (*certain types of it more than others*) tends to resist (*to a greater or lesser extent, depending on many circumstances*) certain kinds of translation." According to him, the association between wordplay and translatability is less a matter of ontology than the mirroring of a whole section of translation criticism.

The translation studies scholar who bets on Saussurian linguistics, for example, will not break away from the duos of signifer/signified, form and content by which he defines wordplay. For linguist and translation studies expert J. C. Catford, wordplay causes issues because it highlights ambiguity in the source language. He says: "The functionally relevant features include some which are in fact formal features of the *language* of the SL text. [...] Linguistic untranslatability occurs typically in cases where an *ambiguity* peculiar to the SL text is a functionally relevant feature — e.g., in SL puns."[38] Either equivocal or ambiguous, and juxtaposing form and function wittily, wordplay stops Catford from getting to his final goal: automatic translation by machines. This form of translation relies on the careful breakdown of languages into unequivocal components. It is thus impossible to ask machines to translate equivocal or ambiguous pairings from one language into an equally equivocal

[36]Shuttleworth and Cowie, *Dictionary of Translation Studies* (Manchester, UK: St. Jerome Pub, 1997).

[37]Delabastita, "Introduction," in *Traductio: Essays on Punning and Translation*, 1–22 (Manchester, UK: Namur, Belgique: St. Jerome; Presses Universitaires de Namur, 1997), 10.

[38]Catford, *A Linguistic Theory of Translation: An Essay in Applied Linguistics*, Coll. "Language and Language Learning" (London: Oxford University Press, 1965), 94.

pairing in another. For Eugene Nida and Charles Taber, whose premises are also those of linguistics, functional equivalency is preferable to a formal equivalency in order to communicate the message of Sacred Scripture. It would be better, therefore, to push the polyvalence of wordplay to the paratext while emphasizing content (for them, the divine word). Catford, Nida and Taber thus position themselves at one of the two axiological poles that orient translation scholars:

> Translation theory oscillates between what Roman Jakobson called the "dogma of untranslatability," the claim that art, above all, is formally and essentially untranslatable, and the "transcreational" practices of the likes of Pound and Joyce, whose motto would appear to be "There is nothing that cannot be translated."[39]

"Both positions are valid," explains Suzanne Jill Levine, who nevertheless adheres to the second pole to "subversively" translate Latin-American literature.

Playful translation also takes position for this second pole: it orients translation in continuity with creation. In the 2009 surtitled performance of the Franco-Manitoban play *Sex, lies et les Franco-Manitobains* by Marc Prescott, for example, the line "moi la seule chose que je râpe, c'est le fromage"[40] becomes "If I'm gonna molest cheese, I at least make it Swiss"[41] in the supertitle. The retranslation makes the pun between "*râpe*" and "*rape*" disappear, but pursues the game of playful translation with allusions to sex and cheese. In the space between the two simultaneous versions, one interpreted on stage and the other on a screen above, there is also a refusal of translation (conceived as a unidirectional transfer) that has nothing to do with untranslatability and a lot to do with a play on reception.

---

[39]Levine, *The Subversive Scribe: Translating Latin American Fiction*, 1st Dalkey Archive ed. (Champaign, Ill: Dalkey Archive Press, 2009), 9.

[40]Marc Prescott, *Sex, lies et les F.-M.*, English surtitles by Shavaun Liss under the supervision of Louise Ladouceur, Théâtre au Pluriel, Campus Saint-Jean, University of Alberta, Edmonton, 5–6 November 2009, in Shavaun Liss, *Le surtitrage anglais du théâtre francophone de l'Ouest canadien: application et expérimentation*, Master's thesis (Edmonton, Campus Saint-Jean, 2021), 60–94.

[41]Ibid., 2009, slide 840.

In this regard, what I have been calling playful translation aligns with three criticisms formulated by Delabastita regarding doctrines of the untranslatability of wordplay. This translation scholar first explains that we probably overestimate anisomorphism between languages, that is to say the degree of semantic non-correspondence between them. This is especially true with French and English, which share a "common substance."[42] Secondly, Delabastita criticizes holders of untranslatability for their too-great focus on the word to the detriment of the text and its context. Kathleen Davis[43] subscribes to this analysis while adding that this is the argument by which deconstructionists also gave their support to untranslatability, which was then built up as an absolute principle. Davis suggests that considerations of translatability engage with readings of the text and its context, on a reading of wordplay as a Derridean signature of the text. Or, as Delabastita states, "puns have a history and that history depends on reading strategies."[44] Finally, Delabastita[45] points out that the discourse on untranslatability of wordplay confirms and maintains strict equivalence at the heart of the definition of translation. The labels "non-translation" and "perversions of translation" are examples of such maintenance. What is also at stake here is the need to conceptualize playful translation in two words ("playful translation"), relegating to the adjective (playful) the role of deconstructing the noun (translation).

Tace Hedrick, who has studied bilingual punning in a similarly diglossic context—Chicano poetry—acknowledges the double effect, formal and polemical, of this practice, but also of a certain refusal of subsequent translations. According to her, the mixing of codes, "always contentious, cannot be re-translated, sorted back out, without again effecting a *re*-territorialisation, a taking back of those linguistic, historical, and cultural spaces and their boundaries which the interlingual text

---

[42]Delabastita, *There's a Double Tongue: An Investigation into the Translation of Shakespeare's Wordplay, with Special Reference to Hamlet*, Approaches to Translation Studies, v. 11. (Amsterdam; Atlanta, GA: Rodopi, 1993), 182.

[43]Davis, "Signature in Translation," in *Traductio: Essays on Punning and Translation*, 23–43. Manchester, United Kingdom: Namur, Belgique: St. Jerome; Presses Universitaires de Namur, 1997), 30.

[44]Delabastita, "Introduction," in *Traductio: Essays on Punning and Translation*, 1–22, 7.

[45]Delabastita, *There's a Double Tongue: An Investigation into the Translation of Shakespeare's Wordplay, with Special Reference to Hamlet*, 186–90.

deliberately (mis) appropriates in punning, playful and ironic ways."[46] We could say that she answers a question asked previously by Derrida: "How is a text written in several languages at a time to be translated? How is the effect of plurality to be 'rendered'? And what of translating with different languages at a time, will that be called translating?"[47] The translation of bilingual wordplay does not institute a new form of untranslatability. To dodge untranslatability, playfulnes generates "new pacts of translation"[48] through retranslation. This playful *re*translation, or playful translation retranslated for metropolitan spectators with uneven capacities in French or English, is a *re*territorialization on the borders of the two same languages. As such, playful retranslation is a crafty reworking of modes of inclusion and exclusion as new modes of reception.

Performing Playful Translation

Many practices have been suggested for the translation of multilingual literature: footnotes, endnotes, bilingual editions, erasing all traces of multilingualism, cushioning loan words, adding italics, transposing or augmenting the multilingualism present in the source text.[49] Theatre practitioners, with their emphasis on performance and embodiment, have tended to accentuate less these textual practices, yet there is a certain resurgence of textual translation in multilingual performances as well. Multilingualism and translation have appeared through the use of supertitles and other theatrical side texts, as Marvin Carlson[50] calls texts that are "produced alongside and simultaneously with the performance

---

[46] Hedrick, *Spik in Glyph? Translation, Wordplay, and Resistance in Chicano Bilingual Poetry*, 154.

[47] Derrida, "Des Tours de Babel," in *Difference in Translation*, edited by Joseph F Graham (Ithaca: Cornell University Press, 1985), 215.

[48] Simon, *Le Trafic des langues: Traduction et culture dans la littérature québécoise*, 184.

[49] Suchet, *Outils pour une traduction postcoloniale: littératures hétérolingues* (Paris: Archives contemporaines, 2009), 180–207.

[50] Carlson, *Speaking in Tongues: Language at Play in the Theatre* (Ann Arbor: University of Michigan Press, 2006), 190.

itself." As a form of "diagonal translation,"[51] supertitles force the eye to crisscross between the oral and the written, while the two stream simultaneously. In French-Canadian theatres, supertitles have been used since the early 2000s to attract more audience members among exogamous couples, partially assimilated francophones, timid francophones and anglophones.[52] As a result of implementing a regular programming with supertitles, for example, the Théâtre français de Toronto and the Troupe du Jour in Saskatoon have seen a rise of 20 to 50% in attendance rates.[53] Guy Mignault, then director of the Théâtre français de Toronto, elaborated on this success: "We are out of the ghetto [...]. Francophones bring in their Anglophone partners or friends. We have Anglophone journalists coming in, even deaf-mute spectators!"[54] Yet supertitles haven't received universal acclaim in French-Canadian theatres. In Ottawa, when the Théâtre la Catapulte inaugurated the use of supertitles, then artistic director Joël Beddows claimed that it was "to open doors" while actor Pierre-Antoine Lafon-Simard showed a reticence that relates firmly to the delays of playful translation: "Comedy is the most difficult [...]. Because all of a sudden you say a joke and you have this two- or three-second delay, because people have to take the time to read the joke you just said."[55]

The place of play in theatre is not as hard to justify as its role in translation. Play crosses disciplinary lines between Drama Studies and Performance Studies as an integral part of what theatre, drama and performance are all about. In this context, it is not surprising that supertitles themselves become playful. As Marvin Carlson explains, the rise of multilingual theatre could only mean a surge in experimentation of its modes of translation:

[51] Gottlieb, "Subtitling: Diagonal Translation," *Perspectives* (1994), 247. https://doi.org/10.1080/0907676X.1994.9961227.

[52] Gagnon, Un milieu sur la corde raide de la viabilité (*Liaison*, Spring 2009), 14.

[53] Nadeau, "La Belle effronterie," *L'Actualité*, février 2013.

[54] Quoted in Nadeau, "La Belle effronterie," L'Actualité, février 2013.

[55] Kate Porter, "Ottawa French Theatre Adds English Surtitles," *CBC News*, November 19, 2009, sec. Arts & Entertainment.

> From the beginning theatre has taken a strong interest in its own procedures and devices, giving rise to the long tradition of metatheatrical expression. It was thus inevitable, once heteroglossic theatre became sufficiently common to inspire various translation strategies and devices for its operation, that these strategies and devices would themselves be converted by practitioners into new material for metatheatrical experimentation.[56]

This "metatheatrical playfulness" in supertitles also extends to other theatrical side texts. Carlson gives the example of Robert Lepage's *Les sept branches de la rivière Ota*, where a translator is staged in an interpreter's cabin. If this translator is not a character, it is still a "neutral, if living, dramatic device."[57] In what follows, I showcase these two forms of theatrical side texts, interpreters and supertitles, as metatheatrical playfulness that emerges from the retranslation of bilingual French-Canadian theatre.

Commenting and Upending Translation: *Le Rêve Totalitaire de Dieu L'amibe*

Patrick Leroux's *Le Rêve totalitaire de dieu l'amibe*, a Franco-Ontarian cybernetic performance from 1995 with four Francophone characters and an Anglophone "Commentator" (La Commentatrice) is an outstanding example of a playful interpreter on stage. Rather than communicating the words of the French-speaking characters, the Commentator held several monologues to vehemently oppose, in English, the postmodern experimentation of the French-speaking characters on stage. She interrupted the action to express herself on the absurdity of the situation:

> La Commentatrice
>
> *Enough! Call me old-fashioned, but I rather like good pure simple theatre, the type you can understand because everything is either explained to you or foreshadowed at least three scenes in advance. I rather like being told what*

[56] Carlson, *Speaking in Tongues: Language at Play in the Theatre*, 213.
[57] Ibid., 184.

> *to think and when to cry and when to laugh. Call me old-fashioned, but I would rather have liked to be told that everything was going on in some parallel world we call cyberspace, or the Internet. I would have liked to be told that the representation of the Internet would not be realistic. How can we understand what's going on if the words aren't understandable? If the situations aren't realistic?!? The nerve of these experimental theatre people! Damn them! Damn them! All of them be damned!*[58]

Other interventions by the English-Speaking Commentator had the following functions: explanation in comprehensible terms, narration, psychological analysis, and dramatic foreshadowing. Like the chorus in Greek theatre, The Commentator sought to be above all "the master Speaker that explains that untangles the ambiguity of appearances, and that brings the gestures of the actors into intelligible causal order."[59] In doing so, she imposes an epic alienation for spectators. In her words, we could also be hearing those of Brecht: "we cannot invite the public to fling itself into the story as if it were a river, and let itself be swept vaguely to and fro, the individual events have to be knotted together in such a way that the knots are easily seen. The events must not succeed one another indistinguishably but must give us a chance to interpose our judgment."[60] As such, the English-speaking Commentator was paradoxically in solidarity with the French-speaking spectators, if not on the linguistic level, then on the level on the incomprehension of the experience of post-identity politics theatre in this performance. This intercultural complicity first relied on a play on two styles of theatre traditionally associated with Anglophones and Francophones in Canada—psychological realism and symbolism, respectively. By being so conservatively Anglophone in her preference for psychological realism, however, The Commentator also gathered alongside her Francophones who were unsure about or resistant to the post-identity politics theatre. In other words, she became a sort of spatial extension of this egregious

[58]Leroux, *Le Rêve totalitaire de Dieu l'amibe: Livret d'anti-opéra cybernétique*, Rappels (Ottawa: Le Nordir, 2003), 123.

[59]Barthes, "Pouvoirs de la tragédie antique," In *Ecrits sur le théâtre*, edited by Jean-Loup Rivière (Paris: Seuil, 2002), 44.

[60]Quoted in Willett, *The Theatre of Bertolt Brecht: A Study from Eight Aspects*. 3rd ed., rev. A New Directions Paperbook; NDP244 (New York: New Directions, 1968), 153.

audience of conservative members, whose commentary she expressed, "at the heart of its intellection."[61]

From Ottawa where the show was performed in a first iteration, the performance traveled to Montreal for an avant-garde theatre festival with French supertitles. In the Montreal performances, the comments of the Commentator broke ranks with Québécois spectators, mocking their position on the sacred place of the French language. Whereas the Commentator said, "Words are not simple play things!" in English, the supertitle above her extrapolated "J'aime comprendre les mots, comprendre les idées, comprendre les gags. On ne niaise pas avec les mots, avec la parole, avec la langue! C'est sacré tout ça! S'il-vous-plaît: on ne fourre pas le chien avec la langue! Mais bon, assez … assez de l'éditorial, je dois commenter, puisque c'est mon rôle."[62] For Montreal spectators who did not understand the spoken English, the translation offered by the supertitle hid the reactionary complicity offered by the Commentator; the supertitle then became a mode of exclusion from this part of the performance.

The supertitle was also used to censor lines that were considered senseless in English. Idiomatic expressions such as "Scratch my back, I'll scratch yours," "Cross your heart and hope to die stick a needle in your eye" and "Step on a crack break your mother's back"[63] are only revealed to French-speaking spectators as "Commentaire gratuit", "Deuxième commentaire pour rien dire" and "Et paf! La gratuité absolue!"[64] The supertitle thus bolstered the "gratuity," or the non-justified, non-motivated, presence of idiomatic expressions in English, positing the French-speaking characters as the only ones allowed language play. The accusation of "gratuité absolue" was also aimed more generally at the English-speaking readers Lawrence Venuti[65] criticizes—those who expect

[61] Barthes, "Pouvoirs de la tragédie antique," 44.

[62] Leroux, *Surtitres (titres de mouvements et sous-mouvements) et traduction des répliques de L'ombre du lecteur anglais*, 6.

[63] Leroux, *Le Rêve totalitaire de Dieu l'amibe: Livret d'anti-opéra cybernétique*, 65.

[64] Leroux, *Surtitres (titres de mouvements et sous-mouvements) et traduction des répliques de L'ombre du lecteur anglais*, 4.

[65] Venuti, *The Translator's Invisibility: A History of Translation* (London; New York: Routledge, 1995).

complete and fluent translations at all costs, no matter the usefulness (or nonsense) of the source text. Bringing translation to light, the performance reverses the legendary invisibility of translators. Here what is highlighted for spectators who don't have access to both languages are the missing pieces of the whole, the supplement as replacement, and for bilingual audience members, the supplement as addition.

When target-oriented practices are discussed in Translation Studies, they are usually associated with equivalence, with the opposite of foreignization. Playful translation, however, helps us understand how target-oriented practices can resemble a bow and an arrow, how translation can be a pointed trajectory toward purposeful exclusion. Such a conception of translation reminds us that translation doesn't have to occur between two languages and cultures, that it can even play across the two to consolidate a single community. In sum, through playful translation, bilingualism and translation intersect in ways that intermingle between the so-called originals and translations, creating different versions of bilingual performance texts catering to specific audiences in a gesture of resistance while accommodating unilingual spectators whose presence is considered to be necessary in their diffusion and legitimization. Thus, the partial translation process points to its own bias, its own partiality and fondness for a particular ideal spectator, its own intended circulation from the margins. It is a jolting reminder that terms need not be deemed Untranslatable, but that translation itself can engage with their resistance to substitution. In other words, it calls on us to take up what Apter refers to as "a linguistic form of creative failure with homeopathic uses" within the context of translation rather than without it.

Works Cited

Aaltonen, Sirkku. 2000. *Time-Sharing on Stage: Drama Translation in Theatre and Society*. Topics in Translation 17. Clevedon, UK; Buffalo, NY: Multilingual Matters.

Apter, Emily. 2013. *Against World Literature: On the Politics of Untranslatability*. London; New York: Verso.

Barthes, Roland. 2002. "Pouvoirs de la tragédie antique." In *Ecrits sur le théâtre*, edited by Jean-Loup Rivière, 35–45. Paris: Seuil.

Berne, Eric. 2004. *Games People Play: The Psychology of Human Relationships*. New York: Ballantine Books.

Bhabha, Homi. 2004. *The Location of Culture*. Routledge Classics. London; New York: Routledge.

Brisset, Annie. 1990. *Sociocritique de La Traduction : Théâtre et Altérité Au Québec (1968–1988)*. L'Univers Des Discours. Longueuil, Québec: Le Préambule.

Carlson, Marvin A. 2006. *Speaking in Tongues: Language at Play in the Theatre*. Ann Arbor: University of Michigan Press.

Catford, J. 1965. *A Linguistic Theory of Translation: An Essay in Applied Linguistics*. Coll. "Language and Language Learning." London: Oxford University Press.

Cronin, Michael. 1995. "Keeping One's Distance: Translation and the Play of Possibility." *TTR: traduction, terminologie, rédaction* 8 (2): 227. https://doi.org/10.7202/037225ar.

———2005. "Identité, Transmission et l'interculturel: Pour une politique de micro-cosmopolitisme." In *Des Cultures en contact : Visions de l'Amérique du Nord francophone*, edited by Jean Morency, Hélène Destrempes, Denise Merkle, and Martin Pâquet, 17–31. Québec: Éditions Nota bene.

Damrosch, David. 2014. "Against World Literature: On the Politics of Untranslatability by Emily Apter (Review)." *Comparative Literature Studies* 51 (3): 504–8.

Davis, Kathleen. 1997. "Signature in Translation." In *Traductio: Essays on Punning and Translation*, 23–43. Manchester, UK: Namur, Belgique: St. Jerome; Presses Universitaires de Namur.

Delabastita, Dirk. 1993. *There's a Double Tongue: An Investigation into the Translation of Shakespeare's Wordplay, with Special Reference to Hamlet*. Approaches to Translation Studies, v. 11. Amsterdam ; Atlanta, GA: Rodopi.

———1997. "Introduction." In *Traductio: Essays on Punning and Translation*, 1–22. Manchester, United Kingdom : Namur, Belgique: St. Jerome; Presses Universitaires de Namur.

Derrida, Jacques. 1985. "Des Tours de Babel." In *Difference in translation*, edited by Joseph F Graham, 209–48. Ithaca: Cornell University Press.

Derrida, Jacques. 1998. *Of Grammatology*. Corrected ed. Baltimore: Johns Hopkins University Press. http://catdir.loc.gov/catdir/bios/jhu052/98129525.html.

Gagnon, Paulette. 2009. "Un milieu sur la corde raide de la viabilité." *Liaison*, Spring.

Gorlée, Dinda L. 1994. *Semiotics and the Problem of Translation: With Special Reference to the Semiotics of Charles S. Peirce*. Amsterdam; Atlanta, GA: Rodopi.

Gottlieb, Henrik. 1994. "Subtitling: Diagonal Translation." *Perspectives* 2 (1): 101–21. https://doi.org/10.1080/0907676X.1994.9961227.

Grutman, Rainier. 2005. "La Textualisation de la diglossie dans les littératures francophones." In *Des Cultures en contact: Visions de l'Amérique du Nord francophone*, edited by Jean Morency, Hélène Destrempes, Denise Merkle, and Martin Pâquet, 201–23. Québec: Nota Bene.

Guidère, Mathieu. 2008. *Introduction à la traductologie: penser la traduction: hier, aujourd'hui, demain*. Traducto. Bruxelles: De Boeck.

Hedrick, Tace. 1996. "Spik In Glyph? Translation, Wordplay, and Resistance in Chicano Bilingual Poetry." *The Translator* 2 (2): 141–60.

Hutchinson, Peter. 1983. *Games Authors Play*. London ; New York: Methuen.

Leclerc, Catherine. 2010. *Des Langues en partage?: Cohabitation du français et de l'anglais en littérature contemporaine*. Montréal: XYZ éditeur.

Leroux, Patrick. 1996. *Surtitres (Titres de Mouvements et Sous-Mouvements) et Traduction Des Répliques de L'ombre Du Lecteur Anglais*. s.l: Traduc.dx.

———2003. *Le Rêve totalitaire de Dieu l'amibe: Livret d'anti-opéra cybernétique*. Rappels. Ottawa: Le Nordir.

Levine, Suzanne. 2009. *The Subversive Scribe: Translating Latin American Fiction*. 1st Dalkey Archive ed. Champaign, Ill: Dalkey Archive Press.

Levy, Jiří. 1967. "Translation as a Decision Process." In*To Honor Roman Jakobson. Essays on the Occasion of His Seventieth Birthday, 11 October 1966*, 1171–82. Janua Linguarum 31–33. The Hague; Paris: Mouton.

Nadeau, Jean-Benoît. 2013. "La Belle effronterie." *L'Actualité*, février.

Paré, François. 1999. "Vers un discours de l'irrémédiable : les cultures francophones minoritaires au Canada." In *Francophonies minoritaires au Canada : L'État des lieux*, edited by Joseph Yvon Thériault. Moncton: Éditions d'Acadie.

Porter, Kate. 2009. "Ottawa French Theatre Adds English Surtitles." *CBC News*, November 19, 2009, sec. Arts & Entertainment.

Prescott, Marc. 2001. *Big; Bullshit; Sex, Lies et Les Franco-Manitobains: Pièces de Théâtre*. Collection Rouge 16. St. Boniface, Man: Éditions du blé.

Ricoeur, Paul. 2006. *On Translation.* Translated by Eileen Brennan. Thinking in Action. London: Routledge. http://catdir.loc.gov/catdir/toc/ecip0612/2006013346.html.

Shuttleworth, Mark, and Moira Cowie. 1997. *Dictionary of Translation Studies.* Manchester, UK: St. Jerome.

Simon, Sherry. 1994. *Le Trafic des langues: Traduction et culture dans la littérature québécoise*. Montréal: Boréal.

———2006. *Translating Montreal: Episodes in the Life of a Divided City.* Montreal: McGill-Queen's University Press.

Sommer, Doris. 2004. *Bilingual Aesthetics: A New Sentimental Education.* Public Planet Books. Durham: Duke University Press.

Suchet, Myriam. 2009. *Outils pour une traduction postcoloniale: littératures hétérolingues.* Paris: Archives contemporaines.

Toury, Gideon. 1980. *In Search of a Theory of Translation.* Meaning & Art 2. Tel Aviv: Porter Institute for Poetics and Semiotics, Tel Aviv University.

Tymoczko, Maria. 2007. *Enlarging Translation, Empowering Translators.* Manchester, UK; Kinderhook, NY: St. Jerome.

Venuti, Lawrence. 1995. *The Translator's Invisibility: A History of Translation.* London; New York: Routledge.

Von Neumann, John, and Oskar Morgenstern. 2007. *Theory of Games and Economic Behavior*. 60th anniversary ed. Princeton Classic Editions. Princeton, NJ ; Woodstock: Princeton University Press.

Willett, John. 1968. *The Theatre of Bertolt Brecht: A Study from Eight Aspects.* 3rd ed., rev. A New Directions Paperbook; NDP244. New York: New Directions.

Wittgenstein, Ludwig. 2009. *Philosophische Untersuchungen = Philosophical investigations.* Translated by G. E. M. Anscombe, P. M. S. Hacker, and Joachim. Schulte. Rev. 4th ed. Chichester, West Sussex, UK; Wiley-Blackwell.

Immigraντ Poetics: Play as Performativity of the Liminal Self

Yiorgos Anagnostou

How does an immigrant make a home in a foreign tongue? How does an immigrant negotiate his foreignness to inhabit the new language, a new linguistic homing?

Immigrants' encounters with the host society display both a displacement, a distance from the mother tongue, and also a process, arduous to be sure, of familiarization with the host language. These encounters entail entering, navigating, and claiming a new linguistic—and therefore cultural—terrain, presenting the wonders of the new and the perplexity of cultural complexity. Nuances, even basic yet historically contingent meanings in the host language, are elusive, creating ground fertile for frustration, irony, and play.

In this work, I undertake an English/Greek narrative and poetic play that speaks to the unstable—and therefore disruptive and creative—encounter with a foreign tongue. Three narrative voices layer the

Y. Anagnostou (✉)
The Ohio State University, Columbus, OH, USA
e-mail: anagnostou.1@osu.edu

V. Rapti and E. Gordon (eds.), *Ludics*,
https://doi.org/10.1007/978-981-15-7435-1_16

text. First, an autobiographical perspective speaks about the speaker's immigrant linkages with English. This angle privileges experience and emotion, though it also ventures into conceptual insights. Second, a theoretical frame of reference directs attention to larger issues about immigrant encounters with a new language. Though this thread marks a departure from the experiential, it is not independent from the speaker's experience of grappling with English. Third, interconnected with the autobiographical and the theoretical, the text features an immigrant persona as a protagonist who narrates in verse. The interest in this telling is to evoke the tension in turning linguistic distance into proximity, including rewriting routines of the host society into playful surprises.

The verses aspire to linguistic dexterity while underlining the anxiety of the persona's linguistic alterity, coupled with accents, misspellings, malapropisms, and all. Languages intertwine in the bilingual plays to signal distance or, in contrast, locate instances of intimate linguistic resonance where none appear at first sight. The persona foregrounds the foreignness of the host language to subsequently trace a trajectory claiming the host as a home language. In this respect, linguistic mistakes, consciously performed, paradoxically underline the immigrant persona's increasing familiarity with the host tongue, offering routes to this homing.

Accents, Passages, de-Fences

> [The] pervasive anxiety that [the immigrant speaker] will get it wrong.[1]

I cannot possibly speak without an accent. I cannot possibly not speak about accents. As an immigrant who has been wrestling with American English, and, as a public speaker too, I have been preoccupied with accents. My own, other people's accents, accents as a problem and

[1]Askold Melnyczuk, Ukrainian-American writer and editor, cited in Henriette Lazaridis, "The Homeland of Stories: On Lingual and Cultural Identity," *The Millions*, September 12, 2013. Accessed 1 May, 2017. https://themillions.com/2013/09/the-homeland-of-stories-on-lingual-and-cultural-identity.html.

accents as a creative potential. Speaking with an accent, as I do, accentuates, it seems, an interest in accents. Writing about them then seems the inevitable next step, my two cents in the discussion over accents.

Like all immigrants, I inhabit my accent. The mechanics of its sounds make it an organic extension of myself. Accents are shadow-like, their scale and shapes being subject to change. In a power-laden situation, say an interview, the accent may choke the Self, dwarfing it. In the informal chat among friends, in contrast, the accent, relaxed, may flicker into liberating playful puns, which one cannot, absolutely not, ban!

One lives with accents the way one lives with one's own body. An intimate companion of fluctuating frustration and fun. Both—the accent and the body—are needy too, a minefield of demands for care and attention.

This much is clear to me: immigrant accents may generate anxiety, charm, or thrill, depending on the individual speaker, setting, and use. The linguistic community within which they are enunciated plays a major role too.

Accents certainly raise the very real problem of effective communication. Signaling unfamiliar sounds, they test the boundaries of a language. They are rarely far from minor slippages or, dangerously, from major communication breakdowns.

"I found it hard to understand what was said to me, and people found it equally hard to understand me," Indian-born author Anita Desai writes about her movement from British to American English. "I could not make the switch from tom-ah-toe to tom-a-to or frag-ile to frag-il; my jaw was too stubborn, my tongue too stiff."[2] Accents may crash their speakers, steely axes decapitating confidence, plunging speakers into powerlessness and even inferiority.

But the enunciation of an accent has a decided yet sometimes inadvertent poetic effect. Because accents flirt with multiple meanings—bad or bud? but or butt?—they infiltrate poetry into the everyday. Oh! The moment the status of a professor becomes the statues of a professor.

---

[2]Anita Desai, "Various Lives," in *Lives in Translation: Bilingual Writers on Identity and Creativity*, edited by Isabelle de Courtivron (New York: Palgrave Macmillan, 2003), 11–17.

Accents elevate the ordinary into the extraordinary. Herein lies a power to motivate working with accents not against them.

As an educator with an accent, I am hyperconscious of language as a series of building blocks—pronunciation, grammar, homophony, vocabulary—that, once accented, may also function as roadblocks to communication. As an immigrant teacher, I cannot afford to be lackadaisical with language, the possibility of disruption keeps me on the alert. Language for me, far from a transparent medium, becomes an object of reflection.

I invest vast amounts of time laboring in the host language, crafting a kind of life vest for its rough currents. A surplus of vests, made to last, keeps me afloat. It's extravagant, I know, the desire to compensate for linguistic limitations. The poetic avalanche overflowing the rim of rhymes, so to speak, creates channels for psychological release. The foregrounding of fluency—perhaps an overkill—is a measure of skill.

Still, let us register this: the surplus of language inevitably adds yet another layer of anxiety, the lurking specter of mistakes.

Building on another language equals bleeding.

–If I am to die in its field, do not bother me brother, have no qualms, dye me with its yield.

–Grant, Grunt, Grand
–Pass ages, pus sage

Words wire worlds
Wires patrol the border
Bleed the old order

Tongue hindered
Racked
Immigrant migraines

Still, I steal
The almost same
Rhymes made of steel
Keep me sane

–Enunciation, Articulation, Locution

It rains grains
Also in Oslo
Pain in Spain
Tears tear ears

In the field of meaning
Tight yield gains
Home run out of sight
Beyond ninth inning

(In retrospect
National metaphors winning)

–Denotation, Detonation

Narco-
pedia paidia[3] amass
Boundaries hunt for bounty
How is an immigrant to pass?

Hey! Home language
Homemade luggage, come to my aid!

　　My voice
　　Hot art
　　My utter stance
　　My pair

Alas! Alien language
Alias for mortgage

　　My invoice
　　Not a part
　　Am I at err nuance?
　　Mighty despair

How does one repair?

---

[3]Minefields, [watch out] fellas!.

Distances, Affinities

> But mostly, the problem is that the signifier has become severed from the signified. The words I learn now don't stand for things in the same unquestioned way they did in my native tongue. 'River' in Polish was a vital sound, energized with the essence of riverhood, of my rivers, of my being immersed in rivers. 'River' in English is cold—a word without an aura. It has no accumulated associations for me, and it does not give off the radiating haze of connotation. It does not evoke.[4]

I remember, or precisely my body remembers, viscerally, my first adult encounter with English. It was with a thick volume on environmental science. It was a frustrating experience, mostly due to the fact that in my early teens I was an indifferent to a lukewarm at best student of English. Like so many of my middle- and low-middle class peers at the time, I was learning the language at one of the few private tutoring schools in my small town. French, which was part of the middle-school curriculum was another language I could not claim passion for at that time. I abandoned both English and French, quickly, now to my regret. They were alluring to some extent but primarily distant. I could not imagine any relevance they could possibly have in my life, which was consumed to my detriment by more pressing problems.

In retrospect, Pierre Bourdieu, a French sociologist, provides me with the conceptual tool to make sense of my former predicament. Though venturing into Western languages was a cultural practice that oriented my imagination toward a future beyond my provincial town, my deep entrenchment—my habitus—in a particular strenuous and therefore consuming social and psychological environment worked against this opening up of the imagination. In fact, it made the step away unimaginable. Sure enough, the tension between opening up away and being closed off within the immediate surroundings must have been simmering, as far as I can tell, deep down in my psyche. The thing is, the objective conditions of my life made a life with English in it unthinkable.

---

[4]Eva Hoffman, *Lost in Translation: A Life in a New Language* (New York: E.D. Dutton, 1989), 106.

I could not imagine then that later, much later, English offered a release route away, toward graduate school in the United States.

I picked the aforementioned book on environmental science in preparation for graduate studies in environmental engineering. My English being barely passable, made reading it a traumatic experience. I should mention that I was able to borderline pass the obligatory GRE (Graduate Record Examination) thanks to my slavish memorization of vocabulary, a mechanical aptitude devoid of a deeper understanding of the language. ("Lackadaisical," a word that I used earlier, came out of the infinite, it seems, pool of infrequently used words international students dutifully memorize for their GRE, and many may still use in ordinary speech, startling native speakers. I still remember the incredulity in the face of my car mechanic when I described a car problem as an aberration.) But I am veering off, my apologies for my circumbendibus detour.

My delving into the book was an exercise in futility. I would read, have a general feel of what I read about, but when I asked myself what was it that I retained I would draw a blank. Five hours of study, dictionary on hand, resulted in a minimal yield, adding a mere couple of words in the vocabulary list I dutifully organized in index cards (and thanks to GRE acquired habits would obsessively memorize):

- Sedimentation: "The process of settling or being deposited as a sediment"; layering of deposits. [Ιζηματαπόθεση ή ιζηματογένεση.]
- Aquifer: "A water-bearing layer of rock or sediment that is capable of yielding useable amounts of water. Drinking water and irrigation wells draw water from the underlying aquifer." [Υπόγειος υδροφορέας.]

Reading Eva Hoffman reflecting on the severance between the signifier and signified, the sound and the meaning, released a current of overwhelming recognition in my mind and soul. At last I could locate, and at least I could name the problem. I fully recognized, I absolutely painfully recognized, how this severance multiplies the distance between the immigrant speaker and the host language; the seemingly unbridgeable distance between the Self and its surrounding world. I recognized with exact precision the toll in labor and in the psyche that this severance extracts. The recognition flooded my being, bringing to the surface the despair of experiencing reading as a process of encountering words as walls. I was lacking, like so many immigrants, the intimate connection between a sound and the meaning it represented. Meaning was elusive, a fleeting flyer in the field of language. I was crashing in thin air.

I cannot resist saying more about the gap in the signifier/signified pair. But I will be switching registers to do so. I learned English through the language of books, engineering books in the beginning, theoretical ones in the humanities and social sciences afterwards, when I was finally able to engineer my dramatic turn into anthropology and cultural studies. No matter how hard I try, my use of English cannot shed its bookish traces. So here it goes.

The juxtaposition between the foreign and the mother tongue renders visible the hierarchy in the experience of accessing meaning. The foreign register resists access, the mother language eases access to it. The dialectic absence/presence of cultural familiarity is the key to make sense of this differentiation. How to conceptualize an American garden in rural Oklahoma or Italian Brooklyn for that matter if one has no visual referent of neither? The mother tongue generates recognizable images of garden falling within an immigrant's cultural repertoire. Certainly not a transparent medium, the mother tongue evokes culturally constituted meanings whose density intertwines with the experiences of its speakers. Its semantic riches reach out to a community that negotiates meaning on the basis of a shared constellation of images, signifiers, and referents. (The severe severing, indeed, of language from every day speech.)

I know intimately, deep down in my linguistic and cultural guts, how this hierarchy in the access of meaning may dwarf an immigrant. How it makes the Self feel inadequate, despairingly so. But when I venture into putting this experience into writing, a golden opportunity presents itself: transport the mother tongue into the foreign text. This move carries the liberating effect associated with the bringing of disparate elements together. Placing the two languages next to each other frames a moment in my immigrant journey across languages. I nest together what ordinary speech separates, what ordinary speech prohibits. I create a space of co-habitation, tense to be sure yet fulfilling for me, in my ongoing negotiation with dual realities.

When I make Greek and English roommates, I introduce my mother tongue as foreign text to the monolingual English speaker. At one level, this gesture obviously juxtaposes the frustration and the delightful affect between experiencing the alienating signifier/signified gap in English and the intimate signifier/signified in Greek. But, as in Annie Liontas's novel *Let Me Explain You*, there is an additional reason for this bilingual coexistence: to manoeuver the native reader into unfamiliar territory, one inhabited with the language resources my immigrant body and mind have smuggled[5] into the national landscape. Neglected and beaten in its travels across the new territory, the mother tongue now makes itself visible, a cameo appearance to be sure, but nevertheless an appearance whose beat leaves a mark. Its presence will most probably startle the reader, creating a defamiliarizing effect (as bookish people would put it). In this move I invite readers to partake in the exasperating and simultaneously enjoyable experience of encountering a new language; its disorienting effect, its surprises, its magnetic power to raise curiosity, its flirting with meanings, its carving sharp turns, its unseen curves.

What does *thalassa* mean? What about *ouranos*? (hint: search close to "uranus," keep away from "uranium"). The strategy of accommodating two different linguistic codes aims to produce a commonality between ourselves, writer and readers, within our differences. You most probably utter *ouranos* and *thalassa* with an accent, even though you may not know their meaning. I no doubt say *sky* (σκάει)[6] and *see* with an accent too. We now have something in common—we speak equivalent words with an accent—we are united in our differences. Sharing the commonality of the strange brings us, strangers, closer together. The struggle for communication across languages ain't going to strangle us.

The mixing of codes inevitably creates a cross-cultural geography prone to missed cues, partial readings, belated responses, delayed or aborted engagements with meaning; all-in-all ruptures or even *mis*communication. But this, evidently, is what makes this multilingual

[5]"[A]ll those bodies and the minds inside those bodies smuggling foreign syntax across the border..." Ariel Dorfman, "The Wandering Bigamists of Language," in *Lives in Translation: Bilingual Writers on Identity and Creativity*, edited by Isabelle de Courtivron (Palgrave Macmillan, 2003), 34.

[6]σκάει (skái): third person singular of the verb σκάω = blow, explode, burst.

and translingual terrain ripe for play. Play lays out multiplicity instead of singularity, which it berates. It layers fluidity. It performs some skill in crossing linguistic and cultural boundaries. It celebrates the cerebral and affects the affective multilingual Self.

Continent of languages
I am not alone in this exile
Not a sole soul, content less, aimless
Connections maimed at an isle

A poet grasps the gap
"He missed," he writes
"words like *thalassa* and *ouranos*
that felt to him much weightier than English"[7]

I gasp

–Gust of wind!
she tells me
–It's about to rain
–It may storm
she lets me
know
(diction slow)

Rain is coming
Storm is coming

Words, matter of appearance
Meaning mere surface
Dictionaries save face
Dictate equivalence
In an instance

Έρχεται βροχή
Έρχεται μπόρα

[7] David Mason, *Ludlow* (Red Hen Press, 2014), 141.

Doors banging
Cold I remain, indecisive
Riders on the storm?
No clue, no cue
Associative valence absent
Distance distills alienation

Gone is the moment
No *retention*, I feel her tension
"Take her by the hand"? Nope... I rot

Bruised, I cruise the intimacy
Of the mother tongue

Έρχεται βροχή, έρχεται μπόρα
Έρχεται μπόρα και παγωνιά.
Στα πόδια μας ζεστή μια θερμοφόρα
...
Κλείσε τις κουρτίνες και πάρε με αγκαλιά[8]

The blinds I did not draw
The raw embrace I failed to cement

Βροχή, όχι
Μπόρα, σπατάλησε την ώρα[9]

[8] Popular song by Dionysis Savvopoulos
«Rain is coming, a storm is coming
Stormy and cold weather are about to fall on us...
Hot water bottle tucked at our feet
–Draw the blinds and cuddle, intimate meet».

[9] Rain, ain't [he didn't take advantage of the rain].
Storm, inability to perform [didn't take advantage of the storm either].

Supply Plus, Surely Surplus!

I now feel compelled to return, to find my way back to the topic of accents. This is a consciously crafted zig zag. My aim is to introduce an element of discontinuity, to fragment the story. This disruption should not come as a surprise to those of you who have cut your … tongue at a new language. Living with a foreign language is about a series of explosive eruptions, definitely not a linear affair. I injected a rupture, to be fair.

I am returning to the question of accents, because accents, please forgive the repetition, inundate my life; they offer to me, you guessed it, an everyday diet of steady dates. And when I stray, when I find myself off guard, others alert me of the poisonous effect, returning me to poise. "Make sure you say 'seamen' in class correctly," a friend cautioned me (teasingly?) many years ago, in my first academic conference—how can I forget—after I presented a paper on merchant seamen; "it can always be *herd* [this is what I heard, I swear, and I am not a nerd], well, differently." He did not mean σεμέν, doily. How can I afford not to be over-conscious of accents? I now have a list of "red flag" words requiring careful handling in the classroom. "Beach" and "sheet" make it on the top, "rip," "heel," and "beet" a close second. Do you hear the fear? Though I can tell the difference between sandal and scandal. My friend, the rascal!

I spoke earlier about accents as engendering real communication problems. But they raise symbolic issues too, with real implications. Marking difference from a norm, they are prone to producing all sorts of negative evaluations by a listener or a national community: placing the speaker as lesser, or as foreign, someone who does not belong. Accents may be marked as heavy, annoying, harsh, ridiculous, incomprehensible, cacophonous. But because of the hierarchies within them, particular immigrant accents may also seduce, provide access. There are cute accents, exotic, sexy, or mesmerizing. Even desirable accents occasionally, particularly if you are sitting in the accent of *a*isles (in the linguistic pyre of the empire). There are surely accents and ax-ends…

Accents in this respect do the work of situating speakers within grids of power. It is others who exercise the power of naming a speaker. It is others who are entitled to do the defining of the accented Self. It is others who interrogate (is this a Mexican accent?)—"the same hurtful, boring, idiotic interrogation—to subsequently label the speaker against her own self-perception."[10] I know of immigrants who opt not to speak in certain situations, if they can afford it. Silence is a telling answer because it is symbolic action. The refusal to speak offers a defense mechanism to avoid facing perplexity, awkwardness, or even humiliation in the accented encounter. It underlines the wish to avoid the ever-present specter of Others' icy ascriptions or genuine bewilderment. Ax-ends contribute to what Gazmend Kapllani registers as an immigrant's butchering of language. "In his hands," he writes, "the language is not spoken, but broken. He doesn't just break it, he butchers it. … Better mute than annoying."[11]

Silence in this case states the desire of skirting away from this grid; it underlines refusal to be evaluated on other people's terms. This strategy, however, is not bullet-proof. It may backfire by placing the Self within alternative grids of power. An immigrant's silences—tongues tied—comes at the risk of someone labeling the nonspeaking person as rude, nonsociable, shy, recalcitrant, or hostile; one erecting boundaries. But the same immigrant tongue, under different circumstances, may join joyfully joke sessions; or contribute to the crescendos of engagement with social talk. Enragement over the specter of rejection leads to electing self-censorship.

If accents put an immigrant speaker on guard, playful manipulation of accents liberates something deep within my writing Self. The play placates my soul, placing me in a position of power. A whole terrain opens up for animating all sorts of poetic devices—alliteration, rhyming, homophony, assonance—surprising at times perhaps, but simple and predictable often. Nevertheless, the devices perform words and concepts that underscore some fluency with the language, some friction with its fiction, some command of its commas and….

---

[10]Nancy Huston. "The Mask and the Pen," in *Lives in Translation: Bilingual Writers on Identity and Creativity*, edited by Isabelle de Courtivron (Palgrave Macmillan, 2003), 57.

[11]Gazmend Kapllani, *A Short Border Handbook*. Translated from the Greek by Anne-Marie Stanton-Ife. (Portobello Books Ltd., 2010), 19.

I relish playing within and across languages. The playing performs the end-result of what has been achieved via enormous investment in the new language. It represents the outcome of immense, excruciating labor translated into playful joy. It underscores some dexterity against the intimidation of anxiety. And it can function as an additional layer of fortification by disguising mistakes as play! As Eva Hoffman notes, "one can play only if one feels a measure of security in the first place. Anxiety does not breed flexibility."[12]

Accents may function as rigid boundaries, but in play they open up metaphorical passages to, and actual passages performing language plasticity, mobility, porousness. Playing with words creates spaciousness for the Self in θάλασσα και ουρανό.

The accent ascents
Moon crescent
Low flow overflows...

Pronunciation, goes without saying,
ain't easy, so I speak my two cents uneasy

–Let us *meat* to eat,
please accept my *envytation*

In the gym of language, I tone
Low class
High glass consonants

Accents lift weights
Grunts in sweaters dripping
Errors, eight attempts

–Wait, newcomer, you temp
Hear is the nation's mission
Trainer raise the bar of admission!

[12] Eva Hoffman. "P.S.," in *Lives in Translation: Bilingual Writers on Identity and Creativity*, edited by Isabelle de Courtivron, 49–54 (Palgrave Macmillan, 2003), 53.

–Please release me, lease me
Time, the least I can do
A form of appeal
Make a list to peel
The pear from
The minimal pair
For real

reel
kiss/keys
luck/lack
word/ward
pray/prey
read/red
hit/heat
sick/seek
lick/leak
feat/fit/feet
pick/peek/peak

Long vowel or short?
Year-after-year
Acid of angst
Uncertainty burns the lungs

To avoid the fear
Of the void in your ear

On the weekend
I forbid myself to make a bid
On a double deck ship where
Well-bred seamen sleep
Bold lips on sparkling sheets
As if a rich ream bids farewell
Reach for a hut, hat in a beach
Each one of them, each
Celebrate the season, in peace!

–Repeat–

On the weak end
I forbid myself to make a bead
On a double deck sheep were
Well-bread, see men, slip
Bald leaps on sparkling sheats
As if a reach rim bids fair well
Rich four a hot, hut inn a beach
Itch one of them, itch
Celebrate the sea son, in piece!

–RIP it–

Fierce swords pierce words
Verbs, nouns
Ailing at pronounciation's tail
Musty curse of the mistake
They announce

m –i –s –t –a –k –Execution

I often subject myself to the discipline of correcting or blurring my accent, of conforming nearer to a norm. Equally often I rebel against this self-subjection. The labor to find my voice translates into an earned accent that refuses to recoil. It demands its volume, it dismantles the minority Self, it mandates the performance of accents.[13] I self-mock to deride when I decide compliance. I self-mock for more: to satisfy a deeply felt drive, an overwhelming force to stage carnivalesque linguistic babels. In this quest, a personal request, I make room, once again, to submit to the need to keep moving away from labels, sneaking bilingual tonal plays against linguistic normalization and conquest.

No choice, must nurse
Sounds of wound

[13]For accent as bold empowerment for bilingual immigrant women (English/Spanish) see, Denice Frohman, "Accents&Poem." *NarrativeNortheast* March 11, 2012. Accessed September 15, 2018. http://www.narrativenortheast.com/?p=1952.

Other, gather your poise
Rather much at stake!

–Let us get it right, let us attain
phonetic transcription

[məˈsteɪk]

–Say Am
she instructs
I say
–Em

–Me
–Mη[14] (Mother tongue distracts)

You say *Am*
I say *Em*

You say *Me*
I say *Don't*

–I see no end in *site*
I cannot retain…
Sound engineer
Heart races, do you hear?

Transcription Is the Prescription

The act of writing accents redirects flows of power in favor to the immigrant speaker. Pen and paper offer me the tools to foreground my anxiety over accents, but also simultaneously repel this anxiety, press it into far recesses (though, true, immigrant writing carries its own accents). In manipulating the problem of the accent, I relish the opportunity

---

[14]μη = do not.

for a symbolic revenge over the specter of linguistic awkwardness that occasionally might disempower me.

In other words, writing accents puts me in a position to control what the undisciplined tongue refuses to do in the act of speaking: to speak back to the colonizing power of the host. Making play out of accents reverses power, emancipating to some extent the Self from their tight grip.

Dexterity in the play of writing performs belonging, homing to the "foreign" tongue. If the play appears awkward at times or excessive in others, it is because the play layers the accumulating traces of the incessant wrestling with the foreign language, evidence of the exhausting and exhilarating engagement (ring and all) with the host language.

How to tell the tale
Refrain meaning from derail?

–Let us get it *write*
I say, me the scribe

m-i-s-t-a-k-e
I inscribe

Again

m-i-stake

–Hay, hold on, do you see?

m-eye-stake

It ain't no miss-take
Missing the norm,
No partner in cr*y*me
Plot of poetic rhyme!

A gain

"I get that feeling"

"It's getting stronger and stronger"

Textual healing!

Language's Mini-Mall[15]

Λες more with less[16]

This
poem
must
be
as
short
as
possible
to
minimize
the
possibility
of
a
missed
ache

Yiorgos Anagnostou
The Ohio State University
November 2018

Acknowledgements I presented an initial version of this work at the Mahindra Humanities Center, Harvard University, in 2017. I thank Vassiliki Rapti for the invitation, and the participants for their lively engagement and feedback.

A participant even came up with a motto for raising funds for Greek/English writings: "Hey Pal, PayPal, Pay Páli!" (páli = πάλι = again).

[15]Originally published as "Immigrant Poetics": Yiorgos Anagnostou, "Immigrant Poetics," *Transnational Literature* 7 no. 2 (May 2015).

[16]λες = you say (singular).

References

Anagnostou, Yiorgos. "Immigrant Poetics." *Transnational Literature* 7 no. 2 (May 2015).

Desai, Anita. "Various Lives." In *Lives in Translation: Bilingual Writers on Identity and Creativity*, edited by Isabelle de Courtivron, 11–17. New York: Palgrave Macmillan, 2003.

Dorfman, Ariel. "The Wandering Bigamists of Language." In *Lives in Translation: Bilingual Writers on Identity and Creativity*, edited by Isabelle de Courtivron, 29–37. New York: Palgrave Macmillan, 2003.

Frohman, Denice. "Accents&Poem." *NarrativeNortheast*, March 11, 2012. Accessed September 15, 2018. http://www.narrativenortheast.com/?p=1952.

Hoffman, Eva. 1989. *Lost in Translation: A Life in a New Language*. New York: E.D. Dutton.

Hoffman, Eva. "P.S." In *Lives in Translation: Bilingual Writers on Identity and Creativity*, edited by Isabelle de Courtivron, 49–54. New York: Palgrave Macmillan, 2003.

Huston, Nancy. "The Mask and the Pen." In *Lives in Translation: Bilingual Writers on Identity and Creativity*, edited by Isabelle de Courtivron, 55–68. New York: Palgrave Macmillan, 2003.

Lazaridis, Henriette. "The Homeland of Stories: On Lingual and Cultural Identity." *The Millions*, September 12, 2013. https://themillions.com/2013/09/the-homeland-of-stories-on-lingual-and-cultural-identity.html. Accessed 1 May, 2017.

Liontas, Anna. *Let Me Explain You*. New York: Scribner, 2015.

Mason, David. *Ludlow: A Verse-Novel*. Pasadena, CA: Red Hen Press, 2014.

Savvopoulos, Dionysis. Erhetai Vrohi, Erhetai Bora (Rain is Coming, a Storm is Coming). In Μπάλλος (Ballos). Athens: LP Lyra, 1971. https://www.youtube.com/watch?v=xHcuFIpg6FQ.

Play(Modes) & Performance as Transgression

Ludics as Transgression: From Surrealism to the Absurd to Pataphysics

Pierre Taminiaux

The issue of ludics has always been a primary concern for my creative work. I firmly believe that it is rooted in an original language that challenges traditional schools of thought and modes of writing. This language rejects the common expression of meaning in order to underline the power of human imagination. Ludics, therefore, always implies for me a definite move beyond reality. It inevitably leads to the exploration of the irrational side of life and reflects the paramount role of chaos in its artistic representation. In other words, ludics does not abide by the order of things: it exceeds it by stressing the splintered nature of the world as opposed to its preconceived unity.

I have authored and published a total of six plays in the past decade. I have read and analyzed most of these works repeatedly with my students in my Contemporary French Culture classes at Georgetown. All these

P. Taminiaux (✉)
Georgetown University, Washington, DC, USA
e-mail: taminiap@georgetown.edu

V. Rapti and E. Gordon (eds.), *Ludics*,
https://doi.org/10.1007/978-981-15-7435-1_17

plays combine surrealist and absurdist influences: they constitute therefore the perfect illustration of my scholarly research of the past thirty years, which has focused on both the literature of the absurd, from Pinget[1] to Beckett, and on Dada and Surrealism, with an emphasis on the relationship between literature and art.

The first play, *Feu noir*,[2] deals with the issue of precarious and short-term labor: it features two male workers who work in the metro at night and who meet a young lady who has just been fired from her job as a secretary. The image of a fire that is raging throughout the city appears several times in the play: It constitutes its main background and represents the ongoing destructive forces that are disrupting everyday life in today's French cities, from riots in the suburbs to widespread vandalism and social unrest.

The second play, *Le Refus*,[3] features a young poet whose manuscript has been turned down by a publisher. It is largely based on a series of tense verbal exchanges between the two characters that often become confrontational. They also involve thorough discussions on the role of poetry and literature in global culture and how it is transformed and even threatened by the almighty power of technology and the Internet. This work constitutes a critical reflection on the evolution of the French publishing world in the twenty-first century under the pressure of mainly commercial and economic interests. But it also questions the reality of a so-called freedom of speech that is a core principle of modern democracy, in France and elsewhere.

The third play, *La Faille*,[4] involves several characters standing on a sidewalk in Paris. It deals in particular with the issue of random violence in contemporary French society and the general decline of traditional social and cultural values. This random violence questions the very meaning of the social contract for the community. This work also features several metaphors of chaos, more precisely that of an earthquake in the final scene. This striking image reveals the destructive

[1]See this regarding my monograph in Pierre Taminiaux, *Robert Pinget* (Paris: Le Seuil, 1994).
[2]Taminiaux, *Feu noir* (Paris: L'Harmattan, 2009).
[3]Taminiaux, *Le Refus* (Paris: L'Harmattan, 2011).
[4]Taminiaux, *La Faille* (Paris: L'Harmattan, 2014).

consequences of climate change for mankind and how it affects the ecological balance of the planet as a whole. Global violence, in this sense, is engendered both by man and by nature.

The fourth play, *Le Grand chambardement*,[5] features several characters who are invited to participate in the election of the President of an imaginary party. It constitutes an allegory of the current French political system, which is dominated by the impossibility of true progressive political and social change: the political change that is promised here by the candidates remains indeed elusive. This work stresses therefore the numerous illusions and deceptive strategies of contemporary democracies. It is being defined as 'neo-pataphysical,' in reference to the playful spirit and language of Alfred Jarry.

The fifth play, *Dire*,[6] which is also defined as 'neo-pataphysical', is the shortest one. It features several participants in an academic conference. The name of each of these participants includes the syllable 'Di,' and each line of the play also includes the same syllable in various forms. I want to emphasize here the void of a certain social language that is shaped by predetermined codes of communication and that is deprived of any true relevance.

I am asking here the following question: 'what does the verb: to say exactly imply?' And how could we say something that does not abide by a strict set of rules? These questions are particularly relevant in a culture that is as rhetorical and formal as France and in which the rules of both oral and written expression remain often dictated by the French academy. In this sense, one should never take for granted the freedom of language.

The sixth and final play, *Les Dormeurs*,[7] features two male and two female characters who spend their time sleeping in a bedroom while there is a war going on outside. The main theme of this work is the issue of collective apathy and indifference toward evil. The casual attitude of these characters stands indeed in sharp contrast with the tragic nature of the situation that surrounds them.

---

[5]Taminiaux, *Le Grand chambardement* (Paris, L'Harmattan, 2016).

[6]Taminiaux, edited by Vasile Robciuc, *Dire* (Cahiers Internationaux Tristan Tzara, 2016).

[7]Taminiaux, *Les Dormeurs* (Paris: L'Harmattan, 2017).

This indifference towards evil constitutes an historical reality in French culture, from the pre-World War II period to the present. In the context of globalization, it refers more precisely to a collective mindset that has for many years ignored the danger posed by radical Islam. But one could also think here of the French people's sometime casual and Munich-like attitude towards the threat of war coming from Nazi Germany back in the nineteen thirties.

Alfred Jarry was the first to explore the ludic dimension of theater at the end of the nineteenth century. It definitely entailed for him a rejection of the psychological tradition that had been particularly powerful In France since the seventeenth century. It shed a new light on the essential role played by the body in the definition of a character. In this sense, he stressed the physical and even the animalistic nature of theater like never before, at least in French culture.

Moreover, his most important work stemmed from the representation of an insurmountable chaos. The world of *King Ubu*[8] was indeed torn apart by violence, madness, and destruction. This chaos had never been exposed before in such a vigorous way: it questioned above all the moral and philosophical value of rationality, which had originally been developed in the seventeenth century by the philosophy of Descartes. This perspective had a profound and lasting influence on French culture as a whole. It is no coincidence, in this regard, if Breton himself celebrated Jarry as one of the main precursors of surrealism, alongside Nerval and Lautréamont, in his Manifestoes. There was no room for the power of reason in this kind of theater. In other words, no human behavior could really be explained in analytical terms.[9]

In my own work, I have attempted to synthesize the influence of three literary movements or schools. The first is Surrealism. One must say that theater played only a minor role in the artistic identity of Surrealism. Breton, in his Surrealist Manifesto of 1924,[10] defined in this regard

[8]Alfred Jarry, *Ubu Roi*, in *Tout Ubu* (Paris: Fasquelle, 1968).

[9]I analyzed Jarry's main play in the first chapter of my book Taminiaux, *Surmodernités: entre rêve et technique* (Paris: L'Harmattan, 2003), 15–40. I studied in particular the metaphor of the machine in *King Ubu*.

[10]André Breton, *Manifestes du surréalisme* (Paris: Gallimard, 2003).

automatism as a form of instant and straightforward poetic writing.[11] In this regard, the founding members of Surrealism were above all poets, from Breton to Desnos and from Eluard to Aragon and Péret. And if they were not writing poetry, they were then focusing most of their intellectual and creative efforts on autobiographical narratives or critical writings.

In *Nadja*,[12] his main work and autobiographical narrative, Breton expressed his fascination and admiration for a young actress, Blanche Derval. She belonged to the world of popular theater, and not to that of the avant-garde. In this book, most of the references to the theater were of the same kind. Breton was only interested in the relationship between theater and the popular culture of the time (the nineteen twenties and thirties). He obviously preferred to see cheap entertainment on the stage, as if theater was just for him a second-rate art form with little esthetic meaning or artistic worth.

It is interesting to notice in this perspective that the most important theatrical work coming from Surrealism was precisely authored by one of the main rebels and dissident figures of the movement, namely Antonin Artaud, who wrote in particular the landmark essay on modern theater entitled *Le Théâtre et son double*.[13] In other words, surrealist theater could only exist and assert its identity against Surrealism, or at least against the authoritarian leadership of André Breton.

If we set aside the domain of literature, we have to say that art was the second most important area of creativity for Surrealism, from painting to collages and photography. One of its main characteristics was its ongoing emphasis on the magic and the supernatural. These notions had to be explored through various visions and images. They were thus primarily visual. Moreover, the rule of automatism also applied to painting and drawing, as demonstrated by the work of André Masson and by Breton's

---

[11] In this regard, Breton's work for the theater is mostly limited to two short plays (*S'il vous plaît* and *Vous m'oublierez*) that he co-authored with Philippe Soupault in 1919, when he was barely twenty-three years old. They are included in Breton, *Les Champs magnétiques* (Paris: Gallimard, 1971), 125–178.

[12] Breton, *Nadja* (Paris: Gallimard, 1990).

[13] Antonin Artaud, *Le Théâtre et son double* (Paris: Gallimard, 1966).

essays in his book of art criticism, *Le Surréalisme et la peinture.*[14] In other words, there was no such thing as 'automatic theater.'

Nevertheless, one should stress the original dimension of Surrealism in its playful perspective on both literature and art, particularly in the field of language, of puns and word games, as demonstrated in particular by the work of Robert Desnos. This unique attitude has inspired some of my own writings: The main issue associated with this approach is the possibility of drifting through language, of wandering aimlessly without any specific purpose or goal. This was exactly what defined the main character of Breton's novel *Nadja*.

The philosophical legacy of the Absurd has also been very important for me. It was rooted in the dark history of the twentieth century, and in particular of World War II. Let us think for instance of Ionesco's play *Rhinocéros*,[15] which stemmed directly from the writer's personal and early experience of fascism in his native Rumania. The Absurd was definitely inspired by the direct confrontation with radical evil and the apocalypse it engendered.

One could quote here the famous question by Adorno: 'is poetry still possible after Auschwitz?' to which the Absurdists answered: 'Is theater still possible after Auschwitz?' which could be translated also as: 'Is meaning still possible after Auschwitz?' The twenty-first century seems to be a bit quieter in this sense. It has yet to produce a major conflict like those of the previous century or an ideology as destructive and deadly as Nazism.

Nevertheless, evil is present almost everywhere around us, from terrorism and random violence to the most obscene forms of materialism and capitalist greed. It is just more disseminated and less easy to grasp. A superficial sense of democracy and freedom has prevailed in the West, making it more difficult for many to see evil and define it in clear terms. This is the reason why the legacy of the Absurd is still largely relevant. Indeed, when one is no longer able to recognize nor to identify evil, one is doomed to meaninglessness.

14Breton, *Le Surréalisme et la peinture* (Paris: Gallimard, 1965).

15Eugène Ionesco, *Rhinocéros* (Paris: Gallimard, 2001).

The Absurd also stressed the profound existential vacuum in which mankind was forced to live in the middle of the twentieth century. In the age of iPhones and the social media, this vacuum has not entirely disappeared. The cultural influence of a purely consumerist approach of life that rose more than sixty years ago has vastly expanded instead.

Ionesco himself did not like the term: 'Theater of the Absurd.' He preferred the notion of 'Theater of derision,' since it was life, for him, that was indeed absurd. In my own case, I have tried to draw the numerous and profound lessons of the creative power of the Absurd. My plays represent a state of cultural, social, and personal confusion that largely stems from the negative impact of globalization on human life. The most fundamental issue that I tackle in this regard is that of a generalized loss of identity and purpose in a world dominated by false values and a deceiving concept of social success and achievement.

In *La Cantatrice chauve*, for instance, the characters do not have a clear identity. They just all look alike, or are searching for a true self that will never be realized. The mainly uprooted lifestyle produced by globalization has also triggered this kind of crisis in the context of the twenty-first century. It is based on the loss of national belonging, of cultural affiliation and in general of community ties that used to define individual existence in the past.

In *La Faille*, a character called L'Humaniste embodies in this regard the longing for a common cultural heritage and strong personal roots. In his solitary quest for both wisdom and truth, he mirrors the decline of humanism in contemporary French culture: globalization has indeed put forward the economy as a new God, according to the notion that the laws of the market are always right.

Anyone who dares to contradict this widespread assertion runs therefore the risk of being ostracized. The values and beliefs of L'Humaniste stand in sharp contrast with those of L'Anarchiste, who deeply mistrusts the redeeming and ethical power of language and thought. Instead, the anarchist dreams of an impulsive and unpredictable action that would solve all human problems by simply eradicating human life around him.

The Absurd unveiled the nihilism of an era in which the very notion of humanity had been denied by various political leaderships. In the twenty-first century, we are actually witnessing a return of the same process of negation in ideologies such as radical Islam. This is happening in the context of a profound economic, political and social decline in the West in general and in France in particular.

In other words, the definition of meaning itself becomes harder to formulate when all former political and religious beliefs have waned, from communism to Christianity. Many people, in this sense, have lost all faith and are therefore deprived of a community that could potentially save them from emotional distress and spiritual emptiness.

The Absurd still asserted the need for a ludic approach to theater, in spite of the surrounding evils. It stressed in this regard the artistic power of laughter and derision, according to Ionesco's own word. *Rhinocéros* represented a world in which virtually anyone could become a monster, due to the constant pressure of social conformity. Nevertheless, it also allowed for a form of playfulness and even lightness.

The ludic perspective can never be confused with an attitude of detachment toward reality. It does not lead to a position of withdrawal: to the contrary, it forces us to confront this reality in its most challenging aspects. In my personal case, I have attempted to tie the representation of chaos to that of twenty-first century French culture in general. This multifaceted chaos is the direct consequence of globalization and of its negative impact on the lives of many French citizens.

There are actually three fundamental dimensions to this chaos: the first is socio-economic, the second is political, and the third is ecological. The spirit of Jarry never ceases to haunt me, in this sense, because the high school student that he was when he wrote his now classical play could foresee a world to come, that of twentieth-century totalitarianism but also of twenty-first century democratic decadence. He perceived it then already in its most grotesque form.

King Ubu, indeed, was only motivated by greed and the search for unlimited power. We all know that a contemporary version of King Ubu has lived in the White House for the past four years. The dark fantasy of comedy has unfortunately become reality. In other words, new monsters and buffoons occupy now the space of a stage that was created more than a hundred years ago: they constitute the ultimate symbol of both moral ugliness and absolute ignorance.

Chaos is therefore an eternal problem: the ludic theater has to address its numerous repercussions in contemporary society, particularly in the West. I stated already three dimensions of this predicament. In the context of contemporary French culture, the one I know the best and study the most, one must face first its social and economic implications.

They have been dictated by the might of global capitalism, an unfair and cruel system that turns many human beings into mere disposable objects and enslaves them for the profit and the financial gratification of a few. This situation is eminently tragic: nevertheless, one can try at least to laugh about it, and there is no better means at our disposal in this regard than the theater. This is exactly what I have been trying to do, in particular in my play *Feu noir*, in which the two main characters are in many ways victims of this system.

What characterizes above all the contemporary Western world is precisely the overwhelming presence of excess in its multiple aspects around us: the excess of wealth, of poverty, of injustice, of stupidity, of nastiness, of arrogance. Without any doubt, excess can only lead to the negation of freedom and equality. Jarry's work was just a constant metaphor of excess, in this regard: the excess of the obese body, that of megalomania and egotism. It rings true even more today than it did back then, at the end of the nineteenth century.

A world without balance is a world without truth, what some even call now the post-truth universe.[16] My own form of ludic theater takes this problem into consideration and tries therefore to underline the utmost nihilism that it necessarily entails. In *La Faille*, for example, the character named L'Anarchiste dreams of going on a shooting spree by using a gun. He is only concerned with spreading terror and mass death. Excess is in this sense the symbol of a system of domination that inevitably engenders violence and the negation of the other.

In the past few years, France has witnessed unprecedented acts of terrorism. One has often related them to the threat of radical Islam. This is certainly relevant. But beyond the ideological roots of such problem, one must also stress the fact that they reflect an irresistible breakdown of

[16] I want to refer here to the Oxford Dictionary Word of the Year 2016, which was precisely post-truth. It is defined as 'relating to or denoting circumstances in which objective facts are less influential in shaping public opinion than appeals to emotion and personal belief'.

the French social contract that was created at the beginning of the fifth Republic, in the late nineteen fifties. In other words, these horrendous acts could only happen because of a profound decline of social values such as public responsibility and solidarity or the basic respect for the other and for human life in general.

In my play, L'Anarchiste wishes to spread chaos by all means. My own philosophical perspective on contemporary French culture emphasizes thus the numerous dysfunctions of a social order that produces exclusion and marginalization, especially among the youth. Violence becomes too often in this context the only solution and escape available.

The second dimension of this current chaos is political. In the case of France, one has seen an erosion of the democratic ideals of the French Republic in the course of the twenty-first century. In this regard, far-right and populist ideologies have gained considerable popular support, a phenomenon that has no equivalent since the nineteen thirties and the rise of fascism. French culture has always had a definite attraction for radical political ideas, especially those stemming from reactionary nationalism. This is clearly the sign of a society plagued by a deep identity crisis.

More and more French citizens, indeed, have become disillusioned over the years with the so-called democratic political process. It has paved the way for the ongoing power of a technocratic elite that has been unable to tackle seriously the labor issues of underemployment and precariousness and improve the living standards of a beleaguered middle class whose insecurity is largely the result of growing socio-economic inequalities. My play *Le Grand chambardement*, which in French means ironically 'The big change,' deals precisely with this new situation: it is largely the result of the deep erosion of the left in contemporary France.

By contrast, right after World War II and at least until the nineteen seventies, the French Communist Party enjoyed a strong popularity and a solid base of followers. It constituted a force of opposition to the status quo and the conservative policies of the French State. Today, though, this Party has become almost entirely irrelevant, due to the universal domination of global capitalism and the collapse of the former Soviet Union.

Moreover, the socialist Party has ceased to be a true left-wing Party in order to embrace the free market and bourgeois individualism. It no longer represents the interests of the workers, as it used to at the time of its foundation in 1905 when it was known as the SFIO, and for many years after that, at the time of the Popular Front in particular, when it was carrying the political legacy of Jean Jaurès, the main historical figure of socialism in modern France.

When no real change is possible, no true democracy is possible either. I try to treat this painful reality with a definite irony in *Le Grand chambardement*. In this play, several characters must choose between various phony candidates. At the end of the contest, an impostor is elected President of the 'Parti des colombophiles récidivistes,' the Party of repeated pigeon-fanciers, which is another word for fools.

He only gets to the top because of a large sum of money that he receives from a character called the queen. The apparently free electoral process has become a farce, since the game is rigged from the start and determined in advance by the diktat of the financial establishment, as demonstrated by the most recent presidential elections in France.

This means that any true critical discourse on French society, one that takes into account all the oppressive mechanisms of social, economic, and cultural domination and denounces them forcefully, is being sidelined. The system no longer tolerates its own contradiction it must eliminate it in order to maintain the same oligarchy and the same interests in power, although sometimes with a different name and a different look.

The third dimension of chaos is now ecological. It is fostered by the pressing issue of climate change and enlightens therefore a profound loss of balance between man and his natural environment. This particular balance is crucial for any substantial personal and social development. In *La Faille*, for instance, all the characters die at the end in a strong earthquake that actually looks more like a Tsunami: their bodies, literally, lose their stability and they end up falling into an abyss that is quite metaphorical. Chaos reveals thus the need for a sensible and harmonious relationship between man and the earth. This relationship is obviously threatened nowadays by all those who carry on the exploitation of natural resources for purely material gains and who also categorically deny the existence of climate change.

The notion of a ludic theater, therefore, implies for me a definite engagement within the community. This engagement is no longer of an idealistic nature, as it was often the case back in the sixties and the seventies. In other words, it does not reflect a form of political activism driven by a specific ideology. Nevertheless, it still rests upon the belief that critical thinking constitutes an important part of literature in general and theater in particular.

Any alternative or non-conventional use of language is somehow political. This is an idea that I have also developed in my book *L'Ellipse et le cercle: art, poésie, politique*,[17] which was published in 2016. It deals primarily with the playful dimension of language as it is expressed in aphorisms and philosophical fragments. This unambiguous statement echoes the spirit of the early twentieth century European avant-garde and in particular of Dada. To speak differently is to think differently, which means that it allows us to imagine and then to create a different world. Language, therefore, is the ultimate revolutionary weapon, because it can transform the social and material conditions of our everyday existence.

The use of an original and unorthodox language is thus a precondition to any original artistic creation. This is what Jarry said when he talked about the need for a pataphysical language, a new 'science of imaginary solutions.' Language is what controls us most of the time, but it can also liberate us if we are truly aware of its potential for radical cultural change.

The norms of language are largely dictated today by the mainstream media and by all-mighty technologies that constantly emphasize instant communication and a purely functional or practical form of verbal expression. Our language is most of the time shaped by an alienating ideology of mere efficiency. In this perspective, our words are not allowed to wander or to drift: they are too often forced to reach an immediate goal and are thus devoid of ambiguity or secrecy.

This is precisely where the legacy of pataphysics makes particular sense. It includes an attitude of transgression that is less moral than essentially linguistic. The ludic perspective is political because it displaces and

[17] Taminiaux, *L'Ellipse et le cercle: art, poésie, politique* (Paris: Les Impliqués, 2016).

unsettles the traditional centers of power of speech. As a consequence, it provides us with the unique opportunity to speak beyond the imperatives of meaning and rationality.

The two major totalitarianisms of the twentieth century, that is Nazism and Stalinism, did exactly the opposite. They repressed any kind of playfulness in the verbal expression of man, since they were obsessed with the strictly ideological and doctrinarian dimension of language. In this sense, the ludic language still represents today a threat to the powers that be, in a world where journalists and politicians impose a form of discourse that is filled with semantic distortions and hollow objectivity. One can talk therefore about the subversive quality of the ludic approach, a quality that I reiterate on numerous occasions in my work.

The eccentric language acts as a means of resistance against apathy and indifference. It stirs our reflection and leads us to a profound questioning of reality. I have represented this attitude of collective detachment in my play *Les Dormeurs*, in which the physical presence of war and radical evil does not seem to touch or even bother the four main characters, who constantly remain in a state of lethargy. It unfortunately characterizes the mindset of many in contemporary society. The new technologies and the media, through their ubiquitous presence, tend to numb indeed the mind in various ways.

They create a situation of psychological and even physical dependency that stifles our ability to think freely and to react against the negative aspects of our closest environment. Moreover, they make us lose our sense of focus and our capacity to concentrate on a particular issue for a long period of time. In other words, a world ruled by technology and the media like ours today is a world of constant distraction and mental dispersion.

The ludic theater never abandons its critical mission: it unveils and denounces in many ways the gap that exists between our most profound aspirations and what the world actually has to offer. One must add that this work is always related to a deeply poetic sensitivity, as it is definitely the case in my plays. It constitutes a product of the imagination and as such, it opens to the hidden domain of dreams and visions. The main point is ultimately to depart from reality in order to reveal the sheer power of ideals and desires.

I have published two poetry volumes and have performed several poetry readings of my own work over the past decade.[18] Moreover, I have written numerous scholarly essays on modern French poetry, from Mallarmé to Reverdy, from Baudelaire to Breton, and from Valéry to Tzara, among others.[19] This strong presence of poetry and of its unique spirit can also be found in my plays.

To put it differently, the necessary representation of reality never obeys the rules of strict realism. One always has to move beyond an objective image of the world, to the extent that such image cannot convey the whole range and complexity of life and of the human psyche or unconscious. Theater allows me therefore to reinvent the tangible and material universe: it asks for a thorough process of allegorical metamorphosis and metaphorical transfiguration that never truly ends.

We never truly know reality: we can only represent it through our personal perception of things and events. In this sense, the so-called realism of theater is largely an illusion if not altogether a misconception. From Surrealism to the Absurd to Pataphysics, this statement is constantly repeated although in different forms. In other words, all three movements imply the questioning of the objectivity of language and of the confusion of theater with the outside world. Language must therefore be defined by its power of transcendence: its ludic identity leads to the revelation of a hidden world that is never the one we actually see.

This identity also speaks for times of crisis and deep conflicts like ours. In many ways, one is forced to play with language when the purely social meaning of language has been exhausted and when traditional or mainstream means of communication fail to express our strongest fears and desires. We then dream about a lost unity and harmony that can only be recovered through the ludic perspective. This perspective reflects the quest for a new order that stems from the construction of an original

[18]See in this regard Taminiaux, *Les Mots de l'art* (Amay: L'Arbre à paroles, 2012), which is inspired by the art of both Hans Arp and Juan Gris, and also Taminiaux, *Poésie bleue* (Paris: L'Harmattan, 2018), which is inspired by Jazz music.

[19]See in this regard Taminiaux, *The Paradox of Photography* (Amsterdam and New York: Rodopi, 2009), which analyzes the critical discourse on photography by Baudelaire, Breton and Valéry, and also Taminiaux, *Littératures modernistes et arts d'avant-garde* (Paris: Honoré Champion, 2013), which includes an essay on Tzara's *Dada Manifestoes* as well as on the esthetic relationship between the poetry of Mallarmé and the late narrative works of Beckett.

esthetics. In many ways, the ludic sensitivity asks for a *tabula rasa*: it forces us to start from scratch and to imagine a language without any master, that of childhood and of the primitive voice that dwells inside us.

This primitive voice is also the voice of origin and of the buried times of language. It has been tamed or even repressed by society because of its raw and unpolished nature. It is the symbol of an absolute freedom of speech, to the extent that it tells us where we really come from. In other words, to play with language is like being born again and looking at this language with the eyes of an infant.

In conclusion, I will stress the utmost seriousness and gravity of purpose of the ludic mind. To play is not merely to have fun, but rather to underline the ridiculous and at the same time tragic character of many situations that surround us in our everyday life. The main point is indeed to cope with what defies common sense. In a world often ruled by insanity, the ludic approach does not bring more insanity but provides us instead with a form of wisdom and moral reason.

Ultimately, its language is what saves us from madness and nothingness: this was already Jarry's belief. It constitutes a powerful weapon, since we can turn it into a mode of resistance against the powers that try to silence us. In this sense, it would be wrong to emphasize the irrationality of the absurdist or of the pataphysical language. On the contrary, they constantly assert their own logic and philosophical coherence.

It is interesting to notice that in the English language, the usual term for a theatrical work is 'a play.' This word inevitably refers to the idea of a performance, but also and maybe more importantly to the issue of playfulness and to its unique spirit. This is not the case in the French language, since a theatrical work is normally called 'une pièce.' Nevertheless, I must say that this term is also quite telling, since it indirectly suggests the existence of fragments and pieces.

Ludics, indeed, entails the strong sense of the fragmentation of both language and representation. In this regard, the suspicion towards the philosophical and the esthetic significance of unity is common to Surrealism, the Absurd, and Pataphysics. Surrealism, for instance, emphasized the poetic intensity of a discontinuous style of writing in automatism. Moreover, the pataphysical use of language implied the search for its heterogeneous nature through the deliberate mixture of scientific, metaphysical, and comic expressions, as in *Docteur Faustroll*. Ludics, therefore, starts when we grasp the meaning of a creative process of dissemination that allows us to reach a state of radical and unbridled freedom beyond the deceiving order of reality.

Bibliography

Artaud, Antonin. *Le Théâtre et son double*. Paris: Gallimard, 1966.
Breton, André. *Le Surréalisme et la peinture*. Paris: Gallimard, 1965.
——— (with Soupault, Philippe). *Les Champs magnétiques*. Paris: Gallimard, 1971.
———. *Nadja*. Paris: Gallimard, 1990.
———. *Manifestes du surréalisme*. Paris: Gallimard, 2003.
Ionesco, Eugène. *Rhinocéros*. Paris: Gallimard, 2001.
Jarry, Alfred. *Tout Ubu*. Paris: Fasquelle, 1968.
Taminiaux, Pierre. *Robert Pinget*. Paris: Le Seuil, 1994.
———. *Surmodernités: entre rêve et technique*. Paris: L'Harmattan, 2003.
———. *The Paradox of Photography*. Amsterdam and New York: Rodopi, 2009.
———. *Feu noir*. Paris: L'Harmattan, 2009.
———. *Le Refus*. Paris: L'Harmattan, 2011.
———. *Les Mots de l'art*. Amay: L'Arbre à paroles, 2012.
———. *Littératures modernistes et arts d'avant-garde*. Paris: Honoré Champion, 2013.
———. *La Faille*. Paris: L'Harmattan, 2014.
———. *Le Grand chambardement*. Paris: L'Harmattan, 2016.
———. *Dire*. Cahiers Internationaux Tristan Tzara, 2016.
———. *L'Ellipse et le cercle: art, poésie, politique*. Paris: Les Impliqués, 2016.
———. *Les Dormeurs*. Paris: L'Harmattan, 2017.
———. *Poésie bleue*, Paris: L'Harmattan, 2018.

2 Sisters, 2 Stories: Breast Cancer, Femininity, and Body Ownership

Catalina Florina Florescu

In memoriam, to beautiful mother

Mia is a play from *The Rebelled Body Plays* catalogued at the Library of Congress and it will have its world premiere next year at HERE: Arts Center in New York, Director Handan Ozbilgin. The play is inspired by my mother's death in the early nineties in Romania. *Mia* is a creative work with a heavy educational component. When my mother was diagnosed with breast cancer, I did not know much about the illness. I have learned about it via memoirs, artworks, medical treatises, etc. Still, outside of academia, women struggle (more) to talk about the illness, the loss of a breast/breasts, reconstruction, etc. I use the play to communicate about all these issues and raise awareness of the benefits of talking more freely about our ill/healthy body.

C. F. Florescu (✉)
Pace University, New York, NY, USA
e-mail: fflorescu@pace.edu

V. Rapti and E. Gordon (eds.), *Ludics*,
https://doi.org/10.1007/978-981-15-7435-1_18

The play happens in the U.S.A. but reaches out to women globally. The protagonist, Mia, is 38 year-old. She was diagnosed with cancer *by accident* when she was 36. According to her doctor, a woman her age would not need to have a mammogram and/or an ultrasound recommended as part of her medical routine since there was no medical history to trace the illness in her family. Because she is under 40, her insurance would not cover for a mammogram/an ultrasound either. Mia insisted on having a medical investigation and this is how she discovered her cancer. When the play starts, we meet her two years after mastectomy. From the moment of her diagnosis, treatments, and surgery, she had a very difficult time accepting her left breast had to be removed. In addition, she wanted to become a mother, but complications resulting from cancer's unpredictable side effects have made her young body develop early menopause.

Meg is Mia's sister and she is 39 years old. When she hears her sister's diagnosis, Meg schedules herself several screenings and tests, including the BRCA. She discovers that she inherited the faulty gene from their never met grandmother who, digging deeper, she discovered had died when she was in her early 40s. Meg would have 90% to develop breast cancer. Unlike her sister, she opts for a preventive double mastectomy without any hesitation. Since she opens up to us about her surgery (and not to her sister whom she feels the need to protect), Meg takes the position of cancer as seen from the legal standpoint. As a lawyer, Meg insists, she owns her body entirely. She says that directly and convincingly anticipating attacks from others who could see her drastic double mastectomy as an extreme, radical measure.

In this chapter, since Mia and Meg have opted for mastectomy that affected their views on femininity, and since they are not real but inspired by reality, I bring into discussion several points by taking advantage of theatrical devices and other palliative activities. For one thing, I talk about "femininity," a noun that seems to have an easy semantics. However, in the context of breast cancer and mastectomy the noun becomes controversial because it opens up several debates on the nature of femininity and ownership of the body. Furthermore, because of Mia's treatments and her early menopause, her body rejects maternity and she adds yet another layer to our discussion on femininity in the context of breast cancer.

"2 Sisters, 2 Stories" is thus an invitation to think collectively about ways to minimize breast cancer; how to raise awareness of prevention; what's the difference between a very well-known noun, "survivor," versus a still rarely used one, "previvor." The chapter uses two fictional characters to show the benefits of medical humanities as integrated approaches toward ameliorating an illness. In a world dominated by fake beauty and increased usage of cosmetic products and plastic surgery, in a world where the body is shamed if it does not follow the pressures of (so-called) social norms, in a world where the body could be politically institutionalized, Mia and Meg, two sisters with (recently found) family history of breast cancer, talk openly about how prevention along with personal choices should be part of any patient's *educated* decisions.

About Marriage

When the play starts, Mark enters running and panting to which Mia replies half jokingly half seriously, "I hear those who jog die." Mark retorts, "Die happy."[1] This borderline tease happens for the most part of the play indicating that the two were once in love, but that that has been tested by cancer and by Mia's body's inability to get pregnant. The couple struggle and this is not an abnormality given that cancer is a mutation in one's body, a mutation whose randomness baffles everybody, from patients to medical teams. An illness followed by various visits at the doctor, poorly slept nights, excessive worrying, changes within the body, emotions churned and churning daily, overwhelm and sometimes may be hard to get over.

Quickly in the play, we sense Mia's vulnerability and anger not only at the possibility of cancer sneaking back into their lives, but also at how cancer already *marked* her body.

---

[1]There are no page numbers after quotes from the play because the author used a revised, acting edition.

MIA (Sharp): Stop using these clichés. Look at your body: vibrant, young, desirable. Look at mine. (*She uncovers her robe and we discover a big, ugly, real scar on her left breast*) I need layers of clothes to keep me warm. I want to take my insides off, throw them, 'cause they've already betrayed me, and put cotton balls inside me. You know, the same way they make stuffed toy animals.

MARK (Consoling): You'd make a perfect stuffed animal. I'd call you Jemima, like the naïve duck from that children's story. (*Laughs*) You still look good to me.

MIA: What the hell do you mean by "still"? Still is a very revealing adverb: it reminds people that the best part of their lives is gone. "Hey, you can't walk like you used to do? Don't worry, what matters is that you're still alive." Don't even get me started with "at least." Better be dead than dying, really.

What bothers Mia is that the adverb is just as revealing as the scar left on her upper left torso, the scar that replaces her breast. As a college professor of literature and writing and as a cancer survivor, semantics and pragmatics weigh strongly. What Mia tells Mark and, by extension to other people whose sympathy's limits have been tested, is to pay attention to nuances within realities, to details that may be overlooked. Mia's body is functional, but it is far from being back to normal. In fact, Mia is aware that she cannot return to her previously intact physicality. She *still* has a long journey to process everything that has been happening both at the physical, cognitive, and emotional levels. She may be cancer-free (for the moment), but she refuses the aggressive however normative rehabilitation process.

Furthermore, she needs time to mourn. She lost a part of her body, a part that, the more we read, the more we realize she associates with motherhood and femininity:

MIA: If you want to feel pain, you do not need to go to a museum; you could touch this instead. (*She points to her scar*) They say when you lose a hand, a leg, or a breast, you're still able to somehow feel them; you have the phantom limb experience.

MARK: Sounds like a fairytale.

MIA: It sounds so fascinating (*faking excitement*), a phantom in your body (*blunt*), but it's not. Because you are not you anymore. There are ghosts inside your body, crawling, itching, eating you alive. (*Change in tone, now neutral*) Anyway, I don't feel my lost breast at all, as if it never existed. I don't retain any left breast memory whatsoever. Perhaps that's because I never nurtured an infant. (*Pause. Then she starts repeating his remark mockingly*) "You still look good."

In the beginning of the play, at home, Mia wears a robe that resembles a medical gown and that suggests that even though she is not in hospital anymore, the hospital room is inside her own (apartment). Her whole universe continues the one from the medical establishment because she is not yet healed but pressured into accepting accelerated normality. From discussion about God to domestic chores, from religion and personal expectations to social roles, little by little Mia realizes that her only chance at recovery is to accept her reality making sure other women are better educated than she was prior to being diagnosed.

MIA: One day I was dressing in my uniform, old jeans and a black sweater, and had an epiphany: who the hell is that dead woman? I felt chills throughout my body. I ran away from the mirror and searched for my measuring tape. Luckily, I found it in seconds. Then, I took up my measures. I went to the store, bought a lovely fabric, and started cutting and sewing. Now all that's left is adding its finishing touches. (*She tries the unfinished dress on top of her suit*) How do I look?
MARK: Alive! (*He kisses her*)

Because the play is listed when I teach "21st century Dramatic Texts as Inter-Cultural Dialogue" as well as "Women in Literature: Theater of Resistance" and because my expertise in medical humanities dates decades ago when I was a graduate student at Purdue University, continued by published books and conference talks, over the years I have been carefully designing several activities and games to be played by and to benefit younger generations of students, activities that can be incorporated when the play is read or staged professionally.

Therefore, a good way to start engaging with these otherwise intimate realities is by playing a game of free associations. Whatever comes to mind should be written down in students' notebooks. The words chosen are introduced in the play: femininity; choices; womanhood; maternity; pressures; norms. Students are encouraged to be sincere and write down responses on the spot, without overthinking. Once the exercise ends, students go back to the list of words only that this time, by taking turns, they read out loud their answers. As group discussion, we need to observe the verbal recurrences in students' answers (if any), if their chosen responses have multiple meanings, and if they have negative or positive connotations. Since the exercise relies on *fast* free association it reveals how our brains operate (i.e., how much we rely on experience versus how much we have absorbed the social definitions on key concepts).

Another exercise that can be developed because of Mia and Mark is taken from Augusto Boal's the machine of rhythm. The instructions are as follows:

> Especially in this exercise, it is important that the actor really plays the internal rhythm: a machine is obviously mechanical so we should not demonstrate the external aspects of people. The aim of the exercise is to reveal inner rhythms, rather than external cliché behaviours. [...] An actor goes into the middle and imagines that he is a moving part in a complex machine. He starts doing a movement with his body, a mechanical, rhythmic movement, and vocalising a sound to go with it. Everyone else watches and listens, in a circle around the machine. Another person goes up and adds another part (her own body) to this mechanical apparatus, with another movement and another sound. A third, watching the first two, goes in and does the same, so that eventually all the participants are integrated into this one machine, which is a synchronised, multiple machine. When everyone is part of the machine, the Joker asks the first person to accelerate his rhythm – everyone else must follow this modification, since the machine is one entity. When the machine is near to explosion, the Joker asks the first person to ease up, gradually to slow down, till in their own time the whole group ends together. It is not easy to end together, but it is possible. For everything to work well, each participant really does have to try and listen to everything he hears.[2]

[2]Boal, Augusto. *Games for Actors and Non-actors*. New York: Routledge, 2002 (second edition), 94.

Students stand up and are ready to participate in the game by building a machine of rhythm for love. Following Boal's precise instructions, at the end of the game students may be asked if the sounds were soothing/intimidating/repetitive. My advice is to follow up the machine of rhythm for love with another one, this time focusing on pain. At the end, students are assigned to write a 500-word reflective essay on the two machines of rhythm and discuss those answers during next class.

From Jo Spence to Flat Sisters

Jo Spence was a photographer who died in 1992 because of breast cancer. She was one of the first women to chronicle the devastation of the illness and expose the body in pain *as is*. Consequently, her photos are very intimate and powerful, however shocking. They request maturity. Last thing Spence would have wanted were to see faces distorted by disgust as if anyone chose cancer. Spence was extremely critical not only of an establishment that kept patients away from the public eye, almost never revealing the brutality of cancer, but also of a medical system that did not want to accept alternative treatments (traditional versus complementary medicine). That is, in addition to allopathic treatments available at the time of Spence's diagnosis, she insisted on trying homeopathic ones. She encountered a lot of resistance from the heavily intertwined medical and pharmaceutical conglomerates.

When she was not ready to go into surgery to remove her cancerous breast, Spence faced the stigma of being considered insane. Through a series of very revealing photos she narrates visually her story, thus leaving an undiluted legacy of pain.[3] In one photo from the series "Cancer Shock," Spence is naked. A white mask blocks half of her face. She holds a sign that reads "Victim?" with a question mark that triggers a discussion on why patients are made even more vulnerable than they

[3]Due to copyright laws, I cannot use Spence's photographs, but I can direct readers to her website: http://www.jospence.org/.

already are. The cancerous breast is taped with Band-Aids. On the background, there are newspapers with headlines and articles dealing with several crises within the healthcare system.

We know that prolonged hospitalization puts patients' social persona on hiatus. Their medical cases become part of an ongoing statistics. But they are *not* victims. In classroom, I invite students to brainstorm the nouns "victim" and "victimization" and the verb "to victimize." Furthermore, students are split into three groups and asked to find where in my play these words are used and/or suggested.

Going back to the British photographer, in another photo from the series "The Picture of Health?," Spence creates a collage of various parts of her body and arranges those photos so that what is written on the body reads, "How do I take responsibility for my body?" When we read it, we become better involved than if we were only looking at the photos. She is aware of the social impact these messages can have on people. Still, she does not feel ready to talk about cancer:

> How do we begin to speak about what it is like to live with cancer? How do we find a language to express ourselves? What are we able to say if we turn to the medical language of tumours, drags, and surgical procedures: a language which is crucial to medical professionals in helping to diagnose and treat cancer but which can only speak of people as mechanical objects? Can we make use of the non medical language of bodies which is obsessed with the idealism of youth and beauty?[4]

The quote has many topics that should be addressed in class. If budget allows, ideally, specialists and cancer patients/survivors should be invited to share their expertise and/or firsthand experiences to advance the understanding on our rights as (future) patients.

In yet another image from the series "Narratives of Dis-ease," we can see her cancerous breast visibly standing out and on top of it the artist writes the noun "monster," a word with a simple but pertinent etymology. According to www.dictionary.com, the word was introduced in English in the thirteenth century and it comes from Latin, *monstrum*,

[4] Spence, Jo. http://www.jospence.org/work_index.html.

"portent, unnatural event, monster." A good exercise is to ask students to return to the assignment when they talked about "victim," "victimization," and "to victimize," and put those answers alongside their new discussions on "monster" and "monstrosity." Back in the nineties, Spence was trying to save her life and also expose the hypocrisy of a medical system that wanted patients dependent on strong drugs and risky treatments. Letting her body act like a diary, she recorded its decline. Undoubtedly, when words become superfluous, the ill naked body proves the ongoing tragedy, sadly without being followed by a Q.E.D.

Had it not been for her desire to open up public discussions, the more recent movement "Going Flat" would have had an even more difficult time destroying clichés. In an article published in 2016 in *The New York Times* and titled "'Going Flat' after Breast Cancer," Roni Caryn Rabin states:

> The nascent movement to "go flat" after mastectomies challenges long-held assumptions about femininity and what it means to recover after breast cancer. For years, medical professionals have embraced the idea that breast restoration is an integral part of cancer treatment. Women's health advocates fought for and won approval of the Women's Health and Cancer Rights Act of 1998, which requires health plans to cover prosthetics and reconstructive procedures. Since then, breast reconstruction has become standard care.[5]

This is a good moment to look at breast cancer treatments historically to notice how much we know and how much has been done, as well as what else needs to be implemented. Furthermore, as the author writes, "While some states, including New York, now require physicians to tell women about the availability of breast reconstruction, women say they often are not informed of the option to remain flat. 'I was never told there was a choice,' Ms. Cuozzo said. 'I went from the breast surgeon to the plastic surgeon, and they said, 'This is what you're going to do.' Another breast cancer survivor, Rebecca Pine, co-founded a photography and writing

[5]Rabin, Roni Caryn. "'Going Flat' After Breast Cancer." *The New York Times*. 31 October 2016. https://www.nytimes.com/2016/11/01/well/live/going-flat-after-breast-cancer.html.

project called "The Breast and the Sea."[6] Featured in the article, Pine declares, "It's a tremendous amount to put your body through, and it's not like we're going to get our breasts back. They don't look or feel, in most cases, like our breasts," she said. "The nerves are cut, so they're not receptive to feel or touch."[7]

Going back to my play, Mia is caught in a crossfire between a medical system that does not encourage her to embrace whoever she wants to be after mastectomy and her perceptions about femininity as translated and/or absorbed via centuries of heavily intoxicated and manipulated patriarchal rhetoric. Moreover, failed attempts at getting pregnant eventually made up her mind and, after a painful journey, she decides to leave the scar where it is and write above it the noun "Dignity." Sam, a tattoo artist, plays a vital role in Mia's transformation because Sam is the Good Samaritan. For students, another game may be to divide the class into two groups. One group should write a 200 word-scenario about a tough situation/problem that, at the moment, seems unsolvable. The other group, hearing the problem for the first time, has to tap into their good Samaritan reflexes or at least try to come up with a solution. The exercise is invigorating because it is created on the spot. No one knows of the other's problem, but together via dialogue and direct interactions a solution is sought. At the end of this game, students are assigned to research a fundamental theatrical concept, *deus ex machina*, and determine why or why not the Good Samaritan game may be better for a play like *Mia*.

Furthermore, close to the end of the play, Mia reveals she is not afraid to be naked in photos anymore and that proves how much she has grown to accept the drastic change. In a discussion with her husband, she says, "We need to record our pain, just as we keep track of our birthdays, weddings, and holidays. Pain plays an equal part in our identity, don't you think?" A game related to this moment in the play is to ask students to think of a difficult moment in their lives and how they managed to get through it. The exercise is meant to be therapeutic and not exploiting anyone's vulnerability.

[6] Site: https://www.thebreastandthesea.com/.

[7] Ibid., 6.

Thedra's Artivism

Continuing the visibility of having options post mastectomy, Thedra Cullar-Ledford is an artist with a unique style. Artivism is a clever reinvention of an old term (i.e., activism) by simply changing one grapheme (-c- with -r-). Most likely coined collectively, the word has been gaining more and more power lately in light of ongoing but stronger women's liberation manifestations coupled by #MeToo, #TheFutureIsFemale and #Time'sUp, three notorious hash tags of our time. In many of her paintings, Cullar-Ledford, a breast cancer survivor herself, does not treat the canvas as linear but as going into various directions that somehow meet. She creates multiple stories within one story of breast cancer, focusing on images and words that linger hours after (Fig. 1).[8]

For example, in "Random Target" (2015), she divides the canvas with the upper left representing a black and white photography of a woman breast-feeding. Adjacent to it and bigger, she paints one breast in a pinkish hue on a brown background. The breast is marked to be cut. Below the two visuals, there is another piece that shows the fresh scars on a woman's chest post mastectomy. A target that remains immobile unites all three parts. While cancer is random, as studies have shown that time and time again, hence a universal treatment is not yet available, the target is stubbornly stuck in one, fixed position. The message being, no one ever knows if they would be the next "target." However, early detection can save more lives, so maybe what the artist targets is the healthcare system itself by pushing it to introduce mandatory screenings to teenagers and women regardless if they had or did not have a medical history, and make this screening available for men since they can also be diagnosed with this illness.

In a more provocative piece, "Bedroom Gaberdine" (2016),[9] the artist combines her technique of dividing the canvas into two parts, of which the one to the left is made out of three distinct subparts. A woman's body is made out of pieces and that in itself is very revealing. Combining mixed media, the woman's head and feet are painted, while her torso is

---

[8]Link: http://www.independenceartstudios.com/thedra/#.

[9]Link: http://www.independenceartstudios.com/thedra/archives/project/bedroom-gaberdine.

Fig. 1 Thedra Cullar-Ledford, *Bedroom Gaberdine* (2016)

a fragment from a photo. That part represents the body of a woman who appears to be in great shape, although intentionally exaggerated as too eroticized. The breasts are too perky and her abdominal muscles so packed that one may take the woman to be a fitness fanatic. Her skimpy black panties fall off of her body. If it were not for that saw added to her left hand, which happens to acquire more and more meaning once we put the painting's elements in context, the woman's made-up body would have veered toward cheap erotica with the saw as phallic symbol.

However, the middle part tells the other story of the woman's body about to undergo massive change. We know this because the larger part of "Bedroom Gaberdine" represents the scars left by surgery because of breast cancer. Furthermore, gabardine was a loose garment worn in the Middle Ages. Later, when Thomas Burberry reinvented it, gaberdine was made out of high quality cotton. Gaberdine may further be connected to medical gauze and if we put the noun "bedroom" into equation, then the piece is full with many recognizable obsessions but also truths that we cover up in bed. Cullar-Ledford's woman is naked, so that we face reality: nothing lasts forever; nothing is foolproof, especially when it comes to our deeply flawed physicality. With the saw claiming the woman's breasts, her former embodiment becomes a loose fabric that falls off of her body. The saw may suggest one last thing, that is, it could be an allusion to one of the surgical tools used by doctors to perform mastectomies. As exercise, students can be asked to compare and contrast the photos of Spence and the mixed media artworks of Cullar-Ledford, and to contextualize the time of their respective works.

The same tough approach happens during the performance titled *Piñata Smashing (F**K Cancer)* (2015).[10] Volunteers, many of whom had or have had cancer, family members, etc., smash huge piñatas shaped like breasts. They follow the same rules of piñata smashing. The result is cathartic because they destroy not only one image of the unbreakable perception on breasts (with all their socio-linguistic constraints), but also the perpetuated hypocrisy that women need breasts to be considered feminine, which downgrades breasts as erotic toys. As exercise/game, students are invited to think of other concepts or images related to my play when characters would (have) like(d) to smash piñatas to release their built up anger and frustration, and, in light of this energetic release, to re-evaluate how Aristotle's concepts of pity and fear may be applied.

Students may also be asked to compose reactions to Cullar-Ledford's piñata smashing since its usage is partly intended to alienate the audience, in a Brecht-like style. For the German playwright and theoretician, the alienation technique (*Verfremdungseffekt*) would estrange the readers and the spectators from what they normally expect from this dramatic genre. In return, by being alienated, they would be able to detach from

---

[10]Link: https://www.youtube.com/watch?v=JPDM7psNkYQ.

their emotions and assess the issues discussed in my play from a more mature, objective perspective, alienated from an excess of emotions.

Meg's Blunt Truth

As Mia's older sister, Meg tries to protect her, even though signs of being worn down show in the play.

> *MEG*: *Why* did you invite me here? I'm terribly sorry you are so stubborn to accept change. Sometimes I wonder if you perhaps find some kind of devilish pleasure tormenting you and the ones who love you.
> *MIA*: The only change I am aware of is my body-progressive.
> *MEG [I am your sister, not your student]*: And what's that exactly?
> *MIA*: Once a body breaks, there is no going back, no matter what you and your loved ones want to believe. *Humpty-Dumpty* all over again, this time for real. Once a piece falls, all the other fall, too. *Domino.* And not the game. A body falls progressively. Ever since cancer, I have been taking pictures with myself naked to adorn my walls with them. I don't need blessed walls. God would contemplate my pictures, and then I would decide if *He* is worthy of my prayer.
> *MEG*: How could you fight with a concept? It's a lost battle!
> *MIA*: I'm a concept, too; an (*emphasis*) embodied concept. My body is at war, remember what you said before?

Of all characters, Meg understands her sister best not because of their blood relationship, but because she has a secret so deep that she paradoxically shares only with us. She prefers to protect Mia who has had a tougher time accepting her diagnosis. In a crucial moment in the play, Sam comes over Mia's house in what can be interpreted as an encounter with a stranger motif. Sam's body has suffered a lot on account of in vitro sessions. She eventually became a mother, but her in vitro sessions deformed her body so drastically that now she is obese, her husband left her alone to raise that child, and because of that she struggles financially and emotionally. When she is done tattooing Mia's scar, Meg is about to get ready. As she takes her robe off, we see something shocking, a reaction that is replicated by Sam. According to stage directions, this moment unfolds as following: "*Meg takes the robe off. We see she has no breasts, but two big scars. The scars attempt to tell a story, but let's face it, they can't do that. It would be too convenient if our bodies could tell what they have endured.*"

In a monologue that is only for us to know, Meg reminisces about a relationship that she had with Carmen, a hermaphrodite, when she was in college. She recounts the heartbreaking story that Carmen had throughout life. Meg falls in love with this complex, beautiful person and wants to run away with Carmen when tragedy strikes.

> *MEG*: I wanted to run away with Carmen, if... (*she wipes her tears*). Why do I cry? These tears... they run down my cheeks and then I have a glass full of them and drink them all. We are a closed circuit. I went to Carmen's apartment. I had a spare key. I opened the door. It smelled divine, of lavender. I have always wanted to make love in the open air, in a lavender field. I called, "Carmen, Carmen." No answer. And then I saw Carmen, on the floor. The mirror, their confident for all those years, was shattered all over Carmen's body. Its huge wooden frame stayed intact. Carmen looked like a painting. So serene. But Carmen wad dead. We push people away and make them feel like shit. We are the cruelest among animals. We think we are kind but the minute we see one who is different, we are terrified.

Meg reminds us of our discomfort when we meet *different* people. Although we speak about sympathy and empathy quite freely, we do not always know how/when to apply them. Ever since Carmen's tragedy, Meg knew how people look and even discriminate against others whose body has been *othered* either at birth or on account of illnesses. Meg tells she took a prophylactic decision to cut off her breasts because she discovered her BRCA test revealed she had 90% chances to develop breast cancer. She is a lawyer and does not accept to be manipulated into believing she needs to have two breasts to function and/or be feminine. She knows the body remains beautiful and functional even when differences appear or when body parts have to be removed. It is those around us who have to accept and respect physical diversity.

MEG: I am a lawyer, I know my rights for own my body. No doctor could tell me otherwise. I was crying tears not because of my decision but because I was thinking of Carmen. I feel more like a woman now that I don't have breasts. They don't define my femininity. But I could not explain this to Mia. She has her own twisted way to manage pain. We all have. That's how we deal with (*with emphasis*) life.

On October 21, 1998, "Women's Health and Cancer Rights Acts" was signed into law. According to it, "The Women's Health and Cancer Rights Act (WHCRA) helps protect many women with breast cancer who choose to have their breasts rebuilt (reconstructed) after a mastectomy. Mastectomy is a surgery to remove all or part of the breast. This federal law requires most group insurance plans that cover mastectomies to also cover breast reconstruction."[11] While it is worth mentioning this particular law, we need to stress out the importance of being accurately informed so that women know they have options. A body that undergoes surgery cannot logically be and look the way it used to be. Point in fact, Meg reminds us that this is the fight we must *win*, namely not to be coerced into doing things to our body because we are cornered and shamed. Instead, to do things to our body that *we* (and not even our closest ones) may want us to do.

Back in 1998 when this law became official, the noun previvor was not part of the lexicon. Sadly, in 2020, the noun is still used in limited circles. This suggests a couple of disturbing realities that are related to what and who control our body. The medical system and the pharmaceutical corporations function to perpetuate myths that hurt, myths that need to be destroyed, or at least be presented in a light that is not exclusive.

For example, in 2014 when Angelina Jolie published her op-ed "My Medical Choice," I was not aware of the BRCA test. In her words,

> We often speak of 'Mommy's mommy,' and I find myself trying to explain the illness that took her away from us. They have asked if the same could happen to me. I have always told them not to worry, but the truth is I

[11] https://www.cancer.org/treatment/finding-and-paying-for-treatment/understanding-health-insurance/health-insurance-laws/womens-health-and-cancer-rights-act.html.

> carry a 'faulty' gene, BRCA1, which sharply increases my risk of developing breast cancer and ovarian cancer. My doctors estimated that I had an 87 percent risk of breast cancer and a 50 percent risk of ovarian cancer, although the risk is different in the case of each woman. Only a fraction of breast cancers result from an inherited gene mutation. Those with a defect in BRCA1 have a 65 percent risk of getting it, on average.

Nowadays, my medical insurance does cover the BRCA test. I have an annual mammogram followed by an ultrasound *if* the former is not clear. In 2017, the mammogram showed increased density in my breasts and became impossible to read. In 2020, my mammogram showed an asymmetry in my left breast. After a second mammogram and an ultrasound, it was ruled out it was not cancerous. Still, even if I am over 40 and my mother died of breast cancer at 45, to this day (if I have to) I fight the bill with the hospital and my medical insurance. I fight over a mammogram, which is considered by many extremely inaccurate! This is another reason why our focus should continue by writing letters to our local hospitals, insurance companies, and most importantly to Congress representatives, as well as by keeping our request in the public eye via social media and rallies. It is nice that we have an annual walk for cancer/cure, but let's face it, it is not what we deserve. When October comes, we do not need to be invaded chromatically by and immersed in pink.

As game, students are split into 3–4 groups, each brainstorming the word "previvor." After two minutes, they would whisper into the other's ear what they think about it. The game is built like a chain reaction. One may say a synonym/antonym, the next continue with another, hence an ad hoc, unscripted chain reaction. At the end, participants are asked to say their series out loud. The fact that we do not know how the chain reaction ends is in a way similar to being taken by surprise by an event. The game is based on context, mood, and on whatever the other whispers into a participant's ear. Therefore, its perspective is fresh and our analytical responses accordingly.

The Humument Technique

In the late 60's, the British artist Tom Phillips had this idea to use a book that nobody read or would be considered irrelevant and reinvent it through a series of steps.[12] He would first spot (apparently) random words on the original page. Those words would be then connected by visuals freshly painted on the paper. The result varies from day to day, from chosen words and visuals to other such ad hoc embellishments. What seems at surface silly, gains a lot of meaning because, through this technique, the reader is empowered to select words that have relevance for them in that particular moment. We all know how important it is not only the context of an (art)work, but also when and how we encounter it: our mood, level of maturity, and so many other factors. This is why, through this technique that seems to have no pressure on the readers, students get closer to a text and, by extension, they make connections between words and images, reaching a more profound meaning.

In one example, a student used the following moment in the play:

MIA: Are you happy as a mother?

SAM: I think I am. There're days, though, when I can barely breathe, tie my shoes, or even sleep comfortably. My husband left me; he said I was repulsive. What about you? What's your story?

MIA (Blunt, italics): It's a boring, textbook example: I lost my breast to cancer.

SAM: My mom died because of breast cancer. She was from a different generation, of docile women, quiet, faithful wives. She was brainwashed to believe a woman had to have two breasts.

MIA: You'd think things have changed. Women are told to get reconstructive surgery to this day. Why are women told they need intruders in their bodies? What the fuck is this?

SAM: You are funny, but with residues of anger. Don't go there! I mean, I am sorry. I just can't deal with women fighting with themselves. Go look in a mirror. "Dignity," that was a clever inscription.

At that point, MARK *enters the room.*

MARK: What are you doing? Who is she?

[12]Link: http://www.tomphillips.co.uk/humument.

MIA: Sam, meet my husband. Mark, meet my friend, Sam. She's a tattoo artist. I've decided to get a tattoo. That scar was too standard. Sam has embellished it. Now I have one breast and one "Dignity." (*She points to her inscription*)

The student divided the paper into two parts. On the upper part, the words selected were: "I've sacrificed," "I was repulsive," "I lost," "I was" "trying" and "I was fighting." If one looks below, one sees that the words can be read in their singularity, but they could also be read together. If the former, one stops to look at each word selected; if the latter, the overall look gives way to the message. In addition, the words are placed against a meshed visual to imply how easily they may slip our minds, or maybe how we cannot see clearly because of all the things too closely intertwined.

The bottom part of the paper is simpler, word-wise. The student chose "Now I have" and "Dignity." The latter is placed on the breast itself. If we go back, we met Mia after mastectomy, so to see the inscription accompanied by the breast, to see the symmetry is perhaps even more intriguing. Moreover, the woman looks schematic. If in the original, the dialogue was longer, now we get to the essence because the pedagogical outcome of this technique is that it gives students permission to eliminate as many words as they see fit and remain with what they consider relevant (Figs. 2 and 3).[13]

In another example, the passage takes place towards the end of the play:

MARK: Why do people always want to hear the truth? To hurt themselves even… more? What's in the past should stay in the past.
MIA: My past misses a piece and that's your *story*. I've heard many bad medical news and predictions, I kind of gained immunity from being hurt. Besides, it's not a matter of getting hurt, as it is witnessing you accepting responsibility for whatever stupid thing you did that night.
MARK [This is the beginning of the end]: Brace yourself. (*More to himself*) Oh, boy, boy, oh, boy, this shit is gonna be tough.

[13]These two visuals were both completed by Belle Krupcheck for my course, "Writing in the Disciplines: The Arts."

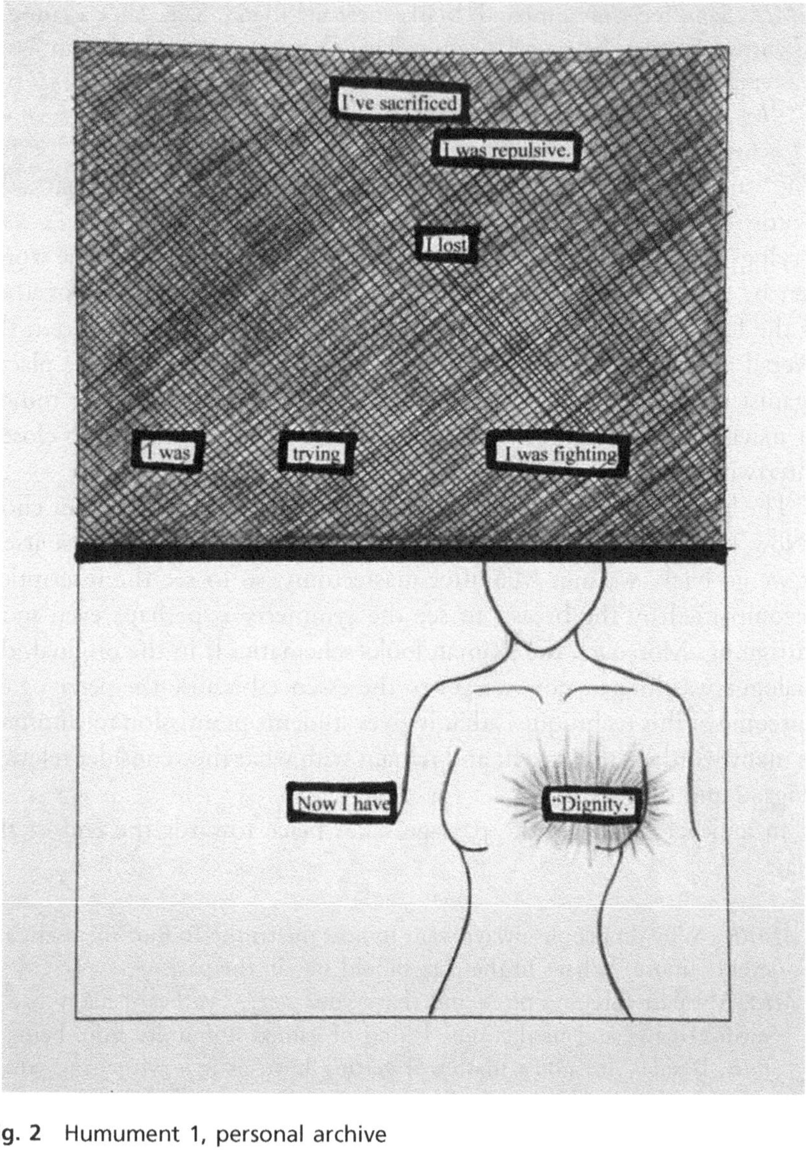

Fig. 2 Humument 1, personal archive

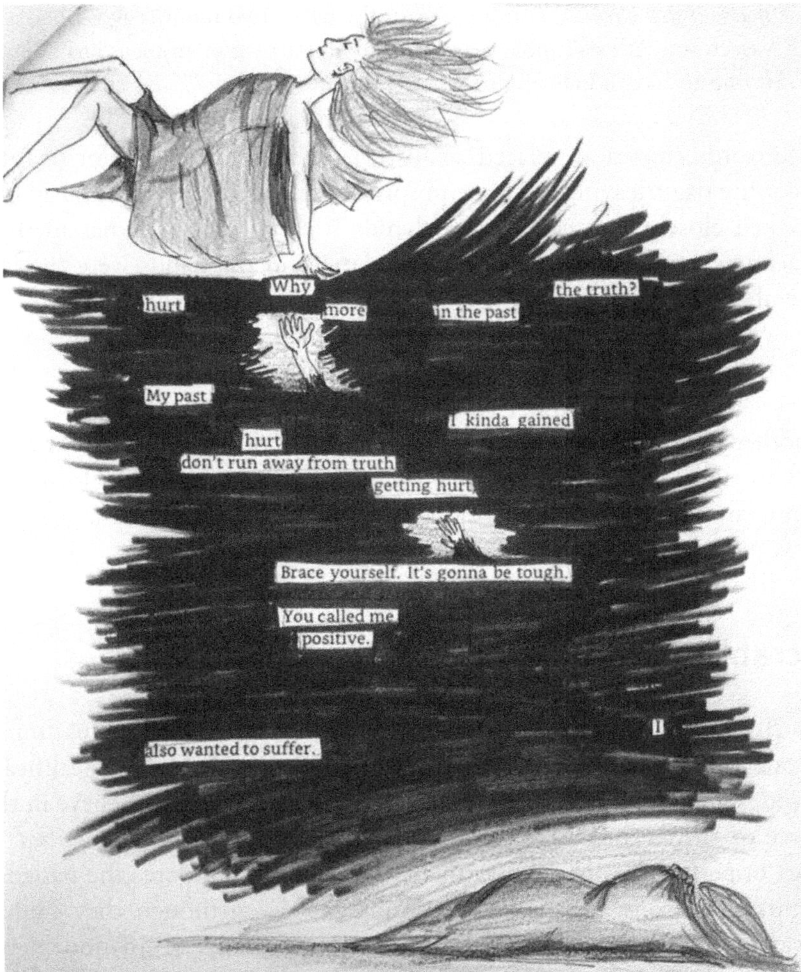

Fig. 3 Humument 2, personal archive

MIA (*Exasperated*): Be a man!

MARK (*He speaks holding her shoulders and staring into her eyes*): That night I drank too much. You called and announced that your pregnancy test was positive. I wasn't happy, but afraid. I ended up with a hooker. I had a one-night stand to prove myself that I was still a free man. (*He makes a step backward*) I didn't want the baby. Two months ago, I had a vasectomy. After all these years, it really doesn't make any sense to hope trying to have a baby. I also wanted to suffer.

The words chosen are placed against black lines that seem not to fully color the page, leaving the hope to spruce back amid sheer marital agony. Looked closely, one can see two hands sticking out as if that meshed blackness was some sort of dark(en) water and the hands were the last members of a person's body before drowning.

In addition, this Humument had two female silhouettes, even though the dialogue was between Mia and her husband. The student created two versions of Mia and I assume the hands are those of Mark. Since another benefit of the Humument technique is that one can read it from left to right, top to bottom, and vice versa, then the woman from this representation may look victorious or in desperate need to figure out her next move.

Scrabble Cancer Project

In 2012, I participated with two posters in an event at the Museum of Modern Art sponsored by New York City Regional Arts in Healthcare Groups and Access Programs at Museum of Modern Art. I believe in the force of stories and artworks and I think they should be *prescribed* as part of patients' palliative treatment. These pieces reinforce the patients' rights as persons and not as medical cases. Even though they cannot treat persons' illnesses, nonetheless artworks can be of an undeniable emotional relief. The poetics of the broken, ill bodies is necessary and unavoidable. It gets us closer and closer, like cells communicating beyond our epidermis. The involutions of the human body ought to be recorded not only medically but also artistically. If we refuse to acknowledge our pain publicly, we continue to perceive our body as erratically out there and, when it breaks, as a medical case, part of the hospitalized and, thus, institutionalized world. My own mom's breast cancer taught me differently. When pain is not synchronized with other people's experiences and reactions, we accelerate its decline, and, in return, illnesses attack patients and healthy people systematically and more virulently (Fig. 4).

"Scrabble-Cancer Project" started as a realization of the playfulness dimension of our lives. Games are collective, social, and inventing. Scrabble-Cancer is a project where I expose and challenge the linguistic impact of this illness. "Scrabble" is a rough word, meaning it has only two vowels and six consonants. The first three are hard consonants (scr-), and, when people pronounce the word, they almost choke. Despite

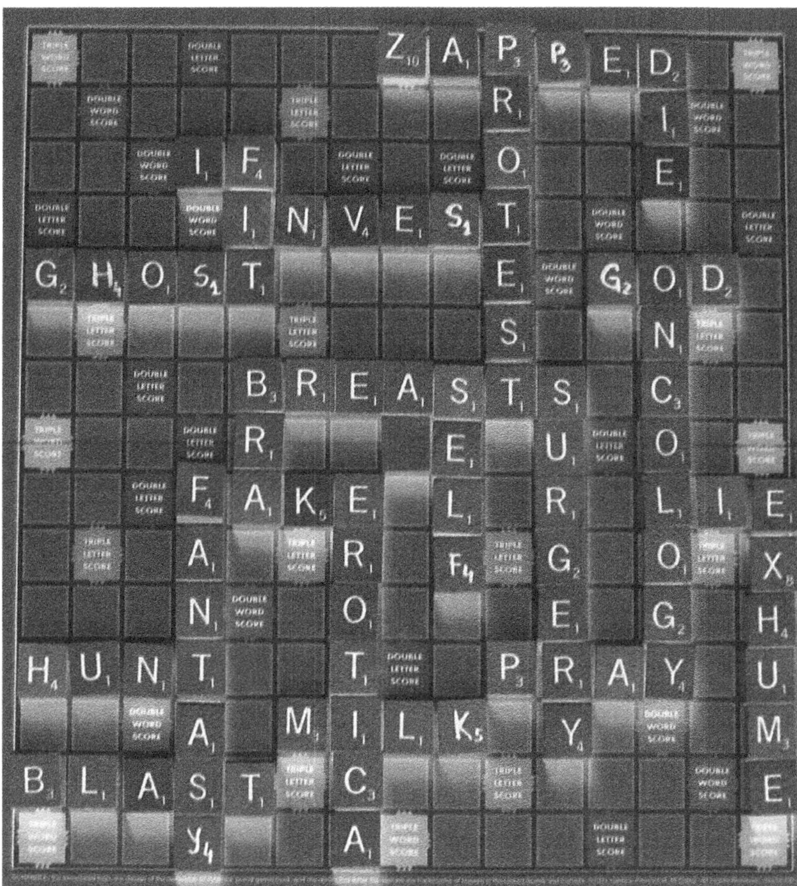

Fig. 4 Scrabble Cancer Project, personal archive

its vocal toughness, it remains open to various combinations of words. Moreover, my project follows the philosophy of artistic installations, in the sense that its main characteristic is fluidity. We tend to believe that our bodies are opaque structures. We also think that words, once written or uttered, remain the same in a given context. Since this is an outdated, fallacious reasoning, what I propose instead is to conceive of bodies and words as open, associative structures. Words connect through people's bodies via sensations and experiences. We are an infinite of connective tissues.

For example, what is the first word that one associates with when they think of breasts? Could it be an adjective, like "big"? A verb, "to touch"? A color or perhaps a shape? Needless to say, the more participants in this project, the better the chances to combine/compare/interpret responses provided they are spontaneous. There is not a definitive response, although unconsciously it is relevant what selection we make when we think of a word in terms of another. Ultimately, the configuration of any Scrabble-Cancer grid changes from users to users because mutability represents its sine-qua-non feature. In classroom, students may be invited to create their own grids placing in center one of the following words used in my play: "cancer," "breasts," "femininity," "embodiment," etc.

Real/Hidden Woman

For the final game, I'd like to return to Boal, this time to his "image of the word." I use the exercise to explore what might be conveyed/understood by woman—a word, but also an idea. I invite 4–5 students to volunteer. They are asked to keep eyes forward so that they intentionally will *not* see and/or be influenced by other volunteers. Students are invited to see in their minds the image of the ideal woman. Next, they are going to use their body to, as closely as possible under the circumstances, create the image that was in their mind. I am not concerned with perfection, I simply want an image to consider and whatever students manage serves that purpose. It may be a still image so, even if this is a figure in action, I ask them to freeze the action. When everyone has stopped moving, I'll take that as a sign everyone is ready. Now, I turn to students who were not involved and ask: "What do you see represented?" "Are there similarities?" "Are there any stark differences?" "Is there an overarching theme?" Once the observers have offered feedback, I return to my volunteers and ask to create an image representing women as they really are. Consider perhaps aspects of womanhood that are usually hidden from the public. All the other steps will replicate the first ones. There is a transition that is important to be played. Students who have volunteered are asked to start in the ideal and slowly change themselves from one image into the "real" image. I snap my fingers seven times and with each snap they slowly transition from one pose to the other.

Those observing are invited to pay attention to the images that are created during the transition. The purpose of the game is to offer a glimpse into what we know about "woman" and how we may feel knowing that there are shifts from person to person, attitudes to attitudes, etc., and that they each, taken together and on an ongoing basis, may improve the stale definitions that we have to otherwise common words—woman being just one of the many examples.

In Lieu of a Conclusion

It's hard for me to write a conclusion for no other reason that I know this book chapter is yet another piece in a continuum that has started when I heard my mother saying: "I have cancer." Still, if I have to write one, I return to the title that was specifically chosen to let us reflect on the numeral two. We have two legs, two arms, two brain hemispheres, two breasts, that is, there is an undeniable symmetry when it comes to our bodies. But bodies are born imperfect and, over the years, they break.

My play underwent several transformations, some on account of direct discussions and games with my students; others because of events at the Romanian Cultural Institute in New York City and at Harvard University. From the beginning, Mia and Meg have been part of the plot. It just happens that they can also be viewed as one. Think about this: when we fall ill, we witness a split. From persons, we become patients: from one, we split into two. I have always wanted this play to be a wake up call to other women who feel cornered not only by the illness itself, but also by very old ways of dealing with pain and key existential concepts. I created two women who come from a lineage of breast cancer, even though they discover that by accident.

Naturally, many other games can be designed to work for classrooms, as well as workshops with breast cancer survivors/patients and their caregivers. If talking about pain is sometimes difficult, the games and exercises ease that embarrassment. Our embodiment has not been designed immortal. We are flawed. But unlike characters in an old Greek play, we rise because of our bodily flaws to discover facets of our constantly shifting identities.

> *MEG*: Suffering should not live inside us. (*Pause*) We can't ask God for anything, except for peace. The moment when you discover that inner peace and elevated tranquility, you notice that all bad things pass you by. (*She mimes as she speaks*) Your body becomes a rowboat and your arms your oars with which you swim farther and farther… (*She opens her eyes*) What bliss! You literally feel your body like a vehicle that transports you toward an unknown realm. Let's try together. (*She puts her hands on Mia*)

Works Cited

The American Cancer Society: "Women's Health and Cancer Rights Act." https://www.cancer.org/treatment/finding-and-paying-for-treatment/understanding-health-insurance/health-insurance-laws/womens-health-and-cancer-rights-act.html.

Boal, Augusto. *Games for Actors and Non-actors*. New York: Routledge, 2002 (second edition).

Florescu, Catalina Florina. *The Rebelled Body Plays*. Ed. Caridad Svich. NoPassport Press, South Gate, California, 2019.

Jolie, Angelina. "My Medical Choice." *The New York Times*. 14 May 2013. https://www.nytimes.com/2013/05/14/opinion/my-medical-choice.html.

Rabin, Roni Caryn. "'Going Flat' After Breast Cancer." *The New York Times*. 31 October 2016. https://www.nytimes.com/2016/11/01/well/live/going-flat-after-breast-cancer.html.

Spence, Jo. http://www.jospence.org/work_index.html.

"Don't Be Mean" and Other Lessons from Children's Plays of the Federal Theatre Project

Leslie Frost

Bad things were happening. To catalogue. In brief.

- In 1934, in spite of an accuser's recantation, the Alabama Supreme Court again upholds the guilty verdict and death sentence against two of nine African-American boys and young men falsely accused of rape. The other "Scottsboro Boys" remain in jail awaiting retrial.
- On October 3, 1935, fascist Italian-led forces under Benito Mussolini invade Ethiopia. Americans, of African against Italian descent, fight in the streets of Brooklyn and Harlem.
- On May 30, 1937, uniformed Chicago police fire on workers trying to set up a picket line under the Steel Workers Organizing Committee. Ten people are killed, seven shot in the back.

L. Frost (✉)
University of North Carolina at Chapel Hill, Chapel Hill, NC, USA
e-mail: lefrost@email.unc.edu

V. Rapti and E. Gordon (eds.), *Ludics*,
https://doi.org/10.1007/978-981-15-7435-1_19

- On November 9 and 10, 1938, Nazis unleash terror upon German Jewish homes and businesses. Properties are destroyed; 91 Jews die and tens of thousands of young Jewish men are incarcerated.

Against racism, fascism, and labor injustice, a broad socio-political coalition formed in the mid-1930s. As Michael Denning has compellingly charted, the cultural apparatuses and broad social movements of this "cultural front" connected concerns of the working class, second-generation immigrants, African-American activists, and artists and émigrés fleeing European fascism.[1] The broad leftist-liberal politics of its social groups shaped the focus and the cultural production of Franklin Delano Roosevelt's New Deal, particularly in the arts projects for out-of-work writers, musicians, artists, and theater personnel, collectively known as Federal One and administered under the Works Progress (later Projects) Administration. In productions of Federal One's most politically active branch, the Federal Theatre Project, one expects to find Popular Front cultural productions for adults. But I am interested in its plays for children, and I explore here how three Federal Theatre children's plays take on and vanquish the psychological terrors and structural inequities of racism, fascism, and labor injustice by actions of tolerance, sharing, and cooperation, values rooted in idealized children's imaginations and socialized play. These plays offer a lesson children know well: Don't be mean.

My focus is on the best known FTP children's play, the ridiculously charming *The Revolt of the Beavers*, as well as the federal *The Story of Little Black Sambo* and an almost unknown anti-war Christmas pageant called *A Letter to Santa Claus*. The extraordinary enterprise that brought these plays into being, the Federal Theatre Project (1935–1939), was led by former Vassar professor Hallie Flanagan, who envisioned building a distinctly American national theater that would grow out of native artistic traditions and be attentive to regional pluralistic voices. Her goal was:

[1]Denning, Michael, *The Cultural Front: The Laboring of American Culture in the Twentieth Century* (New York: Verso, 1996).

> To set up theatres which have possibilities of growing into social institutions in the communities in which they are located ... and to lay the foundation for the development of a truly creative theatre in the United States with outstanding producing centers in each of those regions which have common interests as a result of geography, language, origins, history, tradition, custom, occupations of the people[2]

To this end, its administration structured a federal organization of loosely confederated regional offices. Its staff administered and kept reader responses to scripts, audience and critical responses to productions, detailed production books, internal memos, letters, and reports. The infrastructural groundwork was laid for a permanent American national theater. Taking Kenneth Burke's inclusive symbol of the American worker as its constituency, the Federal Theatre Project *also* aimed to revolutionize art in America. For the FTP's newsletter *Federal Theatre* Flanagan reported that:

> From Maine to Texas, the story is the same. From North Carolina to California, the same public recognition of our work is being bestowed. "The People's Theatre!"—we did not call it that because only the people can make the name appropriate. But where and as the people make it appropriate, we welcome it as describing what the Federal Theatre should be.

This intoxicating vision of an American populace invigorated by its theater would remain an ideal for which Flanagan struggled for four years. It was not to be. Although Federal Theatre produced more than 42,000 performances, its total audience of about 40 million was only slightly more than half the average weekly audience that went to the movies. Federal Theatre's difficulties were legion and its enemies numerous, including the Martin Dies, Jr.–led House Committee on Un-American Activities, established in 1938. The FTP struggled to put on

[2]For more information on the Federal Theatre Project, see my monograph, *Dreaming America: Popular Front Ideals and Aesthetics in Children's Plays of the Federal Theatre Project* (Columbus: The Ohio State University Press, 2013).

plays in the midst of government investigations, the occasional political censorship and audience outrage, budget cuts, union strikes, and WPA/FTP disputes. It was shut down unceremoniously when Congress failed to renew its funding.

And yet, by other measures Federal Theatre performed admirably as a people's theater. At its height, it employed more than 12,700 people. Over the duration of its existence it gave work to more than 30,000. Federal Theatre shows were cheap for many and free for "the underprivileged." The FTP produced new plays, classical plays, children's plays, African-American plays, marionette shows, vaudeville shows, and caravan theater performances in America's parks. Its units produced religious theater and foreign-language theater. Hundreds of thousands of New York City children went to the FTP circus. Companies toured the Civilian Conservation Corps camps across the country. Successful urban productions went to small towns and isolated regions. It played to churches, prisons, hospitals, and orphanages.

While broadly traditional in its production choices, the Federal Theatre Project also took chances that commercial theater did not. It explored the conditions of the disenfranchised and the working class. It mandated that audiences could not be segregated. Its Negro Units produced plays that explored racism and African-American life. It collected anti-lynching play scripts. (But it also collected minstrel skits and shows.) Not only did Flanagan choose an adaptation of Sinclair Lewis's antifascist *It Can't Happen Here* for a dramatic opening simultaneously in 21 cities in 17 states, but also the FTP collected and distributed lists of anti-war plays.

Children's productions were very popular and adults often outnumbered children at *Pinocchio.* Prior to the FTP, children's theater had been the province mostly of education, settlement houses and Junior League activities. From her observations of European and Soviet national theatres, Flanagan theorized that an American national theater would need to build a broad-based audience. A critical aspect of her vision was that children should be socialized and educated to appreciate theater as civic engagement as well as entertainment. Children's Unit director Jack Rennick wrote in 1936, "If America is ever to have a great theatre, she cannot begin too soon to train and establish an audience that will appreciate, demand, and support the best." The New York Unit surveyed children's facilities to determine how much children could pay so that tickets were priced accordingly. Separate children's theater companies were formed and adult units regularly performed children's plays. Like its adult productions, many of the FTP children's plays were fairly traditional productions from fairy and folk tales to didactic plays teaching topics like hygiene and the history of flight.

But not our plays here. The three plays of this essay yoke the dramatic theory of children's drama pioneer Winifred Ward to the ideology of the Popular Front centered on labor justice, anti-racism, and anti-fascism. Developed from John Dewey's education theories, Ward's "creative dramatics" understood drama as a means to stimulate children's interest in experiential learning through creative play.[3] These plays model engaged, inquisitive, imaginative children navigating unjust worlds.

To New York City!

The New York Children's Unit *The Revolt of the Beavers*, as you may imagine, tells the story of two children who lead a beaver labor strike. Press releases in the Federal Theatre Project Collection housed in the National Archives trace a brewing controversy over upcoming production. While some releases remark upon the difficulty actors had adjusting to roller skates and describing the play's street game of "potsie," others link the play to current events. A May 18 exclusive to *the World-Telegram* proposes:

> The furore [*sic*] created by the wave of sit-in strikes has led to considerable speculation as to the origin of labor's new tactic. Who started the first sit-in strike and why is the question that a couple of WPA FTP playwrights, Oscar Saul and Lou Lantz, undertake to answer in a new play.[4]

Historian David Kennedy recounts the story of the great Flint sit-down strike of 1936–1937:

[3]Ward, Winifred, *Creative Dramatics* (New York: D. Appleton, 1930).

[4]Records of the Federal Theatre Project, Records of the Works Progress Administration, Record Group 69, National Archives, Washington, DC.

> UAW captains organized men into squads of 15, insisted on strict adherence to hygiene and safety rules, arranged for food to be delivered, and organized recreation activities to while away the time. Group singing was especially popular … "Sit down, just keep your seat. Sit down and rest your feet. Sit down, you got 'em beat. Sit down, sit down!"[5]

Kennedy notes that after two months, the strikers won the recognition they sought from General Motors. However, by that spring a Gallup poll showed that more than two thirds of Americans thought General Motors should not negotiate with strikers.

New York City responded to a children-led beaver uprising as had Gallop poll respondents to the autoworkers' sit-down strike. Seventeen performances after the curtain rose on *The Revolt of the Beavers*, it descended for the last time. "Meet the Chief," its brightly decorated poster had proclaimed, with a picture of a colorfully clothed, fat, grinning beaver. But *New York Times* critic Brooks publicly branded the play as "Mother Goose Marx." A furor erupted (at least in the newspapers). The response was timid. Federal Theatre shut its *Revolt* down.

The Revolt of the Beavers begins with nine year olds Mary and Paul looking for wood in a vacant city lot and arguing about whether or not they can believe what their teacher says: that beavers can talk. "He thinks just because we're nine years old he can tell us fairy tales!," scoffs Paul. "Well, I don't like 'em… I like real stories about cops and robbers -- and cowboys and Indians -- Where they go bang! bang! bang!" When Mary argues that he'd surely want the wishes promised by fairy tales, Paul replies:

> You know what I would wish for? A blue sweater and a pair of skates. And d'y' know what else? I'd wish that everybody in the whole world was nine years old. Then I'd never be sad. 'Cause then I could go to the candy store and just imagine – Mr. Berger would be nine years old, and I would say, "Mr. Berger, I haven't got a penny – gimme a piece of candy, will ya?" And he'd give it to me! And then I would wish to be as free as

[5]Kennedy, David, *Freedom from Fear: The American People in Depression and War, 1929–1945* (New York: Oxford University Press, 2001 [1999]), 311.

> the wind! So I could do whatever I want – Fly away and have a good time.[6]

Ah Paul. Be careful what you wish for. In a thrice, "Windy" appears and whisks the children away on a "middle" wind to a fantastic forest where the animals talk and all are nine years old except the babies—"and they grow up very fast." Professor Beaver is sleeping on a pedestal; when they awaken him he sings them a song. "Once upon a time…Once upon a time":

> My favorite instrument is the fife/But I'm also fond of the fiddle
> I sit on the left and I sit on the right/But my favorite spot is the middle
> I like to get up in the early dawn,/I'm fond of the morning light
> There's nothing I like as much as the morn/But the beautiful beautiful night – the night ….

The Professor might not know which way he wants to go, but when he realizes Paul and Mary are humans, knows where they should: "Get out of Beaverland! … There's a lot of trouble in Beaverland and you might get right in the middle of the trouble!"

The children's middle wind has landed them right in the middle of trouble as certainly as the professor's inability to choose a side has not kept him out of it. Causing all of the trouble is the Chief. He has a big belly. He controls the bark-producing "busy busy busy" Wheel. He wears a blue sweater and roller skates, sits in a barber's chair pulling levers and he eats all the ice cream he wants. Working beavers can't even eat from the bark they produce. The Chief has not only banished the professor but has banished and "made sad" the Barkless Beavers who "have nothing to eat, no place to go – and they're always crying."

The valiant Oakleaf, played by Jules Dassin, explains:

> You know, Paul, all the beavers are sad, very sad – and me, too – so I got mad and said, "Why don't we make a club for sad beavers to get glad?"

[6]All quotations are drawn from the manuscript housed in the U.S. Library of Congress. Lantz, Lou and Saul, Oscar, *The Revolt of the Beavers* (Library Records, 1932–1940), Playscripts File S1681, Copy 1, Box 753.

> So all the beavers said, "Yaaaaaaaaaay!" But when the Chief heard about it he said, "Oakleaf, you're trying to bust up Beaverland – Get out and never come back! Not even in a million years!"

The children take a side and enlist Professor Beaver in a quixotic attempt to persuade the Chief to change his ways. Professor knows just the tactic to win this battle; he will tell a story, "not a plain story," explains Professor, "but a story with a moral." But a story with a moral, alas, does not produce change. The Chief gets sore and tells his henchmen to bring back the Barkless Beavers to take over the Working Beavers jobs and to "hit 'em all, even the girl." In a startling twist, however, instead of taking over the jobs, the Barkless Beavers join Oakleaf's Club for Sad Beavers to Get Glad. And *then* they stand up to the Chief: "Yeah, we ain't bent over no more. We're going to stick together with the beavers in our club!" The Chief not only banishes the Barkless Beavers for a million years, he gets *really* sore:

> And from now on, a new rule! Any beaver that gets wise, I'm gonna lock him in a cave for a long time – maybe forever! And you human beings and Professor, I'm gonna teach you the biggest lesson there is! And the lesson is – For a hundred years – you're gonna get killed every day starting tomorrow – lunchtime!

Mary is SO SAD: "I don't wanna be killed! I came to Beaverland to have a good time!"

Then follows a glorious battle, a battle engaged with Zippo guns and Bango guns and slingshots and bean shooters. Action does produce change. The Chief is vanquished and banished and the play ends with the united working beavers, hand in hand across the stage singing:

> … There's bark for every beaver
> Who swings a cleaver (At this point, the leading players step forward in a line)
> Or pulls a lever
> There's not a Barkless Beaver
> In all of Beaverland (repeat)

Atkinson wrote in his review that:

> The first lesson in labor warfare is staged against some whimsical settings and in imaginative costumes.... The style is playful; the mood is gravely gay and simple-minded. Many children now unschooled in the technique of revolution now have an opportunity, at government expense, to improve their tender minds. Mother Goose is no longer a rhymed escapist. She has been studying Marx; Jack and Jill lead the class revolution.

An FTP brief prepared for the House Committee on Un-American Activities acknowledged that *Revolt* was "the only Federal Theatre Project play at which the direct charge of 'communistic' has been leveled by anyone other than a Dies Committee witness."[7] And red it was. Saul and Lantz had both been playwrights for the leftist Workers Laboratory Theatre, and cast member Perry Bruskin had performed with the WLT's mobile Shock Troupes, which staged skits and short theater at union events.[8] *Revolt*'s co-director Peter Hyun had become the WLT's Evening Troupe manager in 1934. But the play was also considered visually stunning, complex, and colorful, and it delighted its audiences. "It was so imaginative, so different from any children's theatre at that time," recalled actor John Randolph (who, as Mortimer Lippman, played one of the Chief's toughs). "It still to this day would be considered an extraordinary work ... that was inventive and beautifully directed and beautifully acted by very good actors...."[9] *Revolt* played to full houses of adults and children. The children who saw the play gave vigorous approval. They cheered the Working Beavers and booed the bad beavers; they waited by the backstage door in order to pummel the actor who played the Chief. The *New York American* critic noted that audience children "voted it a grand time and the grownups found it passably amusing," adding that "If

[7]Dies Committee Folder One. Page 58, Box 496. Records of the Federal Theatre Project. Records of the Works Progress Administration. Record Group 69, National Archives, Washington, DC. See Frost, Leslie, *Dreaming America: Popular Front Ideals and Aesthetics of Children's Plays of the Federal Theatre Project* 47.

[8]Williams, Jay, *Stage Left* (New York: Charles Scribner's Sons, 1974).

[9]Interview with John Randolph, George Mason University, oral interview conducted by Diane Bowers, May 20, 1976.

there is any underlying significance to the story ... the children probably will not see it."[10]

But an FTP commissioned survey to test whether audience children understood the class implications of the play or not discovered that they saw many underlying significances translating labor conditions into a moral framework. Comments ranged from "Not to try to [be] a boss over anyone else" to "To show how hard they worked. Also to show that they are just human [*sic*] as us" to "To be kind to animals" to "Don't be selfish," and finally to "It doesn't pay to be mean."[11] (More than a few children also requested memberships in the WPA Children's Theatre Club inaugurated opening night.)

Hallie Flanagan defended the play on the basis of genre. She argued that it was a fairy tale with good beavers against bad beavers and thus, by implication, that the updated elements of character and plot should be read metaphorically. But as Professor Beaver could remind us from experience, a "story with a moral" is not a change agent. What *The Revolt of the Beavers* so successfully demonstrates, with its bright colors and inventive play, is how children's play socializes behavior. Potsie, an urban game similar to hopscotch, and Zippo guns are both children's play and the weapons of class war. A club for sad beavers to get glad focuses Paul's yearning for active role play and even violence. Children's games mimic all too closely adult conflict and games of sharing and cooperation across individual interests different groups create class solidarity that defeats entrenched interests seated at the barber's chair and pulling the levers of power.

Cooperation is emphasized similarly in the Chicago production of *The Story of Little Black Sambo* written by the prolific Charlotte Chorpenning and directed by a young Shirley Graham. An extant play script includes Graham's director's notes for an earlier production at the Goodman Theatre and gives some idea of staging:

[10]Heard, Doreen B., "Children's Theatre in the Federal Theatre Project," in *Spotlight on the Child: Studies in the History of American Children's Theatre.* Ed. Roger L. Bedard and John C. Tolch.

[11]Dies Committee Folder One, Box 496, Records of the Federal Theatre Project. Records of the Works Progress Administration, Record Group 69, National Archives, Washington, DC.

> We stressed the Negro character of the play by the play of brilliant colors, decided use of percussions, intensity of rhythm and in a definite minor melodic line of the music. Thus, again this negroid quality came through without effort and without getting away from the naïve charm of the script.[12]

Before the curtain rises, music is faintly heard; the play begins with Sambo grinding corn near the hut, but looking off into the jungle and gradually ceasing to work as the music swells. Monkeys and tigers, enter the stage and then dart off when one of the monkeys accidentally rolls a drum. Sambo works half-heartedly for a moment, then leaps up and bursts into song:

> I hear the wind./It says it is going away./I am going, too/We go, go, go./Through the cocoanut [sic] trees./Where the monkeys are,/Where the elephants are,/Where the tigers are./I ride on the back of an elephant…To the end of the world,/Then we ride, without ground,/Without tree,/Only on the wind, Only on the water,/Only in a dim place –[13]

When his mother chides him for singing when he should be grinding corn for pancakes, Sambo says his father would grind for him. But when Jumbo returns from the bazaar, instead of buying the food Mumbo has ordered, Jumbo has spent the money on blue and red cloth for clothes Sambo has wanted.

Sambo makes a deal: if his mother will make him clothes, rather than returning the cloth in exchange for food, he will somehow get eggs, milk, sugar, and butter for her. His mother agrees. She thinks Sambo needs to learn to work and to value food. Sambo has no money, so he asks Jumbo where the bazaar sellers get the food and realizes that he can find the raw ingredients or substitutes in the jungle.

So off he goes, where he quickly befriends Malinke the monkey. She agrees to fetch eggs, and as she frolics off, two tigers happen by. "We are

---

[12]Graham, Shirley, Production Book (2), *Little Black Sambo*, Chicago Negro Unit Production, Production Records, 1934–43. Production Title File, 1934–39, Box 1032.

[13]All quotes are taken from the playscript held at the Library of Congress. Bannerman, Helen, *Little Black Sambo*, Adapt. Chorpenning, Charlotte (Library Records, 1932–1940), S1147, Copy 8 Playscripts File, Box 696.

the finest beasts in the jungle," announces one and the other seconds, "No one dare be as fine as we are." Sambo responds, "I never thought of being fine" and the tiger questions, "Then why have you got a black and white and yellow skin like ours?" When Sambo explains that part of his coloring is his clothes and beads, the tigers insist that he remove them, which he politely refuses to do on the grounds that he would then be naked. Tiger: "You wish to make the animals think you are as fine as we." Sambo demurs, but the tigers decide to watch the monkeys' response to Sambo; if the monkeys think the boy is fine and grand, "We will eat you in our burning mouths."

The monkeys do gather round the boy and say he is the grandest of all, but Sambo saves himself by singing a song:

> The tiger walks in the jungle paths,
> The grasses bow as he goes past,
> They bend and whisper praise,
> He stands, he stands in the sun, he shines,
> His beautiful body all patterned,
> The beasts bow low, they sing, they shout, they praise!!!
> I am the tiger. You are the beasts!!
> Everything lives, everything dances, everything sings.

The monkeys bow to him as "the tiger" as Sambo leads the dance to where the tigers are sitting so the monkeys are bowing and shouting to them. "They sing about us. They bow to us," says one. "They don't notice him."

The tigers' jealousy is based on his glorious combination of black skin, white beads, and loincloth, which he tells them (in lines perhaps cut from the production at some point) that "I asked my mother to make my loin cloth yellow because it is beautiful like the moon at night …" "Take it off," interrupts a tiger.

Once the monkeys worship them and the tigers relax from the threat of equality, he asks the mother tiger for a jug of milk. She replies, "You are not grand enough even to look at tiger's milk," and a second adds, "You aren't fit to have a drop of the milk that makes my wee wonderful tiger babies grow their beautiful stripes." Sambo tells them he wants the milk so his mother can make pancakes and sew him blue trousers and a red coat. The tigers come back to find out what the red and blue colors mean:

BOULANE: I want to know what you meant by a beautiful little red coat and beautiful little blue trousers. Are you trying to find something finer than our black and yellow stripes?
BOULANE: Why do you change from colors like ours to be like a parrot or a bird of paradise? Do you think you will get more praise from the jungle folk?
SAMBO: I'm not thinking about praise.
DACURA: Everyone thinks about praise.
SAMBO: I'm thinking about how beautiful, beautiful, beautiful they are. That's all I'm thinking about.

When the tigers ask him why he wants his clothes to be beautiful, Sambo replies, "I don't know. My father never told me. It's the way I am." And Boulane responds, "In your muscles that do not show, you feel that you will be grander than we."

To make a three-act story short, with Malinke's help, Sambo gets all the pancake ingredients except butter. He makes sugar out of sugar cane himself. But when his mother sends his father to the bazaar for butter, his father buys a green umbrella and purple shoes with crimson soles and linings for his son instead. Sambo offers to return to the jungle for the butter. Though he is successful, he must fight off the tigers AND a rival group of jealous monkeys who trap him and set him out for the tigers to kill. While Sambo is lost, his mother chants to drumbeats that she hopes will call him home:

The drum beats
My heart beats
When will my child come home?
I wait, I wait,
My breath comes fast ....

Sambo's safe homecoming brings the play to a close, with Mumbo's, "To all, the drum in my heart beats thanks" echoed by Sambo and Jumbo. The curtain falls as the family begins to eat.

In a decade when modernist primitivism had been too often reduced to inherently racist stereotypes of African-American emotionalism and irrationality, Chorpenning and Graham succeed in creating a black character who is distinctively and positively African and American. In an era when, as David Chinitz notes, "Africa was all but defined by the primitive" Graham's production used African motifs in set, costume, and music, to frame a distinctly American rags-to-riches story wherein a boy's ingenious and plucky self-sufficiency wins him his heart's desire.[14] In a decade where representational mimicry was still almost completely the prerogative of whites at the expense of black autonomy, Sambo's besting of tigers jealous of his black body's fineness to become a free self was radical.

Federal Sambo's jungle is a much more frightening world than *Revolt of the Beavers'* forest. Sambo's disinterested love of beauty is matched by his kindness and sense of fair play that causes him to intervene in the tormenting of Malinke. But meanness isn't located in one being in the world of Sambo's play, but in the predator–prey divide demarcated by skin color. The best that can be hoped for are strengthened alliances that will ensure survival in this violent and fractured social structure. It's really no world for beautiful black boys with sharp minds, big hearts, and poetic souls.

The following year in Chicago another of Charlotte Chorpenning's scripts was used in the fantastic, anti-fascist *A Letter to Santa Claus.* Winston Churchill located the roots of Europe's failure to confront fascism in the refusal of the isolationist United States and the timid League of Nations to stop Mussolini in Ethiopia. A year earlier, Hitler had made is militaristic intentions clear in *Triumph of the Will*, a breathtaking film of the 1934 Nuremburg Rally by Leni Riefenstahl.[15] Children are everywhere in the film's early crowd scenes. They are lifted on shoulders and pushed to the front of crowds lining the streets to see the Führer drive by; they gaze at his passing figure with wide, excited eyes

[14]"The Conservation of Races," qtd in Anthony Appiah's "The Uncompleted Argument: Du Bois and the Illusion of Race" (24), *Critical Inquiry* 12 (1985): 21–37.

[15]*Triumph of the Will* was initially released in 1935. Riefenstahl, Leni, *Triumph des Willens = Triumph of the Will* (Santa Monica, CA: Connoisseur Video Collection, 1993).

as the camera isolates their faces. Riefenstahl's children enact an appropriate emotional response to the Führer's presence; children's symbolic plenitude is harnessed in these scenes to enact national values and model citizen behavior for vaguely defined political ends. *Triumph of the Will* is an explicitly political document; it celebrates a militaristic culture and imperial rhetoric while masking very explicit plans for war. Nazi discourse draws on the symbolic value of children's dynamism, growth, and vigor in service to the state. This relation to power provides a view from which to reflect on the lack of legitimizing authority in an American production for children, the oddest Christmas pageant, perhaps, in American history: *A Letter to Santa Claus.*[16]

Planned for a two-week run in December 1938, the one-act *A Letter to Santa Claus* tells the story of two children who are frightened and confused by the "shadows" that disturb their family and community.[17] Trying to deliver a note to Santa Claus, they see the shadow of a soldier before they fall asleep on the rooftop. When they awaken, Santa is delivering gifts, but the house is now surrounded by more shadows of war and social conflict. Disliking this strife-ridden world, Santa decides to leave. The children hear his call to the wind and repeat it. They too are whirled to the North Pole, where they undergo a series of character tests as Santa is traveling the world delivering gifts. When they pass the tests, Santa gives them a chant to take back to America to make the shadows go away.

> Open your heart
> And shut your eyes
> And I'll give you something
> To make you wise
> Your heart shall be
> The heart of a friend

---

[16]See "Winning over the Young" (261–90) of Richard Evans's *The Third Reich in Power* for a discussion of the Nazi regime's focus on the young, including through pedagogic directives to schools and the takeover of youth groups and activities. See also his chapter "Prosperity and Plunder," particularly the section "The Battle for Work" (322–50), for a discussion of the German economy in the prewar years of Nazi power. Evans, Richard J., *The Third Reich in Power: 1933–1939* (New York: Penguin, 2005).

[17]The play opened about one month after Kristallnacht, which occurred on November 9, 1938.

Your eyes shall see
How love should end.
And now I have made you wise.[18]

Chorpenning wrote *A Letter to Santa Claus* for a series of special matinees staged just before Christmas in 1938. Children were admitted for free. The play was planned for a stadium production but was scaled back for the Blackstone Theatre. For *A Letter to Santa Claus* federal theater ignored its mandate to use only adult actors and used two children to play the leads. According to the production book, the play was originally intended to draw on the resources of all the Chicago units—the vaudeville, ballet, white, and Negro units, and with choruses and the orchestra from the Federal Music Project. Scaled back, it still had a full orchestra and a cast of seventy-five, including acrobats, a snow ballet with thirty dancers, and the entire Chicago vaudeville unit. Almost all of its music was original. Lighting notes by Duncan Whiteside in the production book describe effects intended to emphasize color. "Whatever the scene or the particular demands of the scene, the result was the quality of a Maxfield Parrish canvas."[19] The play also featured dancing penguins and polar bears in a production that was timed to last exactly one hour.[20]

A Letter to Santa Claus stands alone among the FTP children's plays. Its child protagonists as seekers of peace, *A Letter to Santa Claus* links global strife to people's daily conflicts and international fascism to domestic fascism. Understanding that the strife within their home is emblematic of larger conflicts, Joe and Mary seek to rid their world of threats that they only dimly understand as shadows. No other FTP children's play asked its contemporary protagonists to save the world. No other FTP children's play broached the topic of war and the Depression

[18]Production Book (2), *A Letter to Santa Claus*, Chicago Production (Production Records, 1934–43), Production Title File, 1934–39, Box 1031.

[19]Ibid.

[20]According to the production book, each unit that was involved rehearsed separately for two weeks and the whole production came together only just before the opening. Unfortunately, there seems to be no review available for the production; a notice of an upcoming performance in the *Chicago Tribune* is all the record I have been able to find.

realities of hunger and strife outside the framework of comedy.[21] Lowell Swortzell, whose collection *Six Plays for Young People* reprinted the play, wrote in his introduction:

> *A Letter to Santa Claus* is of interest not simply because Chorpenning wrote it ... but mostly because of the anti-war sentiments that permeate almost every scene. References to hunger, poverty, and the "shadows" that cross the land ... convey a sense of national disillusionment.... Surely there has never been a Santa Claus play for "Children Only" written with such a deeply felt and disturbing subtext.[22]

Nor another play in federal children's theater.

A Letter to Santa Claus begins as Joe and Mary have sneaked to the rooftop on Christmas Eve to give Santa Claus a letter Joe has been writing for "weeks and weeks.... I couldn't get the letter to sound right. It's about the shadows." Stage directions call for a shadow to appear "of a soldier (not nationalized), a little larger than life, and not too black."[23] Shadows presage strife both within and outside of their family and thus connect the domestic and the public:

> It isn't just us. You think it's Mother crying, and it's lots of people crying. You think it's just the milkman quarreling with the man that pays him, and it's lots of people quarreling. You think you're hungry, and it's lots and lots of people hungry. They're what you hear when the shadows go by.

---

[21] Charlotte Chorpenning, who studied under George Pierce Baker at Harvard's 47 Workshop, was the most prolific and influential children's playwright through the midcentury, although she did not become active in children's theatre until she was sixty years old. She wrote more than fifty plays, doubling midcentury theatre for children, and taught classes in children's playwriting at the Goodman Theatre, where she was director of children's theater from 1932 to 1951. See her autobiography *Twenty-One Years with Children's Theatre* (Anchorage, KY: Anchorage Press, 1974). See also Roger Bedard's, "Charlotte B. Chorpenning: Playwright and Teacher" (85–98). Bedard, Roger L. and Tolch, C. John, ed., *Spotlight on the Child: Studies in the History of American Children's Theatre* (New York: Greenwood Press, 1989).

[22] Swortzell, Lowell, ed. *Six Plays for Young People from the Federal Theatre Project (1936–1939)* (New York: Greenwood Press, 1986), 22–23.

[23] Dialogue quoted from *Six Plays for Young People.*

As the children watch, more shadows appear. The soldier introduces and outlasts all other forms of conflict in the play, but, the first cause following the soldier is shown to be "children quarreling," with "shadows of children snatching from each other, food, etc. and voices 'It's mine,' 'I want the most!' and 'I don't like you.'" Voices crescendo to include industrial and class conflict, and then the weeping and quarreling voices die down to one. A child: "I'm hungry."

Santa Claus wants no part of the shadow-led strife. He calls out:

> Christmas music on the air
> And so I came.
> Other things are on the air.
> What you think is on the air.
> What you feel is on the air.
> Shadows of your thoughts are marching,
> Shadows of the things you feel, go by.
> I don't like those shadows,
> I don't like the world you're making with the things you think and feel
> So I go away.

Having heard Santa's call to the Christmas winds that help him lift his sleigh, Joe and Mary echo his words and whirl away after him to deliver the letter he has not taken.[24] Santa puts the children through a series of tests and he listens on the radio to determine whether or not they have responded appropriately. The lessons test their ability to share and their ability to cooperate with polar bears and penguins. They enact in simple, didactic terms a complicated childhood innocence. Joe and Mary learn sharing as a civic virtue; they do want all of the gifts offered. But in seeing that the polar bears want them too, they accept only what they need.

---

[24]Interestingly, in light of *The Wizard of Oz*'s filmic effects one year later, "the CHILDREN are whirled around and disappear to reappear on the screen, being whirled madly through space. Snow grows thicker and thicker, the stage lights dance and then dim, and when the lights come up again, the snowy scene at the North Pole is revealed" (185–86). It is unclear whether or not this conceptualized flight was actually staged. Pictures from the production in the production book show very conventional and static moments in the play with polar bears and the snow ballet. The production book notes that the snow ballet appeared three times as a transition vehicle between scenes. The curtain never goes down and it would be consistent with the play that the snow ballet appear as the children are whirling through the air.

The tests point to the rejuvenating possibilities of a childlike faith in social norms. At the South Pole Joe and Mary want to hunt for Santa, but the playful penguins assure them they will only find him if they have fun. Joe is encouraged to slide, but he almost runs through a red flashing light. "Oh! I almost didn't see it! How would I be punished if I hadn't?" The penguins are mystified by the idea of punishment:

NOEL: No one is ever punished here.
NOELITA: We just all agreed together to stop when the red came on.
JOE: What if someone doesn't stop?
NOEL: Doesn't stop? ... Everybody does.
NOELITA: (With finality): We agreed on it.

In a just society, penguins are rationally good (a subject for my next paper ☺).[25]

Joe and Mary's simple representation of childhood enables audience members to equate civic action with innocence and moral purity. The children experience each lesson as if they had no complicating social or familial contexts. In this they are innocent. Free of hate and greed and fear, they confront adult problems with a self-reliant bravery stemming from a certainty about what is right and wrong. In this, they are good. When Santa Claus explains that he cannot banish the shadows and that the light that will destroy those shadows must come from someone else, the children go home alone to rid the world of shadows. Childhood innocence is the basis for a goodness that will produce a just and equitable society.

Thus, the child's innocence becomes trope for a nation's. *A Letter to Santa Claus* explores the role of the American citizen in social transformation. It makes explicit the link between a child's innocence and corresponding morally correct action, and the shift in political

[25]Their innocence creates a profound opposition to the intense emotional strife of the shadows and their accompanying voices. The play's emphasis on the values of tolerance, sharing, and cooperation is amplified by a setting and staging that opposes darkness to light and fearful images with the children's dialogue, which centers on understanding how social interactions can function appropriately. It drew from expressionistic staging of psychological forces and leftist techniques (such as were also used in federal theatre's Living Newspapers) that visually invoke the energy and mass of the crowd.

consciousness necessary for America to produce a response to European war commensurate with its self-image as a moral leader. While both the cause and effect of conflict are rooted in quarreling situated in familial, domestic terms—father, mother, children—the children appeal to the international moral authority of Santa Claus to end the strife. The children provide the link between family, nation, and the world. America, the play suggests, cannot defeat the shadows of war until it addresses the problems of economic inequality. Situating effective idealistic action in such childhood values such as unselfishness and kindness, the play produces a child who stands in for the metonymic, resolute problem-solving American.

But if Joe and Mary enact a simplistic representation of childhood, the manner in which childhood innocence tropes American identity is not simple at all. Many critics have noted that representations of childhood innocence create a condition that is outside of history and knowledge, and therefore outside of accountability.[26] As a longstanding trope of Americanness, innocence is not innocent at all. Rather, it is a thematic that divorces national identity from the social and juridical injustices and inequities the nation has imposed upon individuals. It absolves a nation of accountability. But childhood innocence would not be such a powerfully animating thematic for Americanness if it just served as a deceptive cover for American participation in unjust practices and histories. Childhood innocence also emphasizes America's self-image as a nation united by ideals rather than shared history or blood. Innocence is the condition of being for the ideally principled person who is never compromised by the messy context of lived experience. So while a childlike innocence will mask, for example, America's complicity in the production of arms for war and its low quotas that kept Jews from reaching safety, Joe and Mary's innocence makes operational the values of tolerance and cooperation and thus makes paramount the ideals of liberal democracy.

The three Federal Theatre plays of this essay exemplify what Julia Mickenberg has cogently analyzed as a Popular Front rhetoric that "linked the playful, nonsectarian, and antiauthoritarian consciousness

[26]See Werrlein, Debra T., "Not So Fast, Dick and Jane: Reimagining Childhood and Nation in The Bluest Eye," *MELUS* 30,4 (2005): 53–72.

characteristic of the Lyrical Left … to the strongly prolabor, antiracist, and anti-imperialist views of the revolutionary Old Left.[27] Popular Front cultural production for children combined a progressive emphasis on the child with a radical leftist emphasis on socializing children for a transformed society. As Mickenberg notes, this common emphasis on socializing the child "rejected an authoritarian model of adult–child relations and emphasized freedom, democracy, and cooperation as desirable traits."[28]

> Open your heart
> And shut your eyes
> And I'll give you something
> To make you wise
> Your heart shall be
> The heart of a friend
> Your eyes shall see
> How love should end.
> And now I have made you wise.

Initially, I intended this discussion to focus only on *The Revolt of the Beavers*. But I have been haunted by the shootings of young black men and the chorus of voices rising against this old American violence. And then on a Valentine's Day, 2018, a young man with a gun walked into Marjorie Stone Douglass high school and killed seventeen of his classmates in a matter of minutes. In that shooting's wake we have heard the rise of young voices protesting against the shadows of men with guns stalking our land.

> Your heart shall be
> The heart of a friend
> Your eyes shall see
> How love should end.

---

[27] Mickenberg's, *Learning from the Left*, offers a groundbreaking examination of the connection between modernist and Popular Front works for children. Mickenberg, Julia, *Learning from the Left: Children's Literature, the Cold War, and Radical Politics in the United States* (London: Oxford University Press, 2005), 89.

[28] Ibid., 93.

And now I have made you wise.

I found myself inspired to revisit these three odd little plays, so firmly rooted in their time. When Santa asks, "How should love end?" both children respond, "In doing things, of course." They return to the city with its shadows of the "down and out," who Joe recognizes as "the shadows of what you think and feel." Mary begins the chant and Joe joins in. Those on stage add their voices, but the drums and sounds of grief rise, even as more light shoots across the stage. Joe and Mary start the chant again, until there is only the shadow "of a great soldier and two figures with uplifted fists." At this point, Joe raises his hands for the audience to come in, and as the entire theater chants "Your heart shall be the heart of a friend /Your eyes shall see where love should end," "the last SHADOW is blotted out in streaming Auroras" and the sound of bells is heard.

Action creates change. Engagement, with our fears and the forces allied against us, matters. We must teach our children so, and listen when they try to lead us to this truth. I find myself thinking about how odd it is to think about *playfulness* in the deadly seriousness of our current American political moment. With conservative David Frum,—who I certainly never would have imagined quoting in agreement with eight years ago—"I worry a lot, I think you worry a lot, about democratic breakdown. We're always inspired to think of the spectacular examples from the 1930s."[29]

Yes. We are.

Works Cited

Appiah, Anthony. "The Uncompleted Argument: Du Bois and the Illusion of Race" (24). *Critical Inquiry* 12 (1985): 21–37.

Bannerman, Helen. *Little Black Sambo.* Adapt. Chorpenning, Charlotte. S1147, Copy 8. Library Records, 1932–1940. Playscripts File. Box 696.

[29]Chotiner, Isaac, "David Frum Is Still a Republican. But ..." (*Slate Magazine*, January 22, 2018).

Bedard, Roger L. and Tolch, C. John, ed., *Spotlight on the Child: Studies in the History of American Children's Theatre*. New York: Greenwood Press, 1989.

Chorpenning, Charlotte. *Twenty-One Years with Children's Theatre*. Anchorage, KY: Anchorage Press, 1974.

Chotiner, Isaac. "David Frum Is Still a Republican. But ...". *Slate Magazine*. January 22, 2018. https://slate.com/news-and-politics/2018/01/david-frum-on-how-trumpism-has-changed-him.html.

Chotiner, Isaac. "David Frum Is Still a Republican. But ...". *Slate Magazine*. January 22, 2018.

Denning, Michael. *The Cultural Front: the Laboring of American Culture in the Twentieth Century*. New York: Verso, 1996.

Dies Committee Folder One. Box 496. Records of the Federal Theatre Project. Records of the Works Progress Administration. Record Group 69, National Archives, Washington, DC.

Evans, Richard J. *The Third Reich in Power: 1933–1939*. New York: Penguin, 2005.

Frost, Leslie. *Dreaming America: Popular Front Ideals and Aesthetics in Children's Plays of the Federal Theatre Project*. Columbus: The Ohio State University Press, 2013.

Graham, Shirley. Production Book (2). *Little Black Sambo*. Chicago Negro Unit Production. Production Records, 1934–43. Production Title File, 1934–39. Box 1032.

Kennedy, David. *Freedom from Fear: The American People in Depression and War, 1929–1945*. New York: Oxford University Press, 2001 (1999).

Lantz, Lou and Saul, Oscar. *The Revolt of the Beavers*. Library Records, 1932–1940. Playscripts File. S1681, Copy 1. Box 753.

Mickenberg, Julia. *Learning from the Left: Children's Literature, the Cold War, and Radical Politics in the United States*. London: Oxford University Press, 2005.

Production Book (2). *A Letter to Santa Claus*. Chicago Production. Production Records, 1934–43. Production Title File, 1934–39. Box 1031.

Randolph, John. George Mason University. Oral interview conducted by Diane Bowers. May 20, 1976.

Records of the Federal Theatre Project. Records of the Works Progress Administration. Record Group 69, National Archives, Washington, DC.

Riefenstahl, Leni. *Triumph des Willens = Triumph of the Will*. Santa Monica, CA: Connoisseur Video Collection. 1993.

Swortzell, Lowell, ed. *Six Plays for Young People from the Federal Theatre Project (1936–1939)*. New York: Greenwood Press, 1986.

Ward, Winifred. *Creative Dramatics*. New York: D. Appleton, 1930.
Werrlein, Debra T. "Not So Fast, Dick and Jane: Reimagining Childhood and Nation in the Bluest Eye." *MELUS* 30,4 (2005): 53–72.
Williams, Jay. *Stage Left*. Charles Scribner's Sons: New York, 1974.

The Republic of Childhood: Friedrich Froebel's Kindergarten and *Naturphilosophie*

Diana Ramírez-Jasso

When, in July of 1807—thirty-three years before he coined the term Kindergarten—a young Friedrich Froebel took a job as a private tutor in Frankfurt, his educational plan emulated the anti-urban proposal that Jean-Jacques Rousseau had laid out in his famous *Emile, ou de l'éducation* of 1762. In an unfinished letter to the Duke of Meiningen written in 1827, Froebel recalled his negotiations with the von Holzhausen family concerning the tutoring of its three youngest members two decades earlier. From the outset, his pedagogical demands echoed the first chapter of *Emile*:

> There were … two immutable conditions in our agreement. One was that I should never be compelled to live in town with my pupils, and that when I began my duties, my pupils should be handed over entirely to my care, without any restriction; that they should follow me into the country, and there form a restricted and perfectly isolated circle, and that

D. Ramírez-Jasso (✉)
Tecnológico de Monterrey, Querétaro, Mexico

V. Rapti and E. Gordon (eds.), *Ludics*,
https://doi.org/10.1007/978-981-15-7435-1_20

when they returned to town life my duties as preceptor should be at an end.[1]

Froebel's desire to move his students into a "restricted and perfectly isolated circle" away from the city, where they would be prepared for their subsequent release into the social world, betrays a literal indebtedness to Rousseau. Yet this initial attempt to replicate *Emile*'s protective migration to the countryside also makes it possible to more clearly discern Froebel's later move away from the idea of education as an isolationist endeavor. Contrasting the pedagogical laboratory established in *Emile*, Froebel's mature work presented kindergarten education as an integrative process that aimed to produce ethical, epistemological, and emotional connections between the child and her surroundings.

The purpose of this essay is to examine Friedrich Froebel's kindergarten as a nineteenth-century reshaping of Rousseau's pedagogy in a way that avoided or remediated the profoundly divided understanding of the human subject that had begun to be perceived in the German-speaking context as the most problematic legacy of the Enlightenment. Firmly grounded in the ethics and aesthetics of Romanticism, Froebel's gardens for children set out to reconnect the child with both nature and the social world in a way that echoed the philosophical debates of German Idealism. Aiming to recover an organic link between body and mind, reason and emotion, and subjects and objects of cognition, the garden for children emerged as an ideal arena for the creation and preservation of the Romantic child.

Like most progressive pedagogues in Europe at the turn of the nineteenth century, Froebel was a faithful adherent to the basic principles submitted in both Rousseau's *Emile* and *Julie, ou la nouvelle Héloïse* of 1761. Following Rousseau, he acknowledged the importance of letting the child's inherent powers unfold without external interference and he saw the educator as a mere facilitator of human self-actualization. Setting out to foster the emergence of forms of subjectivity that were unencumbered by received traditions and conventions, Froebel also followed

[1] Friedrich Froebel, *Autobiography of Friedrich Froebel*, ed. and trans. Emilie Michaelis and H. Keatley Moore (London: Swan Sonnenschein, 1886), 66.

Rousseau in rejecting rote learning and the authoritative medium of the book, enthusiastically embracing nature as the ultimate source of enlightenment.

In his mature approach to the garden, however, Froebel the Romantic pedagogue departed from Rousseau, the Enlightenment thinker, in a small but important way. If the isolated garden for individual protection and cultivation had been the cornerstone of Rousseau's pedagogy in *Emile*, Froebel recast it as a productive sphere that immersed young children in collective practices of citizenship from their very first interactions with the social and natural world. If Rousseau's focus was on transforming the autonomous child into a future enlightened adult capable of submitting his personal desires to the rational demands of a social contract, Froebel aimed to promote the emergence of the ideal political community already in the context of the children's garden. A better society would necessarily emerge not on the basis of a rational agreement between enlightened individuals, but as a self-regulating community organically connected through productive interaction and affective bonds.

From his retreat in the outskirts of Frankfurt, Froebel had begun to perceive the cultivation of the land as having the capacity to generate powerful ties between children and the world. Having worked with his pupils in a patch of meadow given to them by Herr von Holzhausen, he noticed that horticulture didn't simply instigate in the child incipient forms of aesthetic or scientific observation, or an awareness of property rights, as Rousseau had suggested. The celebration that children made of their gardening accomplishments by proudly offering gifts of flowers to parents and teachers led Froebel to locate the importance of the garden in its ability to support the development in the human being of an ethics of care and reciprocity:

> ... living cheerfully and joyfully in the bosom of Nature with my first pupils, I began to tell myself that the training of natural life was closely akin to the training of human life. For did not those gifts of flowers and plants express appreciation and acknowledgment of the love of parents and teacher? Were they not the outcome of the characteristic lovingness and the enthusiastic thankfulness of childhood? A child that of its own

> accord and of its own free will seeks out flowers, cares for them, and protects them, so that in due time he can weave a garland or make a nosegay with them for his parents or his teacher, can never become a bad child, a wicked man. Such a child can easily be led towards love, towards thankfulness, towards recognition of the fatherliness of God, who gives him these gifts and permits them to grow that he, as a cheerful giver in his turn, may gladden with them the hearts of his parents.[2]

This early passage conveys the interdependence of divine, human, and natural elements that came to characterize Froebel's later pedagogy. God, teacher, parents, and children were linked by a virtuous cycle of metaphorical cultivation and mutual giving that acquired material form in the child's garden and that was aptly symbolized by gifts of plants and flowers. In this context, gardening made a crucial contribution to the child's trajectory toward self-realization, for the capacity to grow botanical specimens enabled the budding social being to transform itself from a passive recipient of love and attention into an active participant in this universal exchange of generosity and care. Thus, the garden demonstrated that the basis of morality lay primarily in the affective connections forged between human beings, rather than, as late Enlightenment theorists like Immanuel Kant had suggested, in categorical imperatives supplied by the rational mind.

Froebel's appreciation of the connective properties of gardening guided his approach not only to the development of those relationships that linked the child to other human beings. In fact, the first aim of the garden was to lead the child, through a habitual contact with plants and flowers, to a realization of the similarities between botanical growth and her own process of biological development. "Plants," Froebel wrote, "are the center piece of nature because of their similar yet very detailed life cycle. They show men and the child their very own nature by standing in the center and pointing downwards to matter and particles and upwards to animals and man."[3] The capacity of plants to conceptually as well as

[2]Ibid., 72.

[3]Friedrich Froebel, quoted in Joachim Liebschner, *A Child's Work: Freedom and Guidance in Froebel's Educational Theory and Practice* (1992; repr. Cambridge, UK: The Lutterworth Press, 2001), 37.

visually connect the apparently disparate spheres of soil and minerals on the one hand, and the realm of human and animal life on the other, made possible the child's discovery of the universal chain that linked animate and inanimate objects in the natural world. Allowing the child to discern this universal system of connections would ensure, Froebel thought, the rise of a form of subjectivity that was adequately situated in nature and profoundly aware of the fundamental dependence and responsibilities that connected human beings to the world as a whole.

As suggested by these writings, Froebel's pedagogy was defined early on by his attempt to bring together realities that previous models of education had severed or had left to stand in a fractured state. The individual and society, reason and emotion, the body and nature, appeared to him to be the isolated elements that education should bring into a new form of unity in order to ensure the optimal development of humankind. Against what he perceived as the divided subjectivity that had been instigated by rationalism, Froebel grounded his pedagogy on a holistic pursuit of unity:

> All is unity, all rests in unity, all springs from unity, strives for and leads up to unity, and returns to unity at last. This striving in unity and after unity is the cause of the several aspects of human life. But between my inner vision and my outer perception, presentation, and action was a great gulf fixed. Therefore it seemed to me that everything which should or could be required for human education and instruction must be necessarily conditioned and given, by virtue of the very nature of the necessary course of his development, in man's own being, and in the relationships amidst which he is set. A man, it seemed to me, would be well educated, when he had been trained to care for these relationships and to acknowledge them, to master them and to survey them.[4]

This "great gulf" that existed between the individual's "inner vision" and her "outer perception, presentation, and action," was in part the product of educational models that, like those prevalent in late Enlightenment pedagogy, prioritized the mental over the fully embodied and, as it were, geographical or topographical, development of the child. A

[4]Froebel, *Autobiography*, 69–70.

proper education involved, then, offering ample opportunities for the child to practice the kind of reciprocal interactions with both people and nature that were naturally fostered by the garden. Cultivating the soil was seen as a practice capable of breaking down the barrier that separated the human being's mind and her environment.

Despite consistently invoking the concept of unity, Froebel did not leave a systematic account of its pedagogy. Except for his most important pedagogical work, *The Education of Man* (1826), which he wrote fourteen years before founding his first kindergarten, his writings on education are mostly letters and scattered pieces on various subjects that commentators later assembled into volumes. In these writings, very rarely did he directly address the work of other authors, or explicitly situate his own pedagogy in the context of the Romantic response to the Enlightenment. In fact, Froebel resisted the idea that his pedagogical work emerged from theoretical considerations at all, replying to commentators who grounded his work in Fichte's idealism or Hegel's dialectical method by arguing that "it is both of these, and yet has nothing in common with either of them, it is the law the contemplation of nature has taught me, and which I offer to children to guide them in their development."[5]

The basic ideas in Froebel's pedagogical thought, however, have clear affinities with the philosophical project that had been formulated by the early Romantics, who had set out to challenge what they saw as the radically dualistic model of subjectivity established by Cartesian rationalism, a model that they thought Immanuel Kant and Fichte had taken to its ultimate consequences.

Early Romanticism and the Critique of Cartesian Dualism

The main problem that the early Romantics identified in the Cartesian understanding of the mind was that it assigned to consciousness, or the *res cogitans*, properties that were fundamentally distinct from

[5]Friedrich Froebel, quoted by W. N. Hailmann, in Froebel, *The Education of Man*, trans. W. N. Hailmann (New York: D. Appleton, 1906), 42.

those of matter, or what Descartes had identified as the *res extensa*. While the essential mark of matter was that of having a specific length, breadth, and depth—in other words, a capacity to occupy space—the mind was seen as a self-sufficient entity standing outside this sphere and independently of matter. With Kant's Copernican revolution, the mind itself became responsible for providing the very spatiality by which matter or "the thing in itself"—a reality unknowable except through the forms provided by human intuition—was given to perception as an intelligible object. In the early Romantics' interpretation, Fichte's *Wissenschaftslehre* (1797) had pushed Kant's critical philosophy to its most radical conclusions by limiting all forms of knowledge to the representations of the finite subject, while remaining committed to the existence of an essentially unknowable external world.[6] In this scheme of things, the early Romantics complained that nature had remained always an object for, and never a constitutive element of, consciousness. This understanding had brought about, they argued, an unbridgeable rift between body and mind, and between human being—understood as subjective interiority—and the external world of experience.

The alternative that the early Romantics posed to this fundamental fracturing of human experience was often articulated as a recovery of an emotional connection between mind, body, and landscape, a philosophical proyect aptly encapsulated in the notion of *Naturphilosophie*.[7] While this recovery was often expressed in terms of the human response to the most exuberant manifestations of the natural world, it was also deployed through references to agriculture and gardening as symbols of an idealized materialization of the interdependence between human beings and

[6]Frederick Beiser has pointed out that the basis for the anti-subjectivist critique of the early Romantics stemmed from a specific understanding of Fichte as a radical Kantian, which is only one of many possible interpretations of his *Wissenschaftslehre*. For Beiser's discussion of the various possible readings of Fichte's work of the Jena years, see Frederick Beiser, *German Idealism: The Struggle Against Subjectivism, 1781–1801* (Cambridge: Harvard University Press, 2002), 217–221.

[7]In his study of the transformation of geographic knowledge under the influence of Romanticism, Chenxi Tang has called this poetic and philosophical strategy the "humanization of the earth, or the earthing of the human." See Chenxi Tang, *The Geographic Imagination of Modernity: Geography, Literature, and Philosophy in German Romanticism* (Stanford: Stanford University Press, 2008).

nature. In *Die Lehrlinge zu Sais* (1798), Novalis gives an example of this eminently conciliatory character of cultivation:

> In between [those for whom the sentiment of nature is a religion and those for whom it is a jocose fancy] there were other, more contemplative souls, who found in the nature before them only large but neglected gardens, and busied themselves creating prototypes of a nobler nature... some sought to awaken the spent and lost tones in the air and in the forests...others...restored noble plants and beasts to desert regions, dammed the forest floods and cultivated the nobler flowers and herbs, ...taught wood and meadow, springs and crags to join again in pleasant gardens, ... and cleansed the woods of savage monsters, the misbegotten creatures of a degenerate fantasy. Soon nature learned friendlier ways again, she became gentler and more amiable, more prone to favor the desires of man. Little by little her heart learned human emotions, her fantasies became more joyful, she became companionable, responding gladly to the friendly questioner, and thus little by little she seems to have brought back the old golden age, in which she was man's friend, consoler, priestess and enchantress, when she lived among men and divine association made men immortal.[8]

The educational motif, used here to portray the process by which wild nature "learns" to become a willing contributor to the productive and poetic purposes established by humans, becomes, for Novalis, also a potential instrument to instigate the individual's renewed appreciation of nature. Thus, the topic of education returns at the end of Novalis' text, in a way that closely mirrors Froebel's pedagogical theory:

> ... he who feels an inner calling to impart the understanding of nature to other men, to develop and cultivate this gift in men, must first give careful regard to the natural causes of this development and endeavor to learn the elements of this art from nature. Having thus gained an insight he will devise a system based on experiment, analysis and comparison whereby these means may be applied by any individual; this system will become like second nature to him and then he will embark with enthusiasm upon

[8]Novalis [Friedrich von Hardenberg], *The Novices of Sais*, trans. Ralph Manheim (New York: Achipelago Books, 2005), 31–35.

> his rewarding task. Only such a man can rightly be called a teacher of nature, since every other mere naturalist will, like some natural event, only awaken a sense of nature by accident and sympathy.[9]

This double process of education, one directed to nature itself and the other to human beings, was probably also behind Novalis' audacious formulation, one year earlier, of the philosophical project of the young German idealists, a community of which he was a part: "we are on a mission: we have been called upon to the education of the earth [*die Bildung der Erde*]."[10]

The echoes of Novalis and of Romantic Idealism found in Froebel's work are hardly surprising, for he attended the University of Jena as a student of philosophy between 1799 and 1801, that is to say, precisely at the time when Jena became the philosophical epicenter of early Romanticism. Froebel seems to have devoted little time to the study of philosophy per se, as it was here that he took his first courses in architecture and enrolled in other classes ranging from mathematics and physics to land surveying and map drawing. It must have been very difficult, however, to avoid coming into contact with the ideas of the early Romantics, for the environment at Jena was profoundly infused with excitement about the young generation of thinkers who had converged there, and who were quickly changing the direction of German philosophical inquiry at that time.[11]

---

[9] Ibid., 121.

[10] Novalis, quoted in Frederick Beiser, *The Romantic Imperative: The Concept of Early German Romanticism* (Cambridge: Harvard University Press, 2003), 26.

[11] In my discussion of the early Romantics, I am indebted to Frederick Beiser's philosophical and historical analysis. Particularly important for my argument is his emphasis on the important place given by these German thinkers to education (*Bildung*) as a holistic form of self-actualization. Interestingly, attention to Froebel's work along the lines of my study might help qualify what Beiser calls the "paradox" of romantic philosophy, namely, that despite the fact that "there was nothing more important to the romantics than *Bildung*...when it comes to concrete suggestions about how to educate humanity—about what specific institutional arrangements are to be made—the romantics fell silent." Beiser, *The Romantic Imperative*, 105. See also Beiser, *German Idealism*.

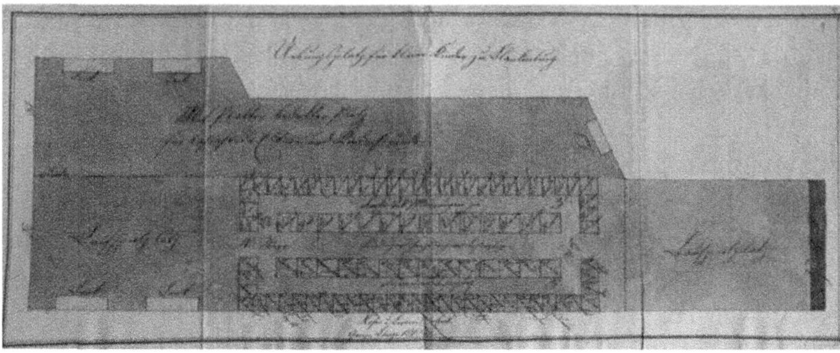

Fig. 1 Friedrich Froebel, "Übungsplatz für kleine Kinder zu Blankenburg" (ca. 1839)

The Children's Garden in Bad Blankenburg

On June 28, 1840, Froebel officially founded the first kindergarten in history in Bad Blankenburg, a small town bordering the Thuringian forest in central Germany. The school had begun operating a year earlier under the name of "*Spiel- und Beschäftigungsanstalt*" or "Institute for Play and Occupations." From the day it opened, the institute for small children had been housed in what the townspeople called the "*Haus über dem Keller*," or "house above the cellar," a three-story building whose basement opened directly onto the street and whose back rooms were carved into a steep hill at the edge of the town. At the top of the hill, connected to the building by a steep flight of stairs, was the school's garden. In this large open space overlooking Bad Blankenburg below and the Thuringian valley in the distance, children played and cultivated vegetables and flowers with their teachers for a space of two hours every day. The garden remained continuously cultivated from the day the school was established until 1844, when the institution was forced to close due to financial problems.

Today, the *Haus über dem Keller* houses the Fröbel Museum, but the garden esplanade is no longer extant. A surviving plan drawn by Froebel circa 1839 provides an idea of what this space contained and how it was laid out (Fig. 1).[12] This colored ink drawing shows the distribution of various programmatic contents within the available land on the esplanade. At either end of the site, the viewer can discern an area for running and active play [*Laufspielplatz*]. At the farthest end on its short axis, the plan shows an elongated area adjacent to the school building where children could meet with visiting parents and friends. Benches appear around the perimeter of the site, and a note along the railings that separate the esplanade from the uncultivated hill indicates a hedge interspersed with roses. In the area of the garden reserved for cultivation, the drawing shows the first iteration of what would become the spatial formula typical of the kindergarten: two rows of square planting beds surrounded by two additional areas for linear cultivation. In each one of the internal beds is a label that indicates the name of a child to whom that particular space had been assigned. In the surrounding beds, rather than young gardeners, the labels describe the exact location of a wide range of vegetables, herbs and flowers to be grown, including cabbages, peas, lentils, parsley, oat, barley, sunflowers, and poppies.

With its representation and distribution of mostly organic material with practically no tectonic elements, this plan may not immediately convey the importance it holds in the material history of early childhood education. Historians, in fact, have paid little attention to the garden as it was spatially imagined by Froebel, and his drawings have remained understudied. This particular drawing constitutes, however, the first practical instantiation of what would become one of the most important components of Froebel's kindergarten theory. Out of this first prototype emerged a garden formula that, soon after the establishment of the original school, began to be enthusiastically emulated and adapted in nearby villages, thanks in part to Froebel's own dissemination. When, a decade later, a revised version of this plan was officially published as a programmatic document, this typology was embraced throughout Europe and the rest of the world.

It is not entirely clear why, despite the garden being such an important part of the theory, the practice, and even the naming of Froebel's kindergarten, it has drawn little attention from historians and commentators

[12] Fröbel Nachlass 209.3, *Bibliothek für Bildungsgeschichtliche Forschung*, Berlin.

as an actual, designed space with a characteristic layout. Most discussions of the gardening practices central to Froebelian pedagogy since the nineteenth century have focused on the practices as such, as if they had been intended to be carried out in any garden setting. Yet for Froebel, it was precisely in the layout of the various planting beds that the function of the garden was expressed and accomplished. It was here, in fact, that the ultimately social, epistemological, and political goal of Froebel's pedagogy was most effectively symbolized and performed.

The garden seems to have been, in fact, the only educational space in his school that Froebel ever considered in detail. The pedagogical importance attributed to cultivation justified his decision to represent and theorize the children's garden as an isolated spatial entity; in other words, independently of any building or interior space used for the instruction of children. In part, this reflected the fact that most small schools at the time were established in adapted pre-existing spaces, giving educators little opportunity to plan their architectural settings; but it also followed from Froebel's own preference for typical domestic layouts as the basis for his kindergartens.[13] Similarly, Froebel's garden emulated the scale of the traditional domestic space for cultivation and was explicitly evocative of productivity within a familiar economy of subsistence.[14] It is interesting, then, that what initially looks like a simple kitchen garden would require abundant and specific theorization, as well as an explicitly prescribed layout, in order to be presented widely as a pedagogical tool. It was perhaps its invaluable contribution to the ambitious project

[13]Even when Froebel had the opportunity to design architectural spaces—he was at one point involved in the design of at least two school buildings—the degree of consideration that went into the children's garden was never matched in his work connected to architecture or interiors. Despite his lifelong interest in architecture—he had briefly apprenticed with an architect in Frankfurt and had thought of this discipline as his true calling for most of his youth—he had little to say about the ideal spatial conditions for education in interior contexts, and archival documents suggest that he relied on traditional domestic layouts and facades for his schools. Several architectural drawings are held in the Fröbel Nachlass, 209, *Bibliothek für Bildungsgeschichbliche Forschung*, Berlin.

[14]Froebel was explicit about his opinion that children should not "be introduced by this garden to the totality of the vegetable world, but only into the part which most closely touches human needs" Friedrich Froebel, *Education by Development: The Second Part of the Pedagogics of the Kindergarten*, trans. Josephine Jarvis (New York: D. Appleton, 1903), 220.

of reuniting the child with nature and society that amply justified this layout's careful revision and broad dissemination.

When an abstracted typological version of this plan was published in Froebel's *Wochenschrift* on April 15, 1850, it came with several pages of writing offering detailed instructions for its implementation as well as discussions of its pedagogical purpose. A decade later, a more formal version of this second drawing substituting Froebel's handwriting with printed italics as if to facilitate its adoption was included by Wichard Lange as an illustration in Froebel's *Gesammelte Schriften.*[15] The original programmatic text announced that "the kindergarten, the completely formed idea, the clearly demonstrated conception of a kindergarten ... necessarily requires a garden, and in this, necessarily, gardens for the children."[16]

The double purpose of this outdoor space is immediately signaled. The garden emerges, Froebel says, out of the "high importance of intimate acquaintance and union with Nature for the development of the child, the education of man, the training of all humanity," but it is also designed to guide the child to recognize herself as a member of society by inciting her active participation in community-oriented practices:

> The human being, the child, as a part of humanity must even early not only be recognized and treated as individual and single, thus as a member of a greater collective life, but must recognize itself as such and prove itself to be such by its action. ... this reciprocal activity between one and a few, a part and a whole, is nowhere more beautifully, vividly, and definitely expressed than in the associated cultivation of plants, the common care of a garden, in which the relation of the general to the particular is clearly shown.[17]

The relation of the general to the particular to which Froebel alludes finds specific forms and measurements in his drawing. The graphic, as much as the textual, components of the article deploy the utilitarian

---

[15]Friedrich Froebel, *Friedrich Froebels gesammelte Schriften*, ed. Wichard Lange, vol. 2, *Die Pädagogik des Kindergartens* (Berlin: Enslin, 1862), 271.

[16]Froebel, Education by Development, 218.

[17]Ibid.

language of regular geometries and precise lengths to convey the reproducibility of the type. Froebel recommends that the garden have, for example, a rectangular shape, and that it be divided into two major areas, what Froebel calls a "part for the general" and "a part for the particular."[18] The area conceived as a tool to introduce the child to the abstract concept of the "general" consists in the peripheral plots that are provided to be cultivated by teachers and children together. This area's function is to "protect" the internal beds, where individual children would take charge of growing their own choice of produce. It is precisely this arrangement that constituted the important difference, Froebel argued, between the regular "house garden" and his own educational space, for "here the gardens and respective beds of the children must be surrounded by the garden of the whole, as the particular always rests protected in the general, and the general protectingly surrounds the particular. … [the garden's] general aim [is that of] representing the relation of the particular to the general, of the part to the whole, of the child to the family, of the citizen to the community."[19]

In representing the individual, the central planting beds were to be clearly labeled with the name of each child and the plant for which she chose to be responsible. This practice ensured that every young gardener would receive "the merited silent praise or blame" for the apparent quality of their work, as one early commentator put it.[20] The symbolic location of the community in the peripheral area, then, was not merely designed to provoke in the child a sense of belonging and safety, but it also ensured that she acquired a sense of responsibility toward nature and of accountability to others. The great emphasis that Froebel placed on the individual child is mirrored in the individuality of the planting bed. Precisely in this section of the garden, a small but significant change was registered as Froebel moved from the tentative, hand-drawn plan for Bad Blankenburg to the diagramatic version published in the *Wochenschrift*. Whereas in his earlier drawing individual beds were laid out in a

[18] Ibid., 219.

[19] Ibid., 219.

[20] William Kilpatrick, Froebel's Kindergarten Principles Critically Examined (New York: Macmillan, 1916), 194.

long line of contiguous squares, the *Wochenschrift* plan prescribes individual plots of land laid out as entirely isolated entities. This would have ostensibly allowed children to move around their plants more easily, but it also underscores a symbolic distinction between the individual and the community. Hence Froebel's recommendation to assign single children to each planting bed, unless space was limited: "Where there is enough land each child must be given four feet in the form of a square. Where there is less land, six square feet, in the form of an oblong, may be given to two children together. Where, however, the number of the children is large and the land small, two children must be content with four square feet."[21]

The separation of the individual planting beds was balanced by the circulation spaces that connected them, for these areas were conceived as settings for social exchange. These paths that "divide and again combine the whole" were thus expected to follow specific design guidelines: while the cross paths between the single beds could be one foot wide, "it is a good plan to make the principal paths, if possible, at least two and one half feet wide, so that two children may walk in them side by side."[22]

The holistic aims of the garden were contained in precisely these seemingly utilitarian details. As is clear from Froebel's text, the child was to be immersed in a carefully designed environment that promoted what he termed "self-activity," that is to say, an engagement with objects, people, and nature that emerged out of the child's own desire. Importantly, that desire was seen as instigated directly by the garden's layout, allowing the teacher to remain a quiet observer at the periphery of the scene. The distinction between the garden for the general and the one for the particular made self-activity immediately practicable: while it was understood that children and teachers cultivated plants together in the surrounding beds, the child learned to associate herself and her work with the individual plot at the center of the space.

> In their own little beds the children can plant what and how they will, also deal with the plants as they will, that they may learn from their

[21] Ibid., 220–221.

[22] Ibid., 221.

> own injudicious treatment that plants also cannot grow well unless they are treated carefully according to laws. This will be shown to them by the plants in the common bed, which they must observe carefully so that they may calmly notice them in their development from the seed through the germinating, growing, blossoming, and fructifying to the seed again.[23]

In offering opportunities for self-conscious and self-directed growth, the garden promoted the ideal of *Bildung*, or what the Romantics had envisioned as a general cultivation of the self that was organically connected to the natural world and the community. The spatial relationships established between the individual planting beds and the collective areas for cultivation were intended to facilitate precisely this reconciliation; they offered an opportunity for children to locate and understand themselves not only *vis-à-vis* the natural world and its dynamic processes, but also with respect to the community at large. While, initially, this community meant the immediate society of children and teachers, the practices carried out in the garden were meant to introduce the child to a wider and more empowered form of adult citizenship. That is the case, for example, of the celebratory exchanges of produce coming from the individual beds that were regularly carried out between teachers and children. Thus, as children came to understand their own contribution to the wellbeing of others, they were also introduced to the basic principles of economic exchange, as well as to the important idea that not only "the whole and general protect the individual and particular" but that also "the latter has a retroactive, beneficial effect on the former."[24]

Froebel's mobilization of cultivation in helping children reach an understanding of themselves as active and valuable members of society brought commentators to refer to the kindergarten as a "miniature state for children" or, as American educator Mary Peabody put it in 1862, "a commonwealth or republic of children [that] may be contrasted in every particular, with the old-fashioned school, which is an absolute

[23] Ibid.

[24] Ibid., 223.

monarchy."[25] Furthermore, with his strong partiality toward women as ideal educators, and his gesture of setting aside a sphere for the free development of both women's and children's "God-given powers and dispositions," Froebel himself thought of his institution as initiating a movement toward social equity that was long overdue:

> Women and children ... are the most oppressed and neglected of all. They have not yet been fully recognized in their dignity as parts of human society. ... I know that this is the work of centuries. The present time demands that the foundation be laid for it by an education corresponding to its demands, and worthy of human dignity. And to lay this foundation is the aim of my kindergarten.[26]

An educational sphere in which women and children utilized domestic and garden settings for the cultivation of civic virtue, held, for Froebel, a powerful promise of social and political reform. It is perhaps not surprising, then, that taking this ambition seriously, the Prussian government came to perceive Froebel's schools as centers of political radicalism, and on August 7, 1851—only one year after the publication of the children's garden in the *Wochenschrift*—a decree was issued banning all kindergartens in Prussia on charges of socialism and atheism.[27] The charge of atheism was perhaps unfounded, for Froebel's pedagogy integrated a form of religious spirituality, however unique, throughout its activities. The institution's reputation for radical politics, on the other hand, was the product of the enthusiastic embrace of the kindergarten by feminist activist groups throughout the German-speaking context. It was also, more generally, a product of its public reception for, as it was later known, the government's decision was justified on "the circumstance that in many confiscated letters of persons politically compromised the

---

[25]Earl Barnes, "Fundamental Factors in the Making of a Kindergarten Community." *Kindergarten Review*, 19, no. 2 (October 1908): 68; Mary Peabody Mann, "Kindergarten—What Is It?" in Mary Peabody Mann and Elizabeth Peabody, *Moral Culture of Infancy and Kindergarten Guide* (Boston: Burnham, 1863), 14.

[26]Friedrich Froebel, quoted in Bertha Maria von Marenholtz-Bülow, *Reminiscences of Friedrich Froebel*, trans. Mary Mann (Boston: Lee and Shepard, 1899), 142.

[27]For the Baroness von Marenholz-Bülow's first-hand account of the *Kindergartenverbot* see von Marenholz-Bülow, *Reminiscences of Friedrich Froebel*, 197–203.

importance of the kindergarten was mentioned as a new foundation for the education of the people."[28] The kindergarten prohibition was not lifted in Prussia until 1860, nine years after Froebel's death, by which time his pedagogy had been taken to, among other places, England and the United States by German kindergarten advocates. In their new settings, kindergartens initially had spaces for cultivation that emulated the layout proposed in 1850, even as they were reinterpreted through other forms of organization, such as concentric circles. Froebel's original typology, however, eventually came to be forgotten, being substituted by all kinds of garden arrangements and other forms of outdoor space, including paved playgrounds.

As the theory was originally conceived, the garden took the form of a conciliatory space for the active development and shaping of human potential in concert with the social and natural worlds. Here, in accord with Romantic theory, the child's engagement with his or her surroundings was meant to be not only intellectual and sensorial, but also embodied, situated, social, and political. The Enlightenment's educational drive had taken a critical turn. In contrast to the emphasis placed on apparatuses, specimens, models, and machines by rationalist pedagogies, gardening practices in the kindergarten provided the opportunity for children to engage with specimens that were, themselves, situated and animated. These living, interactive objects communicated to the child what Froebel saw as the continuous link that connected apparently isolated entities—or what Romanticism theorized as the organic unity of nature.

[28] Marenholz-Bülow, *Reminiscences of Friedrich Froebel*, 202. For the connections between feminism and Froebel's kindergarten pedagogy see Ann Taylor Allen, "Spiritual Motherhood: German Feminists and the Kindergarten Movement, 1848–1911." *History of Education Quarterly* 22, no. 3 (Autumn 1982): 319–339; *Feminism and Motherhood in Germany, 1800–1914* (New Brunswick: Rutgers University Press, 1991).

Bibliography

Allen, Ann Taylor. *Feminism and Motherhood in Germany, 1800–1914*. New Brunswick: Rutgers University Press, 1991.
Allen, Ann Taylor. "Spiritual Motherhood: German Feminists and the Kindergarten Movement, 1848–1911." *History of Education Quarterly* 22, no. 3 (Autumn 1982): 319–339.
Barnes, Earl. "Fundamental Factors in the Making of a Kindergarten Community." *Kindergarten Review* 19, no. 2 (October 1908): 65–71.
Beiser, Frederick C. *German Idealism: The Struggle against Subjectivism 1781–1801.* Cambridge: Harvard University Press, 2002.
Beiser, Frederick C. *The Romantic Imperative: The Concept of Early German Romanti*cism. Cambridge: Harvard University Press, 2003.
Friedrich Fröbels Wochenschrift: Ein Einigungsblatt für alle Freunde der Menschenbildung. Bad Liebenstein, 1850.
Froebel, Friedrich. *Friedrich Froebels gessamelte Schriften, Vol. 2: Die Pädagogik des Kindergartens.* Edited by Wichard Lange. Berlin: Enslin, 1862.
Froebel, Friedrich. *Autobiography of Friedrich Froebel*. Translated and annotated by Emilie Michaelis and H. Keatley Moore. London: Swan Sonnenschein, 1886.
Froebel, Friedrich. *Education by Development: The Second Part of the Pedagogics of the Kindergarten.* Translated by Josephine Jarvis. New York: D. Appleton and Company, 1903.
Froebel, Friedrich. *The Education of Man.* Translated by W. N. Hailmann. New York: D. Appleton and Company, 1906.
Liebschner, Joachim. *A Child's Work: Freedom and Guidance in Froebel's Educational Theory and Practice.* 1992. Reprint, Cambridge, UK: The Lutterworth Press, 2001.
Mann, Mary. "Kindergarten—What Is It?" In *Moral Culture of Infancy and Kindergarten Guide*, by Mary Peabody Mann and Elizabeth Peabody. Boston: Burnham, 1863.
Marenholtz-Bülow, Bertha Maria von. *Reminiscences of Friedrich Froebel*. Translated by Mary Mann. Boston: Lee and Shepard, 1899.
Novalis [Friedrich von Hardenberg]. *The Novices of Sais*. Translated by Ralph Manheim, illustrated by Paul Klee. New York: Achipelago Books, 2005.
Tang, Chenxi. *The Geographic Imagination of Modernity: Geography, Literature, and Philosophy in German Romanticism.* Stanford: Stanford University Press, 2008.

Oscillating Between Tag and Hopscotch: Theo Angelopoulos' Playful Aesthetics

Vassiliki Rapti

"There is always a boy in my movies, a child that discovers, the way I discover in each film. My wife says that she has three girls who are growing up and one boy who will never grow up: That's me!"[1] This confession that endorses the delights of the "child" in the artistic process comes as a surprise from the Greek auteur Theo (Thodoros) Angelopoulos (1935–2012) who is obsessed with bleak Greek History

The title is inspired by Mary Flanagan's article: "Playful Aesthetics: Toward a Ludic Language." In *The Gameful World: Approaches, Issues, Applications*, edited by Steffen P. Walz and Deterding Sebastian (Cambridge, MA and London, UK: MIT Press, 2014), 249–272. https://doi.org/10.2307/j.ctt1287hcd.19. Accessed on May 30, 2020.

[1]Angelopoulos, qtd. in Horton, Andrew, Dan Georgakas and Theodoros Angelopoulos, "National Culture and Individual Vision: An Interview with Theodoros Angelopoulos." *Cineaste*, 1992, 214.

V. Rapti (✉)
Classical Studies, Boston University, Boston, MA, USA

V. Rapti and E. Gordon (eds.), *Ludics*,
https://doi.org/10.1007/978-981-15-7435-1_21

and has left his signature on the history of cinema.[2] To quote film critic Richard James Havis,

> Greece's most famous filmmaker, and a leading light in world cinema until his death in a traffic accident in 2012, Theo Angelopoulos is known for lengthy, aesthetically beautiful films, such as *Ulysses' Gaze* (1995), that examine Greek history, culture and myth from a contemporary viewpoint. *Reconstruction*, his 1970 debut, is smaller in scale, but establishes many of the themes this "auteur's auteur" would revisit throughout his career.[3]

For sure, in his visually stunning epic cinema, Angelopoulos masterfully reconstructs the turbulent history of Modern Greece, primarily during the Civil War (1946–1949), haunted by its ancient myths and history that spans more than three millennia. The paradox of his distinct cinema, that exposes the trauma of History, lies in entrusting his art to children, often as protagonists, and to their play, out of which they painstakingly come of age.[4] Fully embracing children's games, typically associated with the frivolous and the non-serious in the Western tradition, Angelopoulos embarked on a lifelong quest for his ludic language by allowing "the child within him" to take the leap and guide him in his artistic journey. The inexhaustible imagination of the children in his films and their ability to dream and to discover despite their tragic dimension is a common theme. Trauma may have scarred these children and transformed them into adults prematurely, but their games seem always to be present. Puzzled

---

[2]Kris Ravetto-Biagioli summarizes Angelopoulos's impressive career: "During a career that has spanned more than forty years, Greek film-maker Theo Angelopoulos has been feted by scores of awards, including the Palm d'Or for *Eternity and A Day* (1998), the Grand Jury Prize for *Ulysses's Gaze* (1995), the Golden Lion for *Megalexandros* (1980), the Silver Lion for *Landscape in the Mist* (1988), and the International Critics Award for *The Traveling Players* (1975)." In "*O Megalexandros*: Falling In and Out of Dreams." *The Journal of Modern Greek Studies* 29 (2011): 1–26, 1.

[3]Richard James Havis. "Flashback: Reconstruction—Theo Angelopoulos Examines the Relativity of Truth in 1970 Debut: Theo Angelopoulos' 1970 Debut Blazed a Trails for Greek Filmmaking and Put the Director on the Path to Greatness." *Post Magazine*, 27 August 2016. https://www.scmp.com/magazines/post-magazine/arts-music/article/2008907/flashback-reconstruction-theo-angelopoulos. Accessed on May 31, 2020.

[4]Whether in the background as in *Reconstruction* (1970), or in the foreground as protagonists as in *The Landscape in the Mist* (1988), or *Eternity and a Day* (1998), and *The Weeping Meadow* (2004), children are *a sine qua non* in Angelopoulos's films, contributing to their heightened emotional effect.

by these seemingly disjointed ludic moments, I argue that Angelopoulos uses children's games as a cinematic conduit to his cinematic aspirations: by having an important formal role in his films, they serve to structure the narrative, both within each of his films, and more interestingly, across his entire *oeuvre*.

Two universal children's games in particular, tag and hopscotch, which operate in opposite modes—endless free play and calculated play, respectively—allow Angelopoulos to explore a unique playful language that not only allows for autobiographical elements to be expressed but also to seamlessly create for the viewer a world that simultaneously operates on two distinct planes, that of reality and imagination/daydream/memory/fiction. Child's play is the perfect vehicle for a smooth transition from one plane to another. This constant switch is intentional in Angelopoulos's cinema. To quote Andrew Horton, "simply put, we feel the fictive in reality and the reality of fiction simultaneously in Angelopoulos's work."[5] Moreover, children's games, thanks to their inherent performativity, serve as a perfect conduit for Angelopoulos to lead his viewers smoothly from the world of theatricality to that of reality and back again.

Latching onto tag and hopscotch, which are recurring tropes in his *oeuvre*, Angelopoulos weaves all his films into one single film, as he admitted by claiming that in all his life he only managed to create one single film in the form of a work-in-progress.[6] As Dan Fainaru states, "none could claim, as Angelopoulos rightly does, that all his films are basically episodes in one single piece of work, each one engendering the next. For this reason, he says, not one of his films finishes with the classic closing, 'The End.' and as long as he will continue to make films, the last word of each will be the first for the next."[7] Interestingly, this work-in-progress always deals with the tribulations of the artistic process and is perfectly attuned to his favorite aesthetic technique of the long take. The longshot is usually conceived as "a metaphor for History's perpetual

---

[5]Horton, Andrew, Dan Georgakas and Theodoros Angelopoulos, "National Culture and Individual Vision: An Interview with Theodoros Angelopoulos," *Cineaste*, 1992, 14.

[6]See, Dan Fainaru, ed., *Theo Angelopoulos: Interviews* (Jackson: University Press of Mississippi, 2001), xii. Print.

[7]Ibid., xii.

movement and Man's existential journey,"[8] as critic Elie Castiel claims, who further comments on its use by Angelopoulos as follows:

> From this engaged intellectual intention grows a view of the world and cinema as a tool for awareness that is at once social, political and personal. But what is most clear from this hypothesis is that, on the whole, the work of Angelopoulos blends the circularity of the fundamental concepts of a shot with the sociopolitical and existential concerns that stem from the director's idiosyncratic morality. From a purely functional aspect, the long take suggests a notion of *continuity*, thus attributing certain duration to the concept of time.[9]

This almost ritualistic continuity conveyed by Angelopoulos's long take is also characteristic of child play, in which time is suspended as the children-players are absorbed by "the magic circle of play" into which they have voluntarily stepped, to recall the term used by Johan Huizinga in his influential study *Homo Ludens* (1938).[10] There the Dutch cultural historian claimed that "civilization arises *in* and *as* play, and never leaves it."[11] Likewise, I argue that Angelopoulos' art is *sub specie ludi: it* arises *in* and *as* play on multiple levels, besides the endless experimentation with the camera: in each film separately (micro-level) and in his total oeuvre (macro-level); in terms of both content and form. In other words, all the films by Angelopoulos constitute "temporary worlds within the ordinary world, dedicated to the performance of an act apart"[12] in which children

[8]Elie Castiel. The Aesthetics of the Long Take in Theo Angelopoulos's *The Travelling Players* in *Off Screen* 20.2 (February 2016). https://offscreen.com/view/aesthetics-of-the-long-take-the-travelling-players. Accessed on May 31, 2020.

[9]Ibid.

[10]See Johan Huizinga, *Homo Ludens: A Study of the Play-Element in Culture* (Boston, MA: Beacon Press, 1955), 10. The exact reference reads as follows: "All play moves and has its being within a play-ground marked off beforehand either materially or ideally, deliberately or as a matter of course. Just as there is no formal difference between play and ritual, so the 'consecrated spot' cannot be formally distinguished from the play-ground. The arena, the card-table, the magic circle, the temple, the stage, the screen, the tennis court, the court of justice, etc., are all in form and function play-grounds, i.e. forbidden spots, isolated, hedged round, hallowed, within which special rules obtain. All are temporary worlds within the ordinary world, dedicated to the performance of an act apart."

[11]Ibid., 173.

[12]Ibid., 10.

have a key role. By giving room to children in his films either as protagonists or secondary characters and by allowing them to painfully grow as *players*, he simultaneously allows for his art to "arise and unfold in and as play," while engulfing the viewer in timeless Time and an immanent present through the technique of the long take. "The path to greatness" then for Angelopoulos is his invention of his own playful aesthetics through his language of tag and hopscotch that he played as a child and which he skillfully and almost enigmatically embedded in his films both intra-textually (within each of his films) and intertextually (in reference to other filmmakers such as Michelangelo Antonioni, Akira Kurosawa or Lucchino Visconti). Angelopoulos's playful aesthetics makes a skillful use of the embedded scene within a scene or the so-called *mise en abîme* technique, defined by Neil Herz as "[a]n abyssal textual structure [is one] in which an illusion of infinite regress is accomplished by the incorporation of an internal story into a larger diegetic pattern of which it is a mirror or miniature."[13] Angelopoulos uses this embedded technique subtly that is almost imperceptible when it comes to the tropes of tag and hopscotch. Yet these two children's games constitute the glue between the simultaneous planes of reality and fiction on which the action is built in the entire work of Angelopoulos.

These tropes constitute—I believe—the ludic language in game scholar Mary Flanagan's sense that stresses the notions of embodiment and relational aesthetics that lead to "a dynamic disruption of the mundane and reconnect with humanness."[14] Flanagan further clarifies the use of the term "ludic language:" "[it] constitutes a game's cultural conventions, privileging agency with responsive feedback, and connoting meaning through the way in which players take action and authenticate

[13]Herz, Neil, "Freud and the Sandman," *Textual Strategies: Perspectives in Post-Structuralist Criticism*, ed. Josué V. Harari (Ithaca, NY: Cornell University Press, 1979), 311. Print.

[14]Here are the relevant excerpts: "Let me take a moment to unpack experience and the ludic language. To think about notions of embodiment, recall Baurriaud's already cited relational aesthetics, where art is formed through interpersonal relationships. Relationships aren't required to be embodied, but most relational artworks manifest as participants with the work meeting in person, spectating, eating, working, talking, or even sleeping. In this, the people involved in relational works *together craft a dynamic disruption of the mundane and reconnect with humanness.* In a sense, relational works are in direct opposition to abstractions and disembodied experience." (261. My emphasis).

themselves through this action."[15] Thinking of games as sites of action and enaction, Flanagan warns her readers that,

> We must go beyond thinking that games "are about something" and move to "games are about doing something"; then to follow with, "in what context are we doing it?" Further, "is doing this intrinsically satisfying?" The player experience through the type of agency conveyed in the game is the heart of the art of games: this includes nonagency that in unwinnable games, where agency can be thought of as a type of matrix involving decision, ability, affordance, and chance. Games are special precisely because they are an art of doing.[16]

As an art of doing, Flanagan continues, play entails potentiality that brings "always, a sense of experimentation, trial and error, and practice. A ball could be bouncy or it could be heavy, atypical to expectations. In fact, it is the nature of play that it lets us find out what is possible."[17] It is exactly this potentiality of play that Angelopoulos embraced in his films, being in total accord with his inner self—that of the child who never grows. This child lives in an immanent present, as if to resist bleak History and is defined by the ludic drive much like Heraclitus's image of Time as a child who plays pebbles on the beach while the water next to him flows in the opening scene of *Eternity and a Day*, Angelopoulos' award-winning film in the 1998 Cannes Film Festival (Palme d'Or and the Prize of the Ecumenical Jury). Angelopoulos's experimentation with the potentiality of play is an integral part of his singular aesthetics that oscillates between the trope of tag as a constant movement of all his protagonists who are always on a quest attempting to discover something or someone while History chases them no matter their efforts, and the trope of hopscotch that alludes to his cinema of contemplation, as Andrew Horton has labeled it.[18]

[15] Ibid., 265.

[16] Flanagan, "Playful Aesthetics: Toward a Ludic Language," 266.

[17] Ibid., 268.

[18] See, Andrew Horton, *The Films of Theo Angelopoulos: A Cinema of Contemplation* (Princeton, NJ: Princeton University Press, 1997).

In the next section, I will showcase the exploration of the potentiality of play by Angelopoulos in his cinema. I will show his "art of doing" this through the oscillation between tag and hopscotch, which follow the classification of games developed by the French sociologist Roger Calllois in his book *Man, Play, and Games* (1958),[19] which he published in response to Huizinga's *Homo Ludens*. Callois' famous typology comprises these four basic categories or their combinations: *agon* (contest), *alea* (chance), *ilinx* (vertigo), *and mimicry* (mimesis), while all of them stretch along the pole of the so-called *paidia*, characterized by instinctive exuberance, free improvisation and fantasy, and the pole of *ludus*, which is characterized by constraint, rules, and effort.[20]

Tag and hopscotch can be classified as a combination of *agon*, *alea*, and *ilinx*, that is, as games of contest, chance and vertigo, respectively. Their only difference would be that tag stretches along the pole of the so-called *paidia*, while hopscotch stretches along the pole of *ludus*. The definition of the tag game is as follows: "Tag (also called *it*, *tig*, *tiggy*, *tips*, *tick*, *chasey* or *touch and go*) is a playground game involving two or more players' chasing other players in an attempt to 'tag' and mark them out of play, usually by touching with a hand. There are many variations; most forms have no teams, scores, or equipment. Usually when a person is tagged, the tagger says, 'Tag, you're *it*!'. The last one tagged during tag is 'it for the next round.'"[21] Hopscotch, on the other hand, can be played either by one person or two teams and is played on a course that is first laid out on the ground, usually drawn with chalk on pavement or scratched out in dirt. It "is usually composed of a series of linear squares interspersed with blocks of two lateral squares and numbered in the sequence in which they are to be hopped."[22] There are many versions of this game worldwide but usually, the single squares must be hopped on one foot, without touching a line or stepping outside a square. Should this be the case, the player loses. While playing tag requires versatility, swiftness, dexterity, tumult, and agitation, hopscotch requires patience,

---

19 Caillois, Roger, *Man, Play, and Games*, trans. Barash Meyer (New York: The Free Press, 1961).

20 Ibid., see table on page 36.

21 See https://en.wikipedia.org/wiki/Tag_(game). Accessed on May 31, 2020.

22 See https://en.wikipedia.org/wiki/Hopscotch. Accessed on May 31, 2020.

calculation, design, concentration and balance. In that respect, using Caillois' aforementioned typology of games, we may classify tag as *paidia* (free play) and hopscotch as *ludus* (calculated game).

I will now trace some characteristic examples of Angelopoulos' ludic language to show how he employs the trope of the child while playing tag or hopscotch, in order to tell his personal story of discovery that encompasses the collective story of the Greeks. I will focus on two scenes from the films *Reconstruction* (1970) and *Voyage to Cythera* (1984), with a few references to the films *Landscape in the Mist* (1988) and *Eternity and a Day* (1998), to conclude with the pivotal role of children's games in his films.

Tag first appears in the black-and white film *Reconstruction*, the first completed feature film by Angelopoulos, which is a series of reconstructions of the murder of a modern Agamemnon by his wife and her lover. This time, Eleni is the modern Clytemnestra. She lives with her three children in a deserted village of Epirus, after her husband, like thousands of other Greeks, immigrated from Greece abroad, especially to West Germany. Upon his return home, his wife and her lover strangle him to death with a rope. A judge, a policeman, and a journalist attempt to give their accounts of the murder, but receive little help on behalf of the suspects, because they accuse each other and deny responsibility of their act. Amidst several conflicting scenarios and reconstructions, the judge in this noir film then tries to entrap them through his sophisticated and almost sadistic investigation techniques in hopes to finally "catch them" and thus "capture truth," as if he were playing tag along with two other players, the two lovers-murderers.

While this metaphoric tag game is played throughout the film, the final scene offers us a real children's tag game. Taking us back to the moment of the murder, a snapshot that under normal circumstances would look idyllic and innocent, makes its appearance: Eleni's three children, Leni, Angela, and Takis, play tag in circles in their stone house's courtyard patio. Upon their return from school, with their school books nearby, they throw themselves in a breathless game of tag in a series of turns that soon transforms itself into a maze that sweeps even their already-disturbed mother who at that moment exits the house where the heinous act took place. It is ironic that at that very moment, her youngest child, completely scared—either by her mother's look or by her playing siblings' threat—runs to her as a safety base, while the two older children continue their game. Soon, this game, despite the children's unawareness and innocence, will become dangerous for their mother. Her lover—clearly embarrassed and already with qualms of consciousness—exits from the same spot, having hidden the corpse of the children's father. At that moment, the two older children pause before continuing their game of tag, which becomes more and more threatening to their mother. She is suddenly surrounded by them, while hearing repeatedly and pitilessly these lines: "I caught you Leni," "I caught you Taki," "I caught you Angela." The first line in particular, with the name of our protagonist, is particularly disturbing. The tag game transfers the lose state to Eleni and in the eyes of the spectators looks now like another noose, similar to the one that filled the screen during one of the reconstructions of the murder during which Eleni lost her senses. Indeed, Eleni feels with all her senses now that not only is she lost, as she had confessed earlier in the film to her brother Giorgis, seeking his help, but even worse, that her children are lost, that everything is lost.

The power of the innocent children's play reveals to the viewer the powerlessness and tragic dimension of everyone in the film. Unlike the judge who hurried to accuse Eleni as "a woman of immoral qualities," the viewers are less eager now to utter accusations against her, because they see her suffering and feeling to her bones her own tragic fate, as well as that of her children. The spectators may even sympathize with her and tend to find elsewhere those who led her to the murder of her husband, by being responsible for the entire rural Greece's impoverishment and death, including her own house. Angelopoulos' powerful folk song, the "short lemon-tree" that opens and closes the film is very effective, as it sounds like a dirge for the withering of the village and of its population. According to Andrew Horton,

> while Angelopoulos often refers to Brecht and the need for the audience to think as well as to feel in theater and cinema, we do not experience anything close to what could be called an 'alienation effect' in Brechtian terms. To the contrary, the mixing of theatricality and reality in his films

> often leads us into a deeper, fuller emotional bond with the film—one that, we could say, embraces our thinking mind as well.[23]

The innocent children's play of tag not only functions as a clever device of the filmmaker and seeker of discovery of the truth but also as a catalyst that, with its shocking value awakened everybody "in" the film and "outside" the film, those inside and outside the play. The double-coded children's game that addressed both children and adults created a deeper channel of understanding and introspection, one that is way more effective than any direct communication.

The voices "I caught you Eleni," "I caught you Alexandros," will echo again in the opening scene of Angelopoulos's film, *Voyage to Cythera* (1984), another film that again pushes the limits of an artist's experiment with reality, represented reality, verisimilitude and truth. In *Reconstruction,* Angelopoulos displays multiple truths about the desiccation of rural Greece, only to finally disregard all of them for the "truth" of a game of tag. In *Voyage to Cythera,* he recurs to children's games again to find a balance in his artistic concerns about the limits between reality and film or between a reality in which past and present coexist and its reconstruction, in search of understanding. In this film, Alexandros is a filmmaker in search of his characters for a new film and is about to begin a painful artistic journey that starts with the casting of his protagonist, an ex-communist surrogate father-Odysseus who returns home only to be chased away with his modern day wife-Penelope on a raft in the middle of the sea. Like another Telemachus, Alexandros begins his search for his fictional father, Odysseus, with the powerful cast scene with the old men uttering the line "Εγώ είμαι!" (It's me, myself), each one so different yet far from ideal for his casting until the moment he encounters the man who sells flowers, played by the unforgettable Manos Katrakis at the end of his life. From that moment on, the film-within-the-film begins and Angelopoulos seamlessly blends in with the protagonist's own reality as a married man, father of a boy, and as a most hesitant film director. This masterful blurring of boundaries is established in the opening scene of

[23]Horton, Andrew, Dan Georgakas and Theodoros Angelopoulos, "National Culture and Individual Vision: An Interview with Theodoros Angelopoulos," *Cineaste*, 1992, 14–15.

the film which seems awkward at first, yet it effectively sets the tone of the entire film, which oscillates between reality and fiction. These two poles are not presented as opposites, but as part of a continuum, where lines between them are consistently blurred, "as if the present has the past in it."[24] The opening scene zooms in on a boy named Alexandros —the name Angelopoulos consistently gives to the protagonists of all his films—who is attempting to play tag with a German soldier who is on duty at the Hadrian's Arch in Athens during the German Occupation, as the marching music makes it even more plausible. The boy runs through the old Greek streets while the German guard chases him. At the end of the sequence, we see the boy, breathless, holding his face in his hands and uttering these familiar words from *Reconstruction*: "I caught you Eleni! I caught you Alexandros!" Then the director's voice is heard echoing the last threatening sentence: "I caught you Alexandros!" In this way, the newest film embeds the previous one through the tag game, which is brought together as a very effective childhood memory. All in all, the tag game is again present in three interlocking versions: as a chilling experience coming from the distant past and inhabiting the present, as a challenging filmed reality that attempts to incarnate the lived experience, and as a copy of a filmic device that worked effectively in *Reconstruction*, yet this time aims at something else. This fictional film director alludes to the German Occupation in Greece, during which Angelopoulos was six years old and from which his earliest traumatic memories haunt him:

> Born in Athens in 1935 under the dictatorship of General Metaxas, Angelopoulos's earliest memories were images of political turmoil – the Italian and German invasions of Greece during World War II followed by the Greek Civil War that would last until 1949. British and American forces were a key factor in the eventual defeat of the Left, and the American discontinued to support the Right through the military Junta of 1967-1974. Such memories haunt Angelopoulos's films, but also enable

[24]This is how Andrew Horton describes Angelopoulos's obsession with Homer's *Odyssey* in this short video: https://www.youtube.com/watch?v=6c185X6JptE. Accessed on June 17, 2020: "It's as if the present has the past in it and he is telling you that in one visual shot." (6:04).

> them to offer striking insight into the tumultuous history of Greece and the Balkans in the twentieth century.[25]

I am referring to Dimitris Psathas's short story entitled "Oi Pitsirikoi" ("The Little Boys"), where a gang of boys tries to help the adults by sabotaging the Germans by means of their favorite game: tag. Appearing playful and naïve, the little Greek heroes kept the German soldiers busy while their little fellows destroyed their cars and facilitated the adults in their Resistance. Such an endeavor was obviously very dangerous and the little heroes suffered the consequences of their simulated heroic "play." Their tag play, whether seeking pleasure by playing with a real danger or by performing an act of manhood, this game's territory deliberately pushed the boundaries of children's play. Drawing on this new dimension of the tag game, Angelopoulos frames his *Voyage to Cythera* (the title of both the film-within-the-film and of his actual film), he seems to attempt a similar endeavor: to render concrete what a difficult task it is for his film director (and thus for himself) to initiate a link with his traumatic past and come to terms with it, by maintaining a balance and a perfect equilibrium. This idea is further supported by another children's game that also makes its appearance in this film: hopscotch.

The hopscotch game complements the frame that the tag game provided for the *Voyage to Cythera*. The protagonist, fully aware, speaks to himself as follows: "one-two, I am out of step," while using as the course of his hopscotch game the pavement outside his film studio. In a suspended state, he knows very well that every single move that needs to be made should take place in a perfectly calculated manner if one wishes to avoid any trouble. Such suspension and unresolved situation is reminiscent, of course, of Angelopoulos's film *The Suspended Step of the Stork* (1991), where the theme of a border in its many dimensions is magnificently treated. There the protagonist's one foot is in one territory while the other is in the foreign territory, risking to be shot.

Alexandros, the film director of *The Voyage to Cythera*, plays by the rules of the new game. Earlier on, he had made another symbolic move

[25]See Kris Ravetto-Biagioli, "*O Megalexandros*: Falling In and Out of Dreams." *The Journal of Modern Greek Studies* 29 (2011): 1–26, 3.

on the hopscotch-like course of his terrace where his son acted like a music director to the music heard from his father's room while the father acted like a boy when he threw a ball to his son. The child and the adult exchange roles. The child is the orchestra director while the father—the real director in the process of making a new film—is throwing the ball initiating a game, entering thus the mode of child play as a symbolic gesture initiating "the art of doing, the world of potentiality of play in the realm of artistic creation." He will continue being in this modality when he sets out to arrive at his studio. He is playing hopscotch by himself, a game that requires concentration, balance and awareness wherein one bad step may lead to failure. Alexadros' voice echoes then: "one, two I am out of step." This frames the entire film and is repeated again later as a *leitmotif*.

It is clear that these two playground children's games, tag and hopscotch, are far more than superficial. On the contrary, they play a key role in the conception and the structure of these films, while complementing each other. One could even see the hopscotch present in *Reconstruction*, where the outline of a dead body is reminiscent of a hopscotch course. This tomb-like frame is also reflected in multiple shots of the door that appears in every single reconstruction of the murder. Angelopoulos favors both these children's games, that is, playing tag and hopscotch, in which, children always breathlessly seek to reach a goal or to find the perfect balance. Through their games, children become fearless heroes, adventurers, pioneers, challenge seekers, *conquistadore*s, and discoverers.

The last two categories of Callois's typology of games, that of mimicry or make-believe game and games of chance, do appear in Angelopoulos's films, although they cannot be fully addressed in the limits of this chapter. *Mimicry* appears in the form of the fairy tale or *paramythi* of the Creation, prominent in the *Landscape in the Mist* (and surviving also in the *Beekeeper*), while taking on a new version in *Eternity and a Day*. In the *Landscape in the Mist*, two siblings, Voula and Alexandros, find recourse in the fairytale of Creation in order to find their roots in search of their unknown father. Their never-ending fairy tale allows them to keep the quest for their father alive, all the while undergoing a painful rite of passage into deceptive adulthood. The tale of origins is, after all, another articulation of the constant artistic quest of Angelopoulos whose constant main theme is the odyssey of an artist/director toward the conquest of the yet unknown self-expression. As far as the *alea* type of games, there is a reference to the game of playing pebbles at the opening of *Eternity and a Day*, used allegorically for Time which is compared to a child playing with pebbles at the seashore. This would be considered a game of chance. Through all these games, especially tag and hopscotch, children are transformed into little gods and creators, poets, endless storytellers, tireless performers, and daring plot-makers. In other words, their identity is formed through their games. Angelopoulos in his movies re-appropriates children's main mode of self-expression, that of play, through memory and trauma. To recall the words of the leader of Surrealism, André Breton, children's play constitutes a "magnificent field of experience" or else, "a road to the marvelous."[26] It is exactly the quest for this road to the marvelous, one that reveals "a desire to transcend" that Angelopoulos's cinema seeks in children in all his films that are structured as "journeys" of all kinds, either emotional, artistic, geographical or temporal.

Children's games are not meant to offer simple entertainment to the viewer. On the contrary, they reinforce and intensify the emotional effect of each film. Through their essentially irrational and ritualistic character, as Johan Huizinga stressed in his well-known study *Homo Ludens: A Study of the Play Elements in Culture* (1938), play belongs to "the world of the savage, the child and the poet,"[27] while its quintessentially creative character is intimately related to language. Angelopoulos has captured this unique creative quality of children's play not only by masterfully blending reality and fiction through children's play, but also by demonstrating a pure blending of content and form, subverting the cinematic codes together. Angelopoulos dares to accept the challenges that a child's discovery presents and that is why he always becomes a new discoverer in each one of his films. This is how his filmmaking becomes an expression of youthful discovery and creation against bleak History.

---

[26] Breton, André, *Œuvres Complètes*, Vol. II (Paris: Gallimard, 1992), 963.

[27] Huizinga, *Homo Ludens: A Study of the Play-Element in Culture*, 26.

In sum, children's games are the perfect conduit for Theo Angelopoulos's visually stunning cinema—one that oscillates between two planes—reality and imagination. The two children's games, tag and hopscotch that subtly appear in almost all of Angelopoulos' films, showcase Angelopoulos's playful aesthetic with its own ludic language. Through them the Greek auteur explores the potentiality of child play as self-expression, critique, and storytelling that captures life as a journey in all its triumph of hope and understanding. To recall Andrew Horton again when talking about *Eternity and a Day*, he emphasized "the sense of triumph, of some sense of hope he [Angelopoulos] offers; not a Hollywood happy ending but a sense of a coming together and a triumph of understanding."[28] In sum, by latching onto the tag and hopscotch games, Angelopoulos not only remains true to himself as a childlike explorer who constantly discovers against all adversity, but he does so while seamlessly weaving the personal with the collective and the political and while reconstructing Greece's epic history and trauma; a trauma that is experienced viscerally by both the protagonists and the viewers precisely because it stands in sharp contrast to children's games.

Works Cited

Breton, André. *Œuvres Complètes.* Vol. II. Paris: Gallimard, 1992, 963.

Callois, Roger. *Man, Play, and Games.* Trans. Barash Meyer. New York: The Free Press, 1961.

Castiel, Elie. "The Aesthetics of the Long Take in Theo Angelopoulos's." *The Travelling Players* in *Off Screen* 20.2 (February 2016). https://offscreen.com/view/aesthetics-of-the-long-take-the-travelling-players. Accessed on May 31, 2020.

Fainaru, Dan, ed. *Theo Angelopoulos: Interviews.* Jackson: University Press of Mississippi, 2001, xii. Print.

[28]See minutes 0:37–2:12 of the video, "Theo Angelopoulos—*Eternity and a Day*—Andrew Horton—The Films of Angelopoulos (Türkçe Altyazı)." https://www.youtube.com/watch?v=6c185X6JptE. Accessed on June 18, 2020.

Flanagan, Mary. "Playful Aesthetics: Toward a Ludic Language." In *The Gameful World: Approaches, Issues, Applications*, edited by Steffen P. Walz and Deterding Sebastian, 249–272. Cambridge, MA and London, UK: MIT Press, 2014. https://doi.org/10.2307/j.ctt1287hcd.19. Accessed on May 30, 2020.

Havis, Richard James. "Flashback: Reconstruction—Theo Angelopoulos Examines the Relativity of Truth in 1970 Debut: Theo Angelopoulos' 1970 Debut Blazed a Trails for Greek Filmmaking and Put the Director on the Path to Greatness." *Post Magazine*, 27 August 2016. https://www.scmp.com/magazines/post-magazine/arts-music/article/2008907/flashback-reconstruction-theo-angelopoulos. Accessed on May 31, 2020.

Herz, Neil. "Freud and the Sandman." In *Textual Strategies: Perspectives in Post-structuralist Criticism*, edited by Josué V. Harari. Ithaca, NY: Cornell University Press, 1979, 311. Print.

Horton, Andrew, Dan Georgakas and Theodoros Angelopoulos. "National Culture and Individual Vision: An Interview with Theodoros Angelopoulos." *Cineaste* 19.2–3 (1992): 28–31.

Horton, Andrew. The Films of *Theo Angelopoulos: A Cinema of Contemplation.* Princeton, NJ: Princeton University Press, 1997.

Horton, Andrew. Video https://www.youtube.com/watch?v=6c185X6JptE. Accessed on June 17, 2020.

Huizinga, Johan. *Homo Ludens: A Study of the Play-Element in Culture*. Boston, MA: Beacon Press, 1955.

Ravetto-Biagioli, Kriss. "O Megalexandros: Falling In and Out of Dreams." *The Journal of Modern Greek Studies* 29 (2011): 1–26.

Author Index

A
Abrams, J.J. 302, 303
Ackerman, Diane
Deep Play 278, 281
Albee, Edward 52
Arendt, Hannah 1, 2, 4
The Human Condition 1
Aristophanes
Frogs 185
Aristotle 85, 86
Artaud, Antonin 365
Le Théâtre et son double 365

B
Bakhtin, M.M.
Rabelais and his World 297
Berne, Eric
Games People Play 319
Bishop, Claire 90
Boal, Augusto 92, 383
Theater of the Oppressed 92
Bogost, Ian 131
Play Anything 131
Bourdieu, Pierre 127–130
Bourriaud, Nicolas 8
Boyte, Harry 89
Brandon Friend 15
Breton, André 365
Nadja 365, 366
Bryan, Pamela 15
Burke, Ruth E.
The Games of Poetics: Ludic Criticism and Postmodern Fiction 297

C
Caillois, Roger 9, 454

V. Rapti and E. Gordon (eds.), *Ludics*,
https://doi.org/10.1007/978-981-15-7435-1

Les jeux et les homes (*Man, Play, and Games*) 296, 453
Carroll, Lewis
Alice's Adventures in Wonderland 298
Through the Looking Glass 298
Coover, Robert 303
The Child Again 307

D
de Beauvoir, Simone 134, 135
de Coubertin, Pierre 53, 55–58, 68
De Mul, Jos 7
Derrida, Jacques
Writing and difference 297
Deterding, S. 138
Dewey, John 81, 129
Dorst, Doug 302, 303

E
Ehrmann, Jacques 297
"Homo Ludens Revisited" 297
Eliot, T.S.
Waste Land 298
Emilia, Reggio 81
Erikson, Erik 90

F
Flanagan, Mary 8, 451, 452
Ludic language 8, 9
Floridi, L. 22
Freire, Paulo 74, 77
Pedagogy of the Oppressed 74
Frissen, Valerie 7
Froebel, Friedrich 427, 428, 429

G
Gibson, Jeremy and Julian Wolfreys
The Ludic and Labyrinthine Text 298
Goffman, Erving 144
Gordon, Eric 89, 90
Meaningful Inefficiencies 10, 89, 148
Griffin, Jason Douglas 15

H
Halberstam, Jack 149
The Queer Art of Failure 149
Harari, Yuval 82
Harpham, Geofrey Galt 4
Hegel, G.W.F. 49, 50
Phenomenology of Spirit 49
Herzog and De Meuron 100
Hesiod
Theogony 170
Huizinga, Johan 3, 4, 5, 12, 22, 27, 28, 38, 228
Homo Ludens: A Study of the Play-Element in Culture 7, 9, 10, 12, 22, 23, 26–32, 36, 38, 88, 228, 283, 295, 450, 460
Hutchison, Peter
Games Authors Play 298, 320

J
James, C.L.R. 52, 59, 60, 62, 64, 66–69, 72
Beyond a Boundary 9, 48, 51, 59, 62, 66, 71
Juul, Jesper 140

L

Lerner, Josh 90, 92
  Making Democracy Fun 88
Long, Norton 128

M

MacAloon, John J. 57
MacIntyre, Alasdair 70
  After Virtue 70
Marcuse, Herbert 139
Matta-Clark, Gordon 105
Merleau-Ponty, Maurice 230, 231
Montessori, Maria 81
Moschos, John 265
  Spiritual Meadow 265

N

Nabokov, Vladimir
  Speak, Memory 298

O

Obrist, Hans Ulrich 107

P

Pindar
  Pythian 171
Plato 156

R

Raessens, Joost 7
Rancière, Jacques 84
Rawls, John 49
Robert, Fagan 1
Rousseau, Jean-Jacques 427, 428
  Emile, ou de l'éducation 427–429
  Julie, ou la nouvelle Héloïse 428

S

Sappho 168
Schiller, Friedrich 7, 77
Seely Brown, John 6
Sicart, Miguel 131, 133
Staley, David 6, 7
  Alternative Universities 6
Steiner, Rudolf 81
Stout, Jeffrey 49, 50
Suárez-Orozco, Carola 76

T

Theognis 157
Thomas, Douglas 6
Tomasula, Steve
  VAS: An Opera in Flatland 301

W

Walz, S. 138
Weber, Max 80
  The Protestant Ethic and the Spirit of Capitalism 80
Whyte, William 143
Williams, Rowan 83
Wilson, R. Rawdon
  Explorations in Play, Game, and Narrative Theory 298
Winnicott, D.W. 78
Wittgenstein, Ludwig 90–91, 237
  The Philosophical Investigations 90

Z

Zimmerman, Eric 12, 303, 306

Ludic Manifesto 12

The Gameful World: Approaches, Issues, Applications 12, 293, 294

Subject Index

Symbols

αὐλός 156
βέμβιξ 256
γελοῖον 155, 176
γελῶ 155
γελῶντες 159
γελῶσα 171
ἔλως 155, 176
εὐφροσύνη 156
μολπή 156
μουσική 156
ὀρχηθμόν 156
παιγμοσύνη 156
παίγνιον 156
παιδιά 156
παίζειν 156, 157
πλαταγή 249
στρόμβος 256
σχολή 80

A

The Absurd 367
Agon 453
Agônes 53
Alea 453, 460
Animal Crossing 33
Ars poetica 13, 280
Athyrmata (αθύρματα) 256
Audible Toys 249
Auletes/Tibicen 181, 182
Aulos/Tibia 181, 182, 190, 191

B

Brown v Board of Education 65

C

Calculated play 449
Carrus navalis 263

V. Rapti and E. Gordon (eds.), *Ludics*,
https://doi.org/10.1007/978-981-15-7435-1

Children's games 449, 454, 456, 458, 459–461
Children's Toys 248
Child's play/Children's play 258, 449, 456, 458, 459, 460
Civic engagement 87
Comedy 11
Commons 139
Community PlanIt 139
Continuity 450
"The core of humanity" 7
Crepundia 249
Crotala 190

D

Dolls 251
"Don't Be Mean" 14, 403

E

Endless free play 449
Ergodic Ludicity 310
The experience of limit 51

F

Fair play 15
Flâneur 130
Fragwurdig 52
Free to play 36, 37

G

The Gameful World 138
Game of Thrones 32
GamerGate 34
The Games of Fiction 297
Gamification 136
Geist 49
Gelān 156
Geloion 167
Gelōs (*gelō*) 11, 156, 158
Gelotopoios 167
Gentleman's Game 15
Greek Ploiaphesia (πλοιαφέσια) 263

H

Habitus 127
Harvard Mahindra Humanities Center 8
Homo faber 88
Homo poieticus 22, 23, 26, 29, 30, 32, 36, 38, 39
Hopscotch 14, 449, 451–454, 456, 459–461
Hopscotch game 458
Humanistic inquiry 8, 15

I

Ilinx 453
Immigraνt Poetics 12, 339
Infancy Gospel of Thomas 259
Invisible Cities 99

J

Jocari 3
Jocus 3

K

Knucklebones (*astragaloi*) 256

L

Lares ludentes 3
Laughter 11, 12, 224
Leitmotif 459
Life of Simeon the Holy Fool 260
Liminal Self 12
Ludere 3, 4, 16
Ludic action 11
The ludic gesture 11
Ludic impulse 300
Ludic language 448, 451, 454, 461
Ludic moments 449
Ludic Music 11
Ludi/Ludus 3, 9, 296, 454
Ludics 3, 8, 361, 376
  seminar 15
Ludics as Transgression 361
The ludic turn 7
Lysoporta 260

M

Magic circle 5
"The magic circle of play" 450
Metamaquettes 96, 97
Methectic 228
Mimetic 228
Mimicry 453
Mise en abîme 450
Mostellaria 11, 185, 191, 192, 194–197

N

Narthex 261
Naturphilosophie 14, 433
Negative Capability 277

O

Octavia gallery 15

P

Paidia 9, 296, 453, 454
Paizein 156, 157
Participatory Pokémon Go 10
Photodotes 109, 110, 112, 118
Photodotes I: Light Donors 110
Photodotes III: Plug-n-Plant 113
Photodotes V: Cyborg Garden 116
"Playdrive" (*Speiltrieb*) 78
The play drive 7
Playful aesthetic(s) 450, 461
Playful language 13
Playful Translation 327, 330
Play is an antidote to dark times 5
Play (Modes) 13
Playspace 9
Playthings 11
Play within and with 132
Poetic Play 12
Poetry and games 68
Poiesis 29
Poietic 30
Poietically 29
Pokémon GO 127, 142–147
Postmodern Gaming 298
Potentiality of play 452, 453, 459
Pre-Texts 73, 76, 84
Psogos 11
Public 88
Public games 243
Public Work 87–89

R

Red Dead Redemption 2 33, 34

Religio athletae 53
The Republic of Childhood: Friedrich Froebel's Kindergarten 14

S

Schiller's Enlightenment 84
Scrabble Cancer Project 14, 398–400
Separateness 27
Ship of Theseus 302, 303
The Sims 24, 33
Skholḗ 80–82
Social and emotional learning (SEL) 79
Spoudḗ (σπουδή) 156
Stardew Valley 33
Sub specie ludi 450
Symposion 158

T

Tag 14, 449, 451–456, 459–461
Tag game 453, 454, 457, 458
Tag play 458
Technae 98
Technoecologies 105, 106, 117, 121
Techno-utopia 96, 97, 102
Theo Angelopoulos' Playful Aesthetics 15
Theognideia 157
Toys 12, 256
  of Play 12
Twitch 33
Tympanon 190
Typology of games 454

V

Vita activa 2, 81

W

Westworld 32

Y

YouTube 33, 34

The manufacturer's authorised representative in the EU is Springer Nature Customer Service Centre GmbH, Europaplatz 3, 69115 Heidelberg, Germany. If you have any concerns regarding our products, please contact ProductSafety@springernature.com

Printed and bound by CPI Group (UK) Ltd, Croydon, CR0 4YY

30/09/2026

02225327-0017